Nik Software HDR Efex Pro™ After the Shoot

Stan Sholik

WILEY

John Wiley & Sons, Inc.

Nik® Software HDR Efex Pro™ After the Shoot

Published by
John Wiley & Sons, Inc.
10475 Crosspoint Blvd.
Indianapolis, IN 46256
www.wiley.com

Published simultaneously in Canada

ISBN: 978-1-118-06344-6

Manufactured in the United States of America

10 9 8 7 6 5 4 3 2 1

For general information on our other products and services or to obtain technical support, please contact our Customer Care Department within the U.S. at (877) 762-2974, outside the U.S. at (317) 572-3993 or fax (317) 572-4002.

John Wiley & Sons, Inc. also publishes its books in a variety of electronic formats and by print-on-demand. Some content that appears in standard print versions of this book may not be available in other formats. For more information about John Wiley & Sons, Inc. products, visit us at www.wiley.com.

Library of Congress Control Number: 2011935818

WILEY

About the Author

Stan Sholik has spent over three decades as a commercial, advertising, and illustrative photographer in Orange County, CA. During that time he has developed a national reputation in a wide range of technology-oriented specialties for his clients in the computer, electronics, medical device, and food industries.

He has also gained a reputation as a writer on both conventional and digital-imaging topics with articles in *View Camera*, *Shutterbug*, *Professional Photographer*, *AfterCapture*, *Rangefinder*, and other magazines. He has written several books, including *Macro & Close-Up Photography Handbook, Photographer's Filter Handbook: A Complete Guide to Selection and Use*, and *Professional Filter Techniques for Digital Photographers*.

Self-taught as a photographer, Stan holds a BS degree in Physics and an MA in English from Carnegie Institute of Technology in Pittsburgh, PA. Visit his website at www.StanSholik.com.

Credits

Senior Acquisitions Editor
Stephanie McComb

Project Editor
Kristin Vorce

Technical Editor
Josh Haftel

Senior Copy Editor
Kim Heusel

Editorial Director
Robyn Siesky

Vice President & Executive Group Publisher
Richard Swadley

Vice President & Executive Publisher
Barry Pruett

Business Manager
Amy Knies

Senior Marketing Manager
Sandy Smith

Project Coordinator
Patrick Redmond

Graphics and Production Specialists
Andrea Hornberger

Quality Control Technician
Dwight Ramsey

Proofreading
Jacqui Brownstein

Indexing
Estalita Slivoskey

For the women in my life for their patience and support.

Linda, Amelia, and Strawberry

Acknowledgments

My heartfelt thanks to Stephanie McComb for allowing me the opportunity to write this book for John Wiley & Sons. I appreciate her support and humor, but her friendship most of all.

My thanks and appreciation also to Kristin Vorce, my project editor at Wiley, for her insights, suggestions, and successful efforts to keep my style consistent and readable.

To the incredible team at Nik Software, Josh, Kevin, Tony, and Laurie, who put this software together in the first place, and have supported me throughout this project both technically and philosophically, I propose a toast to a job very well done.

And finally to Fr. Robert Gaestel of the Church of Angels, Pasadena, California, and Deborah Schneider, executive chef at Sol Cocina in Newport Beach, California, for providing me with unrestricted access to create HDR images for this book.

Contents

Introduction

The ultimate goal for many photographers is to capture a moment exactly as they saw it with their eyes and share this moment with others. Other photographers strive to interpret that moment and, regardless of the technical accuracy of their image, convey an emotional and personally interpretive response to it.

It is no wonder then that High Dynamic Range (HDR) imaging has so quickly found such a large and passionate following. HDR imaging allows followers of both of these approaches to photography to pursue their creative visions.

However, neither group could exist without the software needed to support its imaging goals. Fortunately, Nik Software's HDR Efex Pro provides the tools needed to create images that are capable of reproducing both the reality that the eye perceives as well as supporting the creative interpretations of our emotional and artistic responses.

This book is designed to guide you through HDR Efex Pro so that you can create a workflow that best suits your personal vision, whether it is to reproduce or interpret reality. Many of the key concepts in HDR imaging may be new to you, so I do my best to show practical examples in images I have taken so that you can choose the best tool to use at the right time to create the image you envision.

If you are new to HDR imaging, I encourage you to read the book from the first chapter, where I discuss the concepts behind HDR. If you can't wait to get started with the actual process, don't begin any further along than Chapter 2, which includes essential information on setting up HDR Efex Pro. Chapter 3 likewise is essential reading to set up your imaging software that works in conjunction with HDR Efex Pro to optimize performance. Then it's on to the magic of the program itself.

The reader

To be perfectly honest, HDR imaging is not for the amateur photographer or casual computer user. High-quality results require creative vision, passion, and technical skill, both with the camera and the computer. HDR Efex Pro is a plug-in for Adobe Photoshop, and some features require the Extended version of Photoshop. Although the integration and workflow of HDR Efex Pro with Photoshop is explained in detail in this book, the reader should be comfortable with Photoshop before loading HDR Efex Pro.

Similarly, HDR Efex Pro can also integrate with other software. These programs include Adobe Lightroom, Adobe Bridge, and Apple Aperture. The reader should be comfortable with these programs before making the adjustments to them recommended in this book.

I have made every attempt possible to keep the technical information to a comfortable level while still providing enough to satisfy the technically minded or simply curious. The purpose of the book is to guide you in creating a workflow that moves from image capture to HDR image output as smoothly as possible. But I personally find some of the technical stuff in between interesting, also. I hope you do, too.

HDR Efex Pro v1.2

I first became familiar with HDR Efex Pro in a prerelease beta version. I began this book shortly after the release of version 1.0. Recently, I downloaded and installed version 1.2 and that is the version I discuss in this book. Owners of versions prior to version 1.2 should install version 1.2, which makes significant performance improvements in some areas. However, no matter which version you have up to version 1.2, this book should be of value.

Mac or Windows?

I am equally familiar with Apple and Windows operating systems. I use HDR Efex Pro on both platforms and find no functional differences between the programs on either platform. The screen captures in this book have all been done on the Mac because that computer was the fastest one I owned when I started the book. That is no longer the case, and my new Windows 7 64-bit computer can run circles around my two-year-old Mac. Chapter 2 discusses system requirements, but trust me, HDR Efex Pro runs well on both platforms. Appendix A includes tables of keyboard shortcuts for both Mac and Windows computers.

Final words

I have done everything I can to ensure that all the information I am presenting is 100 percent accurate. But if you find an error or a little trick or obscure hidden keyboard shortcut that I missed, or if you have a question, I would love to hear from you. Please e-mail me at stan@stansholik.com, and I will do my best to respond in a timely manner.

I hope you find this book as helpful and enjoyable to use as I found it to write.

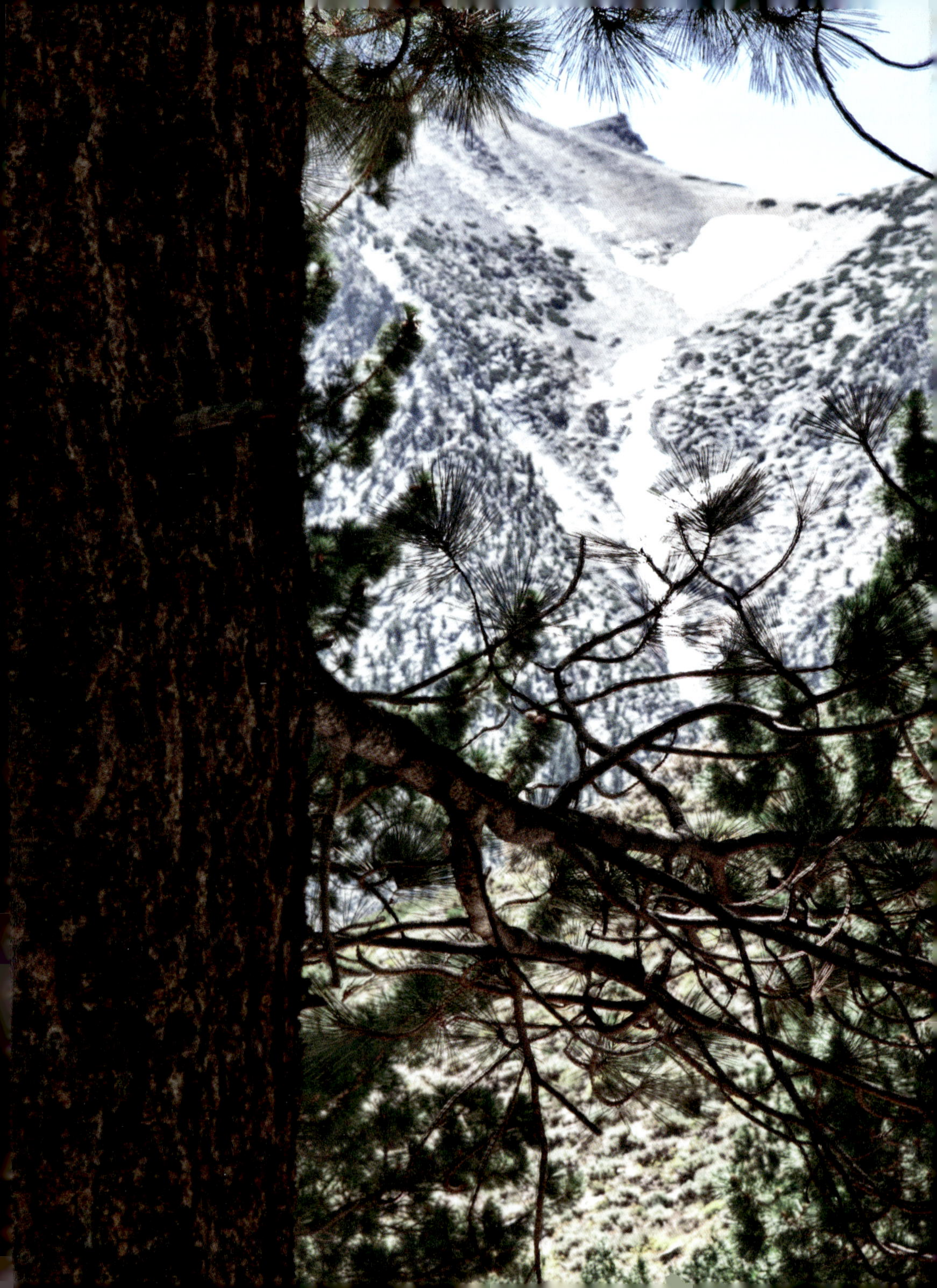

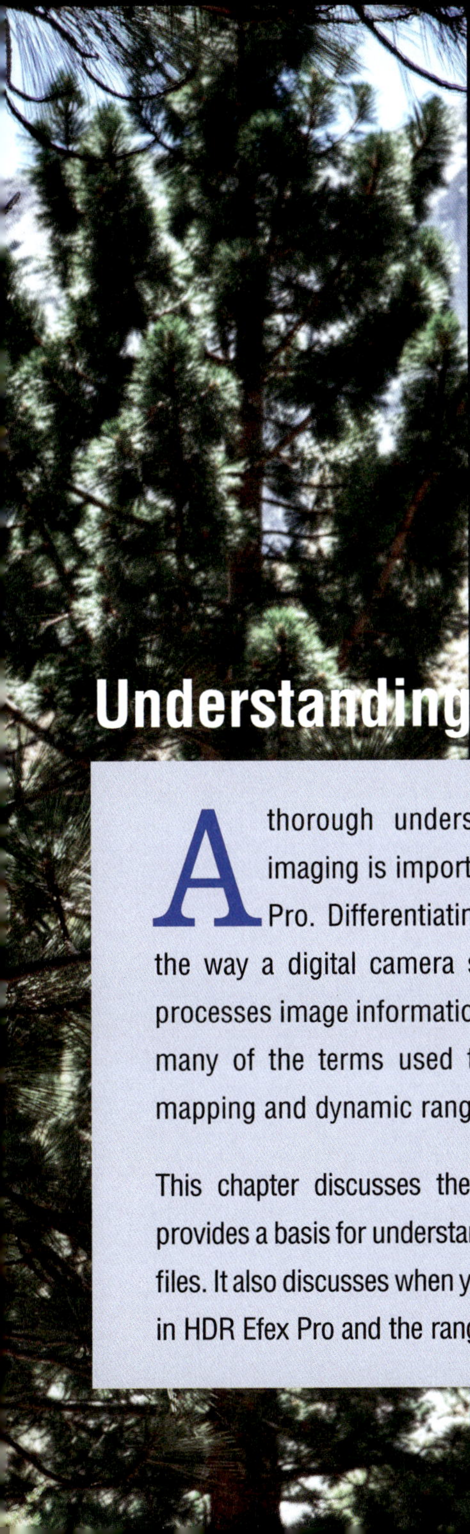

1

Understanding HDR Imaging

A thorough understanding of High Dynamic Range (HDR) imaging is important in order to get the most out of HDR Efex Pro. Differentiating between the way humans see the world, the way a digital camera sees the world, and the way the computer processes image information from digital files can be confusing because many of the terms used to describe these processes, such as tone mapping and dynamic range, are unfamiliar to many photographers.

This chapter discusses the terms and principles of HDR imaging and provides a basis for understanding what HDR Efex Pro is doing to your image files. It also discusses when you would want to capture images for processing in HDR Efex Pro and the range of results that the software can produce.

What Is HDR Imaging?

The goal of most digital photographers is to accurately capture an image that looks like the scene before their camera. Unfortunately, many are disappointed and don't understand the result.

Figure 1.1 is an image captured with a professional digital SLR in *RAW* file format and converted to a *TIFF* file for printing. Despite the care I took to extract as much information as possible from the image, it doesn't begin to approximate the scene as I remember it.

Human vision (eyes and brain working together) processes the scene in Figure 1.1 so that you can see full detail in both the interior and the sunlit exterior. With a single digital capture and processing, you must decide whether you want to hold the detail in the interior or the exterior.

With HDR imaging, however, it is possible to have detail throughout the scene, more closely approximating human vision. The reason is that HDR imaging includes the full dynamic range of the scene. With HDR Efex Pro you can produce the final result shown in Figure 1.2.

What is dynamic range?

Human vision is capable of accommodating a brightness range of approximately one million to one (1,000,000:1) or approximately 20 f-stops. This range of brightness from maximum to minimum of any measurement is called the *dynamic range* of the measurement.

The dynamic range of a typical sunlit scene ranging from deep shadows to bright sunlight,

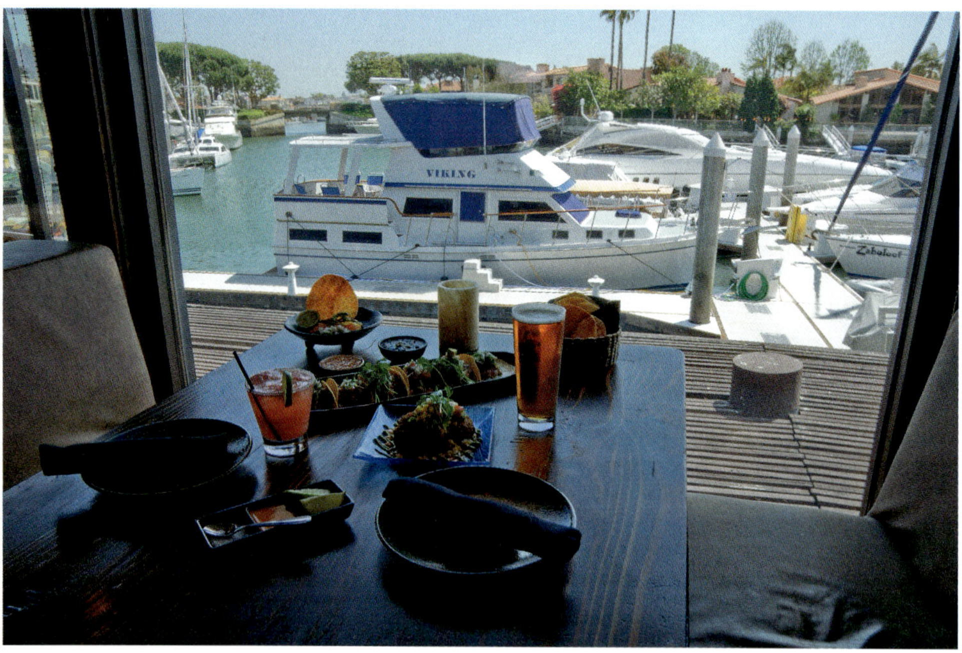

Figure 1.1

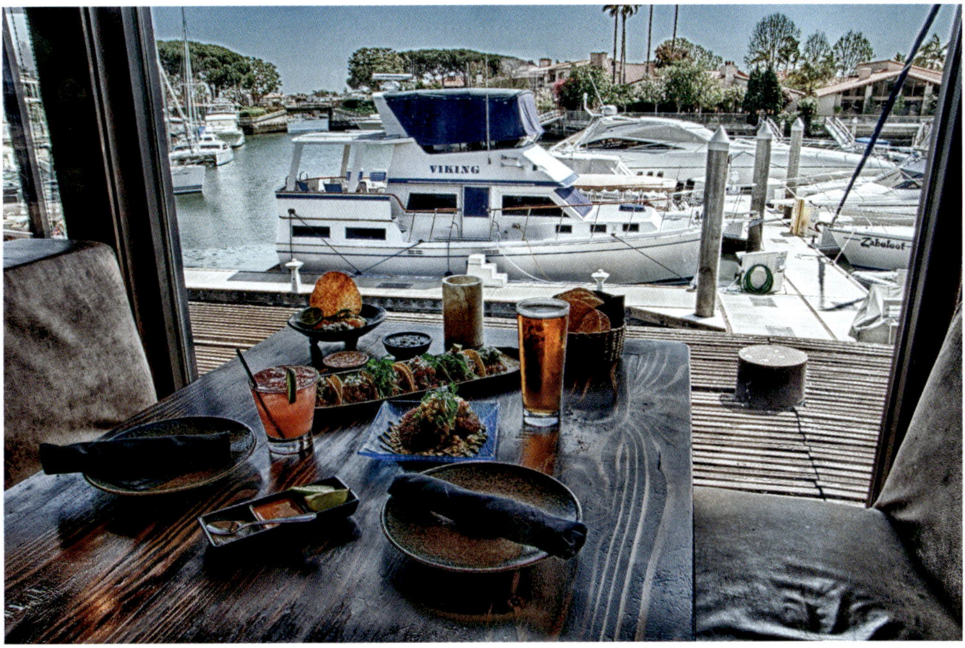

Figure 1.2

such as Figure 1.1, is about 100,000:1 or about 15 f-stops.

However, the dynamic range of a digital image sensor is far less than the dynamic range of a typical sunlit scene. The theoretical maximum dynamic range of the sensor typically found in low- and midpriced digital cameras, or in any JPEG or TIFF capture, may only be 5 to 7 f-stops. Pixels in these cameras capture 8 bits of information per color and are only capable of capturing 256 colors or shades of gray per color channel. Because the pixels' information is processed to three colors, the *bit depth* per pixel is 24 ($8 \times 3 = 24$).

High-end and professional dSLRs provide 12 bits of information per color and a few produce 14 bits of information per color. These bit depths for each color are only available when the capture is saved in the camera's RAW file format. Even with 14-bits of available color information, the sensor can only record 16,384 colors or tones of gray per color channel. This information is summarized in Table 1.1.

But even the sensors in high-end dSLR cameras only produce a dynamic range of 11 f-stops, still far short of your typical sunlit scene. This is the reason that a single image capture will not be able to reproduce the colors and dynamic range of the scene you were viewing.

Table 1.1
Sensor Bit Depth

Sensor Bit Depth per Channel	***Bit Depth per Pixel***	***Theoretical Maximum Colors or Shades of Gray per Channel***
8 bits	24	256:1
12 bits	36	4,096:1
14 bits	48	16,384:1

A single digital image, even one that includes a full range of tones from featureless black to pure white, is a Low Dynamic Range (LDR) image.

What you need to capture the full dynamic range of a scene in the way that human vision sees it is an image with a higher dynamic range than current image sensors provide.

What is an HDR image?

A High Dynamic Range image is capable of capturing the full dynamic range in a typical scene. HDR Efex Pro is software that is designed to create an HDR image and process that image so that it may be viewed on a LDR monitor or printer.

HDR Efex Pro takes the limited dynamic range of at least two separate LDR captures, as many as nine or more, and then merges them into one image with a theoretically unlimited dynamic range.

This book isn't the place to go into the details of capturing the images for HDR processing other than to say that a bracket of exposures covering the full dynamic range of the scene is needed. More information on the photographic requirements for capturing the image series for HDR processing is available on the Nik Software website in the FAQs (www.niksoftware.com/hdrefexpro/usa/help). The FAQs at HDR Labs is also a good source (www.hdrlabs.com).

see also

More information on image input requirements is included in Chapter 3.

Figures 1.3 to 1.8 show the exposures I processed in HDR Efex Pro to create the photo on the first page of this chapter. None of the original captures on its own comes close to capturing the way I saw the scene, but the HDR image, processed with the default settings in HDR Efex Pro, does.

see also

Chapter 3 contains additional information about choosing which images to include for processing to an HDR image.

HDR images are easily capable of accommodating all the dynamic range information in real-world scenes.

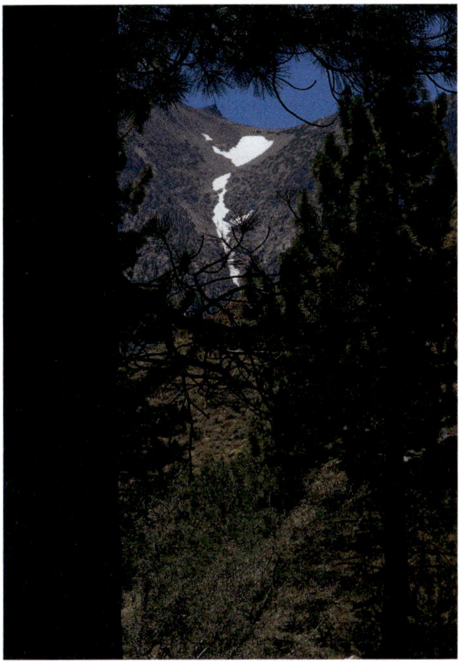

Figure 1.3

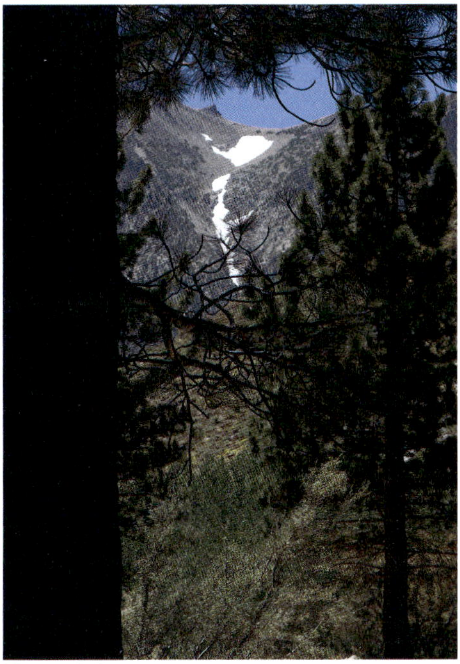

Figure 1.4

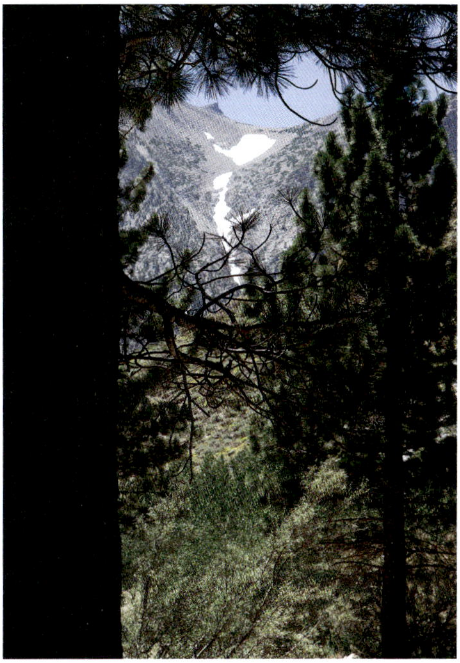

Figure 1.5

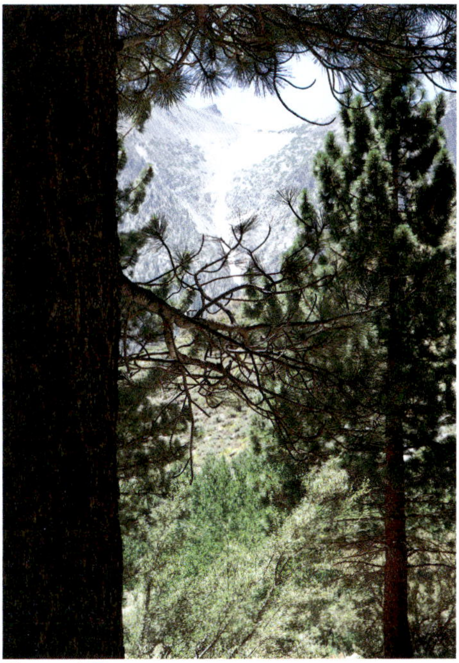

Figure 1.6

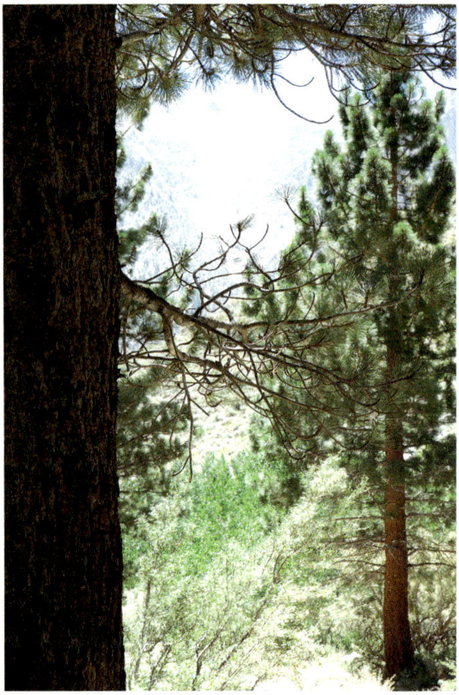

Figure 1.7

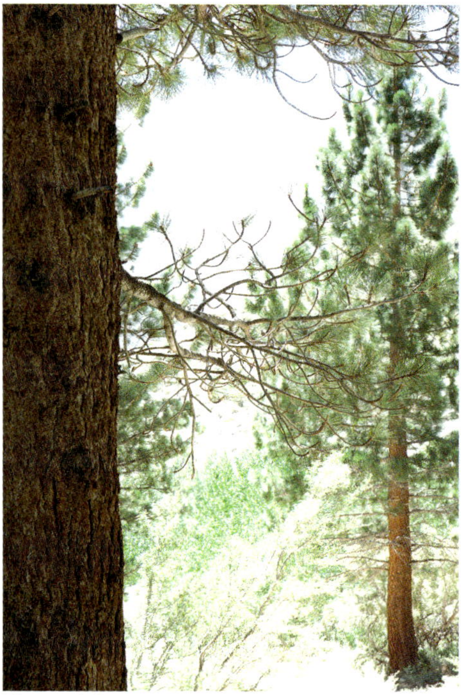

Figure 1.8

The strength of HDR Efex Pro is its ability to create an image that captures the full dynamic range of a scene and save it to be viewed on a computer screen or printed. But you can also use it to combine single captures to create *Extended Dynamic Range* (EDR) images. Processing a single RAW file twice, once for the highlight information and once for the shadow information, is one technique. EDR Images do not have the dynamic range of HDR images, but have a greater dynamic range than a single processed RAW LDR capture.

HDR Imaging Before HDR Software

Before the existence of HDR Efex Pro and other HDR software, photographers used other digital techniques to extend the dynamic range of their images. One technique was to take a bracket of exposures and combine them using complex masking into one image.

While this labor-intensive technique seems to extend the dynamic range of an image, it is seldom practical and rarely creates a believable photograph.

Figure 1.9 is an EDR image created in HDR Efex Pro illustrating this technique. I processed one RAW file in Adobe Camera Raw software, once favoring detail in the highlights and a second time favoring detail in the shadows. The result gains slightly more information in the highlights and shadows than the single process of the RAW file directly to a TIFF without using HDR software. But it is still limited by the dynamic range of the digital sensor and doesn't come close to the look of a true HDR image.

You have another option for creating an EDR image. You can process a single RAW, TIFF, or even JPEG file in HDR Efex Pro.

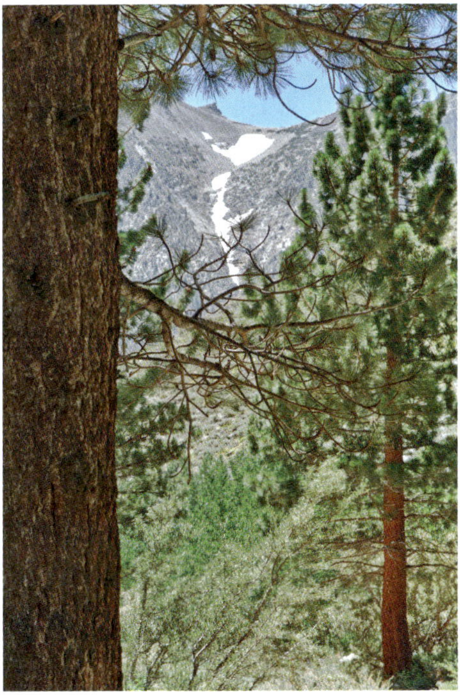

Figure 1.9

Figure 1.10 is an example of the same RAW file used for Figure 1.8, this time without preprocessing it twice in a RAW converter before I created an HDR image in HDR Efex Pro and processed it out for printing. Again, the result contains far less image information than the true HDR processed image.

Starting from an 8-bit TIFF or JPEG yields the least satisfactory results. HDR Efex Pro converts these images to a 32-bit image for processing, but the actual amount of underlying information is limited to the original 8 bits of color data. However, this feature allows you to revisit your photos taken before you began HDR imaging and work creatively with them as I did with a film scan in Figure 1.11.

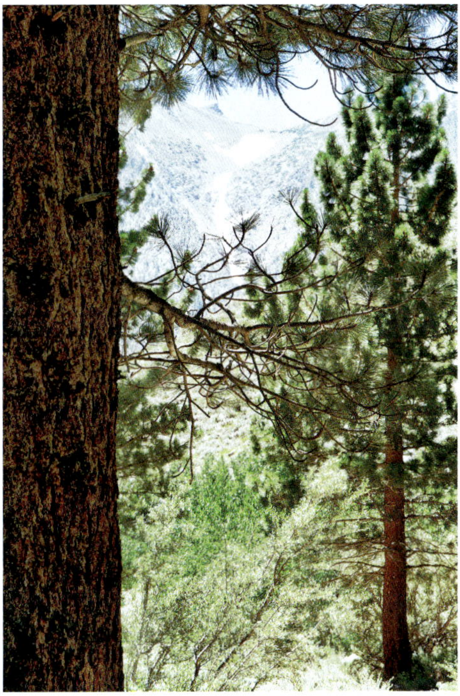

Figure 1.10

see also

Chapters 4, 5, and 6 contain more information about processing single images.

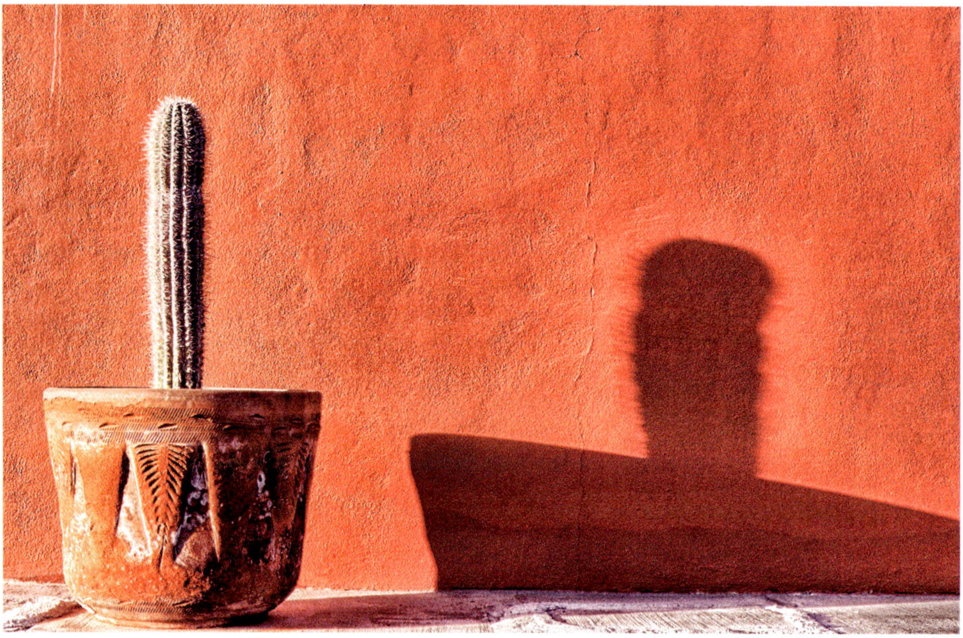

Figure 1.11

Only a true HDR image, created from multiple brackets of the scene, will come close to re-creating the scene as you see it.

What is tone mapping?

A 32-bit HDR working image contains many more tonal values than the multiple images from which it is made. The tones in the source images must be converted to appropriate tones in HDR Efex Pro for manipulation. This process is called *tone mapping.*

Tone mapping is also used to display the HDR image on a conventional computer monitor or to print on any printer. To view or print an HDR image, the image must be converted to a bit depth that is compatible with the output device.

Actually, any time the bit depth of an image is changed, some form of tone mapping is used. A digital camera uses tone mapping to display a RAW file format capture on its LCD screen. RAW converter software uses tone mapping when you save the RAW file as an 8-bit TIFF. But these examples of tone mapping are far less sophisticated than converting an image with a dynamic range of 100,000:1 to around 200:1 for a monitor.

The process of tone mapping is extremely important in HDR software. If you spend the time creating and adjusting an HDR image based on how it looks on your monitor, you need to be confident that it will look the same when you save it and view it in Photoshop.

Ansel Adams and Tone Mapping

Tone mapping is not new to photography, although the use of the term in HDR imaging may be new to you. The Zone System popularized by Ansel Adams is a tone mapping system for black-and-white photography. For scenes with high contrast (High Dynamic Range) or low contrast (Low Dynamic Range), the photographer adjusts exposure and processing to map the scene tones to the range of the negative.

Tone mapping also is used in traditional black-and-white darkroom work. Choosing the grade of paper on which to print or the variable contrast filter to use is a way to tone map the values of the negative to the tonal range of the printing paper.

HDR Efex Pro uses very sophisticated tone mapping. The adjustments you make are carried out in the 32 bits-per-color HDR color space, but you would never know this. As you make adjustments, the preview image on your 8 bits-per-color monitor precisely matches the adjustments made to the 32-bit image. This ensures that the look of the final TIFF image matches the image you see while working in HDR Efex Pro. This is not true with some other HDR software.

Unfortunately, this does not mean that the final image will contain all the tones in the HDR image. Tone mapping makes compromises and approximations in reducing the bit depth. However, the better the quality of your color-managed monitor, the more tones you will be able to see both in HDR Efex Pro and in Photoshop.

HDR Efex Pro also uses tone mapping to convert a single 8-bit or 16-bit image to a 32-bit image for HDR processing. Because there are no multiple images to merge, tone mapping is the only technique available to process the lower dynamic range image to the higher 32-bit dynamic range image needed for HDR processing. In Adobe Bridge, the menu item for creating an HDR image from a single image file is called HDR Efex Pro Tone mapping.

When Do You Use HDR Imaging?

Photographers who expose color transparency film speak almost reverently of the *golden hours* of the day. They are speaking of those hours around sunrise and sunset when the sun is low in the sky. The golden hours are the ideal time to shoot color transparency film because the dynamic range of the scene, exclusive of areas near the sun itself, rarely exceeds the roughly 64:1 dynamic range of the film.

The actual, rather than theoretical, dynamic range of digital cameras is very dependent on the camera model and the bit depth of the capture. The dynamic range of most digital cameras is greater than the dynamic range of transparency film. This is most certainly true with RAW captures made with professional dSLRs. Because this is the case, how do you decide when to use HDR imaging?

Using HDR imaging to capture full detail

Non-HDR photographers are used to getting up to catch early morning golden hour light. The hours around midday are spent traveling or relaxing. During midday in full sunlight, the scene contrast, which is another way of saying dynamic range, is high and often exceeds the dynamic range of single digital captures. Shooting begins again later in the day and continues until it becomes too dark to shoot.

HDR shooters get no breaks during the day. With HDR you can take pictures at any time of day and capture the full range of detail and dynamic range of the scene. This includes midday, as shown in Figure 1.12.

If you shoot using HDR during the golden hour at sunset, there is no reason not to include the setting sun as well as the nearby scenery. As Figure 1.13 shows, it is possible to hold detail from the brightest highlights to deep shadows. HDR Efex Pro provides you with the tools that allow you to decide how much detail to hold throughout the image.

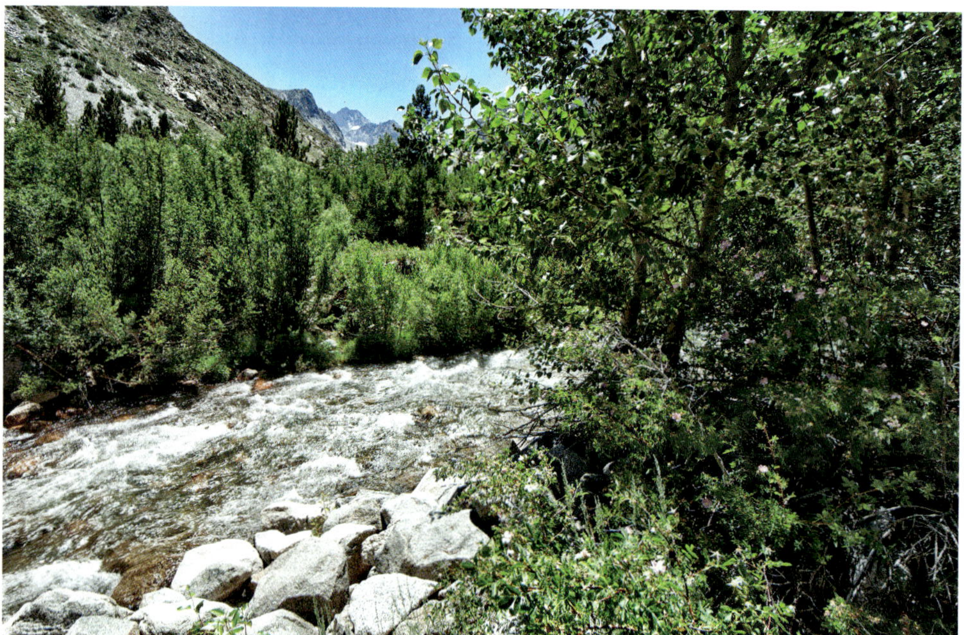

Figure 1.12

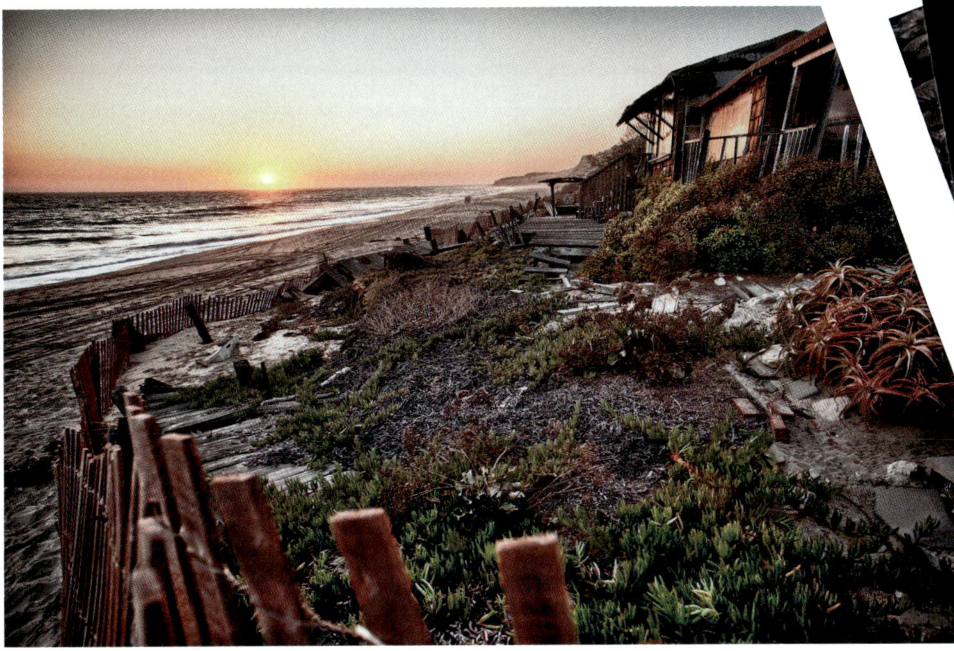

Figure 1.13

While much of my personal HDR imaging involves landscapes, no subject matter is off limits. Portrait subjects may not appreciate having the full detail of their faces revealed, but HDR imaging is used by portrait, wedding, sports, architectural, and still-life photographers with amazing results.

Using HDR imaging for creative effects

HDR Efex Pro does not limit you to HDR images that only present a realistic rendering of High Dynamic Range scenes: quite the contrary.

Using only the tools available in HDR Efex Pro, it is possible to create surrealistic images like Figure 1.14 from the original captures shown in Figures 1.15 through 1.18.

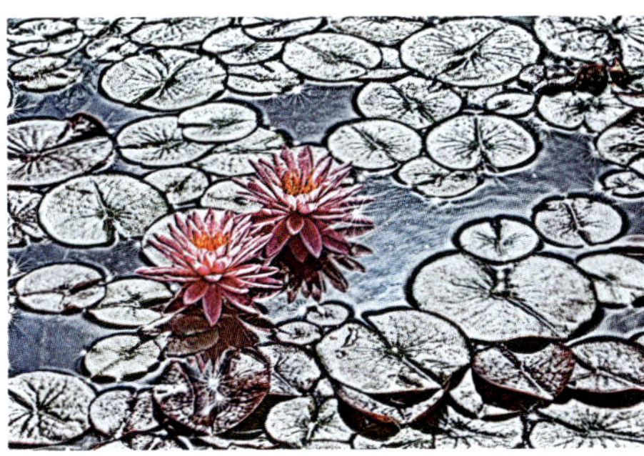

Figure 1.14

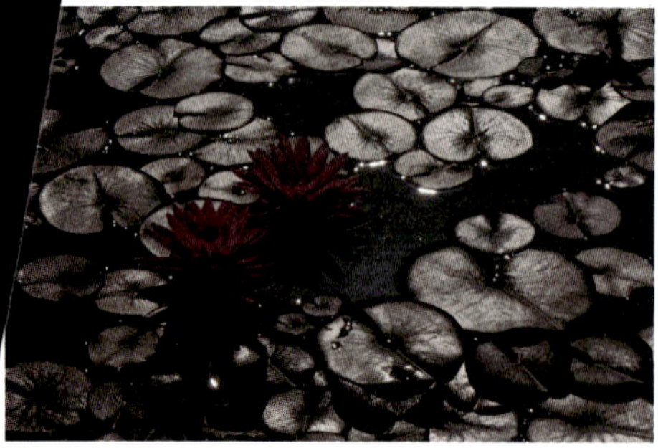

Figure 1.15

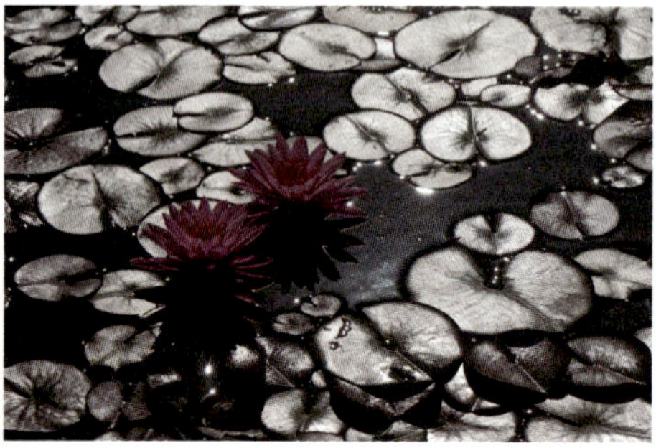

Figure 1.16

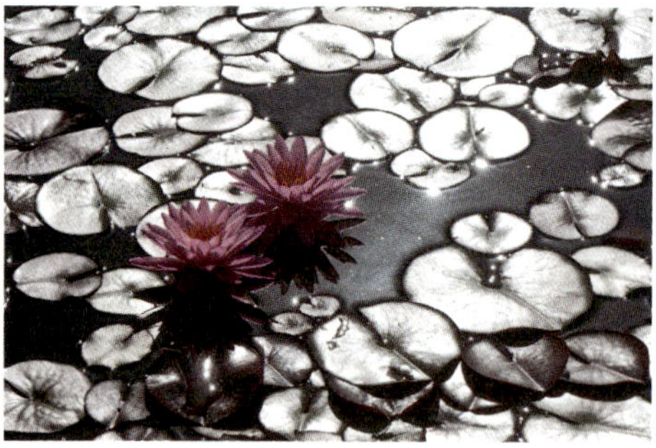

Figure 1.17

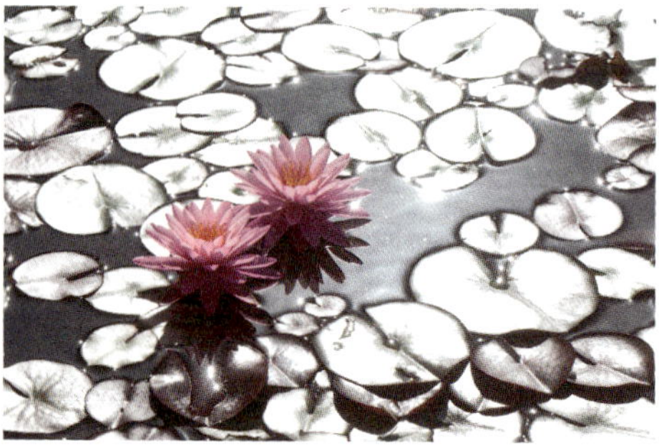

Figure 1.18

If you are looking for subjects that really "pop" using HDR Efex Pro, those with a lot of texture, like the cactus in Figure 1.19, are excellent candidates. It is even possible to make solid blue skies interesting.

There is no subject that I can think of that doesn't lend itself to interpretation with HDR imaging. I shoot a bracket of RAW captures almost every time I take photos. I know the correct exposure is there, and the additional exposures give me the opportunity to create an HDR image.

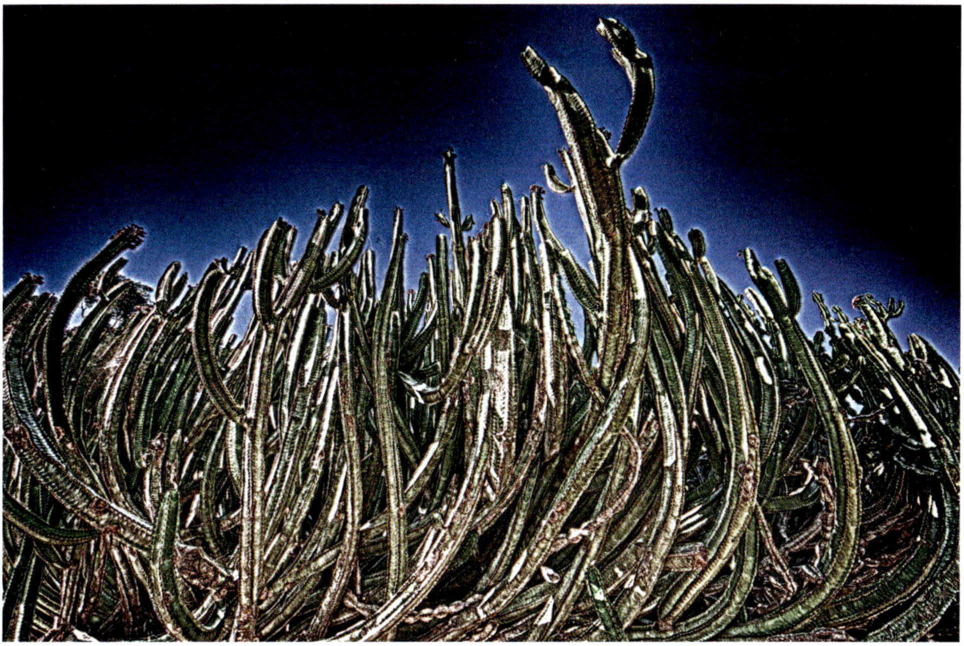

Figure 1.19

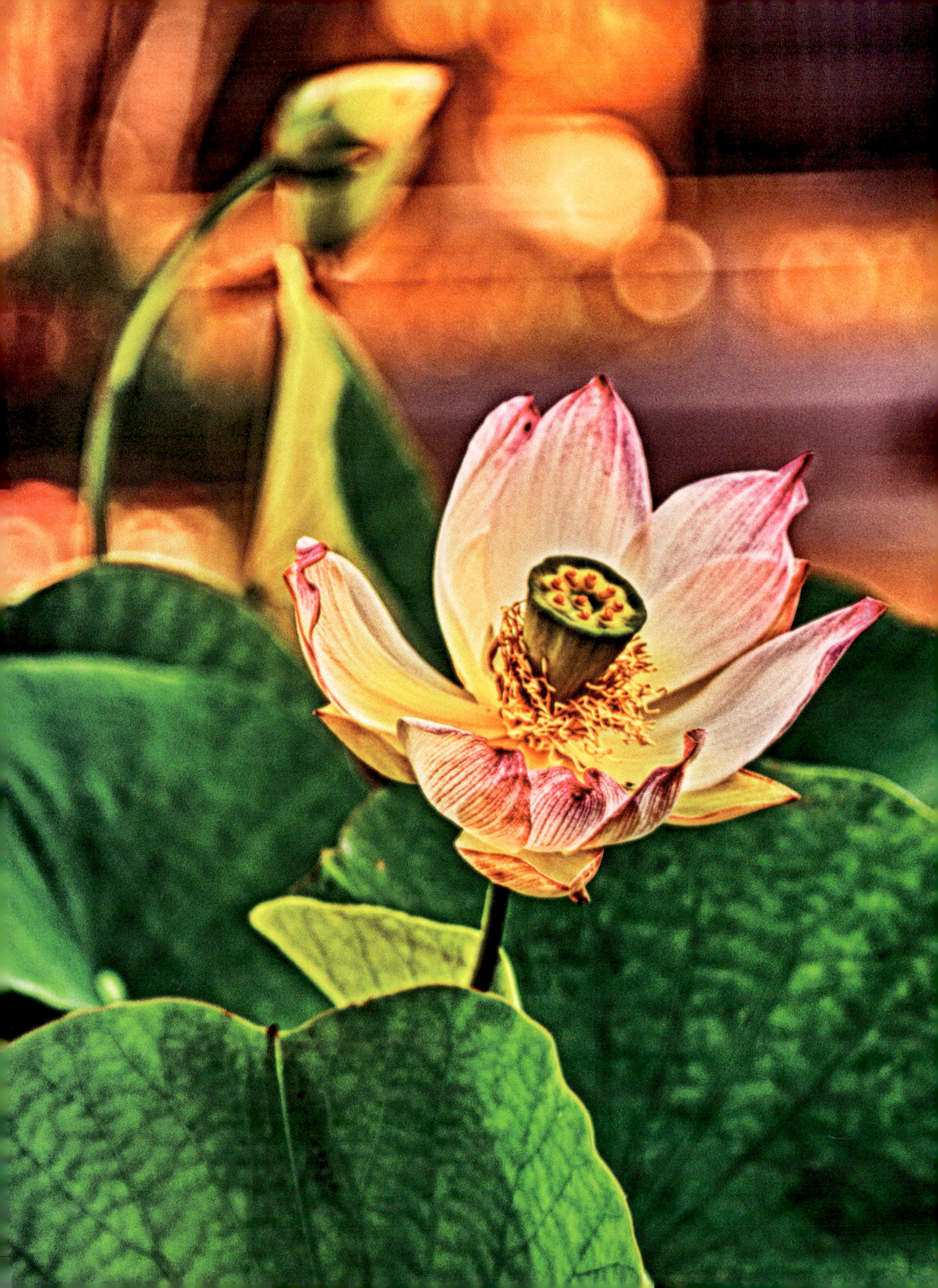

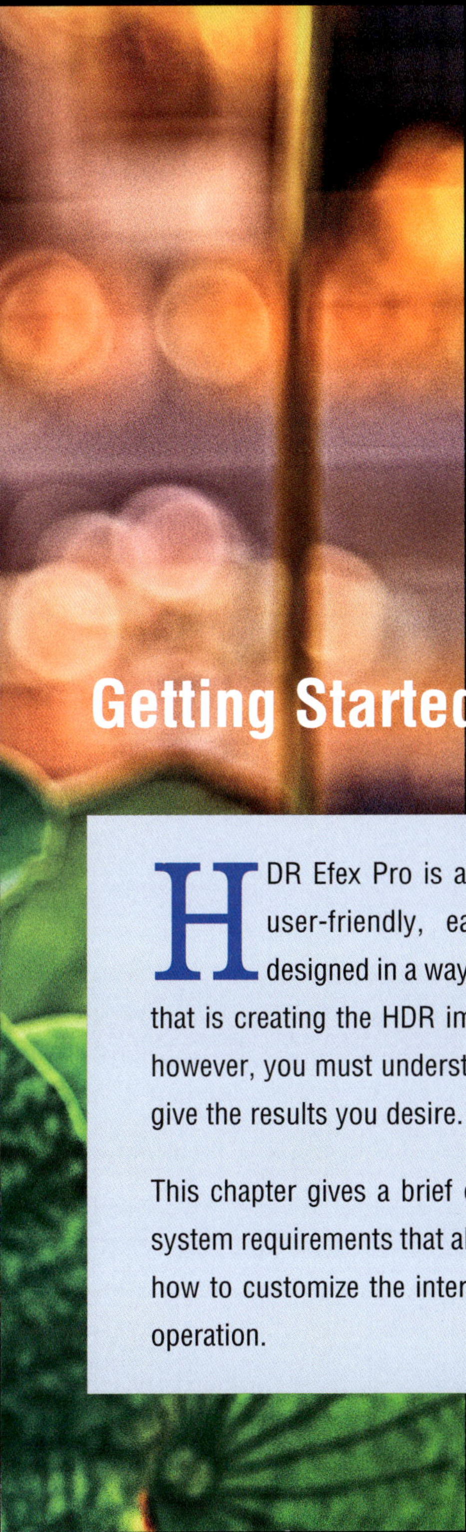

2

Getting Started with HDR Efex Pro

HDR Efex Pro is a powerful and sophisticated plug-in. Yet its user-friendly, easy-to-learn interface and operation are designed in a way that masks the complexity of the processing that is creating the HDR image. To get the most out of HDR Efex Pro, however, you must understand the workflow and set up the program to give the results you desire.

This chapter gives a brief overview of the workflow and the computer system requirements that allow it to run efficiently. I finish by discussing how to customize the interface and adjust the preferences for efficient operation.

Overview of the Workflow

The HDR Efex Pro interface shown in Figure 2.1 is organized in a logical workflow left to right. The interface is divided into three sections called the Preset Browser, the Main Image Window, and the Control Palette. The positions of these sections are fixed; they cannot be undocked and moved to a different area of the interface or moved off to a second monitor.

The Preset Browser is where you choose an initial look for your HDR image. The Main Image Window displays the HDR image with the selected preset and adjustments as it will look when you save the image as an 8- or 16-bit file. The Control Palette contains the adjustment tools to customize the look of the preset that you applied.

see also

Chapter 4 discusses presets in detail. Chapters 5 through 10 contain detailed information about using the tools in the Control Palette.

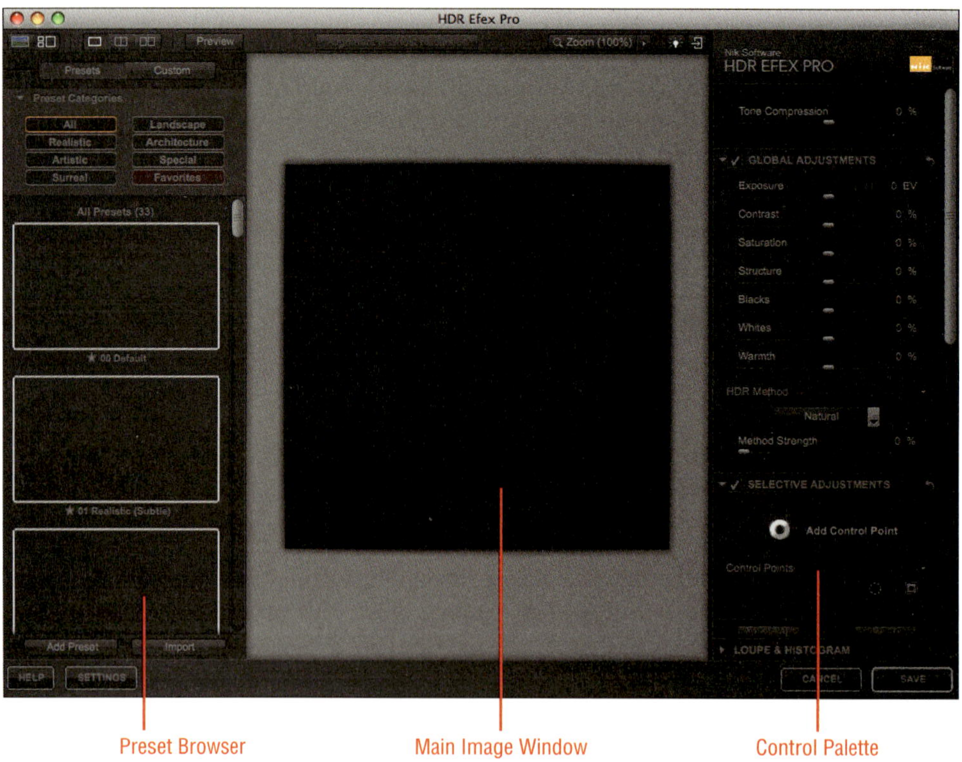

Figure 2.1

Above the Preset Browser and the Main Image Window is a bar containing icons and buttons. These are used to adjust the look of the workspace.

Below all three sections is a bar of operational buttons for accessing help, setting preferences, discarding changes and exiting, and processing your HDR image and exiting.

Presets

Knowing how to begin creating a look for your HDR image can be daunting. Other HDR software programs require that you experiment with tools and sliders and watch while your image slowly redraws on the screen to begin defining an HDR look.

Not so in HDR Efex Pro. Your HDR image opens in the Main Image Window with the 00 Default preset already applied to it, as shown in Figure 2.2.

I prefer to have my preview in the Main Image Window as large as possible. When I'm working with presets, I close the Control Palette by clicking the icon at the far right of the bar above the Main Image Window. This looks like the rectangle with a right-pointing arrow, as shown in Figure 2.3.

tip

To enlarge the workspace to the full screen, press F. To preview the image only without the Preset Browser or the Control Palette, press Tab.

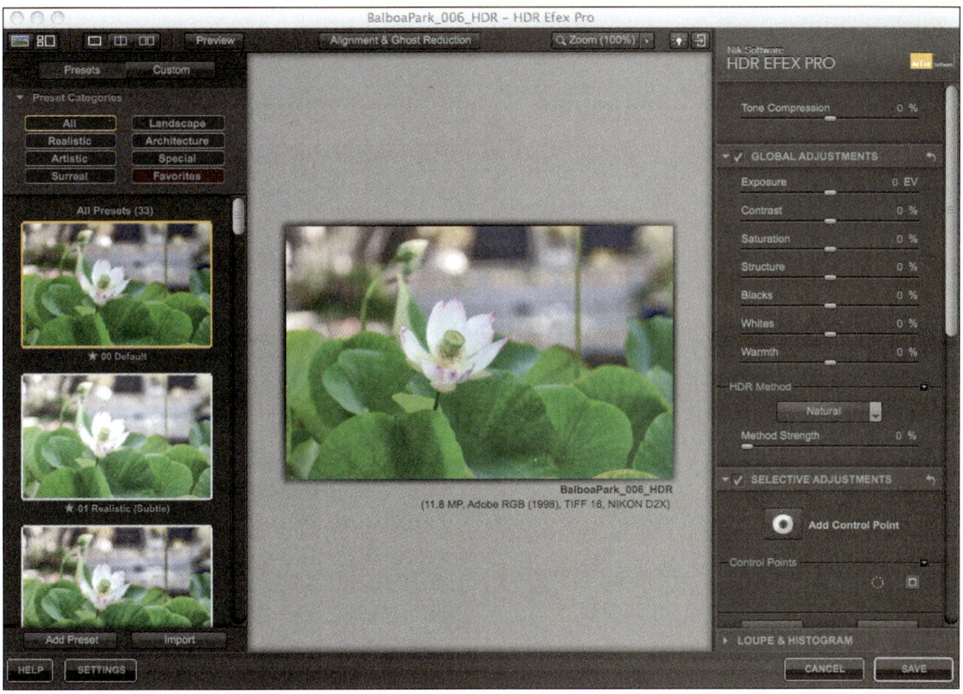

Figure 2.2

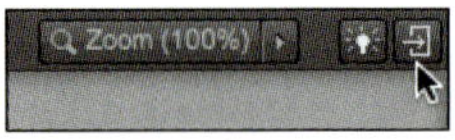

Figure 2.3

see also

A complete list of interface keyboard shortcuts is in Appendix A.

The 00 Default preset is a low-contrast representation of the linear data in the HDR file. This may be the look you are after, but if not, HDR Efex Pro provides 32 other options as prebuilt presets.

You can see these presets in the Preset Browser if the All button near the top of the Preset Browser is highlighted in orange. The All category is active by default.

The prebuilt presets are displayed on a thumbnail of the HDR image on which you are working in the Preset Browser. Seeing them in this way is a huge advantage over seeing them applied to a generic image. If the HDR image is horizontal, the presets are displayed in one column. If the HDR image is vertical, the display will show two columns of images.

Here are the sometimes descriptive, sometimes whimsical preset names:

- 01 Realistic (Subtle)
- 02 Realistic (Balanced)
- 03 Realistic (Strong)
- 04 Realistic Gradients 1
- 05 Realistic Gradients 2
- 06 Fine Structures
- 07 Subdued Contrasts
- 08 Structured Skies
- 09 Vibrant Textures
- 10 Vibrant Textures & Colors
- 11 Monochrome, Contrasty
- 12 Monochrome, Soft
- 13 The Old Cottage
- 14 Night On Earth
- 15 Vintage Colors
- 16 Granny's Attic
- 17 End of the Road
- 18 Bleach Bypass Look
- 19 Full Scene Compression
- 20 Vibrant Scenery
- 21 Gradual Contrasts 1
- 22 Gradual Contrasts 2
- 23 Postcard Paradise
- 24 Clean City 1
- 25 Clean City 2
- 26 Friendly Scenery
- 27 Bright Room 1
- 28 Bright Room 2
- 29 Strong Counterlight
- 30 Very Low Compression
- 31 Single Exposure 1
- 32 Single Exposure 2

see also

Prebuilt presets with examples of each are discussed in Chapter 4.

note

It is possible to create custom presets or import presets that other HDR Efex Pro users have created. Chapter 4 discusses how to do this.

If you don't have a clear idea of where you are headed with your HDR image, it is valuable to look at each of the thumbnails of these presets to see the possibilities. If you feel that one of the presets suits your image or will serve as a good starting point to adjust it, click the preset to apply its settings to the image in the Main Image Window.

If you have an idea of where you are headed and don't want to see all 32 possibilities beyond the default, HDR Efex Pro makes this easy by grouping similar presets together. There are eight preset categories:

- **All.** The All category is available by default when the program opens and contains all 33 available presets.
- **Realistic.** The five presets in the Realistic category are good choices to begin with when you want a natural look in the processed HDR image. These are some of my favorites and I use them often for landscape and nature photos. The Default preset is also included in this category.
- **Artistic.** The Artistic group provides seven presets. They produce a mildly stylized look. Included in the Artistic group are two monochrome presets.
- **Surreal.** As the name suggests, the Surreal group of six presets provides the most extreme HDR looks. Processed HDR images from these presets will never be confused with reality.
- **Landscape.** The five presets in the Landscape group are also good starting places for creating HDR images of landscape captures. This group differs from the Realistic preset category by offering more extreme effects and a darker overall mood.
- **Architecture.** The Architecture group of six presets provides good choices for images of cityscapes, skylines, and interiors.
- **Special.** The three presets in the Special preset category seem to be grouped there because they didn't fit conveniently in any other categories.
- **Favorites.** The Favorites category is empty by default. It serves as a convenient location for you to store your favorite presets. Click on the star next to the preset number to add the preset to the Favorites preset category.

Buttons to access these preset categories are shown near the top of the Preset Browser. If the Preset Categories palette isn't displayed, click the twirler to open it, as shown in Figure 2.4.

note

A *twirler* is Nik Software's term for the arrowhead found in many title bars in HDR Efex Pro. Click on a twirler and it rotates to display or hide available options.

For example, if you know that you want a realistic rendering of the scene in the HDR image, click Realistic. The Preset Browser will only display the six Realistic Presets, as shown in Figure 2.5.

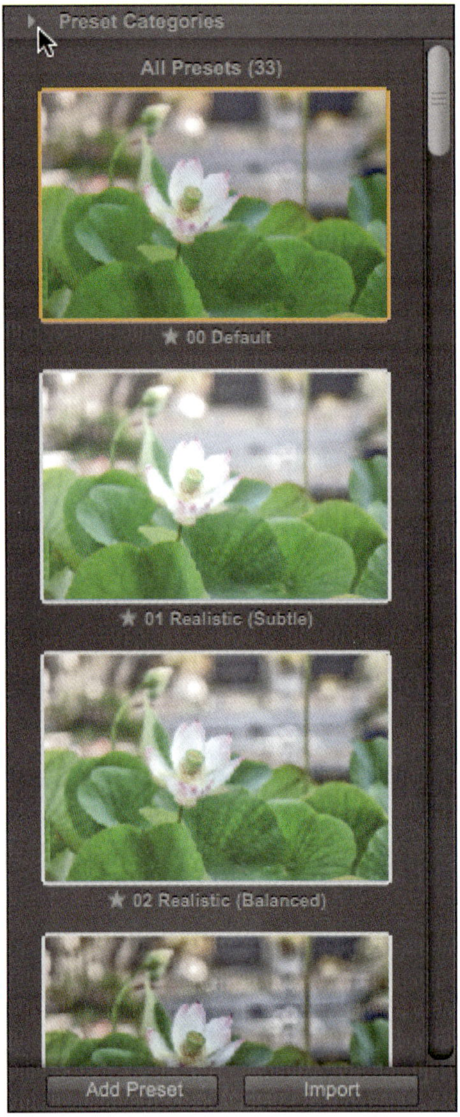

Figure 2.4

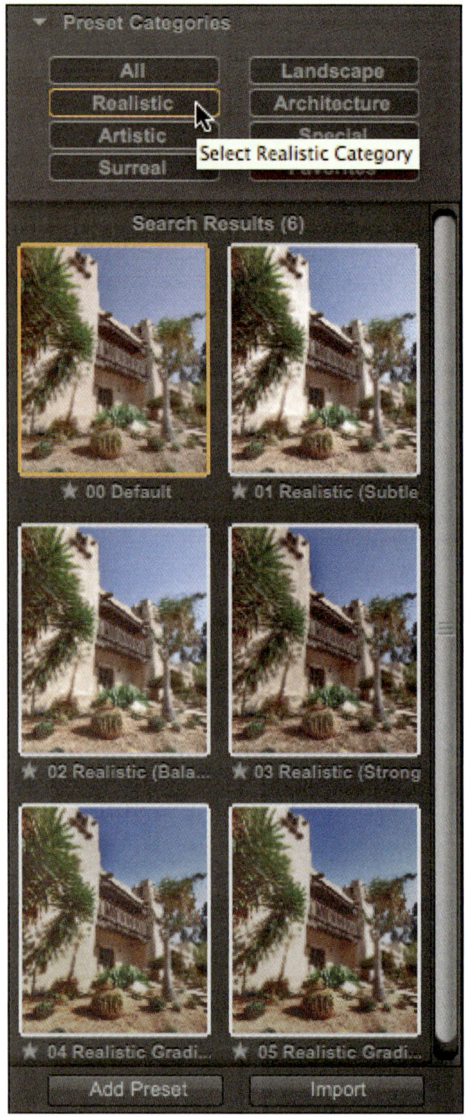

Figure 2.5

If a surrealistic look is what you want, click Surreal to display the six options, as shown in Figure 2.6.

You may be satisfied with the result you obtain by using a preset. But to save your image without at least investigating the options available in the Control Palette is to miss out on the real power of HDR Efex Pro.

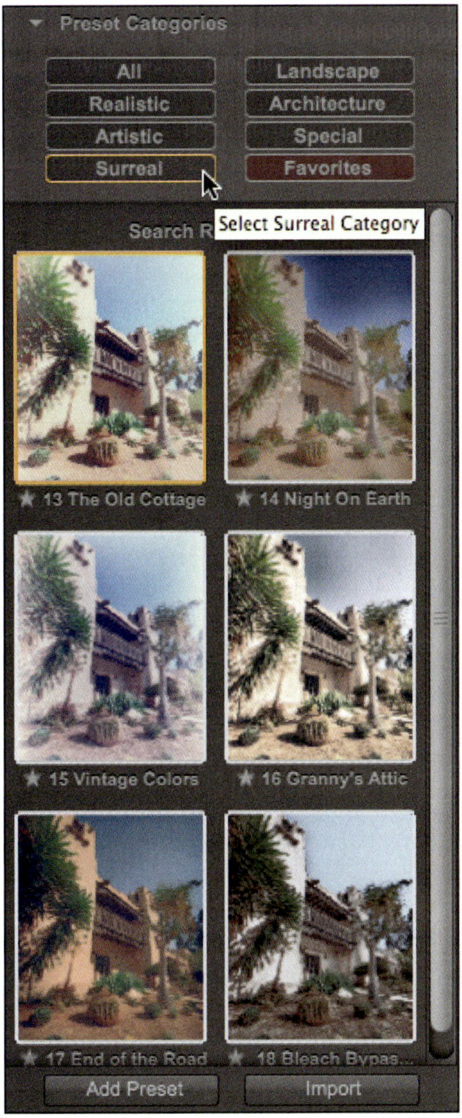

Figure 2.6

The Control Palette, as shown in Figure 2.7, contains the tools for tone compression, global adjustments, selective adjustments, and finishing adjustments, plus a Loupe & Histogram window.

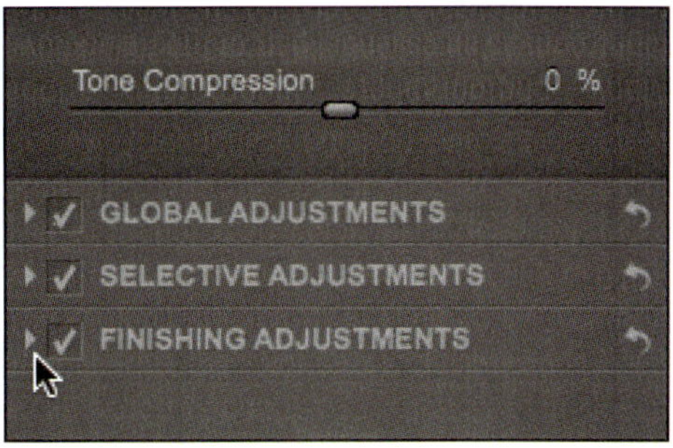

Figure 2.7

If the tool palettes are closed, as shown in Figure 2.7, click on the twirler to open the palette window. The check box next to the twirler indicates whether the adjustments in that palette are active. If a box is checked, the adjustments are active and are displayed on the image in the Main Image Window. The check mark also means that the adjustments are applied if you were to click Save. If there is no check mark, the adjustments are not displayed on the image and would not be applied if you save the image.

note

Chapter 5 discusses the Tone Compression slider in detail.

Global adjustments

After deciding on a preset, click the left-most icon in the bar above the Preset Browser. It is rectangular, as shown in Figure 2.8. This will hide the Preset Browser and create a larger preview in the Main Image Window while leaving the Control Palette open.

With the full image large on the monitor, its overall look may not be the best it could be. Many presets create a relatively low-contrast HDR preview that is too dark or too light or that needs other overall adjustments. The Global Adjustments section (Figure 2.9) contains tools to adjust contrast, exposure, and more. Global adjustments change the look of the entire image.

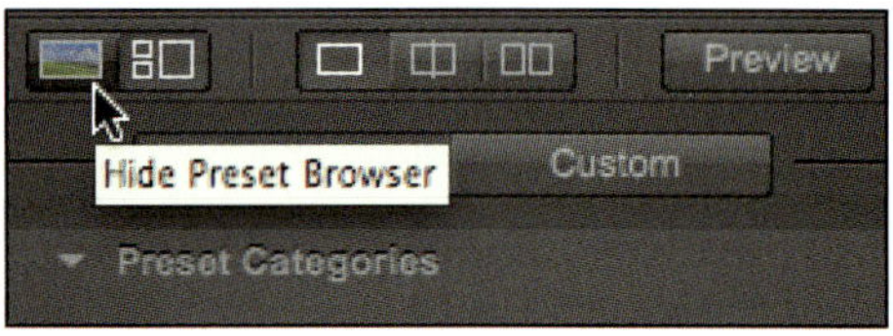

Figure 2.8

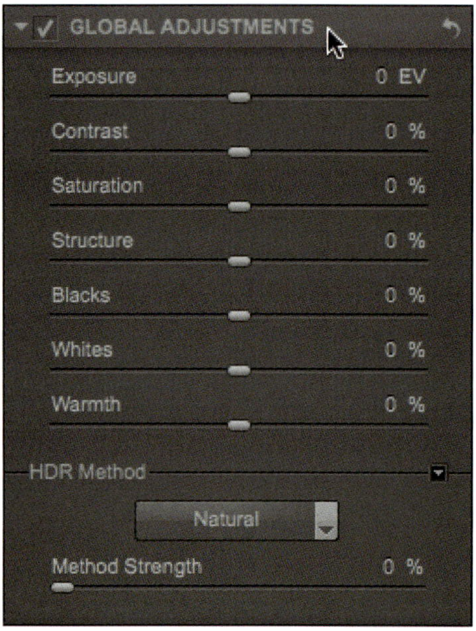

Figure 2.9

The seven sliders available for global adjustments are

- Exposure
- Contrast
- Saturation
- Structure
- Blacks
- Whites
- Warmth

There are two ways to adjust the sliders. You can click on the handle in the slider and drag it to a new position, or you can type a number in the dialog box to the far right of the adjustment name.

tip

If you decide that the image looks better when the adjustment is off, rather than trying to drag the slider handle to the 0 position, either type 0 in the dialog box or double-click the slider and it will reset to 0.

Global adjustments make relatively subtle changes to the look of the overall image. When you want to make drastic changes, use the HDR Method palette directly below the Global Adjustments sliders. Figure 2.9 shows the HDR Method palette. If all you see is the HDR Method title, click the twirler to the right of the title.

tip

To return all the adjustment sliders to their 0 positions, click the curved left-facing arrow to the right of the Global Adjustments title.

Much of the "magic" in the Preset looks of HDR Efex Pro is provided by the HDR Methods built into the program. The 20 methods are shown in Figure 2.10. To see the list, click on the downward-facing arrow to the right of the current method name.

To adjust the strength of each of the methods from 0 to 100%, click and drag the handle in the slider, or type a percentage in the dialog box.

see also

Chapter 6 demonstrates the use of the different HDR Methods. Chapter 7 discusses the Global Adjustments sliders in detail.

When you make a global adjustment, it is often useful to see a before and after view of the adjustment. HDR Efex Pro provides several ways to do this. The icons above the Preset Browser shown in Figure 2.11 control the different views. The icon with a white border is the active view.

The single rectangle is the default view and displays the HDR image with the adjustments applied, as shown in Figure 2.12. In this view, click Preview to change the preview image to the preset on which it is based.

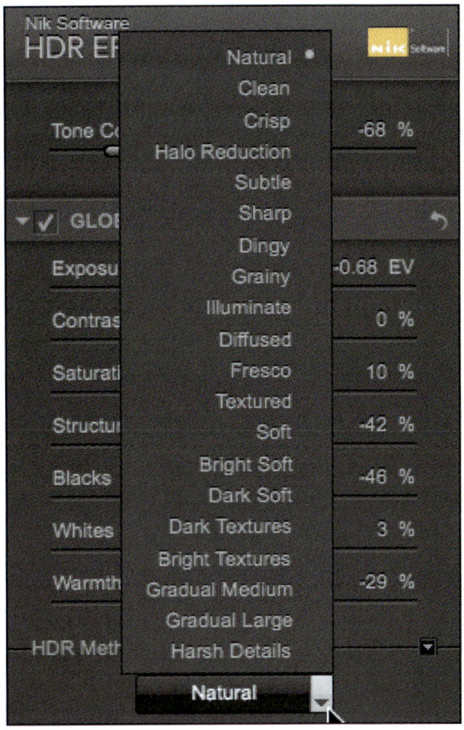

Figure 2.10

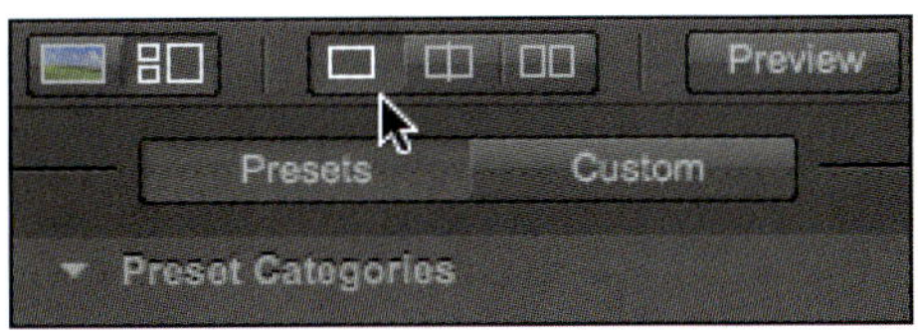

Figure 2.11

The rectangular icon with the vertical line through it displays a split image with the original preset and the adjusted view of the HDR image, as shown in Figure 2.13. The icon with two rectangles side by side displays separate views of the image with the original preset and with the adjustments, as shown in Figure 2.14.

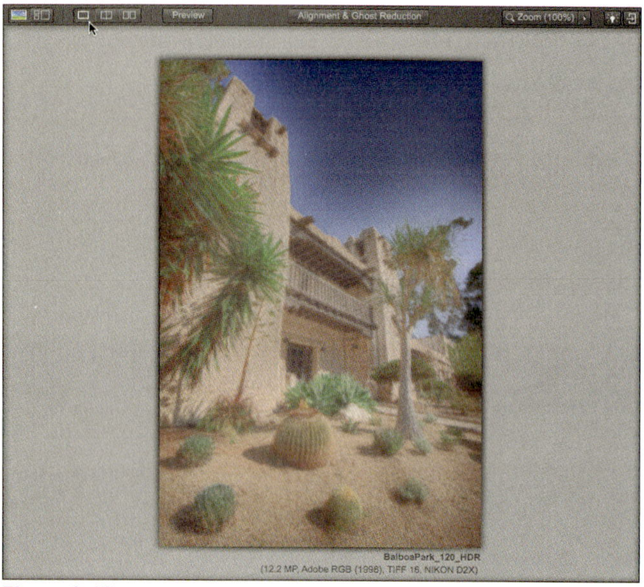

Figure 2.12

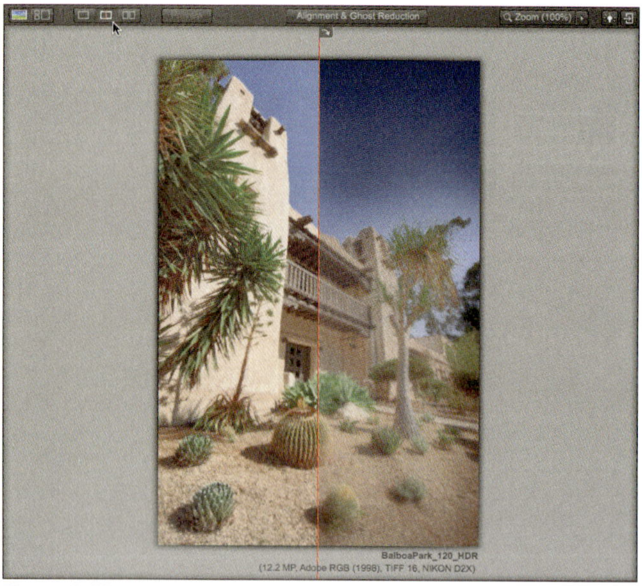

Figure 2.13

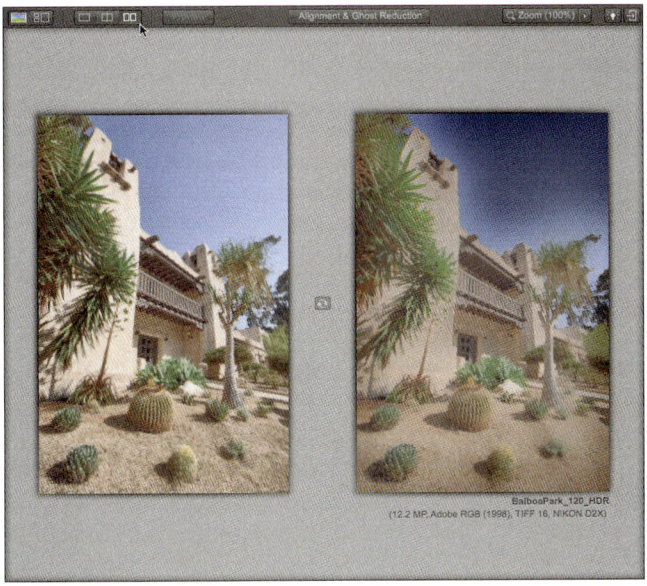

Figure 2.14

Local adjustments

Even after making extensive changes you still may not be satisfied with your image. While it may look great overall, there are likely to be local areas in the image that could use some fine-tuning. The Selective Adjustments section contains the tools to do this. If it isn't open, as shown in Figure 2.15, click on the twirler at the left of the Selective Adjustments title.

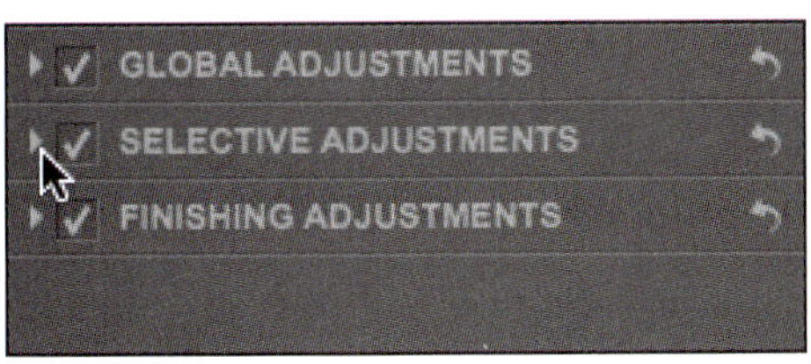

Figure 2.15

Local control in the image is accomplished by using Control Points. If a particular area of the image needs exposure or contrast adjustments, they can be done easily, without masking, by using Control Points.

The same adjustments available globally are available with Control Points:

- Exposure
- Contrast
- Saturation
- Structure
- Blacks
- Whites
- Warmth

see also

Chapters 8 and 9 cover Control Points in detail.

Finalizing your image

With global and local adjustments applied, you may feel that the image is ready to be saved or that it needs a few final adjustments. Perhaps a vignette would add impact and dimension by drawing the viewer's eye into the image. Maybe a final contrast tweak is called for or the color balance of one of the RGB channels needs adjustment.

Once the globally and locally adjusted image is saved, each of these final adjustments can be done in Photoshop or other image-editing software. Why would you do them in HDR Efex Pro?

The reason goes back to the 32-bit workflow discussed in Chapter 1. By finalizing the image in HDR Efex Pro, the adjustments are made on an image with a much higher dynamic range than an image in an image-editing program such as Photoshop. Gradations in the transitions of the vignette are smoother. RGB curves adjustments have more information on which to work so the color changes have little chance of producing banding or other color artifacts.

The Finishing Adjustments section is shown in Figure 2.16. The two tools available are a Vignette tool and Levels and Curves.

The drop-down menu to the right of the Vignette title contains eight prebuilt vignettes. Four of these simulate camera lens vignetting, two are traditional black vignettes, and two are traditional white vignettes.

The Amount, Transition, and Size sliders adjust those properties of the vignette. Each vignette can also be adjusted from circular to rectangular and the Place Center button allows positioning the vignette in the image.

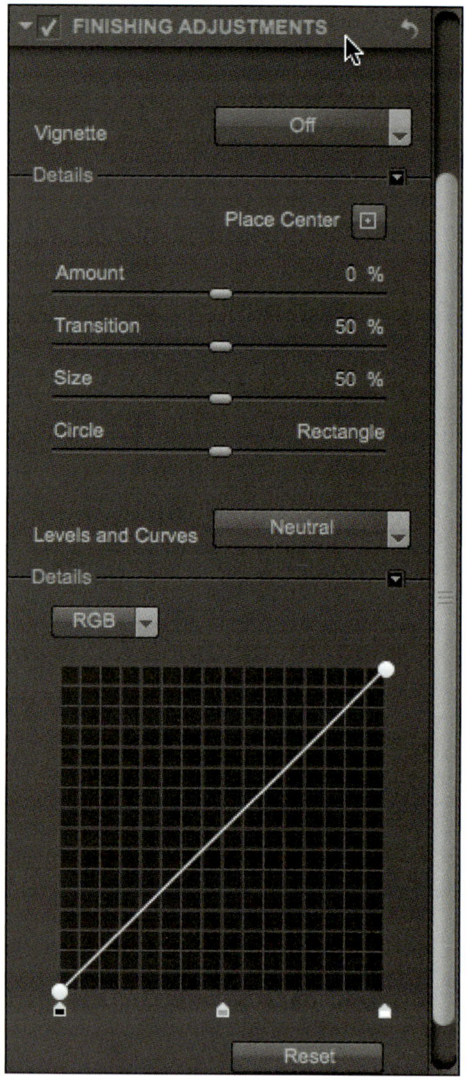

Figure 2.16

The Levels and Curves tool also has prebuilt options as well as full manual control of the separate RGB channels and the composite channel of all three colors. You can click Reset in the Levels and Curves section, and you can reset all the finalizing adjustments by clicking the curved left-facing arrow opposite the Finishing Adjustments title.

see also

Chapter 10 discusses finishing adjustments in detail.

Click Save (below the Control Palette) to save the image or Cancel to discard everything.

System Requirements

HDR Efex Pro is constantly doing complex computations while creating, adjusting, and displaying an HDR image. If you find your screen redrawing slowly, the program operating sluggishly, or error messages appearing and HDR Efex Pro crashing, you may not have computer hardware that meets the minimum system requirements shown in the following lists.

Windows

- Windows XP, Windows Vista, and Windows 7
- AMD or Intel processor
- 2GB of RAM (4GB recommended)
- Adobe Photoshop CS4 through CS5 (32-bit and 64-bit compatible), or Adobe Photoshop Lightroom 2.6 through 3.0 or later (32-bit and 64-bit compatible)
- Adobe Photoshop CS4 or CS5 Extended Edition required for 32-bit per channel Smart Object support

Macintosh

- Mac OS 10.5 through 10.7
- Intel processor
- 2GB of RAM (4GB recommended)
- Adobe Photoshop CS5 (32-bit and 64-bit compatible), Adobe Photoshop Lightroom 2.6 through 3.0 (32-bit and 64-bit compatible) or later, or Apple Aperture 2.1.4 through 3.0 or later (32-bit and 64-bit compatible)
- Adobe Photoshop CS5 Extended Edition required for 32-bit per channel Smart Object support

note

Users of early versions of HDR Efex Pro experienced occasional crashes when creating HDR images from Bridge and Photoshop. Version 1.2 eliminated the problems.

The most important things you can use to speed up processing are a fast processor, lots of RAM, fast hard drives, and the latest generation of video cards. This is especially true when creating HDR images through Bridge and Photoshop, because you have the processing overhead of these programs to support as well as the overhead of HDR Efex Pro.

While the preceding list of minimum system requirements gives adequate performance, I recommend a dual-, quad- or six-core processor of at least 2.6GHz, a 64-bit operating system, and a minimum of 4GB of RAM.

Choosing a Graphics Card

Software writers use every trick they know to make their software as fast and responsive as possible. With graphics- and imaging-intensive software, the latest tricks involve using the ultrafast memory on the graphics card to accelerate not only graphics but other operations as well.

Both AMD and NVIDIA incorporate OpenGL in their higher-end video cards. Both companies offer updated drivers for some older cards that allow them to support the OpenGL specification. Onboard graphics on motherboards generally do not support OpenGL.

When shopping for a computer or video card, be sure to check the specifications to ensure that OpenGL is supported.

Hard drive size and speed are also important. Saving HDR images as Smart Objects creates very large files, and moving these files around your computer can be an issue.

I would recommend a minimum hard drive storage size of 1TB for data files. Internal SATA give the best performance, particularly the faster 10,000 rpm and 15,000 rpm drives, although these faster drives do not have the capacity of the slower 7,200 rpm drives. Fast external hard drives with USB 3.0, FireWire 800, or eSATA II interfaces are also excellent. As always, there is no substitute for speed!

note

The Smart Objects feature is available only in the Extended Editions of Photoshop CS4 and CS5. Smart Objects preserve all the content of the original image as well as all the changes made to it when the Smart Object file is saved.

As important as your hardware is your video card choice. HDR Efex Pro runs best with a video card that supports OpenGL and lots of graphics RAM. Many current and upcoming versions of photo software will benefit from a video card that supports the OpenGL specification.

Installation

Installing HDR Efex Pro is straightforward regardless of whether you download it or use the installation CD. At one point in the installation, all the host programs for which it is compatible are displayed on the screen.

These host programs include Adobe Photoshop, Adobe Lightroom, Adobe Bridge, and Apple Aperture. You can access HDR Efex Pro from any of these programs that you have installed if you allow the installer to automatically access them during the installation.

HDR Efex Pro as a Stand-alone Application

HDR Efex Pro is also installed as a stand-alone application on both Windows and Mac computers during the installation process. However, its functionality is limited because it does not incorporate a RAW file converter.

It is not recommended to use HDR Efex Pro as a stand-alone program. But if you are willing to accept the severe limitations of working with 8-bit TIFF or JPEG originals, it will process single or bracketed files in those file formats to HDR images.

If you process bracketed RAW files to 16-bit TIFFs in a separate RAW converter and import them into the stand-alone program, the results can be very good.

I uninstalled Aperture before I installed HDR Efex Pro. Aperture wasn't shown in the compatible host listing when I installed HDR Efex Pro. When I reinstalled Aperture, HDR Efex Pro was available in it. If you install Lightroom or Bridge after you install HDR Efex Pro, you will need to run the installer again.

Before you can use the software, you must activate it. Select an image or a sequence of brackets in Bridge, Photoshop, or Aperture and open HDR Efex Pro. An activation window where you type your product key greets you.

Some users have issues during activation with version 1.0 of HDR Efex Pro. These are corrected in version 1.1.

see also

Opening images in HDR Efex Pro from the host applications is covered in Chapter 3.

Adjusting Preferences

With HDR Efex Pro successfully installed, it is important to set up the preferences to be compatible with your workflow. Most photographers seem to be afraid of changing the default preferences for fear of messing up some aspect of the software. I assure you that you cannot mess up anything in HDR Efex Pro by changing preferences. When you finish this section, I hope you have the confidence to dive into the preferences and adjust them to your needs.

To set the preferences, open HDR Efex Pro, either the stand-alone version or through Lightroom or Aperture. Opening through Bridge or Photoshop will not show all the preference options.

The preferences are found at the bottom of the interface, next to Help. HDR Efex Pro calls the preferences Settings. Click Settings to open the Settings palette, as shown in Figure 2.17.

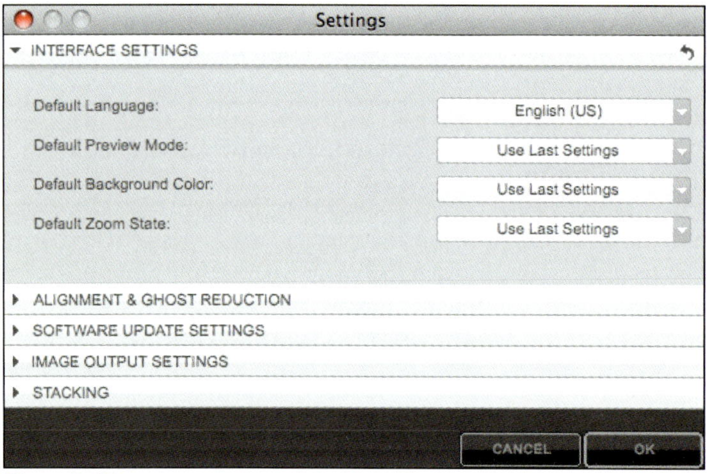

Figure 2.17

The Settings palette displays the following categories:

- Interface Settings
- Alignment & Ghost Reduction
- Software Update Settings
- Image Output Settings
- Stacking

Customizing the interface

Figure 2.17 shows the default interface settings. These open automatically whenever you open the Settings palette. If you don't customize most of these, your interface will likely look and operate differently each time you open an image in HDR Efex Pro.

I recommend changing many of the default settings to ensure that the interface looks the same every time you open an image. If you prefer a different option as you work on an image, you can adjust many of the settings in the program interface, other than the default language. But having a consistent look and operation when the program opens is how I prefer to work.

Setting the default language

For the language setting, the default English (US) is okay to leave unchanged. Click the twirler to view the other options. The available languages are the following:

- English
- German
- French
- Spanish
- Japanese
- Italian

Setting the preview mode

The default preview mode determines the look of the image when it opens in the Main Image Window. Click the downward-facing arrow to display the following options:

- Single image view
- Split preview
- Side-by-side preview
- Use Last Settings

The program default is Use Last Settings. I prefer Single image view. With Single image view, the HDR image always opens to fit in the Main Image Window, and I'm ready to apply various presets to see their effect on the entire image.

The Split preview setting shows the default preset on half the image and the new preset on the other half. Early in the process of selecting a preset, I want to know how it affects the entire image.

The Side-by-side preview shows the default preset and the new preset applied to the entire image, but both images are much smaller and I don't use this as my default for that reason.

If you select Use Last Settings as the default, whenever a new image opens in HDR Efex Pro, it could open with whichever of the other views was active when you last closed the program. This is too random for me, but if you always close HDR Efex Pro with the Main Image Window showing the image the way you want a new image to open, you can use this setting.

Setting the background color

The default background color setting determines the color behind the image when it first opens in the Main Image Window. The following options are available:

- White
- Gray
- Black
- Use Last Settings

Use Last Settings is again the default, but not my choice for the default background color. HDR images, even with the default preset displayed on an 8-bit monitor, contain a wide range of colors and tonal values.

With a white background surrounding the preview, human vision compensates by making the image appear slightly darker, while a black background has the opposite effect. My choice for default is the gray background.

Setting the zoom state

The default zoom state is *not* the level of zoom that the image will have when it first opens in HDR Efex Pro. The HDR image always fits in the Main Image Window when it first opens.

Using a Background Color

When you work with a color image, switch between the black and white backgrounds by using the light bulb-looking icon above the Main Image Window. Comparing image tones to the background shows if you have a pure white and a pure black in the image.

Using a white or black background with a monochrome image helps separate the image from the background if the tones at the edges are very light or very dark.

The default zoom state instead is the level of zoom that the image will have when you press the spacebar with an image displayed. Tapping the spacebar is a handy keyboard shortcut to zoom the image to the level you set here.

The options available are

- 400%
- 200%
- 100%
- 50%
- 25%
- Use Last Settings

I set my default zoom state at 100%. At this setting, the actual pixels of the final lower dynamic range image are displayed as accurately as possible. By panning around the image at 100% using the Navigator window, you can see any artifacts that have been created as well as any exposure, contrast, or other issues.

tip

When working on an image, you can select these same zoom states by clicking the twirler in the Zoom button above the Main Image Window and selecting the zoom level.

My recommendations for the interface settings are shown in Figure 2.18.

Customizing the Alignment & Ghost Reduction options

Creating an HDR image in HDR Efex Pro from an image series requires overlaying a number of images captured at slightly different times. Depending on the shooting conditions, the images in the series may not line up exactly with one another, or there may be subject movement in the scene itself. HDR Efex Pro includes algorithms to deal with these issues. Specifying the options for aligning images and removing subject movement is done in the Settings palette.

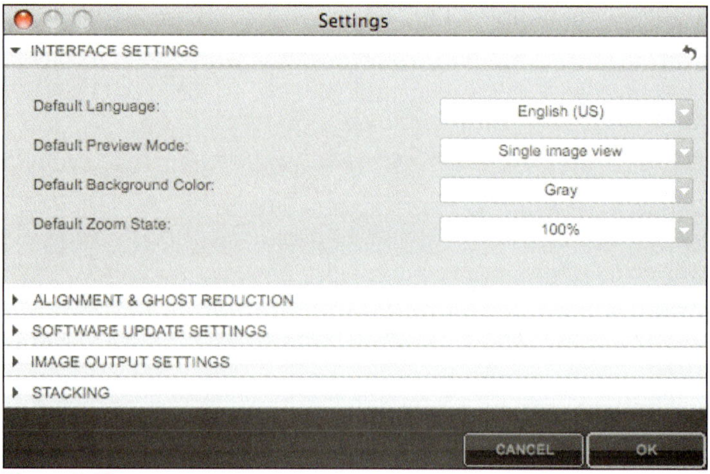

Figure 2.18

In the Settings palette, click the twirler by the Alignment & Ghost Reduction title. The settings chosen here will appear in the Alignment and Ghost Reduction dialog box in HDR Efex Pro when it opens for an HDR image created with Lightroom and Aperture. The settings have no effect on the default settings in the Alignment & Ghost Reduction dialog box in Photoshop. The default settings are shown in Figure 2.19.

Setting Alignment

When you open a bracket of exposures as an HDR image, you want them to overlay exactly on one another to produce a sharp image. HDR Efex Pro includes an alignment subroutine that does this.

Click the downward-facing arrow to see the following options:

- On
- Off
- Use Last Settings

I leave Alignment in the On position, which is the default setting.

note

You can change the setting in the dialog box for HDR images opened in Lightroom and Aperture at any time. The Alignment and Ghost Reduction dialog box is not available in HDR Efex Pro for an HDR image created through Bridge or Photoshop.

Setting the Ghost Reduction Method

Movement of objects within the scene during the exposure sequence produces what is called a *ghost* in the HDR image, because the object appears in a different position in different frames. This movement can be anything from a flag waving or a bird in the sky to a person walking by through the scene. HDR Efex Pro has two subroutines to deal with these problems. They are listed in the drop-down Ghost Reduction Method menu:

- Off
- Global
- Adaptive
- Use Last Settings

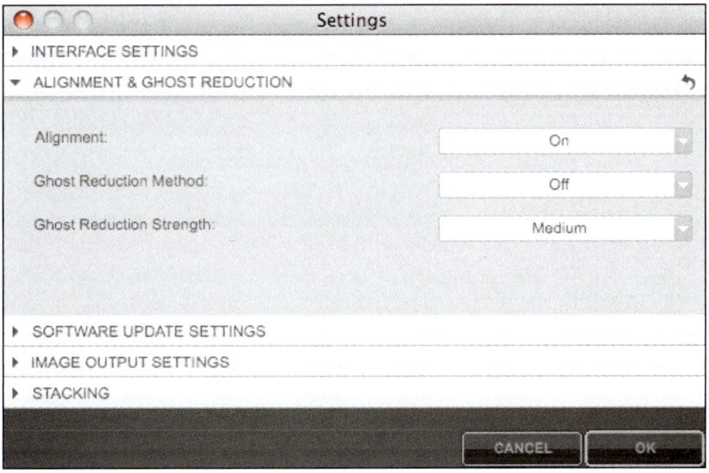

Figure 2.19

The Global option is designed to fix large-scale movement in any direction through the frame. This would include a bird flying by or a person or animal walking toward you or away from you.

The Adaptive option is best for small-scale, random movement of an object that doesn't move through the frame, yet shows motion. It attempts to eliminate the movement of objects such as a waving flag or flowing water.

Because I don't know what kind of ghosting artifact I'm dealing with until the image is open, I leave this turned Off.

Setting the Ghost Reduction Strength

Ghost Reduction is available in three strengths. Use the Ghost Reduction Strength drop-down menu to set the default strength that appears in the dialog box when Alignment & Ghost Strength is opened in Lightroom and Aperture.

The options are

- Low
- Medium
- High
- Use Last Settings

Ghost Reduction is one of the more computationally intensive tasks that HDR Efex Pro performs. When I use it, I first try a Medium setting, unless the ghosting artifact is very small and limited to one area. Medium is my default setting.

However, much of the time the Medium setting isn't sufficient and I switch to High. This often gives me a chance to take a break while the Ghost-Reduction routine does its thing.

My Alignment & Ghost Reduction settings remain the same as the default settings in Figure 2.19.

note

Chapter 3 discusses the Alignment & Ghost Reduction dialog box in all the host applications.

The effectiveness of these Ghost Reduction settings is shown in Figure 2.20, which shows a section of an HDR image processed without Ghost Reduction, and Figure 2.21, which shows the same section processed with Ghost Reduction set to High.

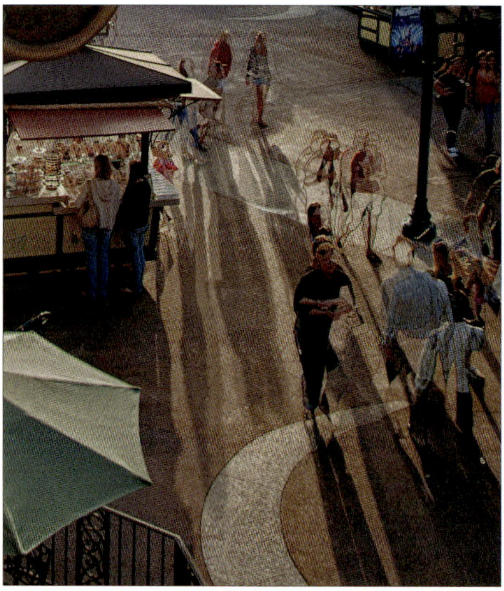

Figure 2.20

Setting the software update interval

The interval between the time that HDR Efex Pro automatically checks for updates is set in the Software Update Settings palette. The default setting to check for updates is Weekly, as shown in Figure 2.22. To me, this is overly aggressive. I recommend changing the setting to Monthly.

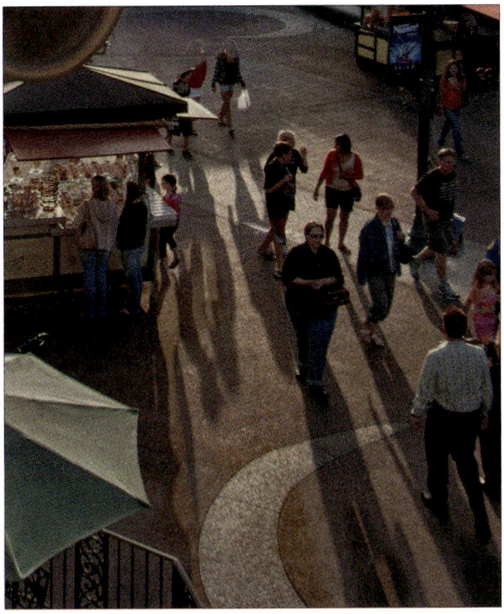
Figure 2.21

If you've been away from HDR Efex Pro for a while and are wondering if updates are available, you can navigate to this palette and click Check for updates now.

Customizing the image output settings

When you are satisfied with your HDR image and click Save in HDR Efex Pro, the file format and bit depth in which the image is saved are determined by the setting in this palette. The setting only applies to images opened through Lightroom or Aperture.

There are three options:

- JPEG
- TIFF 8
- TIFF 16

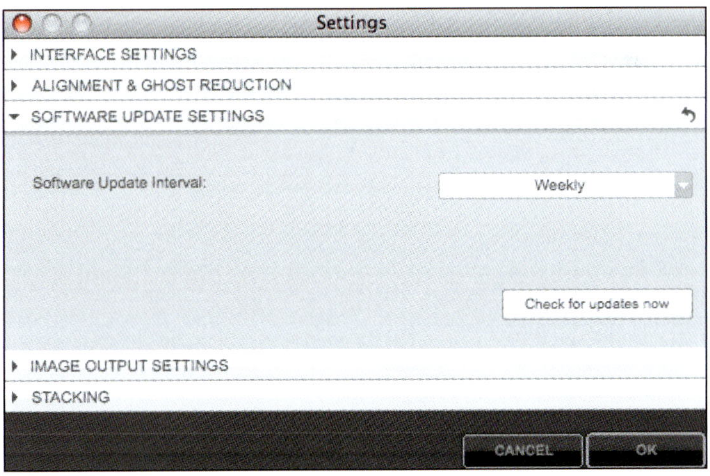

Figure 2.22

The default is TIFF 16, as shown in Figure 2.23, and I don't recommend changing this. The TIFF 16 setting preserves the maximum amount of information possible when the image is saved to a lower dynamic range that can be accessed by image-editing software.

TIFF 8 saves the HDR image as an 8-bit per color file. If you are sure that you will not be making any tonal adjustments to the processed HDR image and only want to save an 8-bit file, choose this option.

If you are only creating HDR images to share on the Internet, you could change the default to JPEG and save disk space on your hard drive.

tip

If you create HDR images from Lightroom or Aperture, you can change this setting before saving the HDR. Image Output Settings are not available in the Settings palette if the HDR image is created through Bridge or Photoshop.

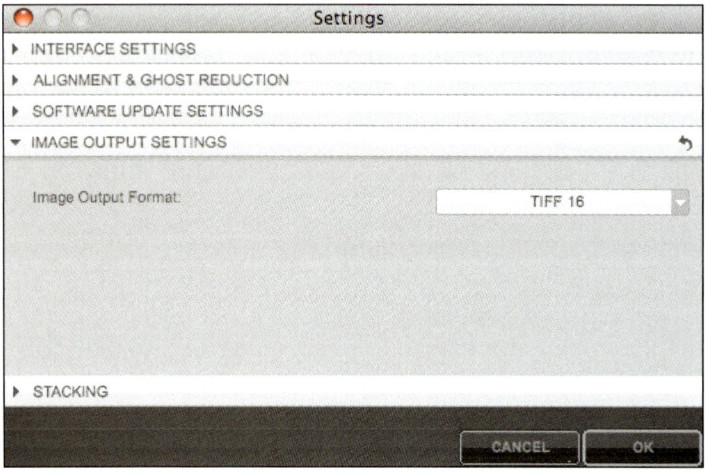

Figure 2.23

Setting stacking preferences

If you are using Lightroom or Aperture as a host application to select files for merging to an HDR image, you may or may not want the final HDR image to be saved back to the host application. The options in the Stacking palette determine where the HDR image is saved and, if reimported to the host application, how it will appear in the host application.

note

Stacking is a feature of Lightroom and Aperture that places a new image created with an existing image in a stack with the existing image. Consult Lightroom or Aperture help for more details.

There are two options in the Stacking palette:

- Automatically Re-import
- Stack With First Image

When you want to save the HDR image to a location on your computer system different from the source images, deselect Automatically Re-import. Stack With First Image becomes unavailable, also. With both options deselected, HDR Efex Pro displays the standard Save As dialog box for your operating system and you must choose a name and the location to save the HDR image.

When your plan is to save the HDR image back to the host application with a new name, but as a unique file not in a stack with the first image, select Automatically Re-import, but deselect Stack With First Image.

My preference is to save the image file with a new name in the same folder as the original images and stacked with the first image I selected to create the HDR image. So I leave the default settings unchanged, as shown in Figure 2.24.

tip

If you are about to save an HDR image that began as files in Lightroom and Aperture and decide that you want to save it with a unique name and not reimport it, open the Settings palette and change the preference in Stacking on the fly before saving the HDR image.

I hope that you now feel comfortable enough with the preferences options that you will adjust them to suit your workflow.

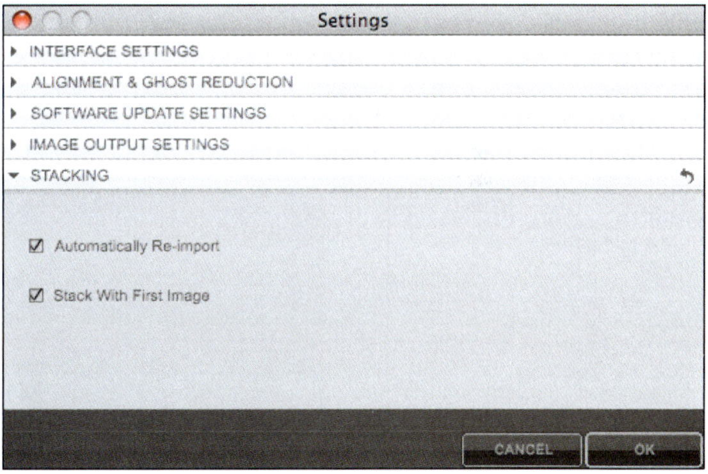

Figure 2.24

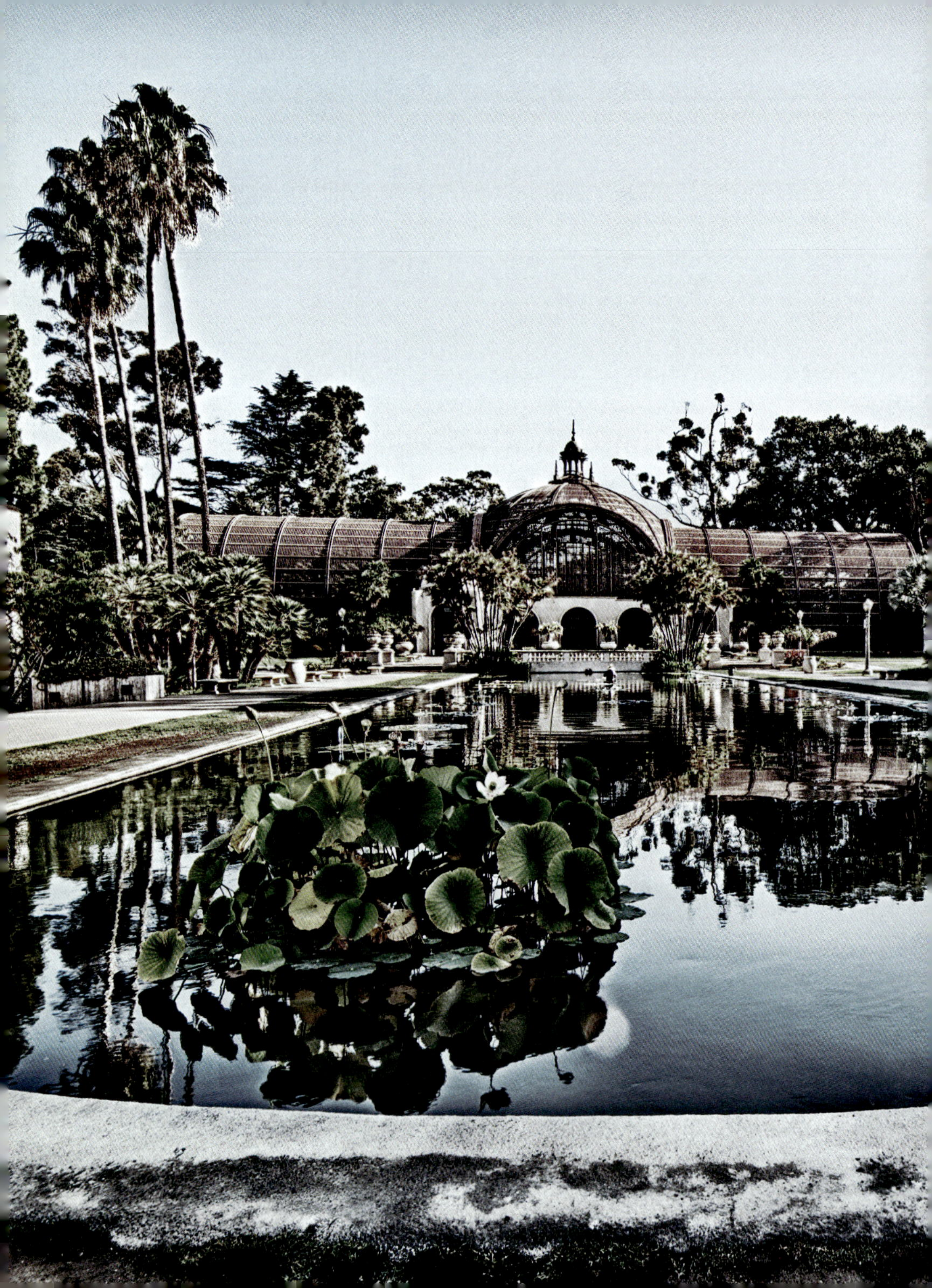

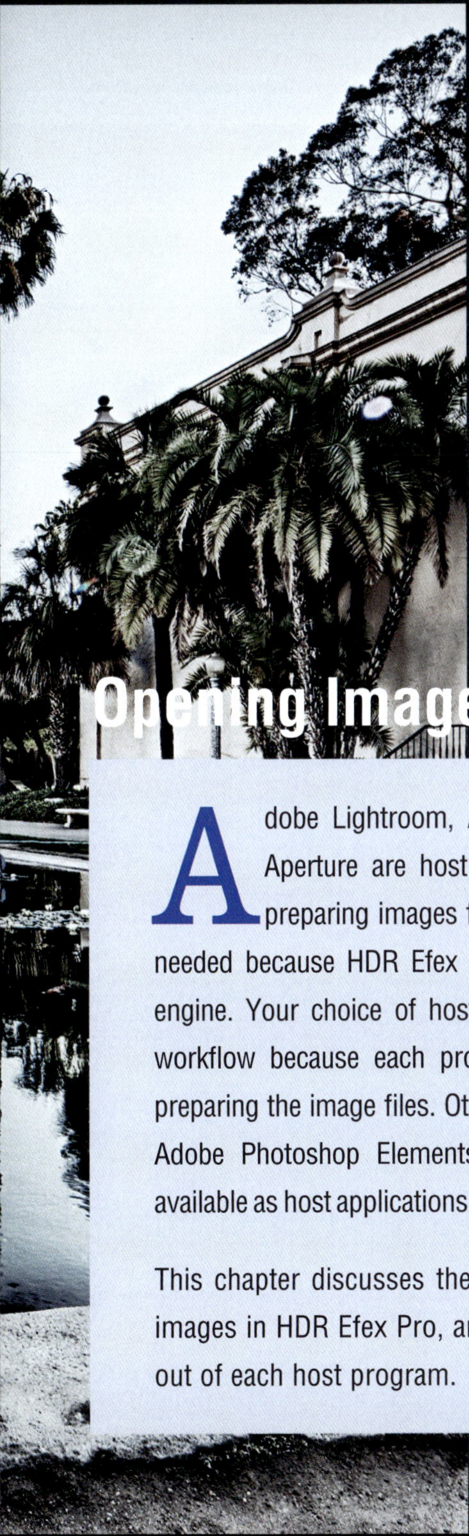

3

Opening Images in HDR Efex Pro

Adobe Lightroom, Adobe Bridge, Adobe Photoshop, and Apple Aperture are host applications that support HDR Efex Pro by preparing images for HDR processing. These host programs are needed because HDR Efex Pro does not have its own RAW processing engine. Your choice of host application has a significant effect on your workflow because each program takes a slightly different approach to preparing the image files. Other programs that process RAW files, such as Adobe Photoshop Elements and Corel PaintShop Photo Pro, are not available as host applications because they do not support 32-bit processing.

This chapter discusses the basic image requirements needed to open images in HDR Efex Pro, and then addresses the steps to get the most out of each host program.

Image Input Requirements

Digital captures needed to create an HDR image have specific requirements. Your choice of camera and camera settings is important, as is image capture technique. A thorough understanding of your camera's controls and the software you use to move the image series to HDR Efex Pro is essential.

Basic image requirements

To get the highest-quality HDR image, it's necessary to have the highest-quality source images. A large number of factors affect the quality of the source images, ranging from the camera and camera settings to the techniques employed while capturing the source images. This section briefly explores these factors.

Choosing a camera for HDR imaging

While it is possible to create true HDR images in HDR Efex Pro from brackets of JPEG and TIFF files, brackets of RAW format image files provide the best starting points, as discussed in Chapter 1. For most scenes, a 5-EV (Exposure Value or f-stop) bracketing series in 1-EV step, or a 3-EV bracketing series in 2-EV steps is adequate. With extremely high-contrast scenes, an even wider bracket may be needed to capture the full dynamic range.

Cameras that contain autobracketing are the easiest to use and generally produce the best results. Autobracketing takes the guesswork out of the bracketing process. Autobracketing also virtually guarantees repeatable results if you need to redo the bracket because of unexpected movement somewhere in the scene.

If only manual bracketing is available, take great care that you do not move the camera when you change settings. Alignment problems can occur if the camera moves.

Image capture technique

Good camera technique is important, also. This includes the proper choice of camera settings as well as careful attention to the physical mechanics of picture taking.

Set the camera ISO to the lowest possible value to minimize sensor noise. Because HDR Efex Pro merges a series of exposures, sensor noise is higher in an HDR image than in any of the images from which it is made. This is especially true in shadow areas and becomes even more apparent when the shadow tones are brought higher in exposure value in the HDR image.

Leave the camera aperture (f-stop) fixed and bracket with shutter speeds. At different aperture settings, the *depth of field* changes. This causes the size and sharpness of objects in the scene to vary, making it difficult for HDR Efex Pro to align the images accurately. Bracket by setting the camera's functions to change the shutter speed while leaving the aperture constant. Consult your camera manual if you are unsure how to do this.

Use a tripod while exposing the bracket. If the camera moves during the exposure series, this can also cause alignment problems. Securing the camera to a stable tripod during exposure and even using the mirror lockup function stabilizes the camera system.

HDR Efex Pro incorporates excellent alignment algorithms to merge images accurately. Proper bracketing and camera technique make it easier and quicker for the software to work, and may even allow you to skip using the alignment function for a further speed gain in your HDR workflow.

Finally, turn off all the automatic camera functions such as auto white balance, autofocus, and flash. Set the essential functions such as focus and white balance manually. HDR Efex Pro performs best when only the shutter speed changes between captures.

Exposure values dialog box

Most digital cameras automatically store information about each capture in an *EXIF* file that travels along with the image. Included in this metadata are both the exposure settings and the EV steps used in the bracketing sequence.

Automatically setting exposure values

To merge a series of bracketed exposures, HDR Efex Pro needs to know the relative exposure values of each image. The program automatically reads this information from the EXIF information that most cameras store in the image metadata.

Lightroom (Figure 3.1), Bridge (Figure 3.2), and Aperture (Figure 3.3) display this exposure bias information in different locations in their respective workspaces. If this information is not displayed, or reads 0 when you view the images in any of these programs, the camera has not recorded the exposure bias data in the field. In Figures 3.1 to 3.3, the cursor points to the exposure bias information.

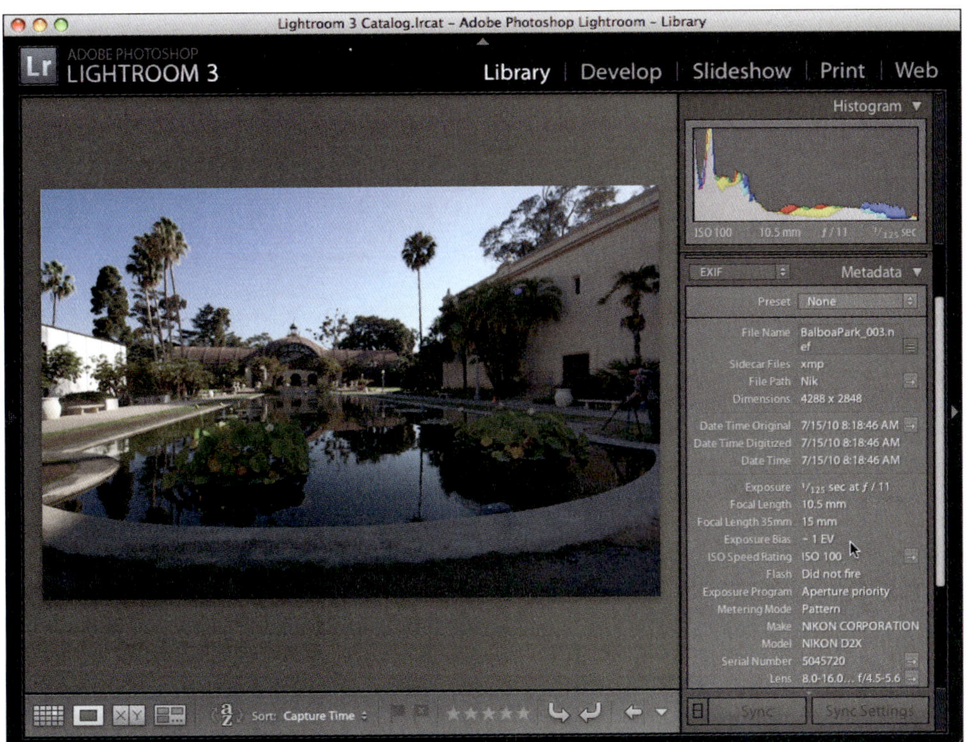

Figure 3.1

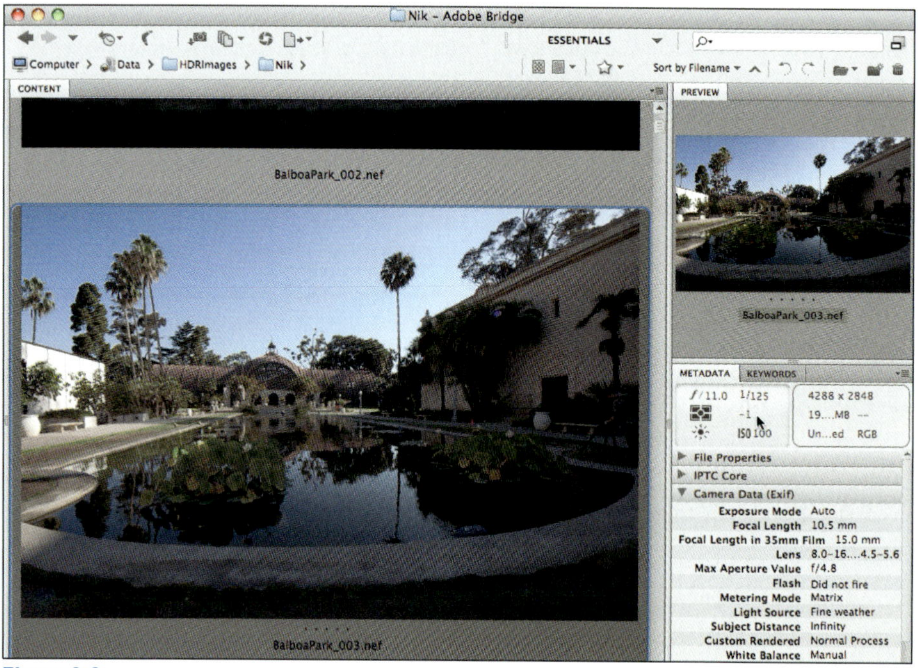

Figure 3.2

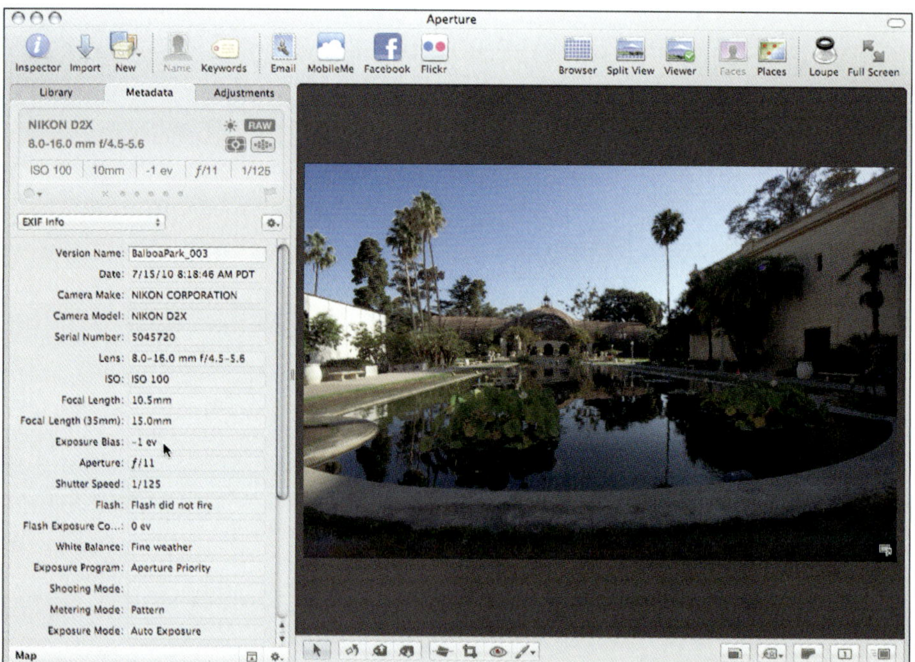

Figure 3.3

If your camera stores the exposure bias information in the EXIF metadata, HDR Efex Pro will process the images correctly and you need never think about it. But even if this is not the case, all is not lost because you can set exposure values manually.

Manually setting exposure values

HDR Efex Pro will still allow you to create an HDR from the brackets even if the EXIF data is missing for any reason. When you select the images and attempt to export them, the Exposure Values dialog box appears, as shown in Figure 3.4.

Click the downward-facing arrow next to E.V. Spacing to display the drop-down menu shown in Figure 3.5, and click the EV step amount that you used during the bracketing.

HDR Efex Pro analyzes the image and generally fills in the exposure values for each image, as shown in Figure 3.6. If it does not, enter the exposure values manually. After the values have been selected, click OK to continue.

note

Nikon professional dSLR models offer autobracketing up to +/– 3 EV, in 1/3-, 1/2-, and 1-EV increments over a range of nine exposures. Canon professional dSLR models offer autobracketing up to +/– 3 EV, in 1/3- or 1/2-EV increments for seven exposures.

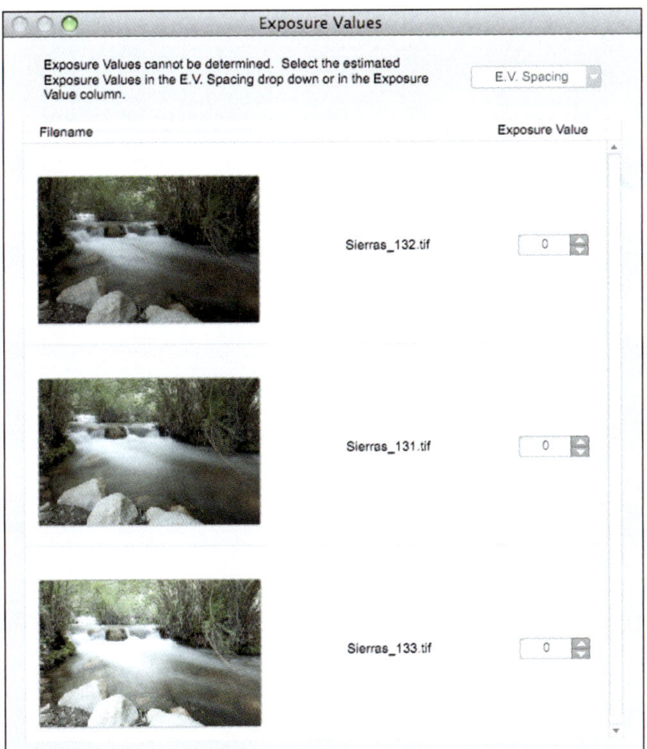

Figure 3.4

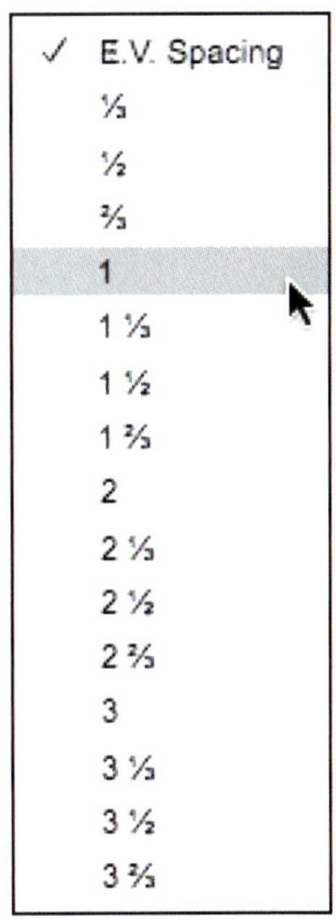

Figure 3.5

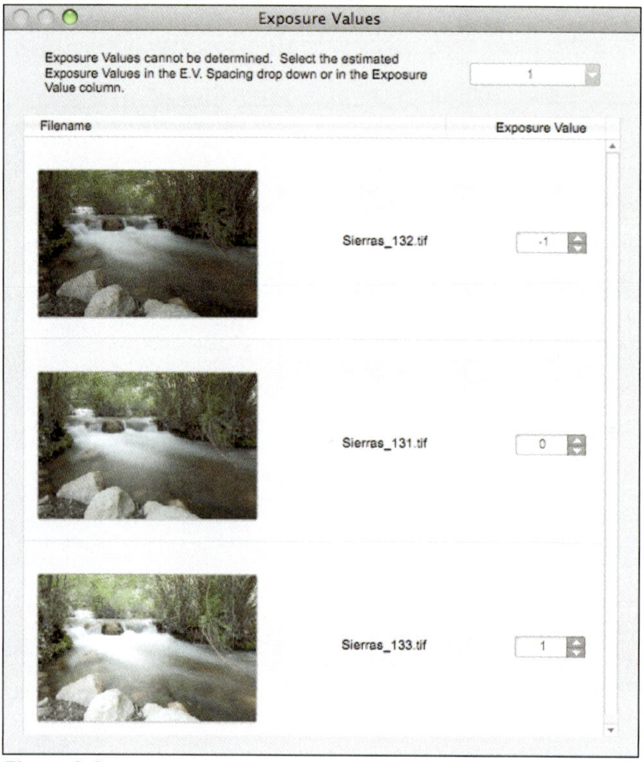

Figure 3.6

Opening Images from Adobe Lightroom

Many photographers incorporate Adobe Lightroom as an essential part of their workflow, from transferring image files into their computers from their cameras to outputting images for printing or sharing. The integration between HDR Efex Pro and Lightroom is excellent, so there is no need to abandon a Lightroom workflow to do HDR imaging. It is only necessary to make a few initial adjustments to incorporate HDR Efex Pro into your Lightroom workflow.

Even though Lightroom uses Adobe Camera Raw for RAW file processing, just as Bridge and Photoshop do, Lightroom process files totally independently of Photoshop. In fact, Photoshop does not even have to be loaded on your computer in order to use Lightroom to process RAW files and open images in HDR Efex Pro.

Because Lightroom is independent of Photoshop, it is not bound by the preferences set in Camera Raw in the way that Bridge and Photoshop are, as discussed later in this chapter. For this reason, Lightroom needs to be set up properly to interact with HDR Efex Pro.

Lightroom and Digital Asset Management

Adobe Lightroom, now in version 3, is one of the most popular photo software programs among professional and advanced amateur photographers. It isn't an image-editing program like Adobe Photoshop, and it isn't a file browsing program like Adobe Bridge. Although it has some of the features of both of these types of software, it is primarily a digital asset management (DAM) program.

DAM software is designed to help you organize your digital assets, as photos and videos are known to software engineers. Lightroom allows you to view, edit, and manage your digital assets and even perform some of these operations if the assets are offline and not directly accessible to Lightroom. To interact with HDR Efex Pro, however, your photos must be accessible to Lightroom.

Setting up Lightroom for HDR Efex Pro

When HDR Efex Pro installs in Lightroom, it adds the default set of export properties shown in Figure 3.7. To see these, choose File→Export→Nik Software→HDR Efex Pro, or simply click Export at the bottom of the left pane in the Library module. These properties are what Lightroom uses when it processes the RAW files to export to HDR Efex Pro.

The four processing options are

- Format
- Compression
- Color Space
- Bit Depth

The default options for each of these selections are excellent and will not create any problems if you decide to use them.

However, I suggest creating one other set of properties with the *ProPhoto RGB* color space. The ProPhoto RGB color space incorporates a wider gamut of colors than the RGB color space. The settings are shown in Figure 3.8. Click Add after altering the color space to name and save it as an export option.

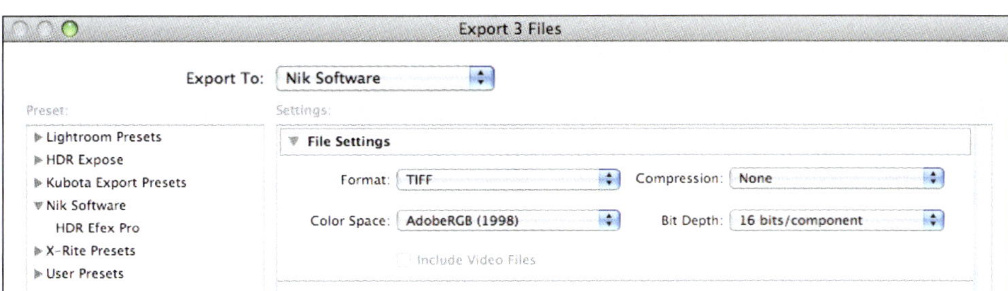

Figure 3.7

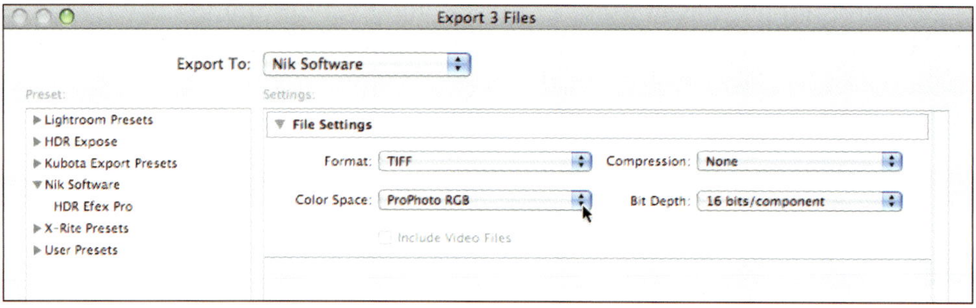

Figure 3.8

The ProPhoto RGB color space includes more colors than the Adobe (1998) RGB color space. And HDR imaging is all about packing the widest dynamic range and color range into the image.

Furthermore, ProPhoto RGB is the color space of the future. In time, monitors and printers will offer support for larger color spaces like ProPhoto RGB. When HDR images are archived in ProPhoto RGB they have more color information available and are ready for the future. To use those images in the present, you can change the color space to Adobe RGB (1998) or sRGB in an image-editing program when the HDR images are complete.

Importing and selecting images in Lightroom

Many photographers apply a Develop Settings preset when importing images into Lightroom as a normal part of their workflow. This preset might be a Lightroom built-in, one of their own creation, or a third-party preset. However, when you import photos into Lightroom that you plan on processing to HDR images, "None" is the safest setting for all but the most advanced users. Applying a preset during import with the wrong choice of settings will cause problems when the HDR image is created.

While you don't want to make any exposure or tonal adjustments to the imported images in the Lightroom Library module, the histogram, as shown in Figure 3.9, is one tool there that is very useful.

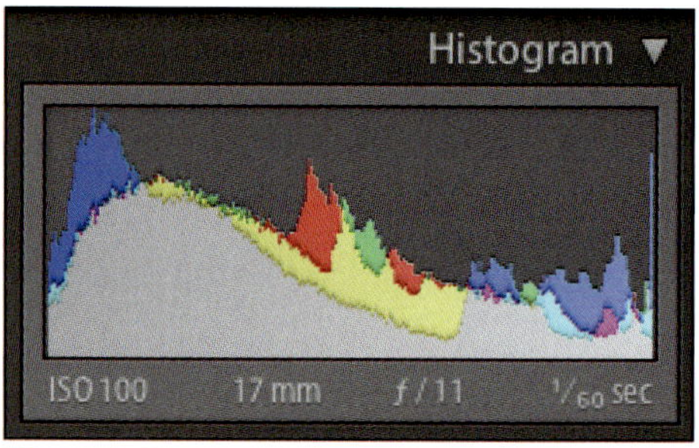

Figure 3.9

The histogram in Figure 3.9 extends all the way from clipping in the shadows on the left side of the histogram to clipping in the highlights on the right side of the histogram. A histogram shaped like this is as you would expect from one of the middle brackets, and graphically shows that this scene has high dynamic range.

What HDR Efex Pro needs to create a true HDR image are images like this one and others. The others need to include one image where the shadow values stop short of the left edge of the histogram (Figure 3.10) and one image where the highlight values stop short of the right side of the histogram (Figure 3.11). The histograms show the tonal information for the image with the lighter border.

While it is possible to create an HDR image from two captures whose histograms look like those in Figures 3.10 and 3.11, I recommend using a minimum of three captures exposed as follows:

- One image overexposed such that the values stop just short of the left side of the histogram
- One image exposed such that the values extend all the way across the histogram
- One image underexposed such that the values stop just short of the right side of the histogram

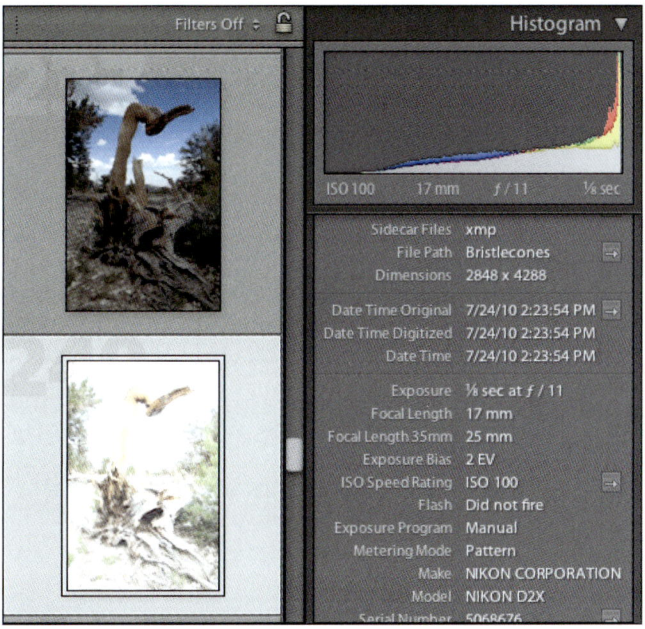

Figure 3.10

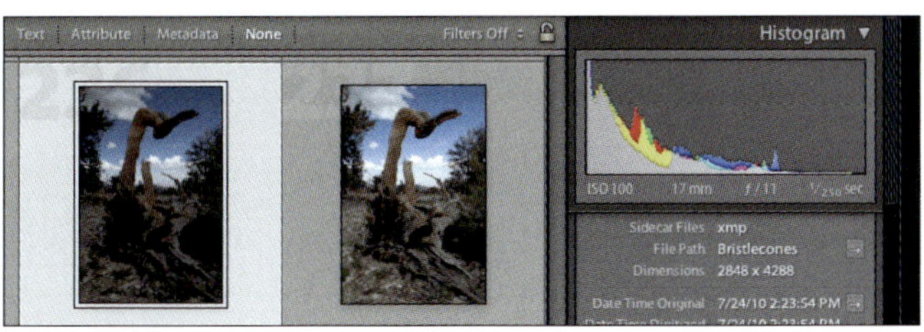

Figure 3.11

Any images whose tonal values lie between those of the overexposed and underexposed images will contribute local tonal information to the HDR image.

Images that are more underexposed than the ones described previously will contribute no usable information, but will contribute noise. However, images that are more overexposed than the three described previously are useful because their dark values are in the middle of the camera's exposure range where there is less noise. Don't limit your bracket to two or three exposures if you want the lowest noise in the processed HDR image.

You could also use the histogram in the Develop module for the same purpose. The Develop module histogram provides an even easier, more visual way to select the overexposed and underexposed files for each end of the bracket.

Press J in the Develop module or click the upward-facing arrows on each side of the histogram window. This activates the Lightroom clipping indicators. Clipped shadow values are displayed in the image with a blue overlay. Clipped highlights are indicated in red.

Double-click each image in the bracket. The first overexposed image that does not show a blue overlay indicates it is good to use for one end of the bracket. The first underexposed image that does not show a red overlay is good for the other end of the bracket, along with all the images between.

Any bracketed images outside of these add processing time but no tonal information to the HDR image. If none of the images falls short of the limits of the histogram, the HDR image won't contain all the dynamic range in the original scene, but it will still be interesting.

There are also a couple of other reasons to leave the Library module for the Develop module, though not to make exposure or tonal adjustments.

One is to run noise reduction. Because processing files to an HDR image builds up noise, it is best to add instructions to reduce noise from the RAW files before exporting the files to HDR Efex Pro. Do not be too aggressive when you do this to avoid softening image detail.

New in Lightroom 3 is a much-improved noise reduction algorithm. If you know that your camera produces even a moderate amount of noise at the ISO speed you use, run at least a small amount of noise reduction on all the brackets in the series. When the HDR image is complete, you may want to run noise reduction again. Nik Software Dfine 2.0 is an excellent choice for noise reduction on the final image.

Noise is reduced in Lightroom from the Develop module. Scroll down until you find the Detail palette. Click the twirler to open the palette if it isn't open. A preview window showing an area of the image at 100% is visible as are controls for sharpening and noise reduction. Drag the window around to a shadow area where the noise is more apparent. If the noise looks like gray dots, use the Luminance slider to lower the noise. If the noise looks like colored dots, use the Color slider to lower the noise. Stop the sliders before the 100% view starts to look out of focus.

Another reason to leave the Library module is to remove any chromatic aberration in the image. Chromatic aberration looks like red and cyan or blue and yellow outlines around objects in high contrast areas of the image. These outlines are most obvious near the edges of the image. Even the smallest amount of chromatic aberration in the source images is compounded in the HDR image. If chromatic aberration is at all noticeable in the source images, remove it before you export the files to HDR Efex Pro.

You can use the Chromatic Aberration tool to remove the color outlines in Lightroom. The tool is found in the Lens Correction palette just below the Noise Reduction tool.

Click the Manual title to open the manual Chromatic Aberration sliders and adjust them to correct Red/Cyan and Blue/Yellow outlines. Turn on and use the Defringe tool to remove color fringing that appears at the edges of grossly overexposed areas and isn't related to chromatic aberration.

When you export your source images using Lightroom, these corrections are incorporated into the files.

Exporting from Lightroom

There are three paths available to export images from Lightroom to HDR Efex Pro. All three are available from the Library module, but only two are available from the Develop module. Choosing the appropriate path depends on your personal Lightroom workflow.

Using the Export button

After you have selected the images in the filmstrip or in the Grid view, click Export at the bottom of the left pane in the Library module. This opens the same dialog box shown in Figure 3.8. Choose one of the presets under Nik Software HDR Efex Pro, either the default preset or one of your own creation, and the export process begins. This method is only available in the Library module.

Using the File menu

If you are in either the Library or Develop modules of Lightroom, you can export images using the File menu in two possible ways.

Choosing File → Export takes you to the dialog box in Figure 3.8, just as clicking Export in the Library module does.

Another method using the File menu is to choose File → Export with Preset → Nik Software, and select one of the presets shown in Figure 3.12. Either method begins the export process.

The fastest way

The third option for exporting from Lightroom, available in both the Library and Develop modules, is to select the image series from the thumbnails in the film strip, right-click, and select Export → HDR Efex Pro.

Summary of export steps

To export a series of bracketed exposures from Lightroom to HDR Efex Pro, follow these steps:

1. **Import files into Lightroom.** Do not apply any presets that change exposure or tonal values.
2. **Select each image and look at its histogram.** Click a selection of images ranging from underexposed to overexposed, as described previously.
3. **Reduce noise and color fringing in the Develop module if needed.**
4. **Export the images to HDR Efex Pro.** Use one of the three paths described previously.

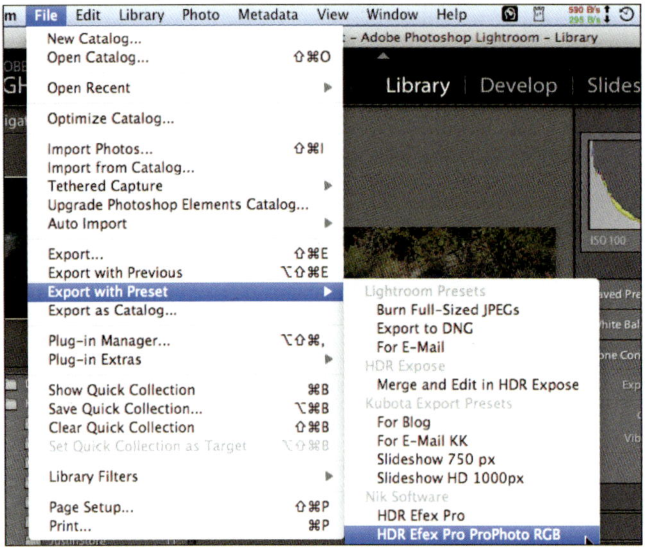

Figure 3.12

note

You can also export a single image to HDR Efex Pro using the Export button or using either of the options from the File menu.

Alignment & Ghost Reduction with Lightroom export

Opening a series of exposures from Lightroom opens the HDR Efex Pro software directly. As you see in Figure 3.13, the upper bar holding the viewing options has an Alignment & Ghost Reduction button.

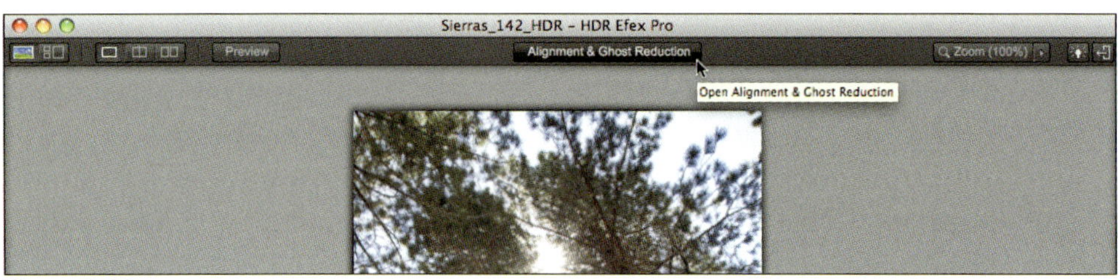

Figure 3.13

When an image opens in HDR Efex Pro through Lightroom, the HDR image has been aligned if On is selected for alignment in the Alignment & Ghost Reduction palette in Settings and Ghost Reduction has not been performed. Press the spacebar or click the Zoom button to zoom to 100% and use the Navigator to pan through the image.

If the image needs further alignment or ghost removal, click Alignment & Ghost Reduction to open the Alignment and Ghost Reduction dialog box, as shown in Figure 3.14. The default settings are those you chose when setting up your preferences in Chapter 2. Make the appropriate selections in the dialog box and click OK. The subroutines process the image and a reprocessed preview appears with the default preset active.

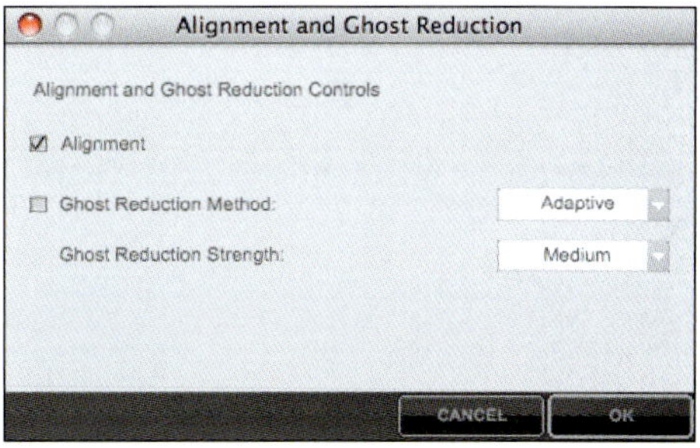

Figure 3.14

Opening Images from Adobe Bridge

While some photographers prefer a Lightroom-based workflow, others prefer centering their workflow on Adobe Bridge. There are advantages and disadvantages to each approach that are beyond the scope of this book. What is important is that HDR Efex Pro supports both workflows.

Adobe Bridge works with Adobe Photoshop to open images in HDR Efex Pro. Because of differences in the software architecture between Bridge and Lightroom, the path that Bridge takes is somewhat different than that of Lightroom and more closely aligned with the Photoshop path covered later in this chapter.

Setting up Bridge for HDR Efex Pro

Bridge processes RAW files using Adobe Camera Raw. Therefore, it is important to set up the Camera Raw preferences before you select and process the RAW files. If you do this in Photoshop, Bridge uses the same preferences. But you can also set Camera Raw preferences directly in Bridge. As a minimum, it is a good idea to check the Camera Raw preferences before you begin processing your images to be certain they are set properly.

To open the Camera Raw preferences in Bridge, select one of your RAW files and then choose File→Open in Camera Raw. The dialog box in Figure 3.15 appears.

Below the preview image are the current processing parameters set in Camera Raw. The processing parameters are highlighted in blue and underlined. Click on the blue type to open the Workflow Options dialog box, as shown in Figure 3.16. The settings you select in the dialog box determine the processing parameters in Camera Raw.

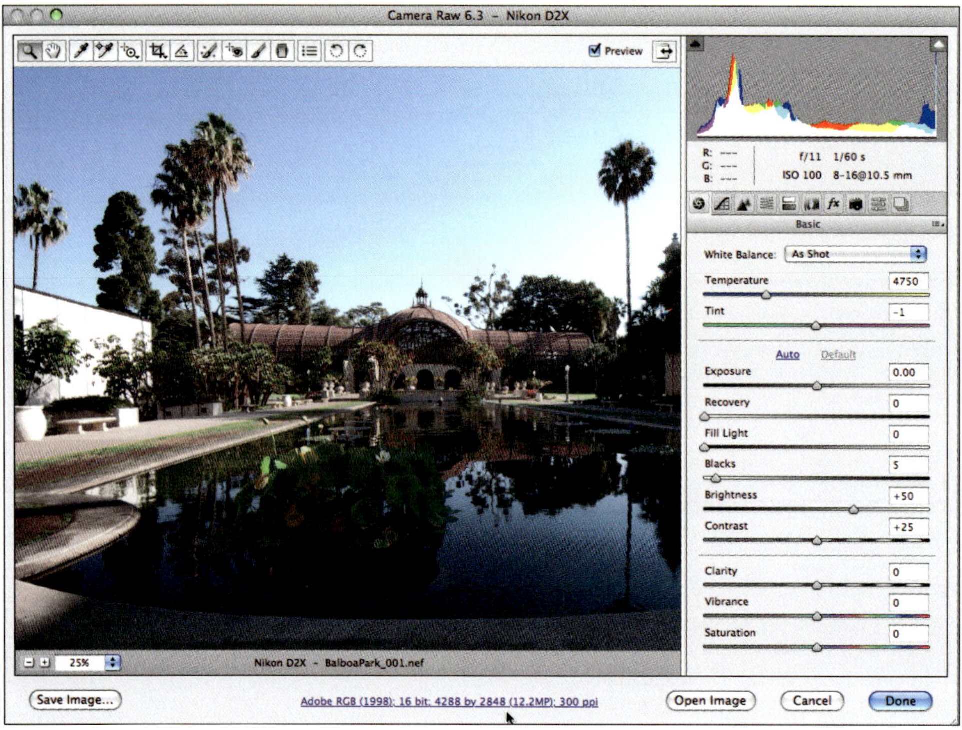

Figure 3.15

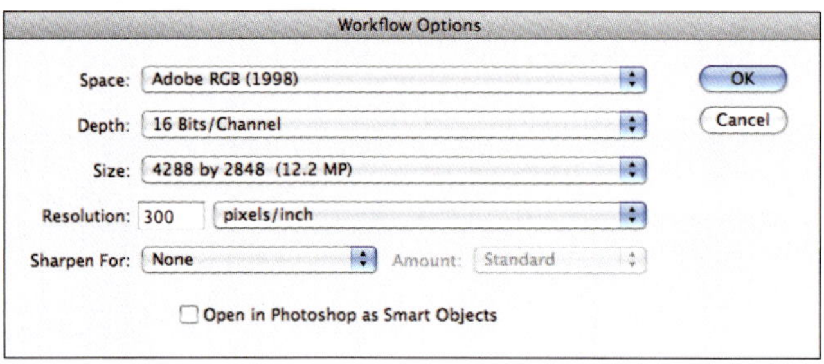

Figure 3.16

Set the color space of the processed file by clicking the Space drop-down menu. The options are

- Adobe RGB (1998)
- ColorMatch RGB
- ProPhoto RGB
- sRGB IEC61966-2.1

Choose either Adobe RGB (1998) or ProPhoto RGB. These are the two color spaces with the largest color gamuts. I prefer working in

ProPhoto RGB for HDR images because it includes more colors than Adobe RGB.

You want to process the RAW files to the largest bit depth available. Choose 16 Bits/Channel in the Depth drop-down menu.

The available Size options depend on the camera used to capture the images. There are five options listed in the drop-down list. These are the pixel dimensions available when you process the RAW image.

Choose the listing that doesn't have a "+" sign or a "–" sign. This is the native pixel dimensions of the image and results in the best image reproduction. To produce any of the others, Photoshop must downsample or upsample the image pixels.

The next setting is Resolution. The number you set in the first box determines the image file resolution of the processed file in pixels/inch (or pixels/cm). Resolution operates along with Size to determine the final output dimensions of the image. This relationship can always be adjusted later in Photoshop using the Image Size dialog box, but I prefer to save the step and set the numbers here.

The Photoshop default is 240 pixels/inch, which is the minimum resolution appropriate for inkjet printing. Because most of my work is destined for commercial printing, I set the Resolution to 300 pixels/inch.

You do not want to sharpen the RAW file at this point. Select None from the "Sharpen" drop-down menu.

Finally, leave the Open in Photoshop as Smart Objects check box deselected.

My preferences for Workflow Options with my equipment and needs are shown in Figure 3.17.

Opening an image series

With your image folder open in Bridge you can see all the brackets that are available for HDR processing. Bridge, unlike Lightroom, does not have a histogram directly available in the interface that can help you select which images to process. You could process the full bracket, but there is a way to save processing time by only selecting the range of images really needed.

You may have noticed when setting Camera Raw defaults that the Camera Raw dialog box has a histogram. The dialog box also has some other useful tools and some tools to avoid.

Choose the images to process in HDR Efex Pro by selecting all of them in Bridge and opening them in Camera Raw by choosing File → Open in Camera Raw. The Camera Raw window now looks like Figure 3.18.

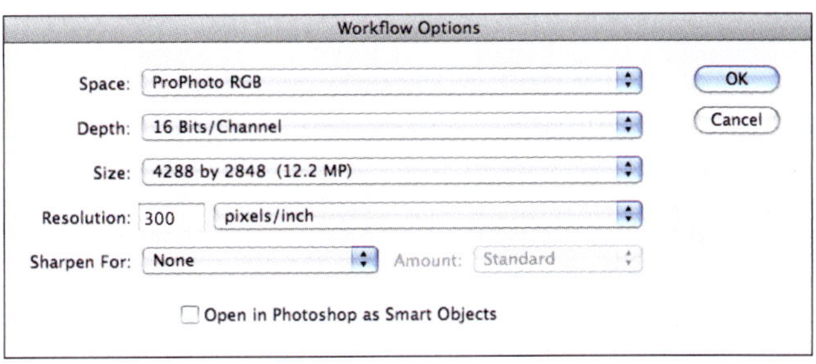

Figure 3.17

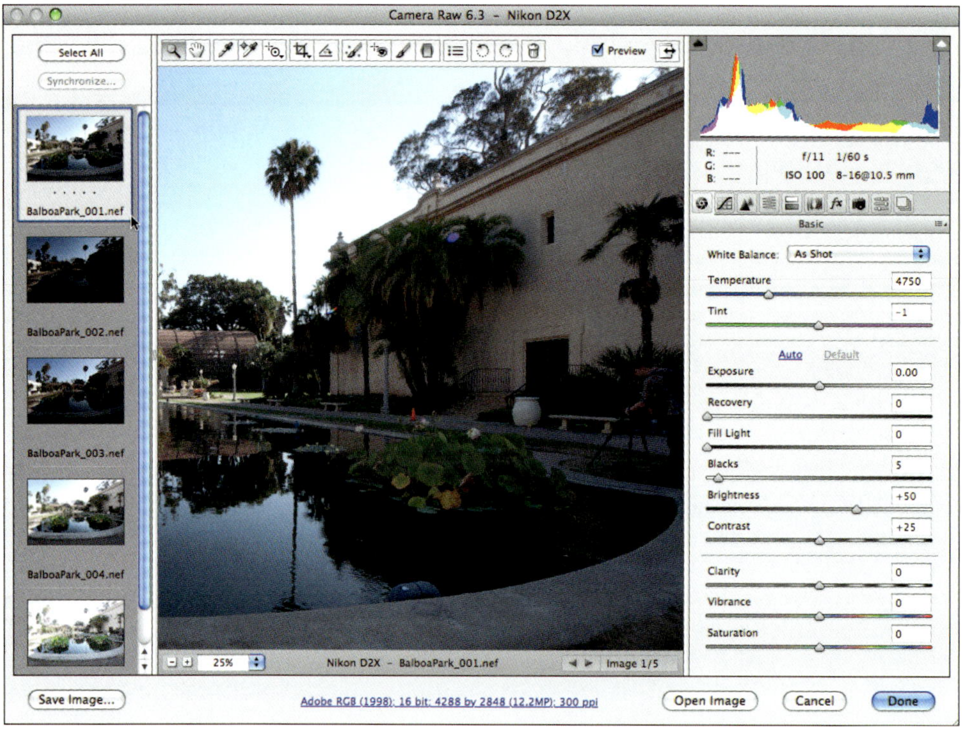

Figure 3.18

As you click through the images, the histogram changes to show the tonal range. Look for the first underexposed image whose histogram does not extend all the way to the right and the first overexposed image whose histogram does not extend all the way to the left. These images and all others between them are the minimum number to export to HDR Efex Pro. Disregard any others that are more underexposed because they will only add noise to the HDR image. Include others that are more overexposed if you want. They will add to the processing time, but will reduce noise.

At times it is difficult to tell whether the image information stops short of the ends of the histogram. If this happens while looking for an underexposed image, press O or click the upward-facing arrow at the upper right of the histogram. This displays clipped highlight values with a red overlay. Note the filename of the first image that does not display a red overlay. This will be your underexposed image.

To find the overexposed image, press U or click the upward-facing arrow at the upper left of the histogram. This displays the clipped shadow values with a blue overlay. Note the filename of the first image that does not display a blue overlay. This will be your overexposed image.

If none of the images stops short of clipping at either end of the scale, the bracket isn't wide enough to cover the full dynamic range. In most cases this still produces a great HDR image. Just be sure to use all the images in the bracket.

Below the histogram, the Basic image adjustment panel is open. Do not make any adjustments in this panel or in the Tone Curve panel.

If the images show significant noise when zoomed to 100%, open the Detail panel. Select all the thumbnails by pressing Ctrl/⌘+A and adjusting the Noise Reduction Luminance and Color sliders to lower the noise level.

With the image still at 100% view and all the thumbnails selected, hold down the spacebar and pan to the corners of the image. If you see or suspect color fringing like that in Figure 3.19, open the Lens Corrections panel. You may need to zoom the active image to 200% to see the color fringing if your lens is well corrected. The color fringing usually looks like a red or reddish-purple outline on one side of a high-contrast area and a cyan (blue-green) fringe on the opposite side, although sometimes the fringing appears blue and yellow. Use the Chromatic Aberration sliders to eliminate the color outlines.

Now you are ready to save these adjustments and get on with the HDR processing. Click Done at the bottom of the Camera Raw dialog box, not Save Image. The Done button saves the adjustments in the RAW file metadata without processing the images. The adjustments are applied when the images are processed and exported to HDR Efex Pro. If you click Save Image, Camera Raw processes the images to 16-bit TIFFs according to the preferences you set earlier.

The export process for an image series from Bridge to HDR Efex Pro is straightforward after checking or setting the Camera Raw preferences and making any adjustments needed. Select the exposure bracket files and choose Tools→Nik Software→Merge to HDR Efex Pro, as shown in Figure 3.20.

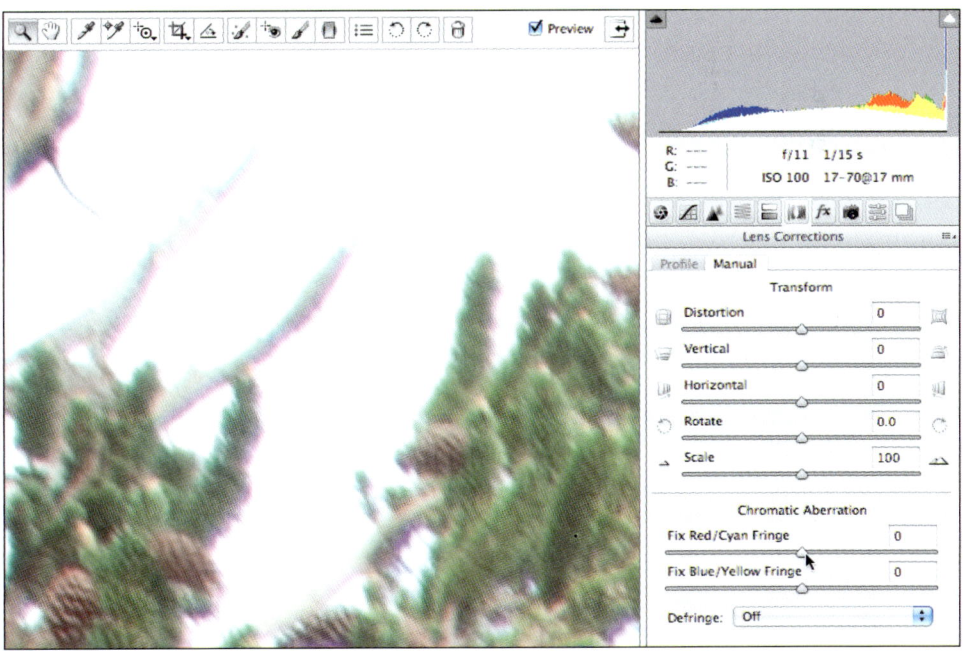

Figure 3.19

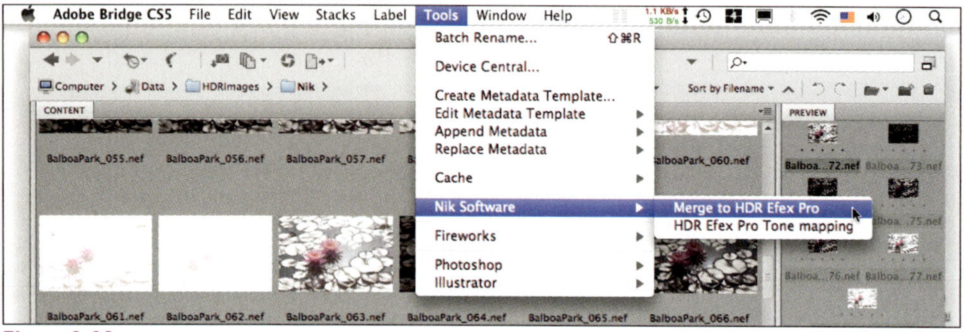

Figure 3.20

Using the Image Merge dialog box

If Photoshop is not already open, choose Tools → Nik Software → HDR Efex Pro to launch Photoshop and open the HDR Efex Pro Image Merge dialog box, as shown in Figure 3.21. The selected images are listed at the top with some options below. The options are the same as the options used the last time the Image Merge dialog box was open. The default options are displayed the first time you open it.

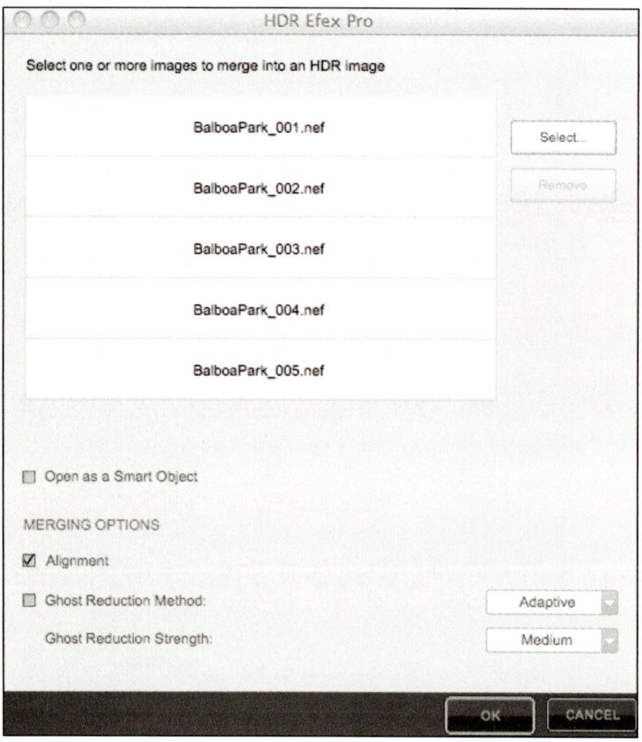

Figure 3.21

File list

The first few times I exported files through Bridge, I thought it was necessary to click each image name in the list, then click Select Image to select them. After all, when you click them, they highlight in red! But I discovered it isn't necessary to select them in this dialog box. If the image names appear in the box, they are selected.

If you scroll through the list and find a file that made its way there in error, you have the option to remove it. Select the file from the list — it will highlight in red — and click Remove.

It isn't time to click OK yet. There are several very import options in this dialog box.

Open as a Smart Object check box

The first option below the file list is the Open as a Smart Object check box. If you are unfamiliar with Photoshop Smart Objects, they are layers that preserve an image's source content with all of its original characteristics and the changes made to the original content. By default, Open as a Smart Object is deselected. Select the check box and Photoshop opens the HDR image as a Smart Object after you save the image in HDR Efex Pro.

note

The extended versions of Photoshop CS4 and CS5 are needed for 32-bit-per-channel Smart Object support.

There is a real advantage to selecting the Smart Object check box. Saving the HDR image as a Smart Object saves the original image file and all the adjustments made to the image, including the Control Points.

see also

Chapters 8 and 9 address working with Control Points.

For example, when you make a print of the HDR image, you may find an area that you wish you had adjusted differently. Or after living with the HDR image for a while you may decide that a different approach is more appropriate. With the image saved as a Smart Object, there is no need to reconstruct the file. Believe me, I have tried to re-create images that I did not save as a Smart Object and it is impossible.

When your image is saved as a Smart Object, you can revisit it at any time in the future. Click on the HDR Efex Pro layer, and the image reopens in HDR Efex Pro. From here you can make additional adjustments and the Control Point selections remain intact.

There is also a disadvantage to Smart Objects. The file size is often as much as ten times larger than the file size of one of the original source images. Many of my HDR images saved as Smart Objects from 12 megapixel digital cameras approach 300 megabytes. This makes them slow to save, slow to move to another drive, slow to archive, and slow to reopen on all but the latest computer hardware and operating systems with lots of RAM.

Despite this, I select the Open as Smart Object check box in the Image Merge dialog box and it remains selected when I import images into HDR Efex Pro from Bridge and from Photoshop directly, which opens the same Image Merge dialog box.

The other options in the Image Merge dialog box, Alignment and Ghost Reduction, are equally important. Unlike with Lightroom and Aperture, these options are not available once HDR Efex Pro creates an image from the source files when you import through Bridge. Alignment & Ghost Reduction options are not available in HDR Efex Pro for images opened through Bridge and Photoshop. You must make the correct choices in the Image Merge box now. If not and there are alignment and ghosting problems with the image in the Main Image Window, you must cancel out and begin again with different Alignment and Ghost Reduction settings.

Alignment check box

Chapter 2 discusses alignment when setting preferences. The HDR Efex Pro Settings dialog box for Alignment & Ghost Reduction only affects files opening through Lightroom and Aperture, not Bridge and Photoshop. For images that open in Bridge, you must choose to set or disable Alignment in the Image Merge dialog box.

Alignment is selected by default in the Image Merge dialog box. I recommend leaving it selected when importing a series of images through Bridge, even for those image series shot with the camera on a tripod. There are so many possible ways for the images to be out of alignment that this is the safer option. Although it is possible to create a misalignment when the images are taken with the camera on a sturdy tripod and using a remote release, the additional time that HDR Efex Pro spends performing the alignment is far less than the time it would take to cancel out of HDR Efex Pro, return to Bridge, and begin the process again.

Ghost Reduction Method and Strength

Chapter 2 also discusses setting the Ghost Reduction Method and Strength for images opening through Lightroom and Aperture. As with Alignment, the Ghost Reduction settings must be set in the Image Merge dialog box for opening images through Bridge to eliminate or at least minimize ghosting.

Ghost Reduction is disabled by default. The options are

- Global
- Adaptive

For large-scale movement in any direction through the frame, use the Global option. This type of movement would include a bird flying by or a person or animal walking.

For small–scale, random movement of an object that is fixed in the frame, like a waving flag or flowing water, use the Adaptive option.

Enabling Ghost Reduction by selecting the check box and selecting a method allows you to set the strength of the method. The options are

- Low
- Medium
- High

Medium is the default and generally a good choice. However, when you view the images in Bridge, if you notice just a slight change in position of a small object between two frames, then the Low setting will probably work fine and save processing time.

If there are many people moving in random directions, however, select the High setting initially to prevent you from having to cancel out of HDR Efex Pro once you see the preview and begin again.

Now that the options are set for this image series, click OK to apply the options, merge the source files, and open HDR Efex Pro.

Summary of export steps

Here are the steps to export a series of bracketed exposures from Bridge to HDR Efex Pro:

1. **Import files into Bridge or open Bridge and navigate to the folder holding the images.**
2. **Check that the Camera Raw preferences are set as described previously.** If not, adjust the settings.
3. **Select the image series to export to HDR Efex Pro.** If you aren't sure which images to use, open Camera Raw and use the histogram to help you decide.
4. **Reduce noise and color fringing in Camera Raw if needed.**
5. **Click Done to save the images from Camera Raw.**
6. **Export the images to Photoshop by choosing File→Tools→Export to HDR Efex Pro.**
7. **Select the options in the HDR Efex Pro Image Merge dialog box.**
8. **Click OK to export the images for merging in HDR Efex Pro.**

Opening a single image

To create a true HDR image, an image series of bracketed exposures is needed. But there are times when it is interesting to see what a single image would look like as a Extended Dynamic Range (EDR) image. Using a single image also allows you to investigate what HDR processing can add to photos already in your image library, even images scanned from film.

Bridge allows you to open a single image in HDR Efex Pro, and there are fewer steps than opening an image series.

Select the image to process. If the image is in a RAW file format, check that the Camera Raw settings are set to your liking. You can create EDR images from single TIFF or JPEG files, also. These file formats won't be processed in Camera Raw unless you choose File→Open in Camera Raw, but this isn't necessary unless you want to make noise or color fringing adjustments.

When you are satisfied that the RAW, TIFF, or JPEG image is ready for export to HDR Efex Pro, choose Tools→Nik Software→HDR Efex Pro Tone mapping, as shown in Figure 3.22.

Because this is a single image and not an image series, there is no need for Alignment or Ghost Reduction, and the image opens directly in HDR Efex Pro with no other dialog box. Follow these steps to export a single exposure from Bridge to HDR Efex Pro:

1. **Navigate to the folder holding the image.**
2. **Check that the Camera Raw preferences are set as described previously.** If not, adjust the settings.
3. **Select the image to export to HDR Efex Pro.**
4. **Reduce noise and color fringing in the Camera Raw dialog box if needed.**
5. **Click Done to save the image from Camera Raw.**
6. **Choose File→Tools→Export to HDR Efex Pro.** Click OK.

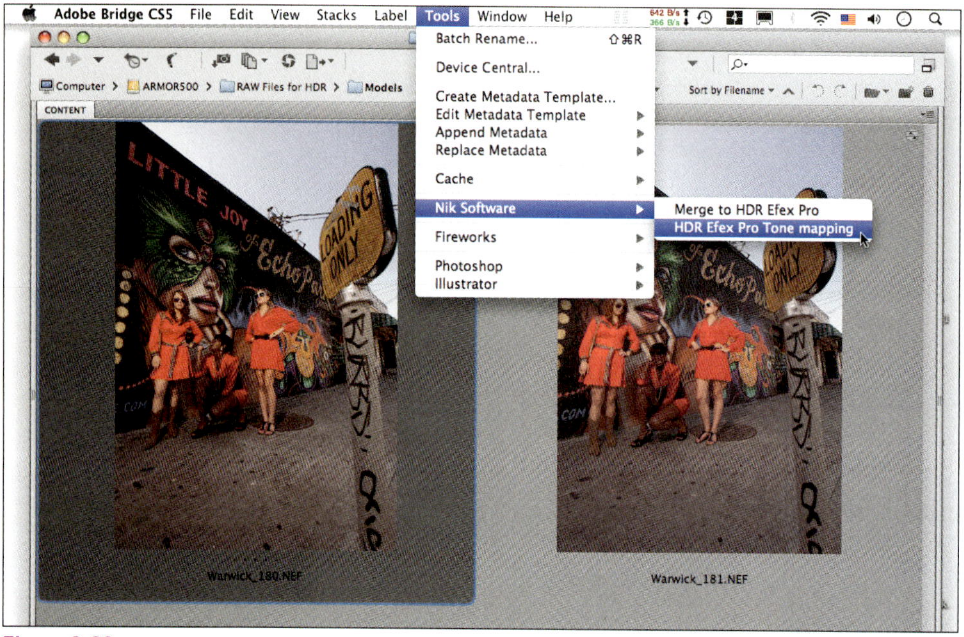

Figure 3.22

Opening Images from Adobe Photoshop

For those photographers whose workflow centers on Photoshop, HDR Efex Pro adjusts nicely. There are two Photoshop paths available for opening a bracketed image series in version 1.1 of HDR Efex Pro, both by choosing File→ Automate. These paths also open a single image for HDR processing, along with a third path for a single image through the Filter menu.

Opening an image series

With Photoshop open, choose File→Automate → Merge to HDR Efex Pro. The HDR Efex Pro Image Merge dialog box opens. The options selected are those used the last time the dialog box was used.

The difference between opening the Image Merge dialog box through Photoshop rather than Bridge is that, through Photoshop, there are no images listed in the box at the top, as shown in Figure 3.23.

You must navigate to your image folder and select images, as shown in Figure 3.24, to populate the box.

When image selection is complete, select the other options and click OK to merge the images and open HDR Efex Pro.

This path to opening image files was the only path available in version 1.0 of HDR Efex Pro. Version 1.1 added another option.

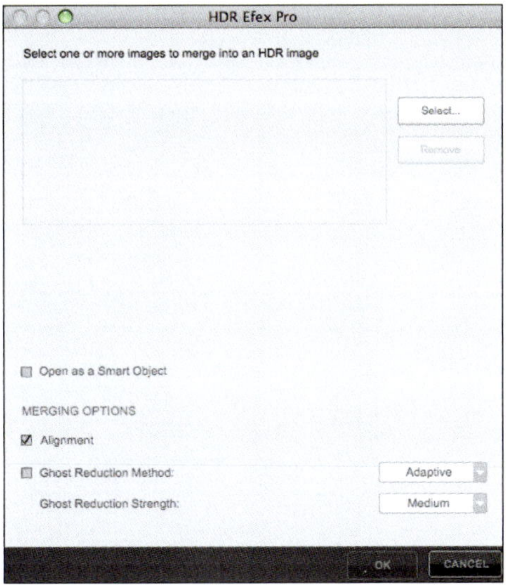

Figure 3.23

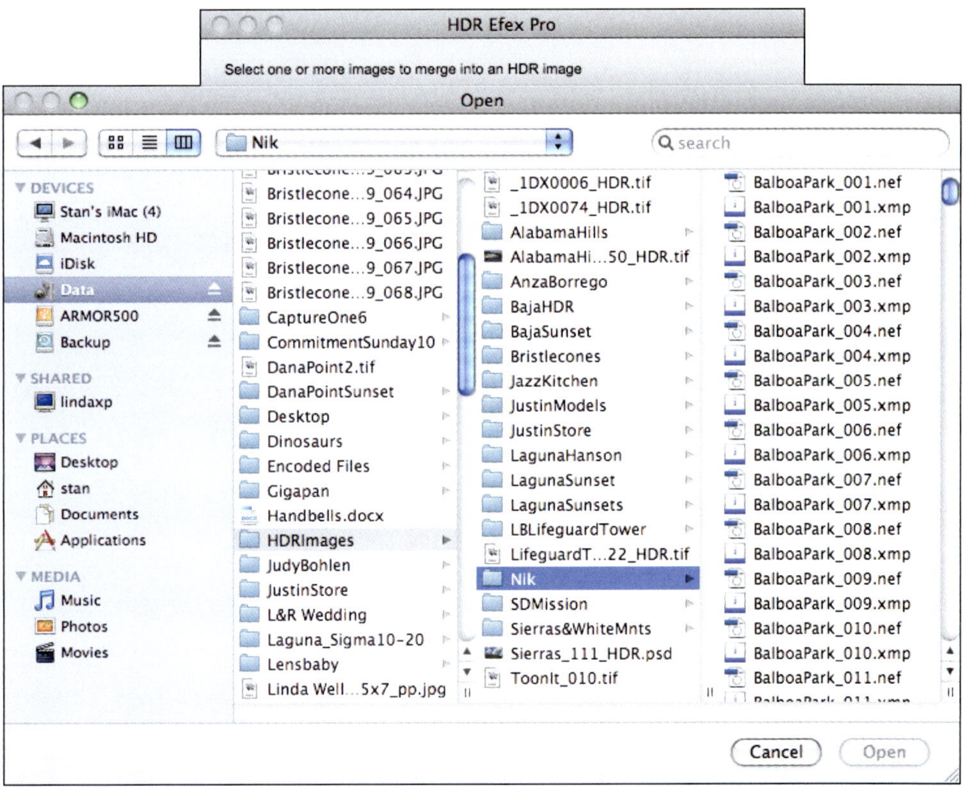

Figure 3.24

Nik Software Selective Tool Preferences

In the lower-left corner of the Selective Tool is a Settings button. The first option is When Photoshop launches. The selections available are

- Automatically open the Selective Tool
- Do not automatically open the Selective Tool

The first option is the default and the Selective Tool opens each time Photoshop opens. If you don't want this to happen, select the second option. It's always possible to open the Selective Tool when you need it by choosing File→Automate.

Ignore the other options. They have no effect on HDR Efex Pro.

If you use any other Nik Software plug-in, you are familiar with the Nik Software Selective Tool, as shown in Figure 3.25. Version 1.1 added the HDR Efex Pro application as an option to the Selective Tool if the Selective Tool existed on your computer, or created the Selective Tool if it wasn't there already.

Click the twirler to the left of the HDR Efex Pro title to open the options in Figure 3.26.

Click the first option, Merge (Multiple Image Series), to open the Image Merge dialog box. Select the images to export and set the options as you would have done had you chosen File→Automate to open the dialog box.

To merge a series of bracketed exposures from Photoshop with HDR Efex Pro, follow these steps:

1. **Choose File→Automate→Merge to HDR Efex Pro and click, or choose Nik Selective Tool→HDR Efex Pro→ Merge (Multiple Image Series).**
2. **Select the image series to merge with HDR Efex Pro.**
3. **Select the options in the HDR Efex Pro Image Merge Dialog box.**
4. **Click OK to export the images for merging in HDR Efex Pro.**

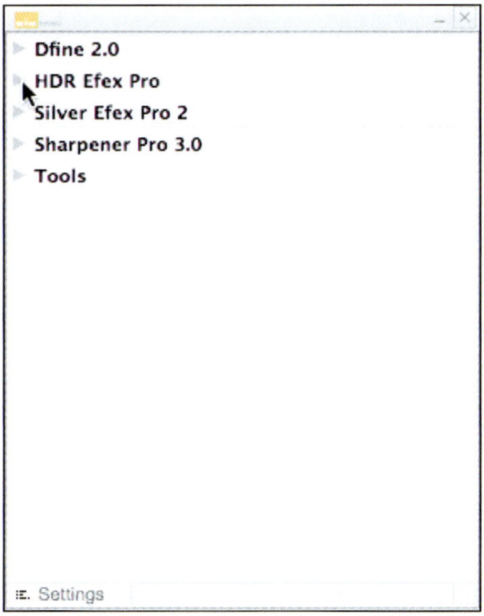

Figure 3.25

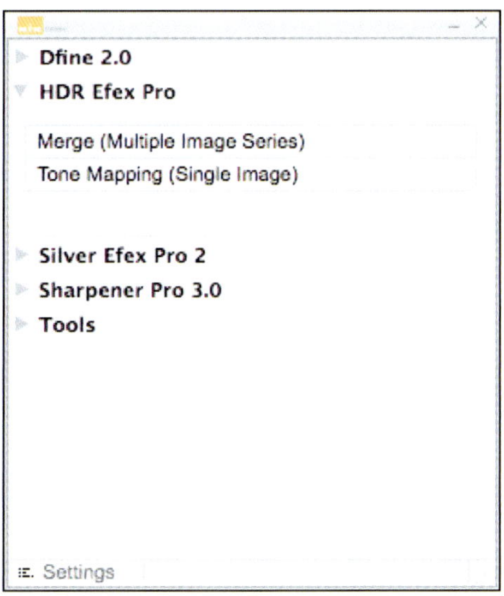

Figure 3.26

Opening a single image

If the single image on which you want to work isn't open in Photoshop, use File→Open to open it. Navigate to Filter→Nik Software and click HDR Efex Pro. The image opens in HDR Efex Pro.

note

If the image is a layered TIFF or PSD file, this route flattens the file before creating the HDR image.

While choosing File→Automate→Merge to HDR Efex Pro route is quick, there are other routes that open some interesting possibilities that are only possible when you open a single image in Photoshop and export it to HDR Efex Pro.

You may find yourself working in Photoshop and suddenly wonder what the image would look like if it were converted to an EDR image. There are two ways to find out from within Photoshop when an image is open.

The first is through the Selective Tool. Open the Selective Tool if it isn't open. Click Tone Mapping (Single Image), the second option under HDR Efex Pro, as shown in Figure 3.27.

Processing begins immediately and the image opens in HDR Efex Pro.

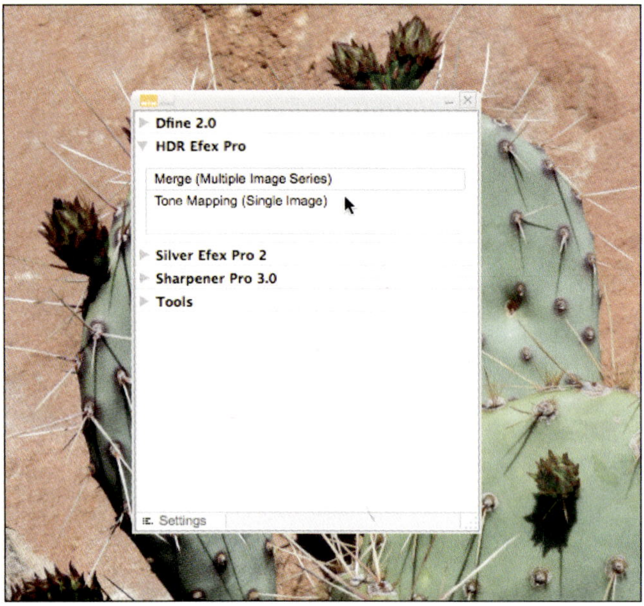

Figure 3.27

A similar route is available using the Filter menu. As long as the single image is open in Photoshop, you can choose Filter→Nik Software→HDR Efex Pro and export the image through that route, as shown in Figure 3.28.

To enhance a single exposure with HDR Efex Pro, follow these steps:

1. **Open the image in Photoshop.**
2. **Duplicate the background layer.** Make adjustments on the duplicate layer.
3. **Use the Selective Tool and click Tone Mapping (Single Image) or choose Filter→Nik Software→HDR Efex Pro to open the image in HDR Efex Pro.**

Using layers and masking with HDR Efex Pro

To this point, all the options mentioned in opening an image series or a single image would result in the entire image being processed and require saving it with a new filename to avoid writing over the source files.

But you may have an image file with layers of adjustments that you want to look at as an HDR image but not have the adjustment layers flattened. Or perhaps you are wondering what the background or the sky and clouds would look like when processed in HDR Efex Pro, but you don't want the rest of the image processed. It is possible to work with layers and masking on a single image open in Photoshop in HDR Efex Pro.

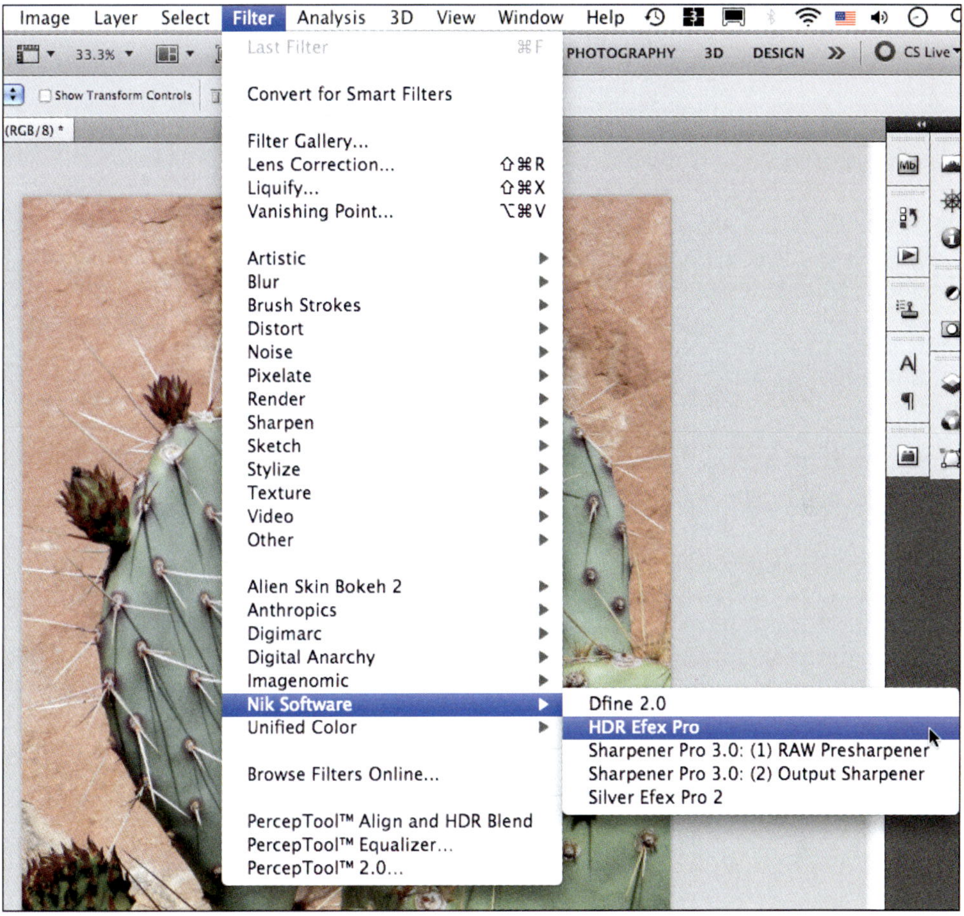

Figure 3.28

note

Chapters 8 and 9 discuss making local adjustments to the HDR image in HDR Efex Pro using Control Points, but Control Points do not allow the complete removal of the HDR effect.

Open the image in Photoshop and create a copy of the Background layer by pressing Ctrl/⌘+J. This preserves the original image. HDR Efex Pro operates on the top layer. If the open file already has layers above the original image, HDR Efex Pro flattens the image internally to create the HDR effect, and then saves the EDR image back to Photoshop as a new layer above the original layers, so no underlying layers or adjustments are lost.

With the EDR image back in Photoshop, create a layer mask on the HDR Efex Pro layer to remove the HDR effect.

Another route to the same destination is to select the area in the image on which to apply the HDR effect first. Leave the selection (marching ants) active and open the image with the Selective Tool or the Filter menu and create the HDR image. In HDR Efex Pro, it will look like the entire image is being processed, but when the image is saved back to Photoshop, only the selection will have the HDR effect applied to it, as shown in Figure 3.29.

HDR Efex Pro opens all kinds of creative possibilities when you open a single image in Photoshop, including the ability to apply HDR effects to single images from your existing image library.

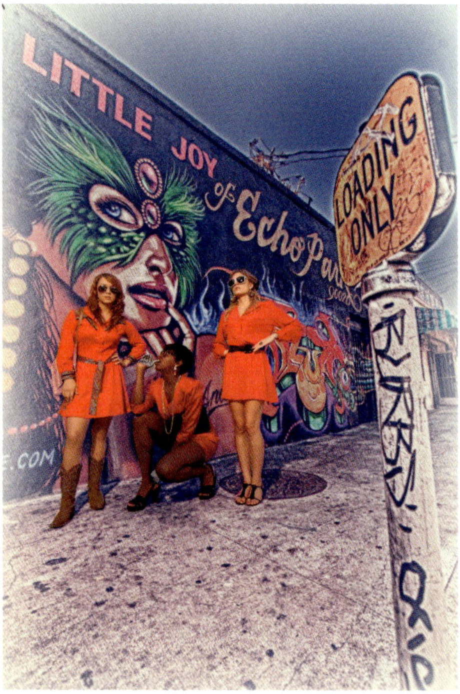

Figure 3.29

Opening Images from Apple Aperture

One other host application for HDR Efex Pro is Apple Aperture. Aperture is not available to Windows users, but some Mac owners are sure to center their workflow on Aperture. HDR Efex Pro also integrates well with an Aperture workflow.

The Aperture workflow with HDR Efex Pro is similar to the Lightroom workflow, but there are differences. For one thing, there are fewer options in Aperture.

When HDR Efex Pro installs into Aperture, it sets up all the properties to export RAW files for HDR processing. There is no need to customize the relationship between the programs further. Aperture uses its own RAW processing engine under the control of HDR Efex Pro to convert the RAW files to full-resolution 16-bit TIFFs for HDR processing.

Importing and selecting images in Aperture

As in Lightroom, it is possible to apply adjustments to images when importing files into Aperture. When you select Import in Aperture, the Library tab shown in Figure 3.30 opens. If the Adjustment Presets palette is open in Aperture, check to make sure that None is showing in the drop-down menu. Applying a preset during import can cause problems when the HDR image is created.

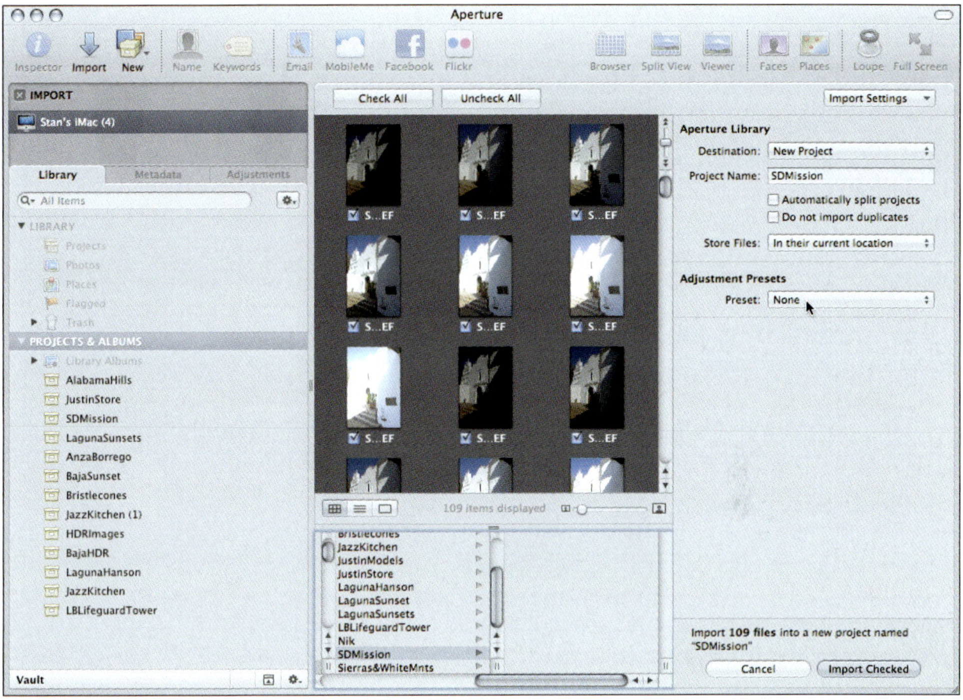

Figure 3.30

To select images for HDR processing, click the Library tab and press V to cycle through the view options until you are in the Browser view, as shown in Figure 3.31. Here you can see thumbnails of the exposure series.

If you have any doubts about where each image series begins and ends, open the EXIF Info palette in the Metadata tab shown in Figure 3.32. Click through the images and watch the Exposure Bias box. If your camera writes the bracket exposure information into the metadata, the information is displayed here. Most brackets begin with the 0 exposure bias by default.

If the Exposure Bias box is empty, your camera doesn't write bracketing information into the EXIF data. When you export the images to HDR Efex Pro, the Exposure Values dialog box discussed previously opens and you must enter the bracketing information manually.

HDR processing builds up noise from the files that are used to create the image. It is best to eliminate as much of this noise in the RAW file as possible, but not so much that the image details become soft.

To view the noise level of an image, double-click on one of the dark images that has some shadow detail to enlarge it to full screen, and then press Z to zoom to 100%. Use the navigator to move around the image and look for noise.

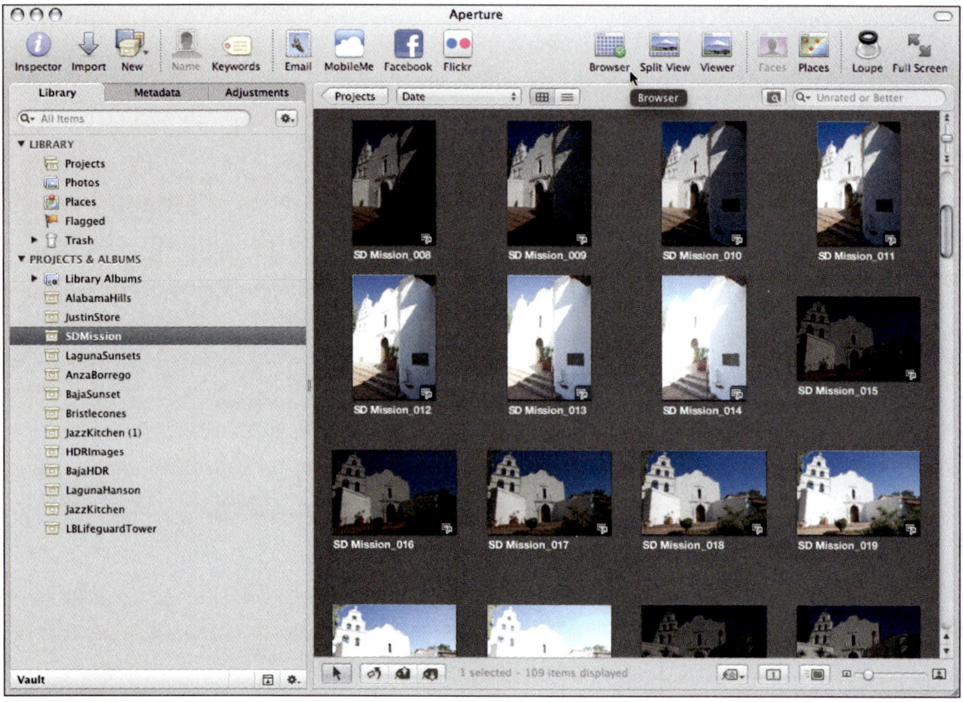

Figure 3.31

Figure 3.32

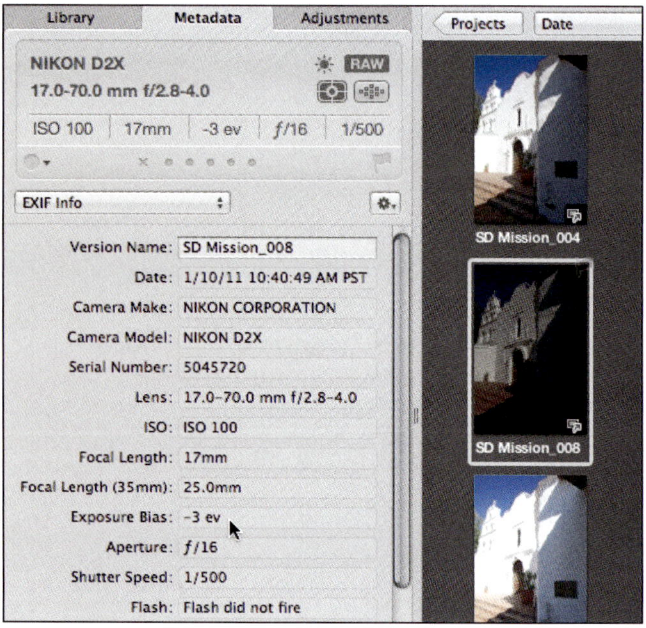

Double-click and zoom one of the lighter images. This time use the navigator to look for color fringing in the image. HDR imaging multiplies the color fringing. I've seen color fringing in my HDR images where there is none visible in the source images. If you can see it in a source image, it is best to eliminate it from all of them before proceeding.

If there is no noise or color fringing, the image series is ready for export to HDR Efex Pro. But if you find either, it is best to correct these issues before creating the HDR image. Aperture has tools hidden in the Adjustments tab to correct noise and color fringing.

Click the Adjustments tab to open the Adjustments palette. At the top of the palette is the histogram of the selected image. Before you correct image problems, you can use the histogram to narrow down the number of images to export to HDR Efex Pro.

To make it easier to select the images to export to HDR Efex Pro, click the gear icon and select Luminance under Histogram Options, as shown in Figure 3.33.

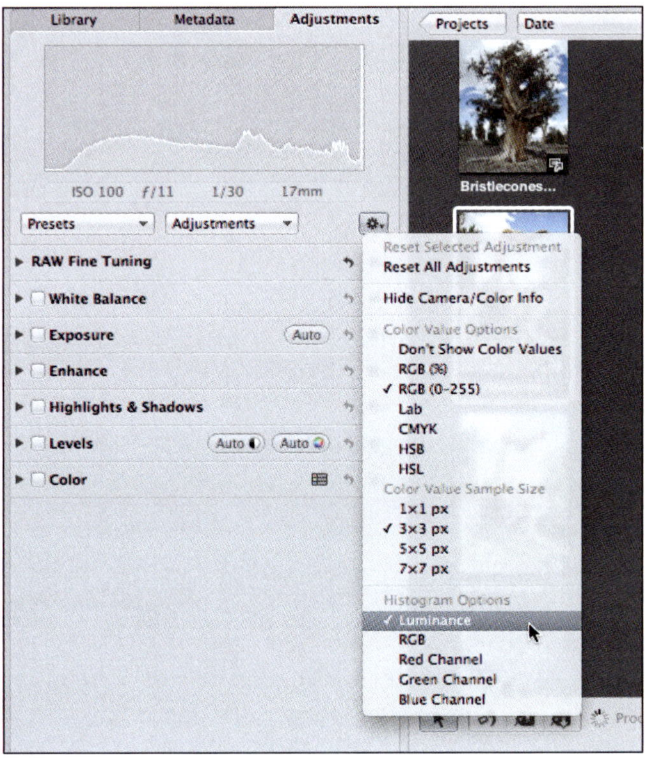

Figure 3.33

The images you need for a true HDR image range from one where the histogram curve stops short of the left side (Figure 3.34) to one where the histogram curve stops short of the right side (Figure 3.35) and including those that fall between these two. Any images that are more underexposed than the image in Figure 3.35 should not be used. They only extend the

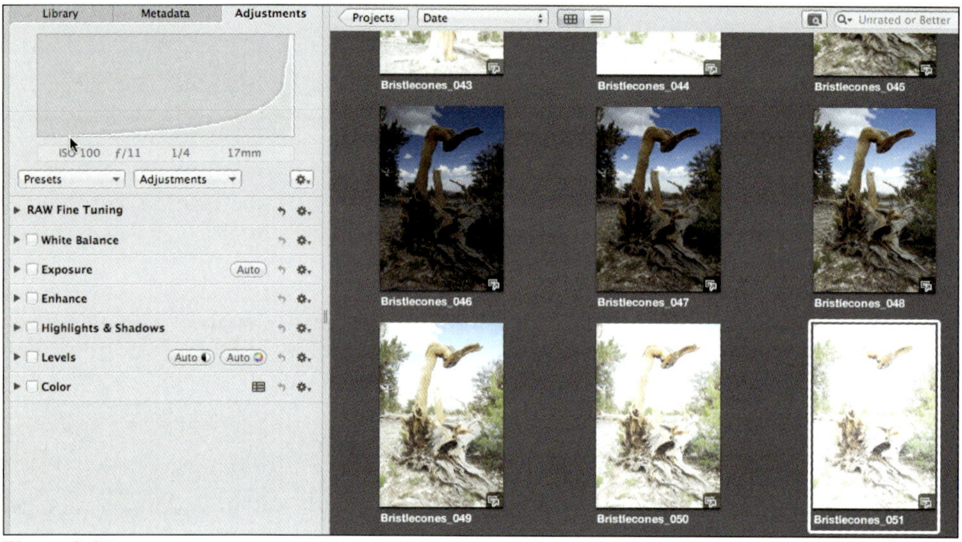

Figure 3.34

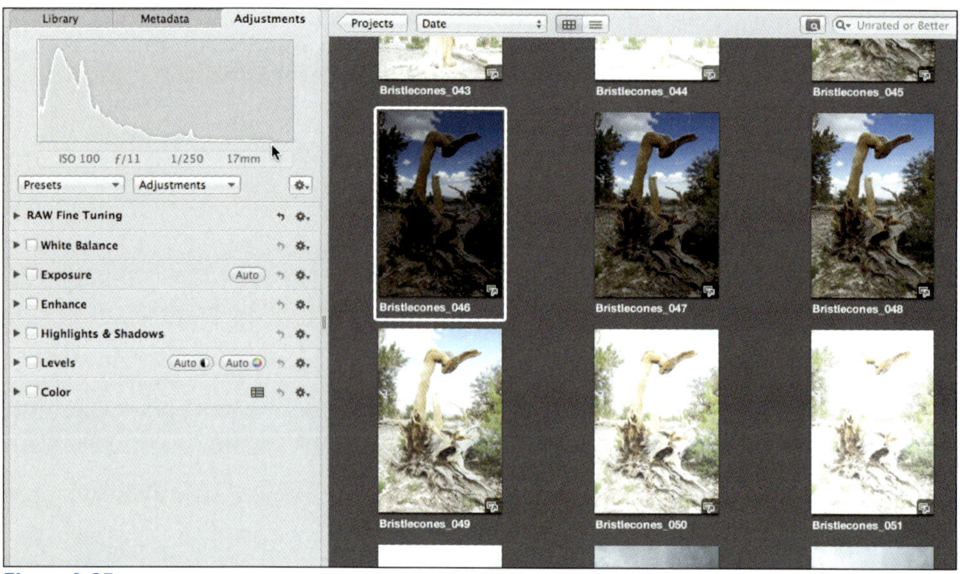

Figure 3.35

processing time and add noise to the final HDR image. Images lighter than the image in Figure 3.34 can be used. While they add processing time, they will reduce noise.

While it is possible to create an HDR image from two captures whose histograms look like those in Figures 3.34 and 3.35, I recommend using a minimum of three captures exposed as follows:

- One image overexposed such that the values stop just short of the left side of the histogram
- One image exposed such that the values extend all the way across the histogram
- One image underexposed such that the values stop just short of the right side of the histogram

Of course, include any others that fall between the limits to add detail information to the image.

Now that you know which images to use, you can reduce the noise and correct the color fringing in those images. First, close all the default adjustments by clicking the downward-facing arrow if the adjustment brick is open.

Now you need to open the noise and color fringing adjustment bricks. Click the Adjustments button to open the list of available adjustments, as shown in Figure 3.36.

Select Chromatic Aberration and Noise Reduction from the list of available adjustments. This adds those bricks to the Adjustments list, as shown in Figure 3.37.

Select Chromatic Aberration to correct the color fringing. Adjust the Red/Cyan and Blue/Yellow sliders until the color fringing disappears.

Now select Noise Reduction to correct noise. Zoom to 100% and adjust the Radius and Edge Detail sliders to eliminate as much noise as

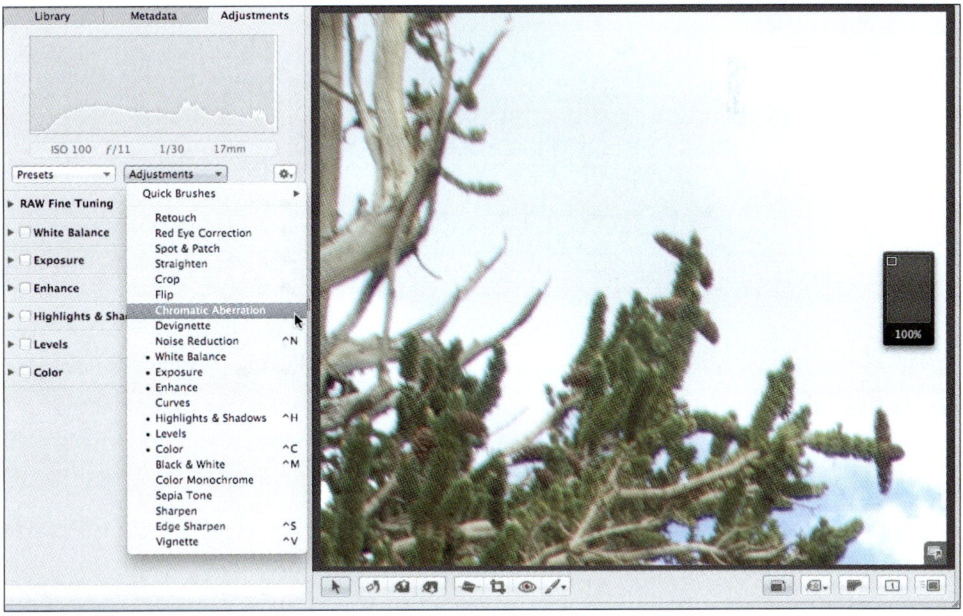

Figure 3.36

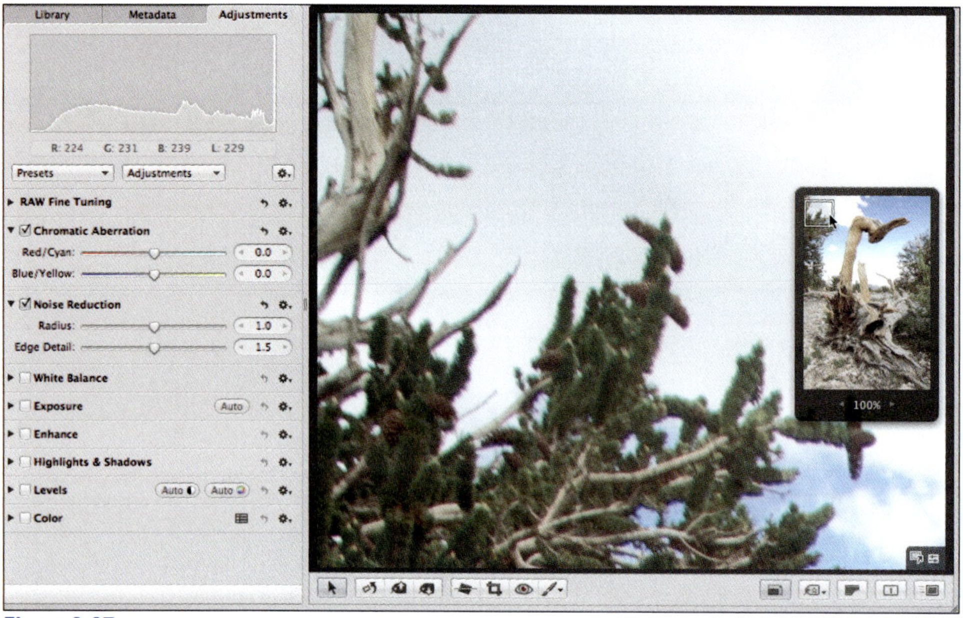

Figure 3.37

possible without softening the image. When the final HDR image is complete, you may need to run noise reduction again, either in Aperture or a third-party application such as Nik Software Dfine 2.0.

Now that you have decided on the images and made these two important adjustments, you are ready to export the images to HDR Efex Pro. When you do, the adjustments are incorporated into the files.

Exporting from Aperture

The export procedure from Aperture to HDR Efex Pro is straightforward with no options. Select all the images to export and choose Photos → Edit with Plug-in → HDR Efex Pro (Figure 3.38).

Here are the steps to export a series of bracketed exposures from Lightroom to HDR Efex Pro:

1. **Import files into Aperture.** Do not apply any presets that change exposure or tonal values.
2. **Select each image and look at its histogram in the Adjustments tab.** Click on a selection of images ranging from underexposed to overexposed, as described previously.
3. **Reduce noise and color fringing in the Adjustment tab if needed.**
4. **Export the images to HDR Efex Pro.**

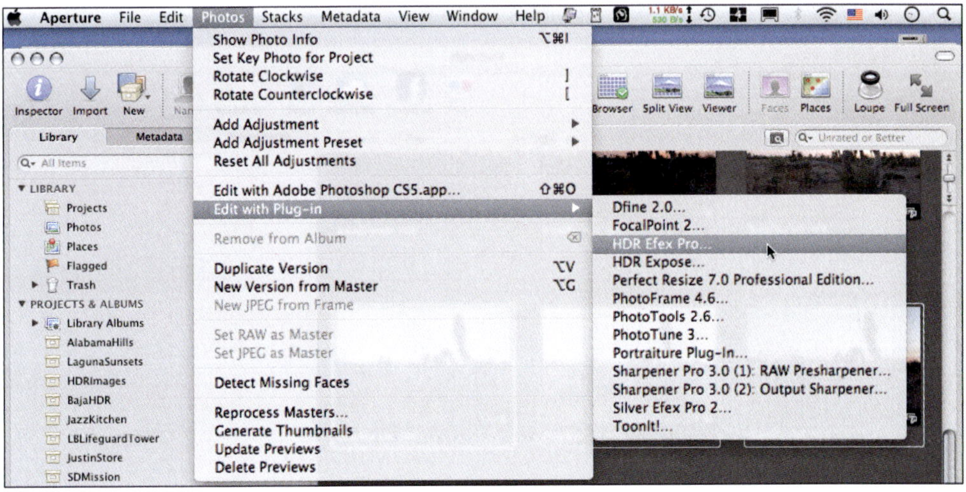

Figure 3.38

Alignment & Ghost Reduction with Aperture export

Opening a series of exposures from Aperture opens the HDR Efex Pro software directly. As you see in Figure 3.39, the upper bar holding the viewing options has an Alignment & Ghost Reduction button.

An image opened in HDR Efex Pro through Aperture is already aligned if On is selected for alignment in the Alignment & Ghost Reduction palette in Settings, and Ghost Reduction is not performed. With the preview HDR image open, press the spacebar or click the Zoom button to zoom to 100%, and use the Navigator to pan through the image.

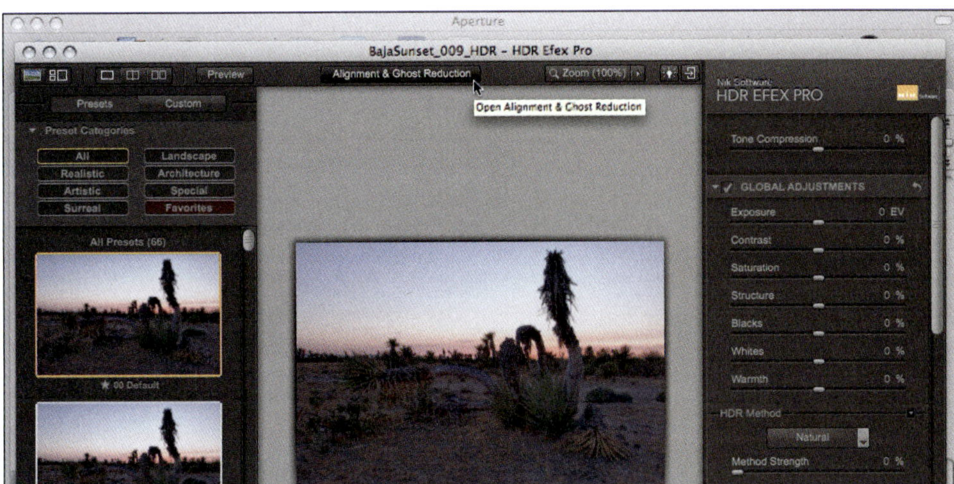

Figure 3.39

If the image needs fine alignment or ghost removal, click the Alignment & Ghost Reduction button. This opens the Alignment and Ghost Reduction dialog box, as shown in Figure 3.40. The default settings are those you chose when setting up your preferences in Chapter 2. Make the appropriate selections in the dialog box and click OK. The Alignment and Ghost Reduction subroutines process the image and a reprocessed preview appears with the default preset active.

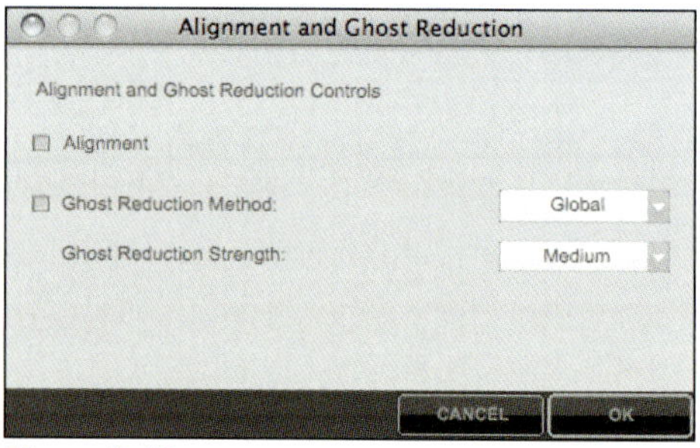

Figure 3.40

Choosing a Workflow to Open Images

With the availability of the preceding host application options, choosing which application to use to open images in HDR Efex Pro can be confusing. This section summarizes the options and makes some recommendations.

The first consideration in choosing a host application is to choose the one that best suits your present workflow. HDR Efex Pro integrates well with Lightroom, Bridge/Photoshop, Photoshop alone, and Aperture. If you are locked into one of these applications, either by choice or because it is the one you currently own, then there is probably no overriding reason to change.

However, if you own and are familiar with several applications, the choice becomes more complex.

The next most critical consideration is whether you would want to revisit the HDR image to adjust it in the future without having to process the source images again. If so, you need to save the final HDR image with its adjustments as a Smart Object. To do this, the Extended version of Photoshop CS4 or CS5 must be loaded on your computer, and you need to use the Bridge/Photoshop or Photoshop only workflows.

If speed is critical to you, then a Lightroom or Aperture workflow would be a good choice. These applications are capable of processing an image series much more quickly than Photoshop, which processes images one at a time.

Finally, although all the host applications allow the creation of an EDR image from a single image file, only Photoshop allows you to begin with a layered file or to make complex selections and apply the HDR effect only to the selection.

Table 3.1 summarizes many of the advantages and disadvantages of the various host applications.

Table 3.1
Advantages and Disadvantages of Host Applications

Feature	*Lightroom*	*Bridge/Photoshop*	*Photoshop Alone*	*Aperture*
Smart Object	Not available	Available (requires Photoshop CS4 or CS5 Extended)	Available (requires Photoshop CS4 or CS5 Extended)	Not available
Alignment	Depends on choice in Settings	Depends on choice in Image Merge dialog box	Depends on choice in Image Merge dialog box	Depends on choice in Settings
Ghost Reduction	Depends on choice in Settings	Depends on choice in Image Merge dialog box	Depends on choice in Image Merge dialog box	Depends on choice in Settings
Noise Reduction	Available, directly in Lightroom	Available, in Camera Raw	Available, in Camera Raw	Available, directly in Aperture
Color Fringing Reduction	Available, directly in Lightroom	Available, in Camera Raw	Available, in Camera Raw	Available, directly in Aperture
View Images While Selecting	Available	Available	Not available	Available
Histogram	Available, directly in Lightroom	Available, in Camera Raw	Available, in Camera Raw	Available, directly in Aperture
Single Image to HDR	Available	Available	Available	Available
Masking and Layers	Not available	Not available	Available	Not available
Speed	Faster	Slower	Slower	Faster
Workflow Customizing Options	Many	Available	Available	Fewer

Since the release of HDR Efex Pro, I have created many EDR and HDR images. My workflow has progressed to the point where I use the Bridge/Photoshop route almost exclusively when I have the image files back in my studio. The main reason for this is to take advantage of saving the final HDR image as a Photoshop Smart Object.

With the images as Smart Objects, I have the ability to revisit them after printing, or after just living with them a while, to make additional tweaks and adjustments. But I already owned Photoshop CS5 Extended, fast computers, and lots of hard drive storage.

When I shoot on location and I'm anxious to see what I've done, I go the Lightroom route on my laptop. Because I use a tripod whenever possible, alignment is rarely an issue, and I'm usually shooting where Ghost Reduction isn't needed. So opening images in HDR Efex Pro through Lightroom is fast. Adjusting the HDR in HDR Efex Pro is also fast without the overhead of Bridge and Photoshop using up resources.

For most photographers using good photographic technique during image capture, I recommend the Lightroom workflow.

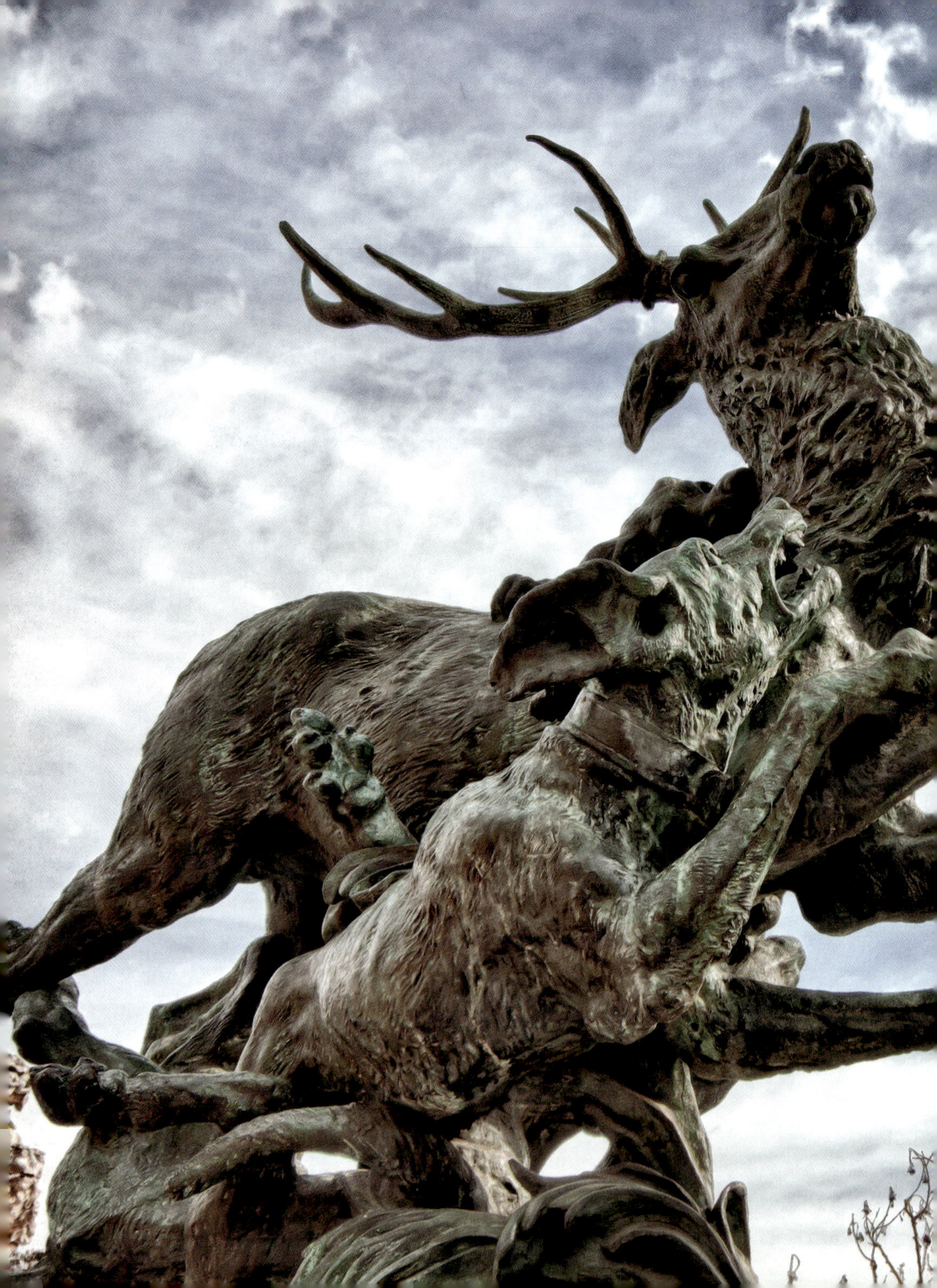

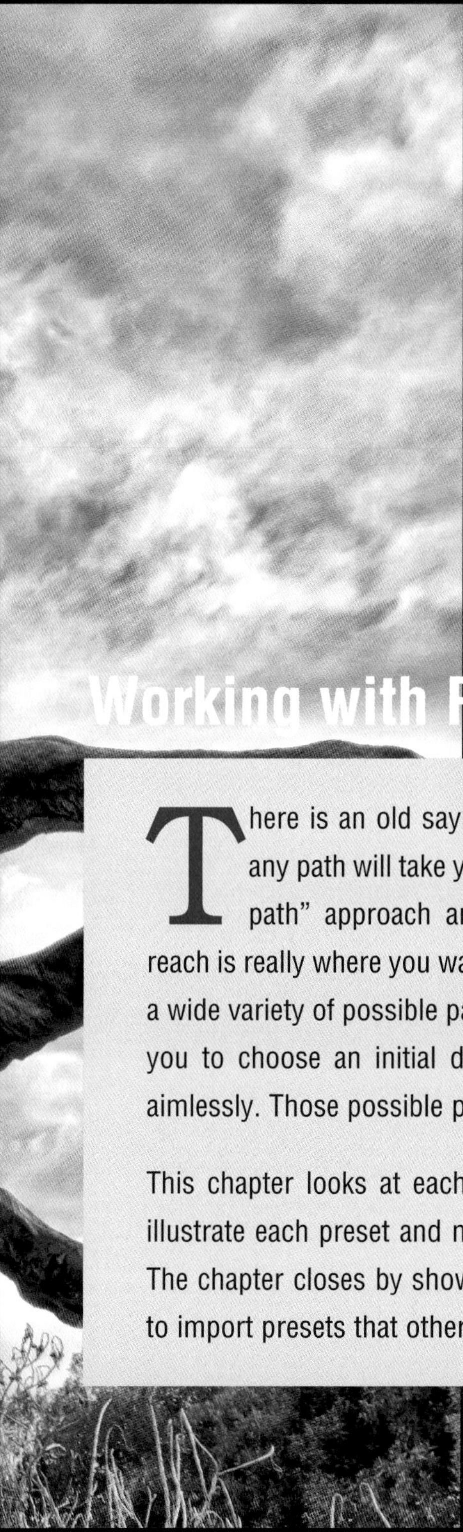

4

Working with Presets

There is an old saying, "If you don't know where you're going, any path will take you there." Most HDR software takes the "any path" approach and leaves you wondering if the result you reach is really where you want to be. Not so with HDR Efex Pro. It shows a wide variety of possible paths as soon as the program opens, allowing you to choose an initial direction for your image without wandering aimlessly. Those possible paths are called *presets*.

This chapter looks at each preset in detail. I use the same image to illustrate each preset and make no adjustments to the default settings. The chapter closes by showing how to create custom presets and how to import presets that other HDR Efex Pro users have created.

Prebuilt Presets

With all the data available in a true HDR image, the possibilities for manipulating it are limitless. You can interpret any scene from the literal to the totally abstract. The range of possibilities can be especially daunting if you're new to HDR imaging. Even with experience, it is sometimes difficult to know the best direction to take an HDR image.

HDR Efex Pro takes the stress out of getting started by presenting you with a range of possibilities called presets. These are displayed as thumbnail interpretations of the active HDR image in the Preset Browser on the left of the interface. Above the presets are Preset Category buttons that display subsets of the presets when activated.

see also

Chapter 2 discusses the HDR Efex Pro interface in detail.

When you open an image series using any of the techniques discussed in Chapter 3, the resulting HDR image is displayed in the Main Image Window with the 00 Default preset applied to it. In the Preset Browser, the 00 Default thumbnail is shown with a gold outline. The active preset always has a gold outline around its thumbnail.

As you click on each preset, the frame around the thumbnail turns to gold, and the Main Image Window updates, showing the result of applying the default settings for that preset.

But other less obvious things are happening in the interface, also. The adjustment tools in the Control Palette on the right of the interface are changing to indicate what settings are used to create that preset.

The next three chapters discuss the tools in the Control Palette in detail. In this chapter, by way of introduction to the detailed discussions, I mention significant adjustments that contribute to the HDR effect for each preset.

It is very important to realize that presets are not intended to produce the final HDR image, although at times they may. Presets are designed to be starting points for your own personal interpretation of the HDR image.

You will see this as you go through each preset at its default setting. A few will look really good, many will look pretty bad, and all could use further global adjustments to exposure and contrast as a minimum. This isn't the result of any defect in the preset; it's just the way that the particular preset's settings interact with the data that makes up the image.

Figures 4.1 through 4.6 show the six exposures that I used to create the HDR image for this chapter. They are 1 stop apart in exposure and range from 3 stops underexposed to 2 stops overexposed. I shot a seventh at 3 stops overexposed, but looking at the histogram of the 2-stops-over image, I didn't need to use the 3-stops-over shot.

It is clear that not one of the six exposures contains the cloud detail, bright sunlit foreground, and shadow detail that I saw while taking the photos. This scene is an excellent prospect for HDR interpretation.

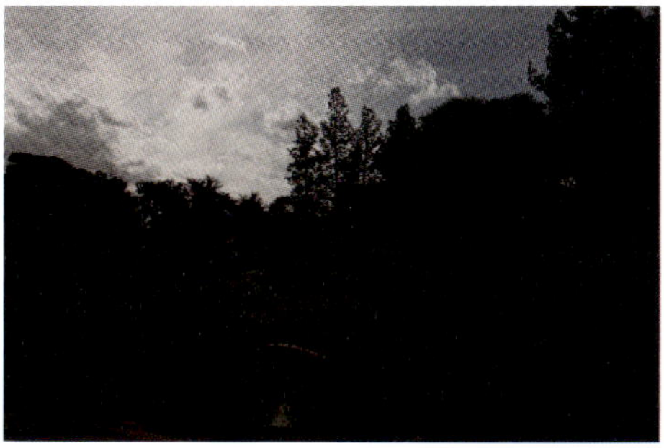
Figure 4.1

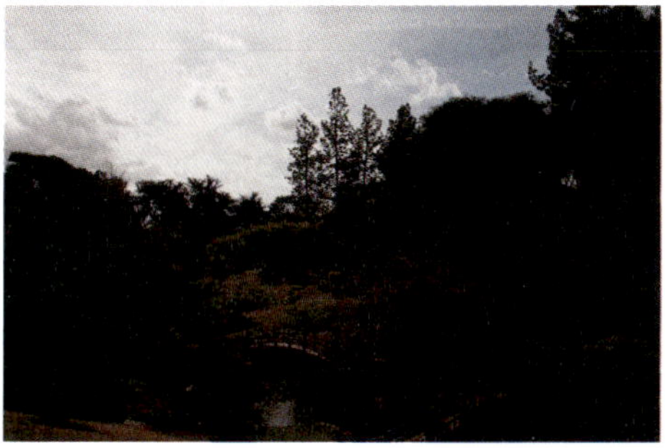
Figure 4.2

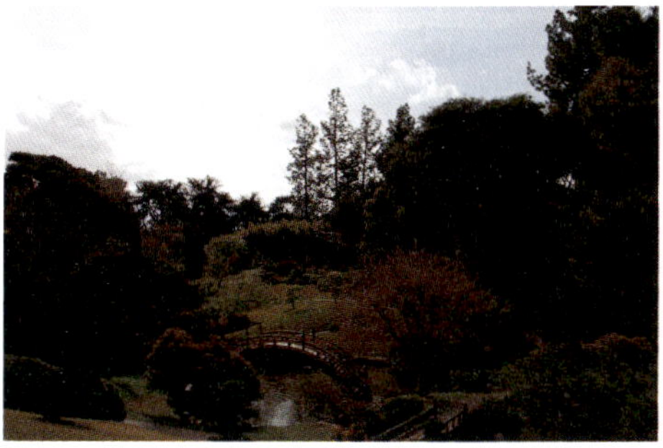
Figure 4.3

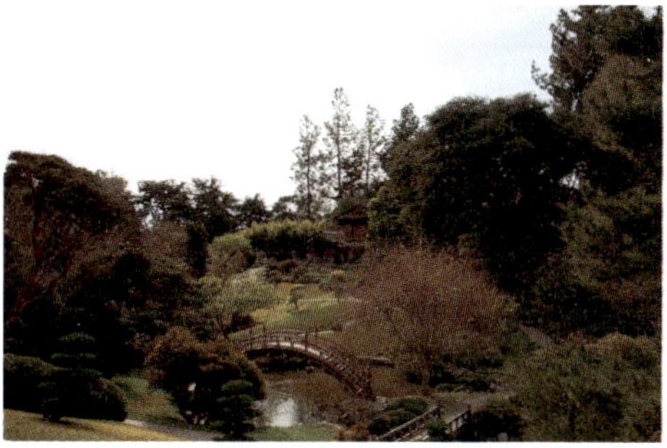
Figure 4.4

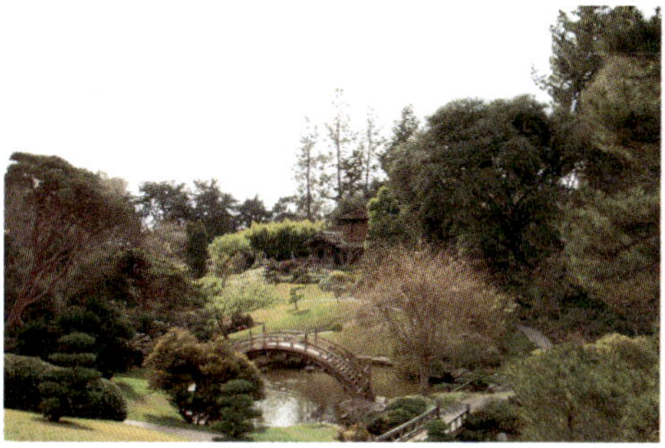
Figure 4.5

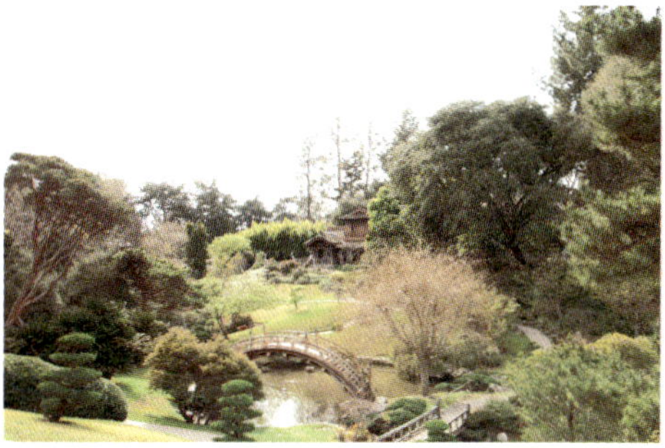
Figure 4.6

00 Default preset

Figure 4.7 shows the Default preset for the HDR image series. The algorithms used in creating the Default preset are designed to create a realistic HDR image using the full range of exposure information in the source images. There are no global adjustments, or finishing adjustments applied to the data. Only minimal tone compression needed to display the image on the monitor is applied. The HDR Method used is Natural, but its Strength slider is set to 0.

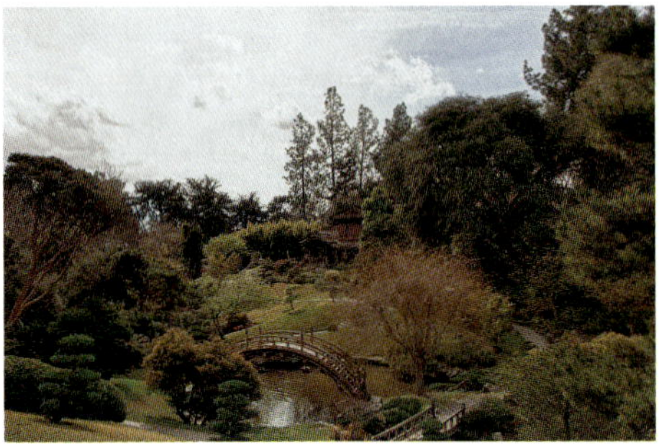

Figure 4.7

see also

Chapter 5 discusses tone compression and Chapter 6 discusses HDR Methods.

As an interpretation of the original scene, it's not terrible, although the sky could use more separation and detail, the overall contrast is too low, the sunlit foreground is too dull, and it lacks a good black in the shadows.

HDR Efex Pro has tools that are covered in later chapters to handle each of these issues, both globally and locally. But the need for these adjustments is what you should look for once you like the basic look created by the preset.

Each preset takes you only so far, and each acts differently on each HDR image you create in HDR Efex Pro. Adjusting and finalizing the image is where the fun is in HDR imaging after you capture the image series.

note

The 00 Default preset is also found in the Realistic Preset Category.

01 Realistic (Subtle) preset

The Realistic (Subtle) preset interpretation of the image series is shown in Figure 4.8. The Control settings for this preset are not that different from the Default preset. The HDR Method is the same and the Strength slider is still set to 0. However, the Tone Compression slider is now set at –50%.

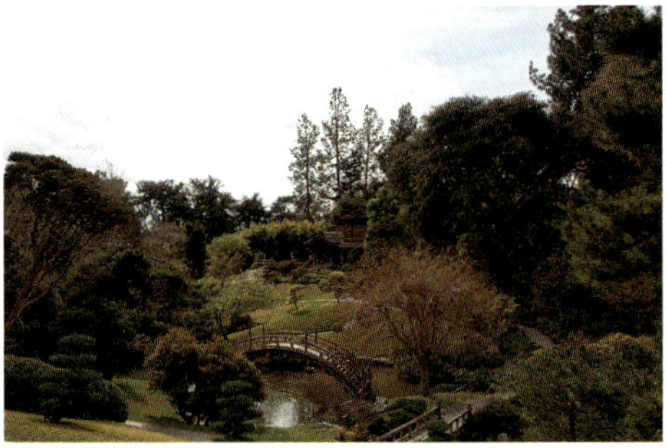

Figure 4.8

With the Tone Compression setting in Realistic (Subtle), the sky loses even more detail. The shadows also lose information, but the Blacks slider is adjusted to –40% to compensate, so it isn't that obvious. There is also a subtle S curve applied. An S curve boosts highlight values and lowers shadow values to increase contrast.

With this preset, this HDR image looks further from reality than the one using the Default setting. The loss of information in the sky bothers me most, but it is still dull and low in contrast compared to the sunlit scene I photographed.

note

The 01 Realistic (Subtle) preset is also found in the Realistic Preset Category.

02 Realistic (Balanced) preset

Figure 4.9 shows the image series with the Realistic (Balanced) preset. As with the Default preset, the Tone Compression slider is set to 0. But the HDR Method is changed to Clean at a setting of +20%. This cleans some of the dullness of the previous presets and applies an S curve to add contrast. The biggest improvement is to the sky, where an adjustment of the Structure slider to +20% adds detail in the clouds.

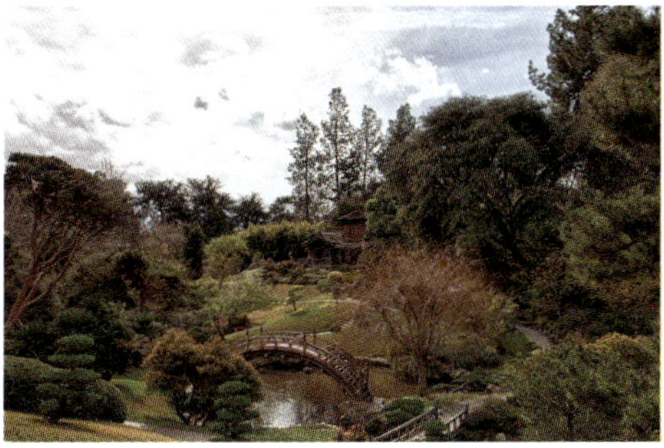

Figure 4.9

Using this present shows a lot of improvement in the image. It's not nearly far enough for me, but it's a good starting point for a realistic rendering of the original scene. It still needs contrast, but you need to be careful not to lose detail in the clouds. Compressing the tonal information in the clouds will help.

note

The 02 Realistic (Balanced) preset is also found in the Realistic Preset Category.

03 Realistic (Strong) preset

With the Realistic (Strong) preset used for Figure 4.10, the sky is definitely dramatic, but now more so than in the actual scene. This is caused primarily by the Tone Compression slider setting of +50%.

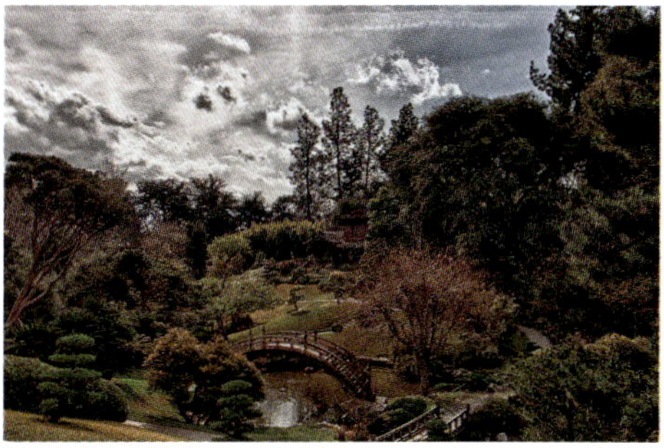

Figure 4.10

The HDR Method is different again. This time the HDR Method is Sharp at a setting of 22, and it also contributes to the drama in the sky. Contrast is better with the Realistic (Strong) preset and the shadows start to look like shadows. Other than the somewhat overdone sky, this is closer to reality.

note

The 03 Realistic (Strong) preset is also found in the Realistic Preset Category.

04 Realistic Gradients 1 preset

Both of the Realistic Gradients presets cast a moody darkness over the scene, which I like for some reason. Figure 4.11 makes me think of an old, faded oil painting of the English countryside (if you forget about the Japanese bridge).

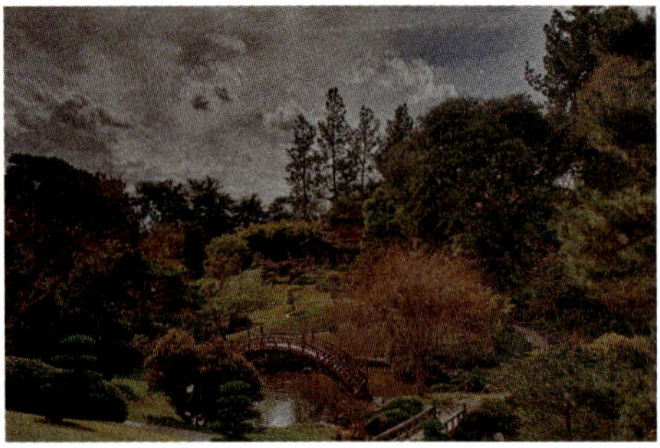

Figure 4.11

Realistic Gradients 1 achieves this effect with a fairly large amount of tone compression (+67%) and an HDR Method of Gradual Medium at a low setting (+12%). The moodiness is enhanced further by adjusting the Whites slider to –100%.

How realistic this effect is could be debated, but it's interesting to create an old oil painting look for this image and other landscapes. I'm sure I would try some more adjustments, but I like it.

note

The 04 Realistic Gradients 1 preset is also found in the Realistic Preset Category.

05 Realistic Gradients 2 preset

The Realistic Gradients 2 preset in Figure 4.12 uses many of the same settings as Realistic Gradients 1, but with even more tone compression. The big change is in the HDR Method, from Gradual Medium to Gradual Large. The foreground is darker and the sky lighter in Realistic Gradients 2.

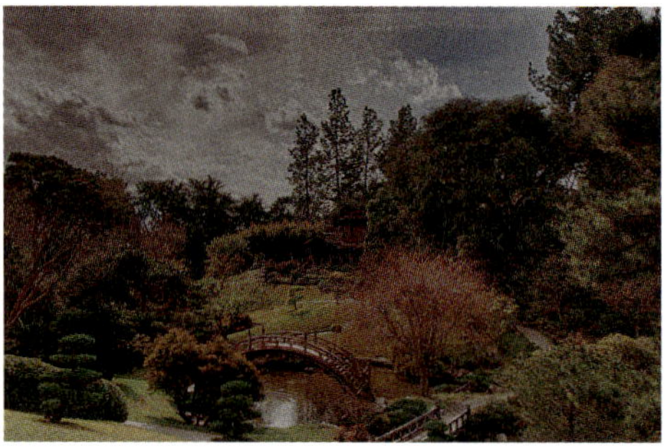

Figure 4.12

Still, it's a nice interpretation for landscapes. With a few tweaks I would use it for this image.

note

The 05 Realistic Gradients 2 preset is also found in the Realistic Preset Category. It is the last of the Realistic presets.

06 Fine Structures preset

With the Fine Structures preset in Figure 4.13, you move away from realistic interpretations to more artistic ones. The sky is much more structured due to the Bright Textures HDR Method and the Tone Compression slider set to +45%.

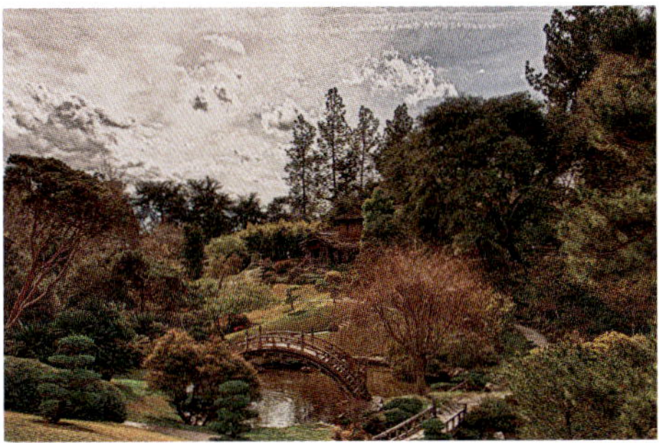

Figure 4.13

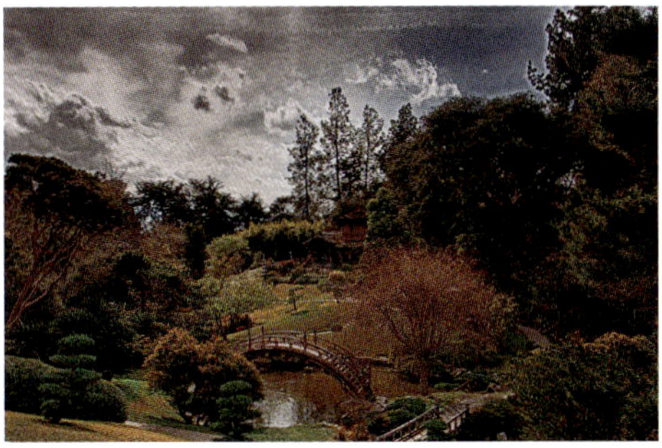

Figure 4.14

Contrast is low with both the Whites and Blacks sliders set to about –50%. The Warmth slider setting of +12% adds some warmth to the clouds and the overall scene.

note

The 06 Fine Structures preset is also found in the Artistic Preset Category.

07 Subdued Contrasts preset

You see some haloing for the first time in the sky around the trees to the right in Figure 4.14. *Haloing* is fairly common in HDR imaging and looks like a light border between two dark areas.

Haloing is actually present in many digital images. You can see it in areas of high contrast, such as a tree against a strong blue sky, if you crank up the contrast. The HDR process overlays multiple images, and this can multiply the natural haloing effect.

But haloing also results from the tone mapping algorithm that is used. The Subdued Contrasts preset uses the Crisp HDR Method at a fairly strong level (+38%) and tone compression of +50%. These algorithms are similar in some ways to those used in unsharp masking, which also relies on local contrast to produce its effect.

Because haloing is considered unnatural by most observers, HDR Efex Pro makes a lot of effort to suppress the effect. There is even a Halo Reduction HDR Method. However, in the Artistic Preset Category especially, you will see some haloing.

note

The 07 Subdued Contrasts preset is also found in the Artistic Preset Category.

08 Structured Skies preset

The Structured Skies preset in Figure 4.15 is the only preset that uses the Fresco HDR Method. As you increase the Method Strength, the effect of the Fresco HDR Method becomes even more pronounced in the sky, but less so in the rest of the image.

Along with enhancing the sky, the settings in Structured Skies also enhance noise and other fine structure, giving a bit of that gritty HDR look.

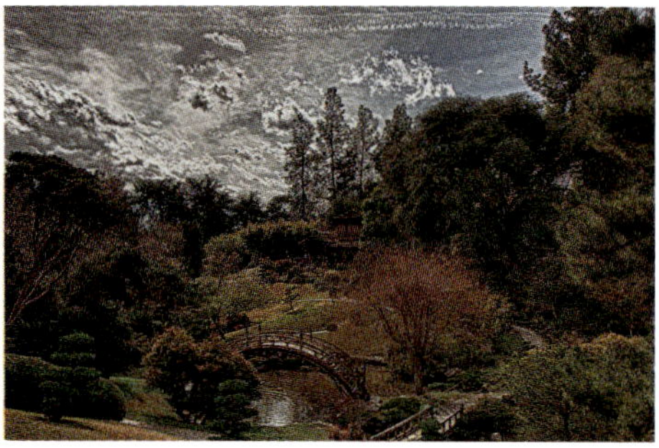

Figure 4.15

Contrast is low as a result of the Blacks and Whites sliders being set to negative values.

If you are looking to really bring out the local contrast in your sky, this is the preset to try first.

note

The 08 Structured Skies preset is also found in the Artistic Preset Category.

09 Vibrant Textures preset

There is a strong family resemblance between the Vibrant Textures preset in Figure 4.16 and the Realistic (Strong) preset. Both use the Strong HDR Method, but Vibrant Textures uses a slightly stronger Method Strength.

Comparing these two presets gives further insight into the Control Palette sliders. With the Vibrant Textures preset, the image is brighter than the Realistic (Strong) preset primarily due to less reduction in the Exposure slider and the setting of a higher black point with the Blacks slider.

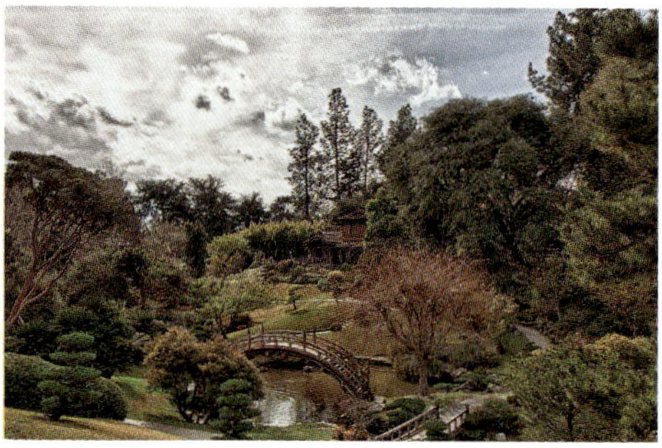

Figure 4.16

While you could create Vibrant Textures from the Realistic (Strong) preset with a few adjustments, HDR Efex Pro has done it for you.

note

The 09 Vibrant Textures preset is also found in the Artistic Preset Category.

10 Vibrant Details & Colors preset

The Vibrant Details & Colors preset in Figure 4.17 adds a strong S curve to enhance the contrast and an increase in saturation with the Saturation slider.

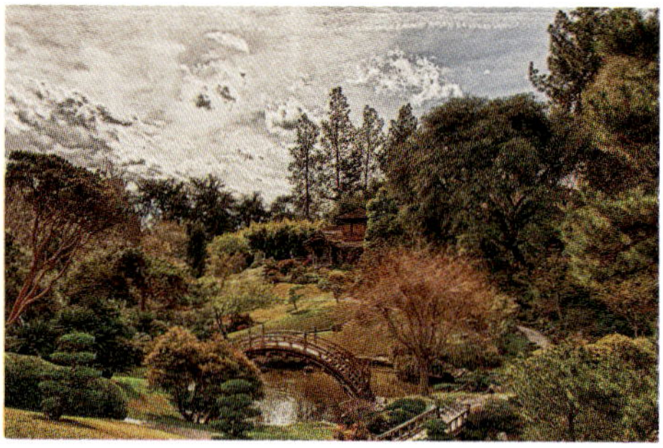

Figure 4.17

This preset increases exposure to brighten the image, but it lowers the black and white points with the Blacks and Whites sliders, so the exposure increase happens primarily to the midtones.

The Warmth slider is set at +12% (as it is for the Fine Structures preset) to add warmth to the clouds and the overall scene.

note

The 10 Vibrant Details & Colors preset is also found in the Artistic Preset Category.

11 Monochrome, Contrasty preset

With digital cameras set up by the manufacturers to capture images in color, interest in monochrome (black-and-white) image capture has virtually disappeared. So it's nice to see HDR Efex Pro paying homage to monochrome imaging with the Monochrome, Contrasty preset in Figure 4.18 and the following Monochrome, Soft preset.

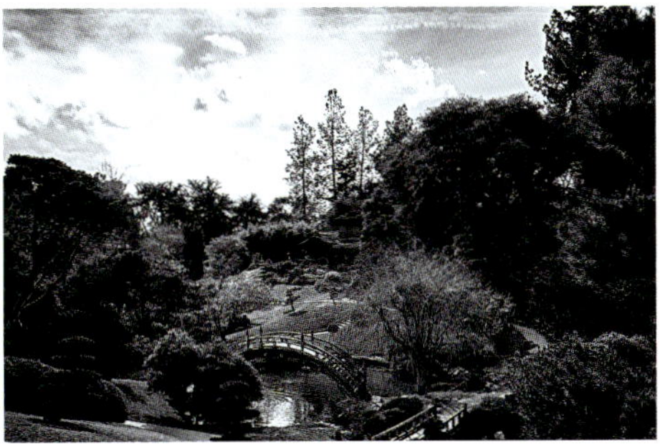

Figure 4.18

Somewhat unfortunately, however, HDR Efex Pro achieves the monochrome look by simply setting the Saturation slider to 0, adjusting a rather nicely adjusted color HDR image fairly crudely to monochrome.

While it's nice to have these monochrome adjustments available so you don't need to use another program to convert the color HDR to monochrome, I use the monochrome presets just to give me a preview of how the image might look as a black and white. If I feel it has potential as a monochrome image, I make the best possible color interpretation that I can, output the HDR image, and then perform the monochrome conversion in Nik Software Silver Efex 2, which gives me total control, including the ability to tone the final image.

note

The 11 Monochrome, Contrasty preset is also found in the Artistic Preset Category.

12 Monochrome, Soft preset

With a lot more tone compression than the Monochrome, Contrasty preset, the sky in this image using the Monochrome, Soft preset in Figure 4.19 is much more interesting. But the rest of the image is pretty bad and needs a lot of work to make it usable.

As with the Monochrome, Contrasty preset, I would save the monochrome conversion until I export the HDR image, and then perform it in Silver Efex 2.

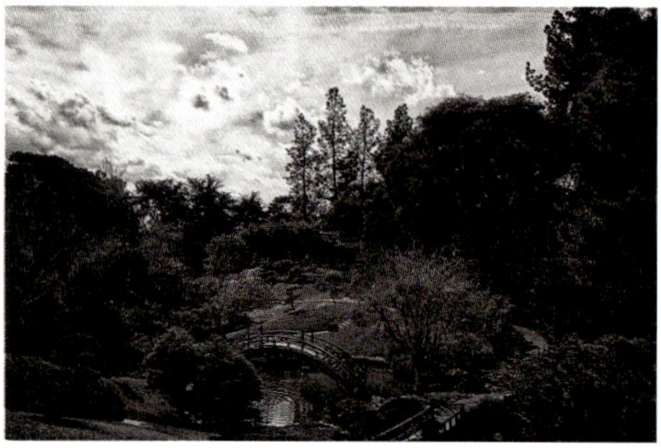

Figure 4.19

note

The 12 Monochrome, Soft preset is also found in the Artistic Preset Category. It is the final Artistic preset entry.

13 The Old Cottage preset

The Old Cottage preset in Figure 4.20 begins the Surreal Preset Category of effects that people either love or hate about HDR. With every HDR image I create I look at the thumbnails in this category to see if there is a potential image there. Most of the time I'm interested in a more realistic interpretation, but there are times when one of the Surreal presets strikes me as just right.

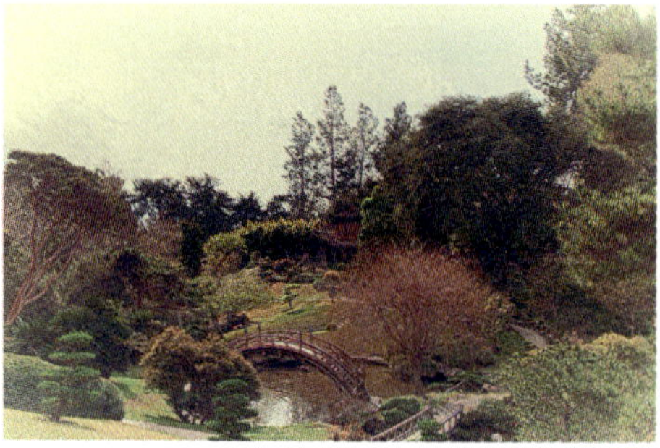

Figure 4.20

With tone compression and HDR Method Strength boosted, but most of the other sliders lowered, the Old Cottage settings produce a result that reminds me of a faded color print, and that may have been the logic behind its name. In fact, the names of all the Surreal presets are fairly whimsical, but the effects are real and often interesting.

note

The 13 The Old Cottage preset is also found in the Surreal Preset Category.

14 Night On Earth preset

It's interesting to compare the result of applying the Night On Earth preset in Figure 4.21 with the Default preset in Figure 4.7 to see just how far you can push an image in HDR Efex Pro.

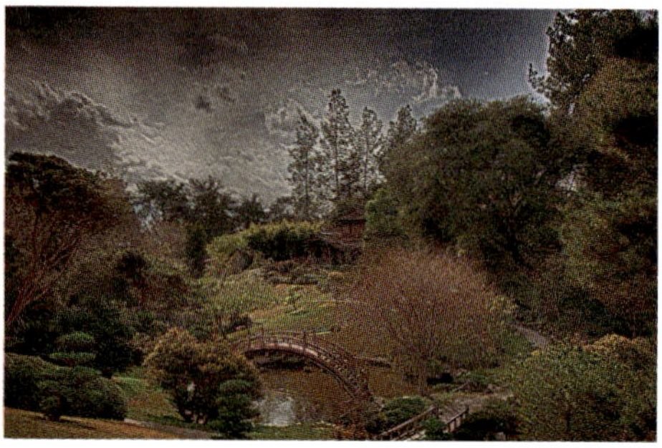

Figure 4.21

With Night On Earth, the Tone Compression slider is set to +100% and the Structure slider to –100%. The Dark Soft HDR Method is set to a high +60% and for the first time a preset includes a prebuilt vignette, which is named Black Frame 1.

see also

Chapter 10 discusses the vignettes that are included as part of the Finishing Adjustments section.

Someday I hope to find an old graveyard or battered and abandoned Victorian house that seems to me to be an appropriate HDR subject for the Night On Earth preset.

note

The 14 Night On Earth preset is also found in the Surreal Preset Category.

15 Vintage Colors preset

I admit that I like what the Vintage Colors preset in Figure 4.22 does to this scene. It could be a print from a faded Ektachrome slide taken 50 years ago in Japan.

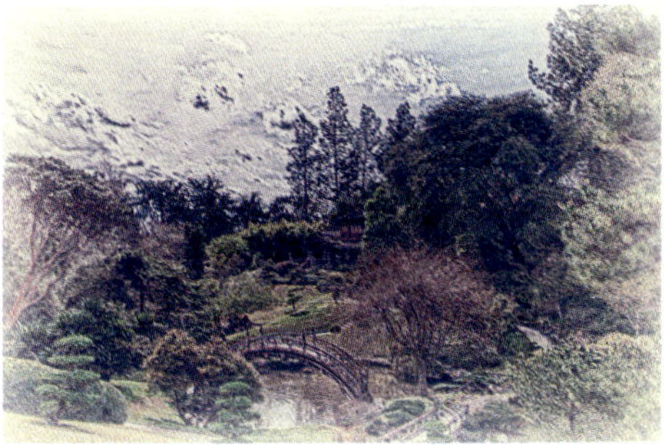

Figure 4.22

In the Vintage Colors preset, a White Frame 1 vignette frames the scene. And unlike in the presets previously described, a prebuilt curve, Vintage 1, rather than Neutral is applied. The Vintage 1 curve lowers the Red and Green curves slightly and changes the Blue curve radically. Together these curves changes produce the color changes in the image.

see also

Chapter 10 discusses the curves that are included as part of the Finishing Adjustments section.

Tone compression is at +100% and the other sliders are all over the place with their settings. I wouldn't need to make too many adjustments to this preset to create a result that I can live with.

note

The 15 Vintage Colors preset is also found in the Surreal Preset Category.

16 Granny's Attic preset

The Granny's Attics preset shown in Figure 4.23 is a classic and probably my favorite Surreal preset. The overall effect is somehow natural and unnatural at the same time.

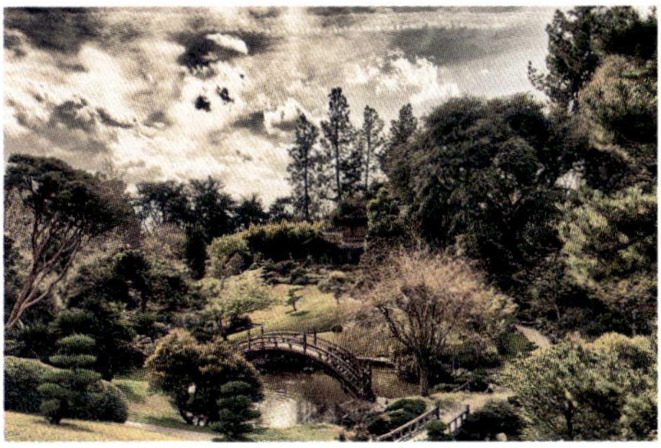

Figure 4.23

Granny's Attic uses the same Vintage 1 curves preset used in Vintage Colors, but with a less radical adjustment in the Blue layer. The Blue curves adjustment adds a touch of overall warmth that works well with this image. Contrast is very good with nice highlights and strong, yet open, shadows.

note

The 16 Granny's Attic preset is also found in the Surreal Preset Category.

17 End of the Road preset

The End of the Road preset uses a different set of adjustments to the Vintage 1 curve of the previous two presets along with a rectangular Black Frame 1 vignette to create the look in Figure 4.24.

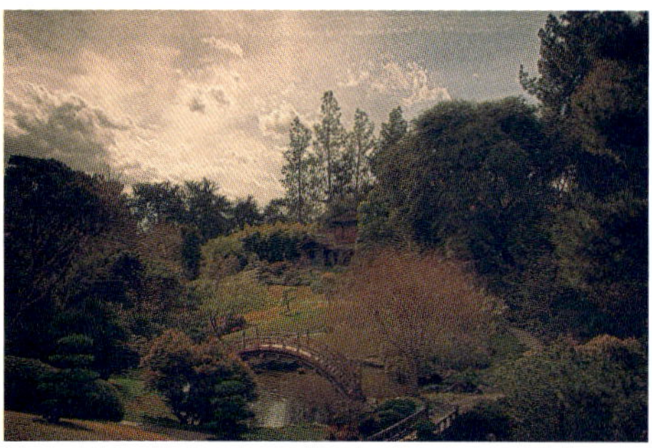

Figure 4.24

It has some of that old British landscape painting look with this image, with a stormy sky and muted land that you saw in Realistic Gradients 1.

The Soft HDR Method and low tone compression setting work together to create a quiet, romantic look.

note

The 17 End of the Road preset is also found in the Surreal Preset Category.

18 Bleach Bypass Look preset

Bleach bypass is a technique used in the motion picture industry. It involves partially or totally eliminating the bleach step in film processing. When the bleach step is bypassed, some or all of the silver remains in the film, overlaying a monochrome image on the color image. This increases contrast and graininess while decreasing dynamic range and saturation.

The HDR Efex Pro Bleach Bypass preset in Figure 4.25 does a very good job duplicating this cinematographic effect. The Contrast slider is set higher and the Saturation, Blacks, and Whites sliders are decreased. These, along with fairly high setting for the Harsh Details HDR Method and for tone compression, create the effect.

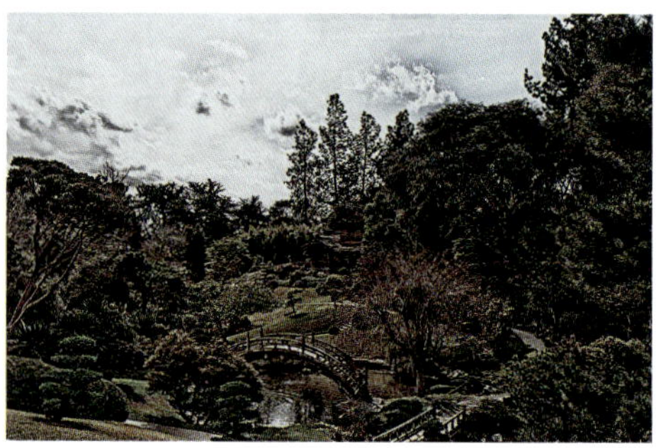

Figure 4.25

note

The 18 Bleach Bypass Look preset is also found in the Surreal Preset Category. It is the last Surreal preset thumbnail.

19 Full Scene Compression preset

I find it a little strange that the preset named Full Scene Compression shown in Figure 4.26 doesn't use the Tone Compression slider at all. Rather, the effect is created primarily with a high (+90%) setting of the Natural HDR Method. This is the same HDR Method used for the Default preset, but in the Default preset the strength is set at 0%. Low settings of the Blacks and Whites sliders add to the effect.

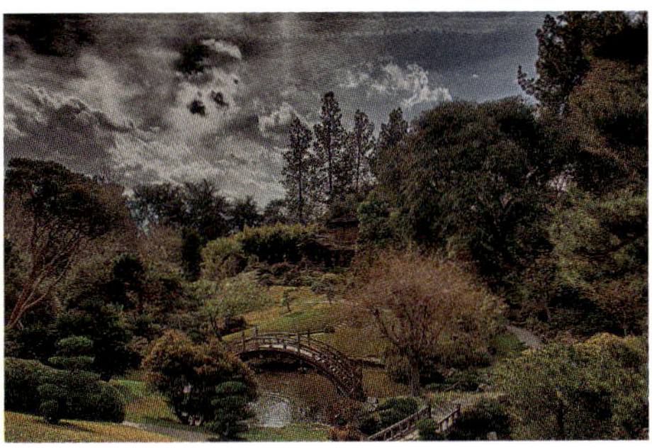

Figure 4.26

Full Scene Compression works well with this image and other landscapes.

note

The 19 Full Scene Compression preset is also found in the Landscape Preset Category.

20 Vibrant Scenery preset

The Vibrant Scenery preset in Figure 4.27 is a relative of the Realistic (Strong) preset. Both use the Sharp HDR Method although Vibrant Scenery couples this with less tone compression than the Realistic (Strong) preset uses.

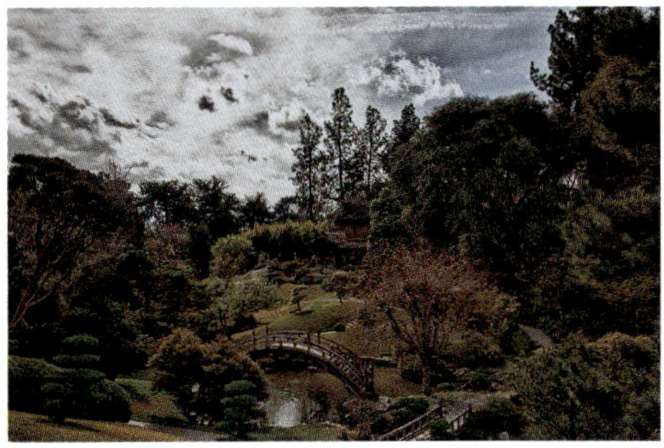

Figure 4.27

With a little less drama in the sky and a little more brightness to add luminance to the midtones in the center of the scene, this would be a realistic portrayal of the original scene.

note

The 20 Vibrant Scenery preset is also found in the Landscape Preset Category.

21 Gradual Contrasts 1 preset

Gradual Contrasts 1 in Figure 4.28 and Gradual Contrasts 2 that follows are closely related, and both are related to Realistic Gradients 1 and Realistic Gradients 2, which were discussed earlier.

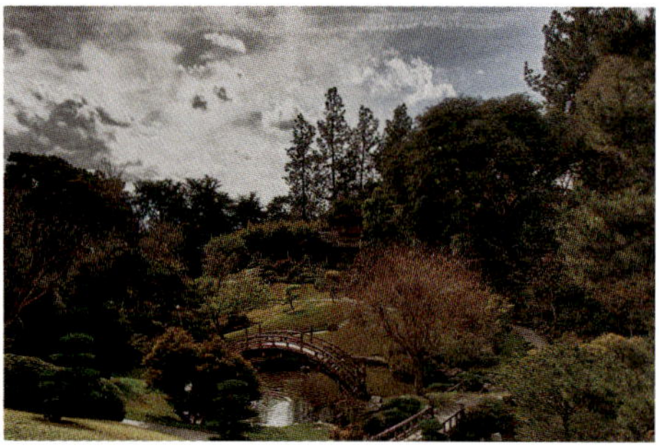

Figure 4.28

Gradual Contrasts 1 uses the same Gradual Large HDR Method at a low setting that Realistic Gradients 2 uses. Settings on the other sliders in the Gradual Contrasts 1 preset produce a brighter image with more accurate color than the settings in Realistic Gradients 2.

note

The 21 Gradual Contrasts 1 preset is also found in the Landscape Preset Category.

22 Gradual Contrasts 2 preset

By using less tone compression and the Gradual Medium HDR Method rather than the Gradual Large, Gradual Contrasts 2 produces a slightly moodier result (Figure 4.29) than Gradual Contrasts 1. The sky is less structured with the reduction in tone compression, and the midtones are darker. I can imagine this working very successfully on a high-contrast desert or snow scene in bright sunlight.

note

The 22 Gradual Contrasts 2 preset is also found in the Landscape Preset Category.

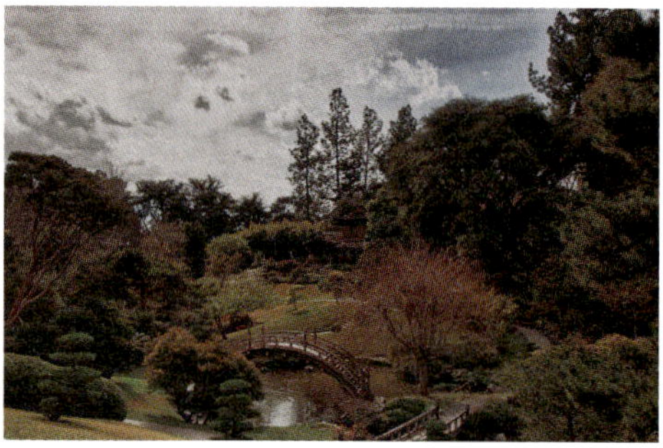

Figure 4.29

23 Postcard Paradise preset

The Postcard Paradise preset shown in Figure 4.30 doesn't look much like the glossy, saturated-color postcards produced today. But the preset does produce results resembling postcards produced from illustrations in the 1920s and 1930s.

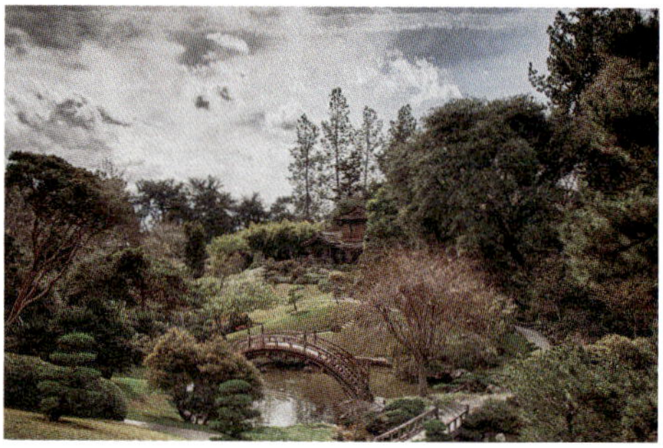

Figure 4.30

The colors are accurate but muted because of a decrease in saturation. The Dark Soft HDR Method at medium strength adds a nice softness while making the scene more two-dimensional. Postcard Paradise is aptly named and consistently produces a pleasing result with landscape images.

note

The 23 Postcard Paradise preset is also found in the Landscape Preset Category. It is the last preset in the Landscape Category.

24 Clean City 1 preset

The Clean City 1 preset used to create Figure 4.31 is very closely related to the Clean City 2 preset, which follows. They both use the same Clean HDR Method and only differ substantially in tone compression.

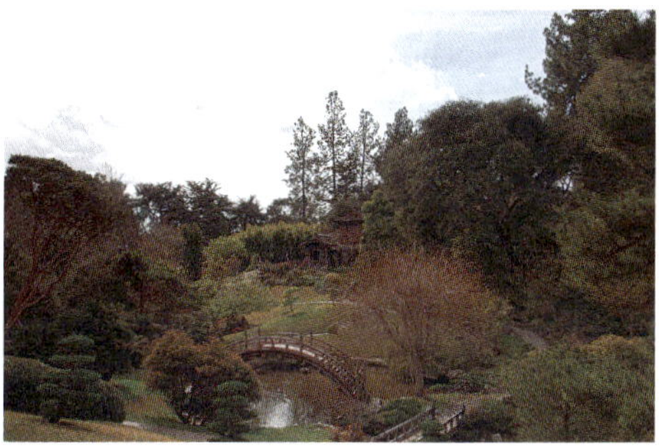

Figure 4.31

Clean City 1 uses a low value of tone compression, –50%, resulting in a washed-out sky and little separation in the shadows with this image.

note

The 24 Clean City 1 preset is also found in the Architecture Preset Category.

25 Clean City 2 preset

The Clean City 2 preset (Figure 4.32) uses virtually the same settings as Clean City 1 other than tone compression, which is set to 0 in Clean City 2. This increase in tone compression results in more detail in the sky and better separation in the shadows.

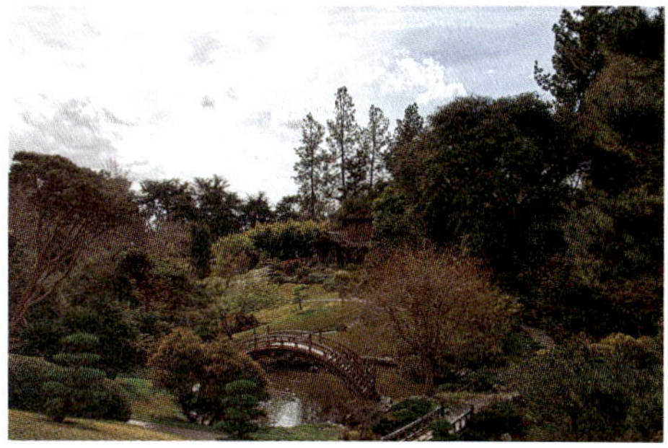

Figure 4.32

note

The 25 Clean City 2 preset is also found in the Architecture Preset Category.

26 Friendly Scenery preset

The Friendly Scenery preset used to produce Figure 4.33 also uses the Clean HDR Method used in the Clean City presets, but at a higher setting and coupled with a tone compression setting of +67%.

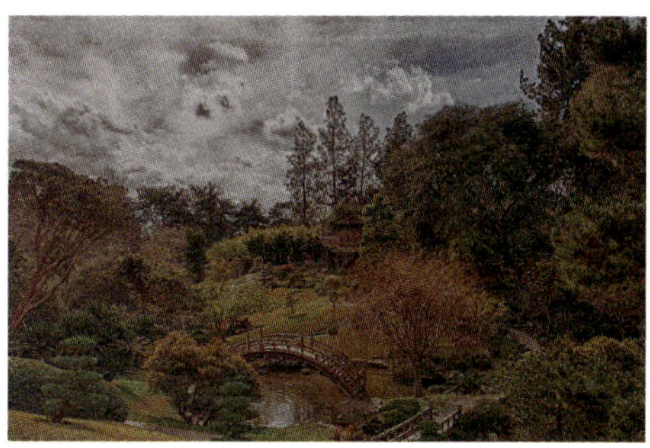

Figure 4.33

With the Whites slider at –99% and the Blacks slider at –76%, the separation between tones in the highlights and shadows is very low.

note

The 26 Friendly Scenery preset is also found in the Architecture Preset Category.

27 Bright Room 1 preset

Photographers who shoot architectural interiors and need to balance the interior with the exterior exposure require a lot of tone compression to hold separation in both areas. The Bright Room presets provide that, along with softening for a more romantic look.

The Bright Room 1 preset in Figure 4.34 uses the Bright Soft HDR Method at a medium setting along with a tone compression of +81%. It also uses a new preset tone curve adjustment, Bright Contrast. Bright Room 1 produces a nice full dynamic range with this image and works well.

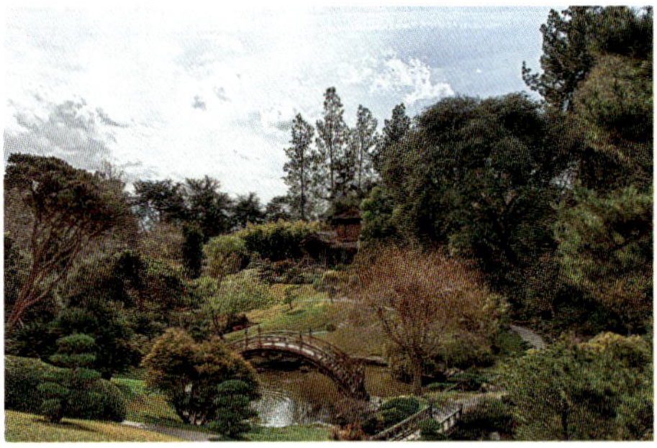

Figure 4.34

note

The 27 Bright Room 1 preset is also found in the Architecture Preset Category.

28 Bright Room 2 preset

The Bright Room 2 preset used for Figure 4.35 is very similar to Bright Room 1, except that it uses the Soft HDR Method rather than Bright Soft. Soft is the same HDR Method used in the End of the Road and The Old Cottage presets but the result is far different in Bright Room 2, which uses the Bright Contrast tone curve preset.

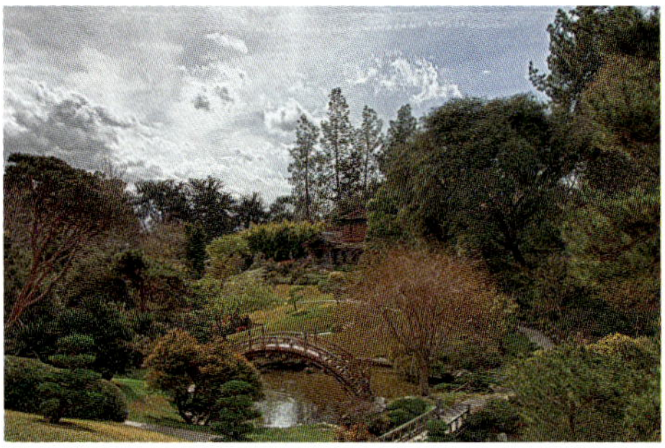

Figure 4.35

note

The 28 Bright Room 2 preset is also found in the Architecture Preset Category.

29 Strong Counterlight preset

One of the most dramatic uses of HDR imaging is photographing into the sun at sunset and being able to retain the drama of the sky and clouds along with a well-exposed foreground and middle ground. The Strong Counterlight preset used for Figure 4.36 is designed for this situation. *Counterlight* is another term for backlight, or light coming directly into the camera lens, such as the sun at sunset.

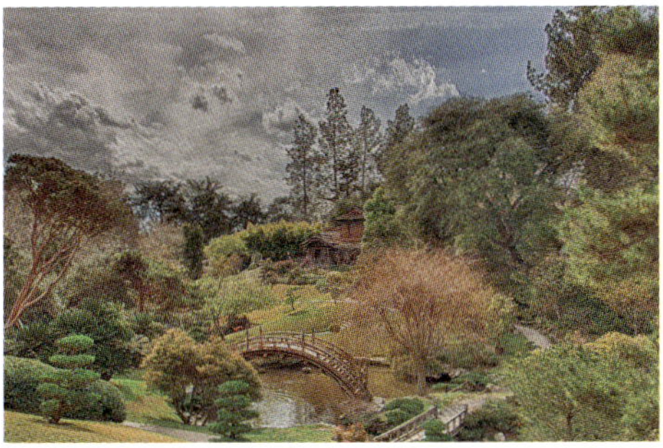

Figure 4.36

The Strong Counterlight preset uses a very high tone compression setting of +96% to hold information in the highlights and shadows. There is not enough contrast in this scene, so the result is lacking in dynamic range. With a high-contrast scene, the Strong Counterlight preset works very well.

note

The 29 Strong Counterlight preset is also found in the Landscape Preset Category. It is the last of the six Architecture presets.

30 Very Low Compression preset

There is no need to guess what effect the Very Low Compression preset delivers. As shown in Figure 4.37, the result is an HDR image with very low compression.

The slider settings for this preset are not much different from the Default preset. The major difference is the Tone Compression slider that was set to 0 in the Default preset is now set to –66%. There are also adjustments to the tone curve to add contrast and a reduction in the Whites slider that serve to darken the image and compress the tonal values further. The result is a poor choice for this scene.

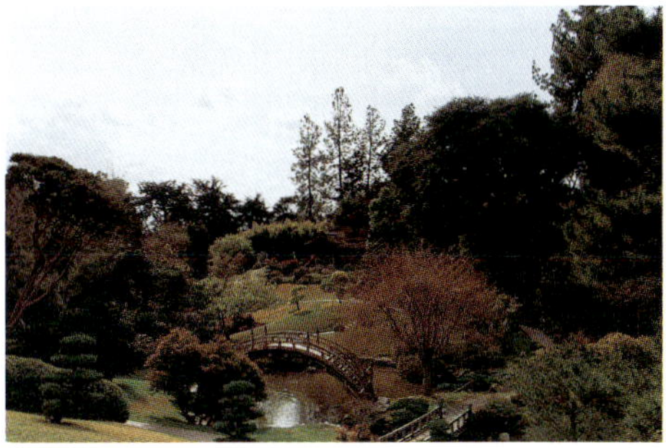

Figure 4.37

note

The 30 Very Low Compression preset is also found in the Special Preset Category.

31 Single Exposure 1 preset

I'm not sure why these next two presets are titled Single Exposure 1 and Single Exposure 2. Certainly they are an option when creating an Extended Dynamic Range (EDR) from a single RAW image, but so are any of the other presets. They also work well when you are creating an HDR image.

The Single Exposure 1 preset is used to create Figure 4.38. It uses a fairly high amount of tone compression (76%) and the black and white points are set quite low, so the dynamic range is very compressed. With this image, the result is a bit flat and dark in the midtones.

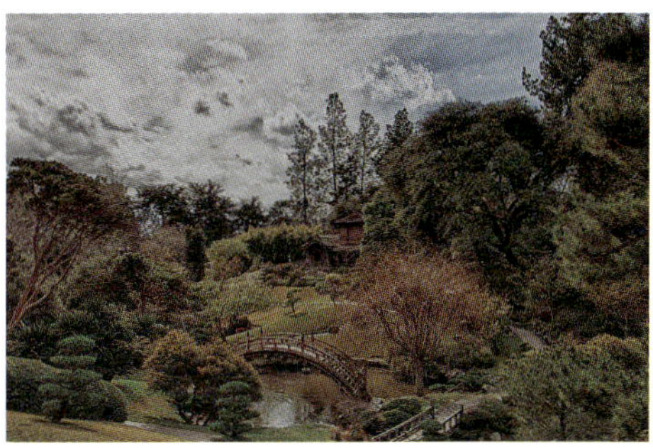

Figure 4.38

note

The 31 Single Exposure 1 preset is also found in the Special Preset Category.

32 Single Exposure 2 preset

The Single Exposure 2 preset (Figure 4.39) is something of an improvement with this image over the Single Exposure 1 preset. The HDR Method is now Sharp rather than Subtle and that opens up the midtones. The Whites slider is set a little higher and that helps, too.

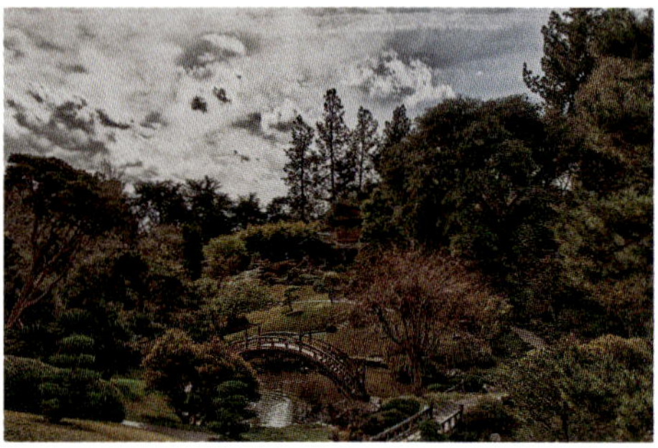

Figure 4.39

note

The 32 Single Exposure 2 preset is the third and last preset in the Special Preset Category.

see also

Appendix B contains a table of the HDR Efex Pro presets along with their Preset Category and HDR Method.

Favorites

As you work with HDR Efex Pro you find that there are presets you use often and some that you don't use at all. If you are interested in creating realistic interpretations, you may only need those in the Realistic Preset Category and you may only use a few of these. But you may also often use one or two Architecture presets. That can mean a lot of extra mouse clicks and scroll bar dragging to navigate through categories. There is one other Preset Category that allows you to gather the prebuilt presets together that you use most often, and it is called Favorites.

The Favorites Preset Category is empty when you install HDR Efex Pro. To add presets into the Favorites, click the star icon that precedes the preset name. The star turns red and remains red to indicate that the preset is added to the Favorites. Open the Favorites by clicking the Favorites button and you will see the thumbnail. The star next to the preset name is red there, also.

Custom Presets

Having seen each of the presets in action, I hope you see the value of having a group of presets to get you started with the creation of your HDR image.

I also hope you see two other things. The first is that a preset seldom gives you the best possible HDR image. Each preset needs some adjustment to create the best possible HDR image from your image series. HDR Efex Pro provides the means to make those adjustments in the Control Palette. The remainder of this book discusses how to make global and local corrections to your image and apply any finishing adjustments you feel necessary before you output your final HDR image.

The other thing that I hope you are seeing is that it is virtually impossible to re-create the same effect from scratch and apply it to another image. There are just too many tool options and too many possible settings for each tool.

But there are times when you will want to apply the adjustments from one HDR image to another image series. Perhaps you exposed several image series of the same scene at different times and you want to see the same tool settings applied to each one. Or perhaps you like what you've done, but you want to try some other adjustments without losing the current ones and without processing and saving the HDR image to a final output. Or maybe you just want to save the settings to apply to images in the future.

HDR Efex Pro provides a way to save your settings by allowing you to create a custom preset. Once you create and store a custom preset you can use it just like any of the prebuilt presets that are provided in HDR Efex Pro.

Creating a custom preset

Creating a custom preset is easy. The first step is to open an image in HDR Efex Pro, and then apply a preset and adjust the Control Palette settings to your liking.

When you are happy with the image, click Add Preset at the bottom of the Preset Browser, as shown in Figure 4.40.

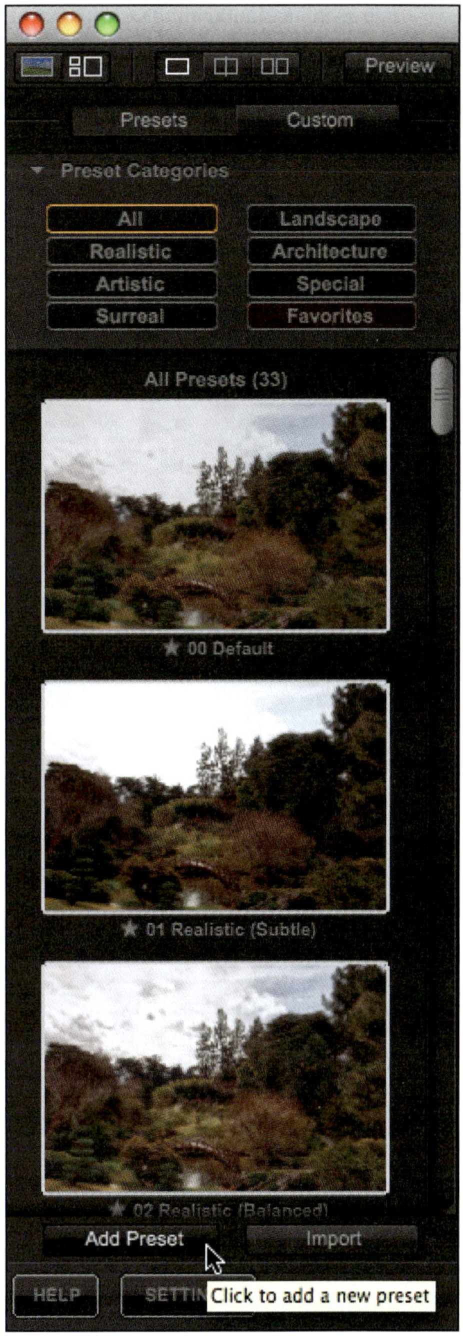

Figure 4.40

Type a name for the preset in the Custom Preset dialog box, as shown in Figure 4.41, and click OK.

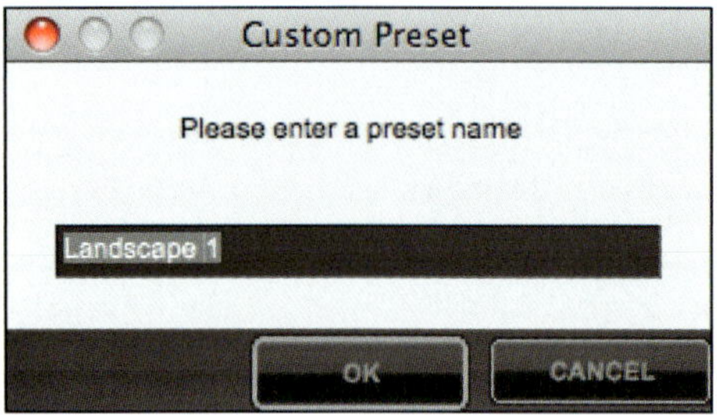

Figure 4.41

When you click Custom, as shown in Figure 4.42, near the top of the Preset Browser, the prebuilt preset thumbnails disappear and the new custom preset is displayed, as shown in Figure 4.43.

There is another path that produces the same result. With the image containing the look you want to use as a preset open, click Custom to open the Custom Preset palette.

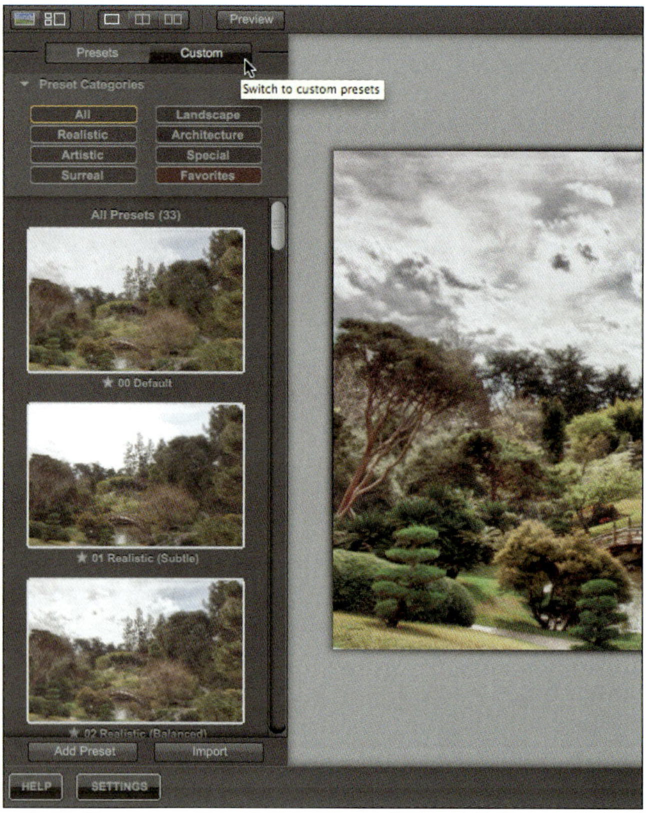

Figure 4.42

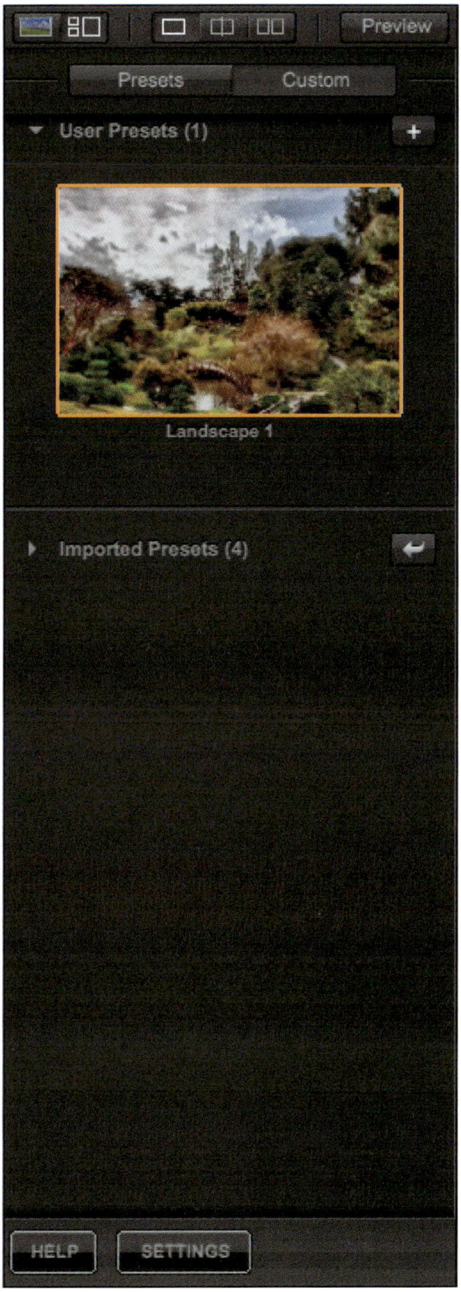

Figure 4.43

Click the + button, as shown in Figure 4.44, to open the Custom Preset dialog box. Type a name and click OK, and a thumbnail of the new custom preset appears in the User Presets palette.

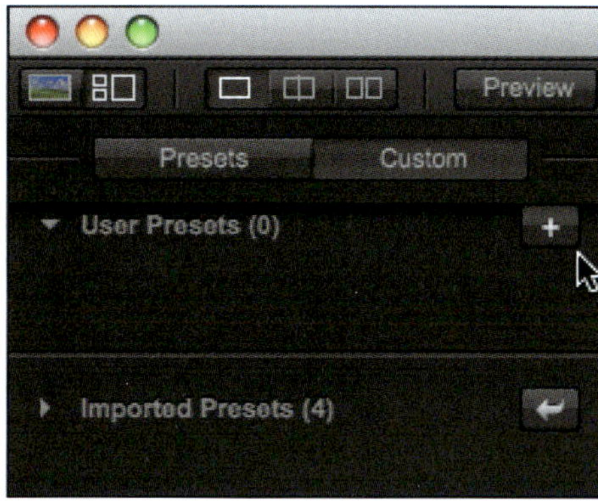

Figure 4.44

In summary, to create a custom preset, follow these steps:

1. **Open an image series or a single image in HDR Efex Pro.**
2. **Apply a prebuilt preset.**
3. **Adjust the image using the control tools.**
4. **Click Add Preset at the bottom of the Presets Palette.** Alternatively, open the Custom Preset palette and click the + button to the right of the User Presets tab.
5. **Type a name in the Custom Preset dialog box.**
6. **Click Yes to save the custom preset.**

You can add as many custom presets as you want to the User Presets palette. Custom presets function the same as the prebuilt presets. When you open the Custom palette, the thumbnails for the custom presets display your open HDR image adjusted according to the settings of the custom presets. Clicking on a custom preset highlights it in gold and applies the settings to the HDR image in the Main Image Window. You can use these settings as a basis for adjustments to further customize the image. You can even save the newly adjusted image as a new custom preset.

Deleting a custom preset

In time, you may create a large number of custom presets and find that you want to delete some that you aren't using or are too similar to others you have created. This is easy to do directly from the Custom Preset palette.

Roll your mouse cursor over the thumbnail of the custom preset you want to delete and icons appear in three of the corners, as shown in Figure 4.45.

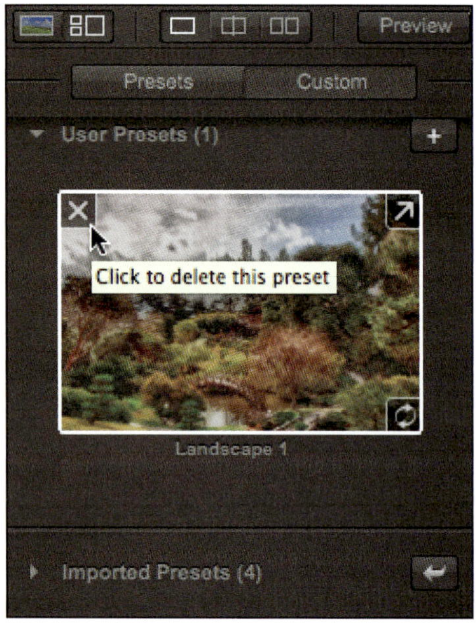

Figure 4.45

Click the X in the upper-left corner. In the dialog box shown in Figure 4.46 click Yes and the preset is deleted.

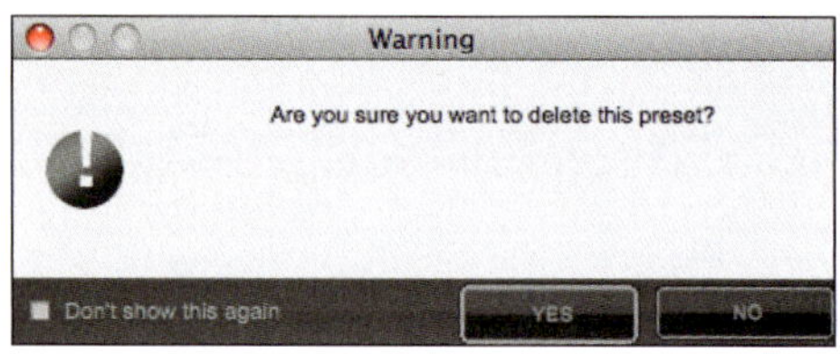

Figure 4.46

Modifying a custom preset

Once you start creating custom presets you may find yourself applying one to an image, making a few adjustments, and saving the new image as a new custom preset just to have it. Actually, there is nothing wrong with this, but you will find that each image usually requires some sort of adjustment to a preset, so you may want to reevaluate the strategy of saving changes to a custom preset that are not radical changes.

One option is to not save the changes at all. But perhaps there are other image series that you shot at the same time and you want to apply the adjusted custom preset to them. Rather than creating a new custom preset it is possible to save the adjustments in the existing preset to use with other images.

Roll your cursor over the custom preset thumbnail you want to modify. In the lower-right corner are two arrows formed into a circle, as shown in Figure 4.45. Click this icon and the dialog box in Figure 4.47 appears. Click Yes and the changes are written into the custom preset, overwriting the previous adjustments.

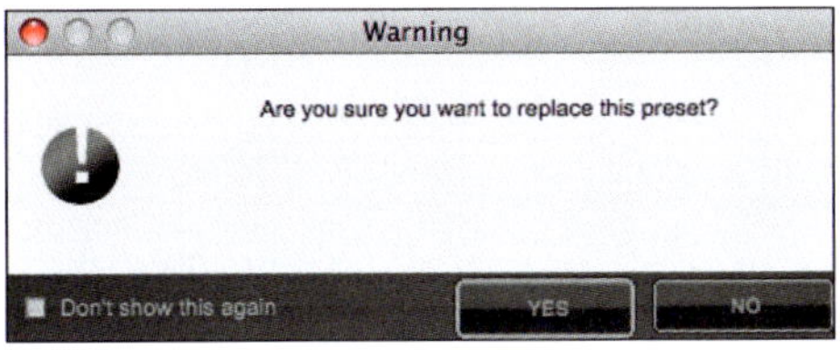

Figure 4.47

Exporting a custom preset

There is a growing community of HDR Efex Pro users, and you can find links to the social networks of users on the Nik Software website. These users share images and ideas along with their tips and problems. They also share their custom presets because HDR Efex Pro makes it easy to export them.

To export a custom preset, click the icon in the upper-right corner of the thumbnail in Figure 4.45. This opens a dialog box (Figure 4.48) that allows you to export the preset to share with others or to move the custom preset to another computer, either Windows or Mac.

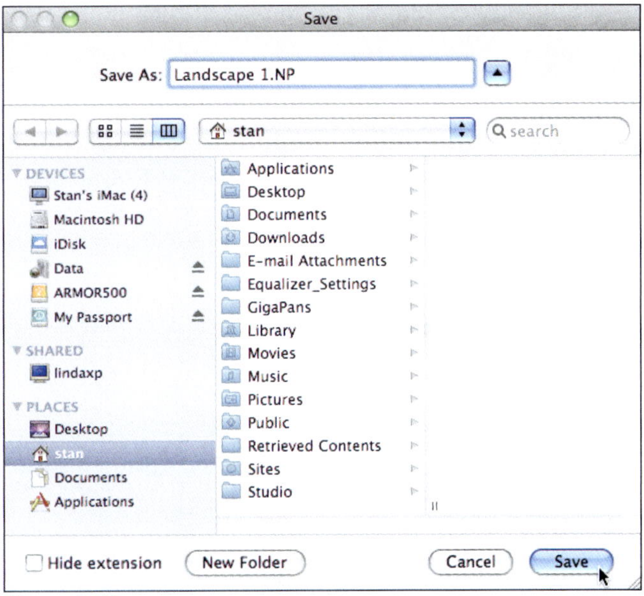

Figure 4.48

Importing Presets

Even if you aren't interested in exporting your presets, you may be interested in seeing presets that other users of HDR Efex Pro have created. Nik Software has a few interesting presets on its website that are free and worth downloading and checking out.

After you download the presets, open HDR Efex Pro with a single image or an image series. You need to have an image open to import presets. Click Import at the bottom of the Presets Palette. This launches the Open window in the operating system shown in Figure 4.49.

Navigate to the location where you downloaded the preset and double-click the filename to import. The thumbnail for the new preset is in the Imported Presets palette in the Custom Presets palette.

You can also import presets directly from the Custom Presets palette. Click the left-facing arrow in the Imported Presets tab, as shown in Figure 4.50. This also displays the operating system Open window. Navigate to the preset and double-click the filename to import.

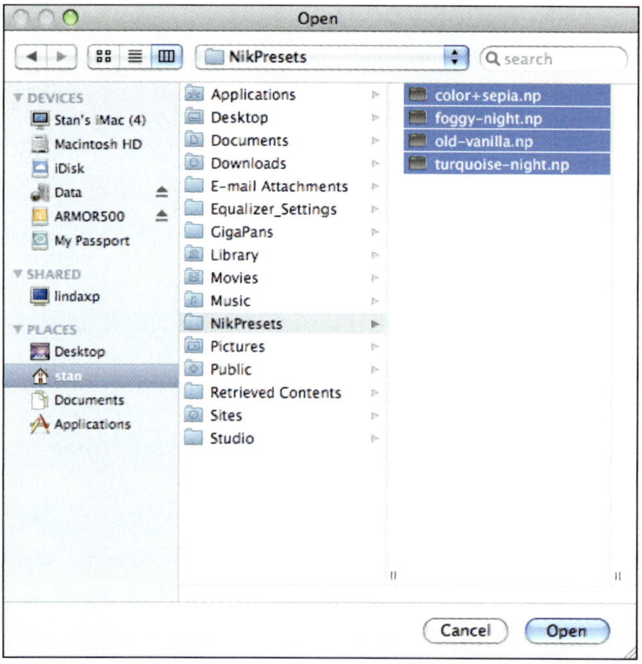

Figure 4.49

The imported presets appear in the Imported Presets palette, as shown in Figure 4.51.

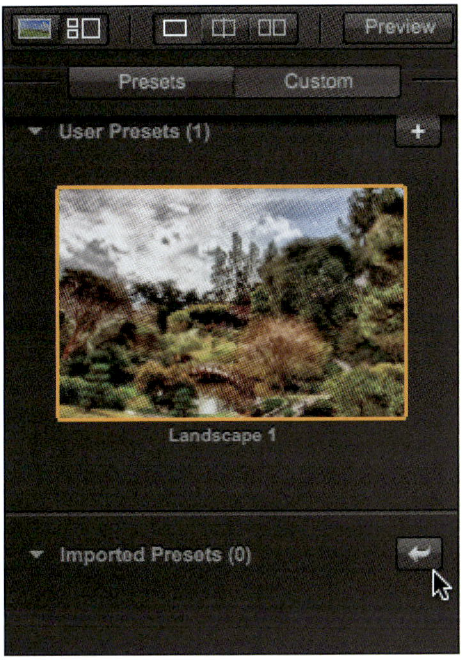

Figure 4.50

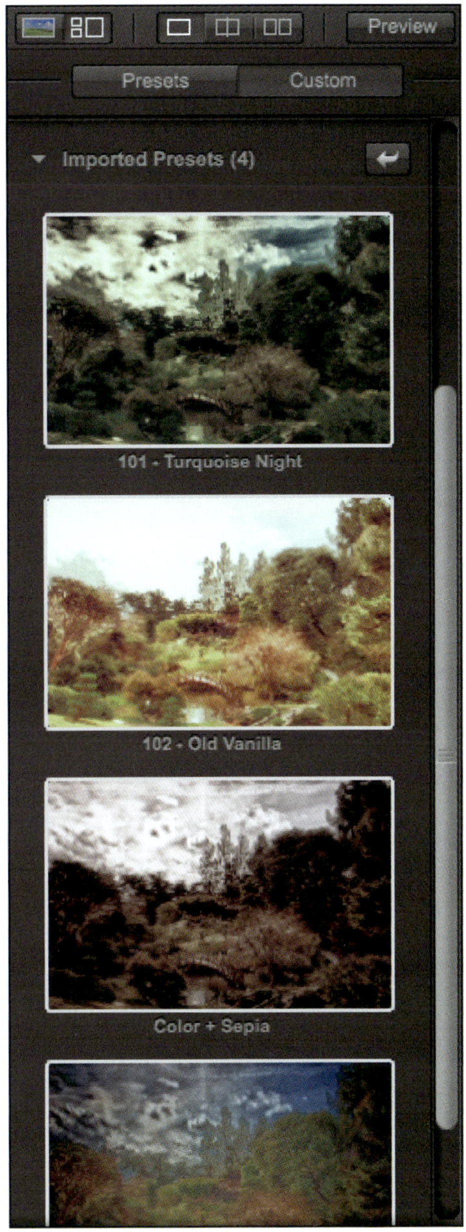

Figure 4.51

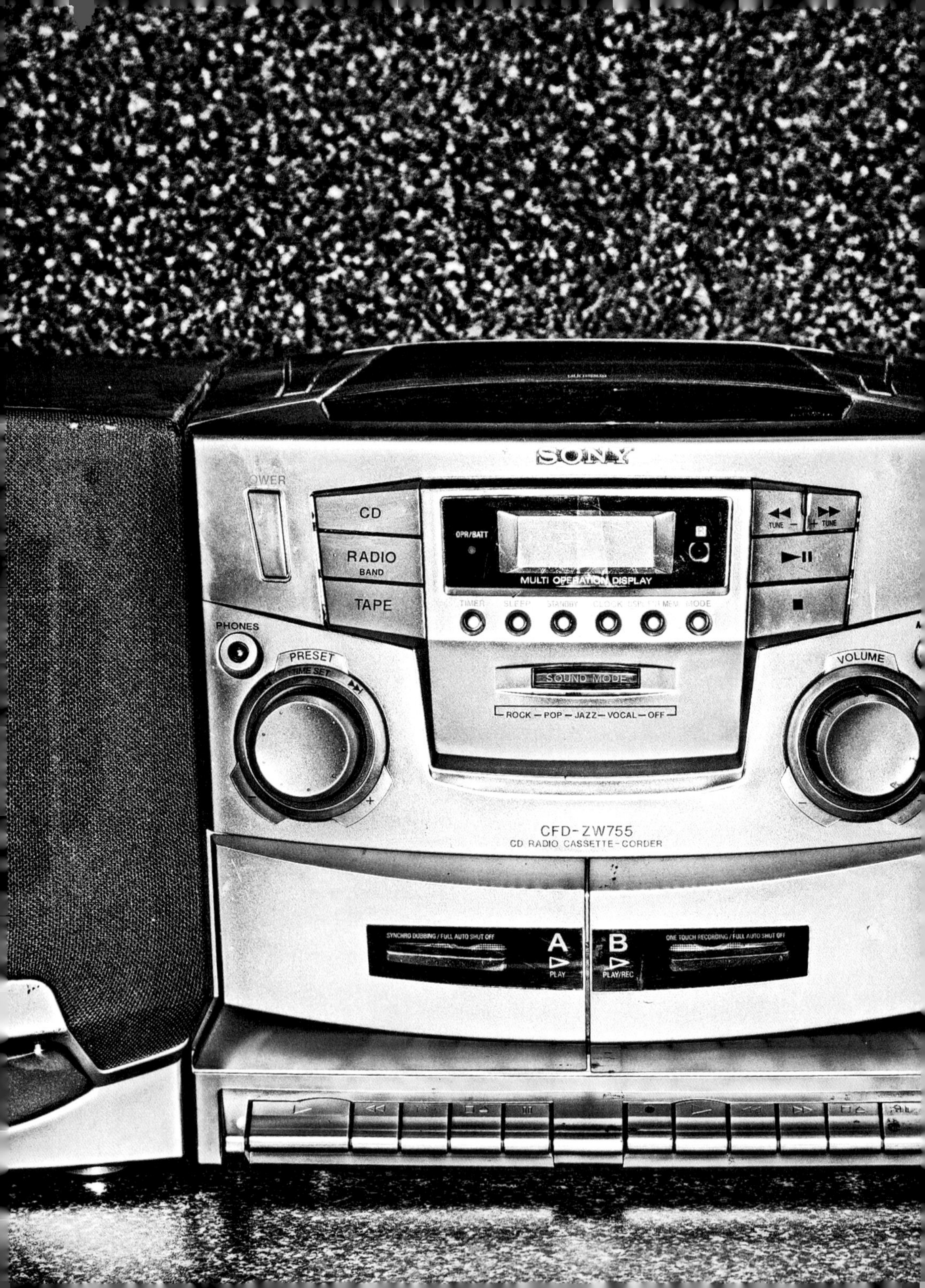

SONY
CD
RADIO
BAND
TAPE
OPR/BATT
MULTI OPERATION DISPLAY
PHONES
PRESET
TIME SET
VOLUME
SOUND MODE
ROCK — POP — JAZZ — VOCAL — OFF
CFD-ZW755
CD RADIO CASSETTE-CORDER
SYNCHRO DUBBING / FULL AUTO SHUT OFF
A
PLAY
B
PLAY/REC
ONE TOUCH RECORDING / FULL AUTO SHUT OFF

5

Adjusting Dynamic Range with Tone Compression

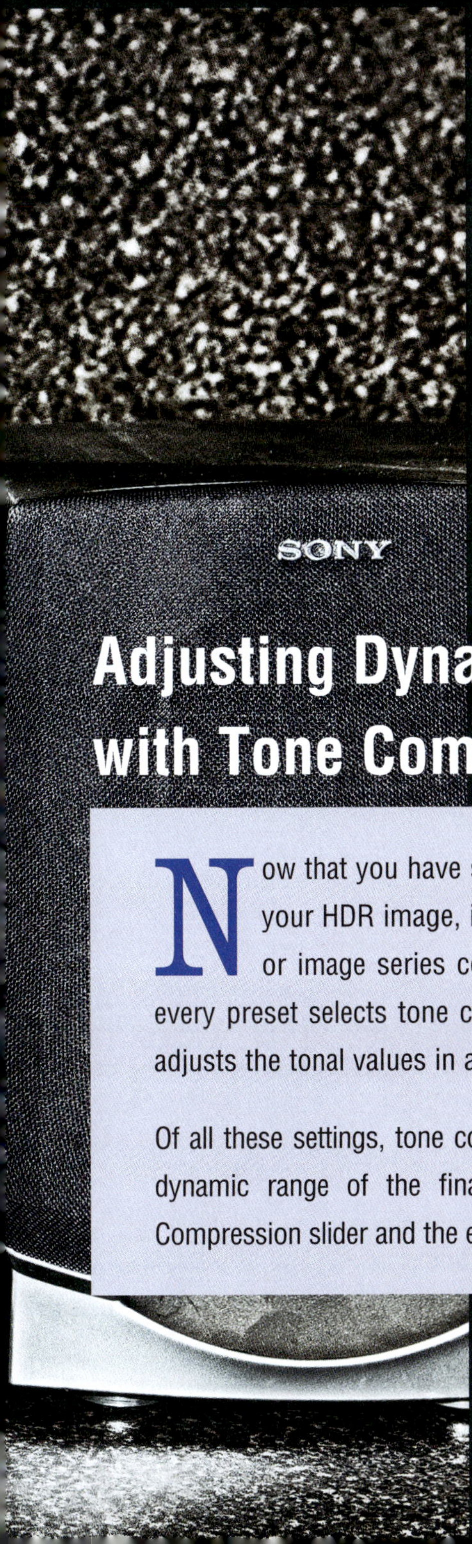

Now that you have selected a preset that gives an initial look to your HDR image, it's time to fine-tune the image. Every image or image series contains a different mix of tonal values, and every preset selects tone compression, chooses an HDR Method, and adjusts the tonal values in a particular way.

Of all these settings, tone compression is the most important. It sets the dynamic range of the final image. This chapter looks at the Tone Compression slider and the effect that adjustments to it have on the image.

Understanding Tone Compression

Tone compression is simply a new term for a photographic concept that has been used since the early days of photography.

Photographers who have worked in a black-and-white wet darkroom *burned in* bright areas of their prints and *dodged* shadow areas to limit the dynamic range of the print. These techniques worked well as long as there was information in the negative that could be revealed. Burning and dodging are a form of tone compression.

The Zone System that Ansel Adams and Fred Picker devised is an even better example of tone compression (and expansion). By making adjustments during exposure and later during development of black-and-white negatives, Adams and Picker showed that it was possible to more closely match the dynamic range of the scene to the dynamic range of the paper on which Adams made prints.

In color photography using film, there are fewer options, both in exposure and processing. The need for tonal compression in color transparency film in particular gave rise to the use of graduated neutral density filters to hold back exposure in bright skies. The effect of using a neutral density filter is to compress the dynamic range of the scene to more closely match the capture medium.

With HDR photography, tone compression takes the enormous dynamic range of the 32-bit HDR image and, using tone mapping, compresses the tonal information to display on your monitor and ultimately in your output.

In HDR Efex Pro, converting the 8- or 16-bit originals to a 32-bit HDR image and compressing the tones so that the image displays on your monitor is all done automatically. During this compression process, it is easy to lose microcontrast, or local contrast between fine details, as tones are compressed, so HDR Efex Pro includes the HDR Method tool to add microcontrast into the compressed image. Tone compression and HDR Method work together to create the overall look of your HDR image.

see also

Chapter 6 discusses HDR Methods in detail.

Adjusting Tone Compression

Each of the presets includes a setting for tone compression. It may be 0 or a positive or negative value. You are free to change the settings to any value you feel suits the HDR image.

Tone Compression slider

Setting the overall maximum dynamic range of your image is the single most important adjustment you make to your HDR image. It is also the first adjustment you should make.

In honor of its importance, the Tone Compression slider resides at the top of the Control Palette, as shown in Figure 5.1. The default setting is 0% and the adjustment range is –100% to +100%.

The default setting of 0% is an arbitrary figure that works well with a large number of images.

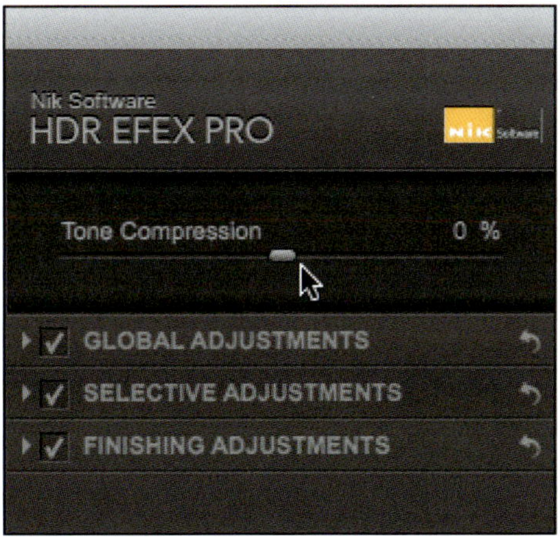

Figure 5.1

It tends to distribute image tones throughout the tonal range from shadow to highlight without losing tonal information at either end of the range (see Figure 5.2).

This distribution of tones is shown in the histogram of the image, as shown in Figure 5.3.

Extreme negative values of tone compression drive the tonal values of the shadows and darker tones to the left of the histogram and drive the highlights and lighter tones to the right. The HDR image at –100% tone compression is shown in Figure 5.4 and its histogram in Figure 5.5.

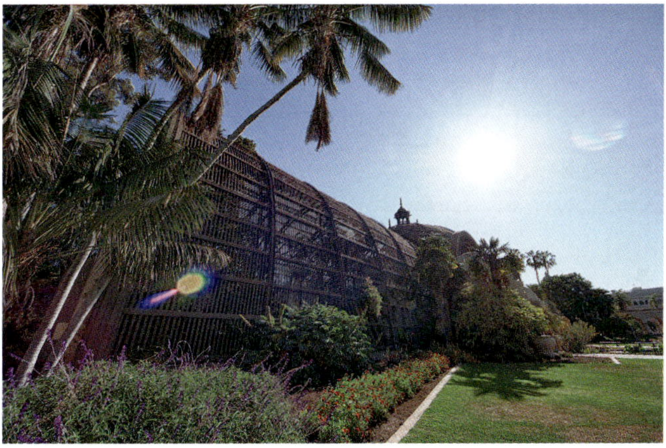

Figure 5.2

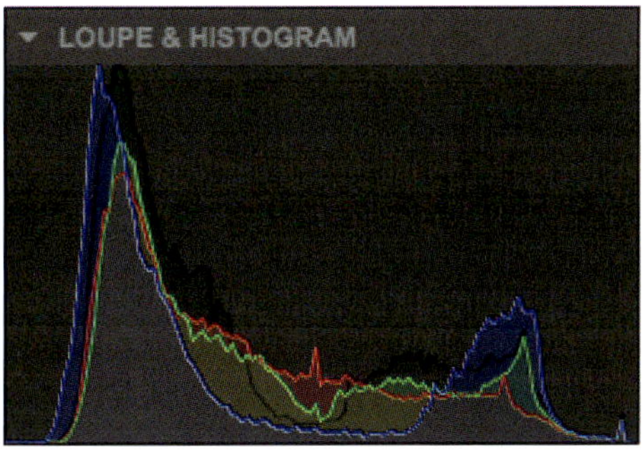

Figure 5.3

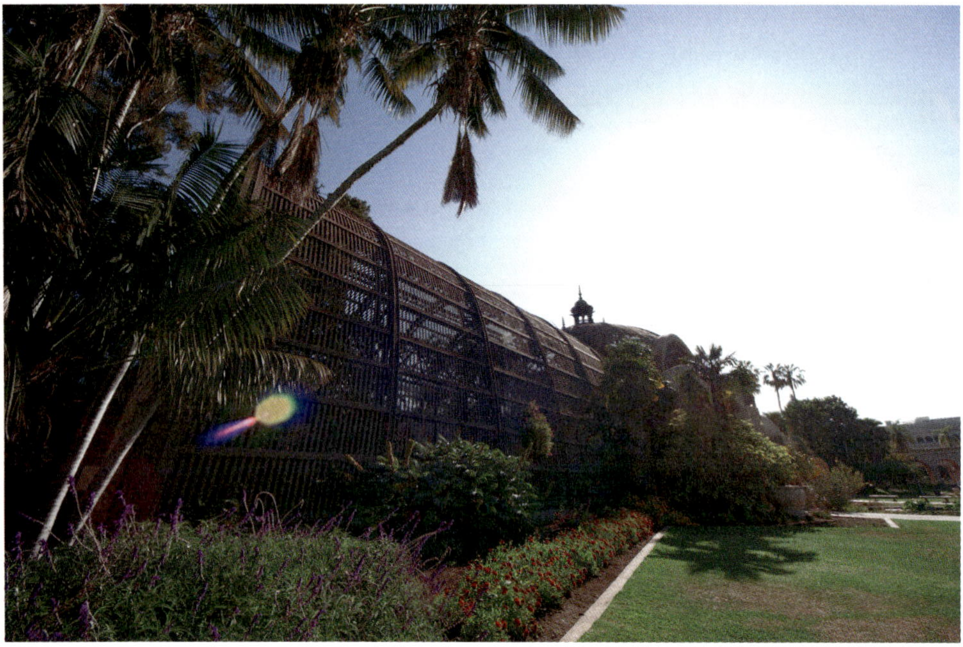

Figure 5.4

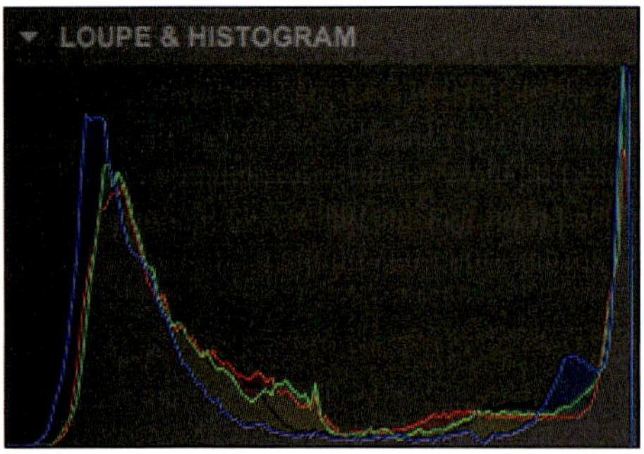

Figure 5.5

Full −100% compression often results in *clipping* of shadow information, highlight information, or both. With clipping, tonal information is lost, and the shadow values reproduce as black without detail while the highlight values reproduce as white without detail.

Extreme positive values of tone compression drive the tonal values of the shadows and darker tones away from the left of the histogram and highlights and lighter tones away from the right. The result moves the shadow and highlight values closer to the midtones, lowering the contrast. The HDR image at +100% tone compression is shown in Figure 5.6 and its histogram in Figure 5.7.

Full +100% compression produces an unnatural-looking result with most HDR Methods — definitely showing that HDR adjustments are present. But this may be the look you want. Several of the Surreal presets set tone compression to +100% to achieve their distinctive look. The Night On Earth preset in Figure 5.8 is one that uses +100% tone compression.

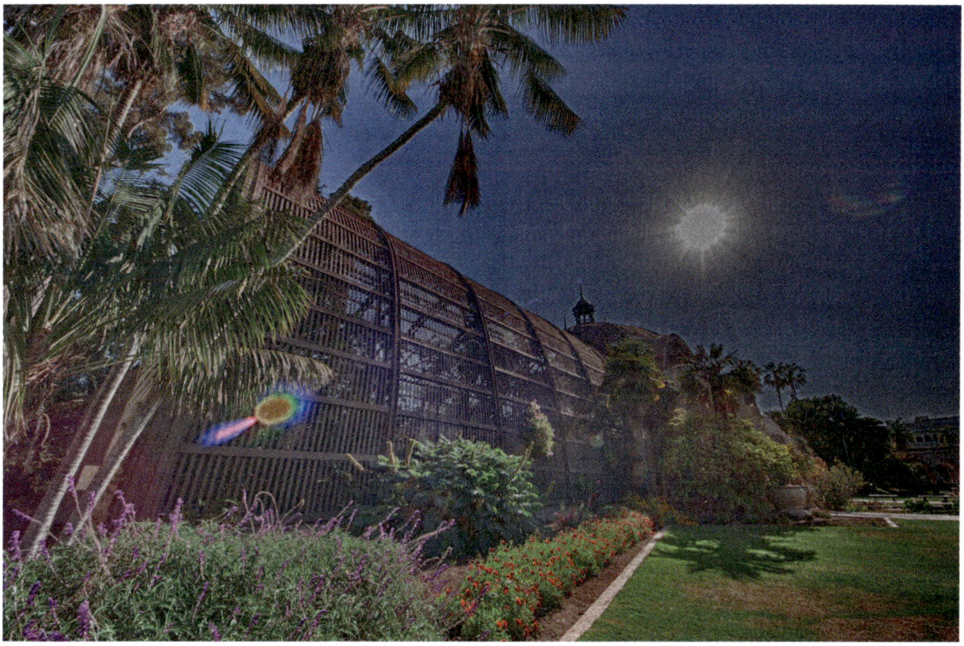

Figure 5.6

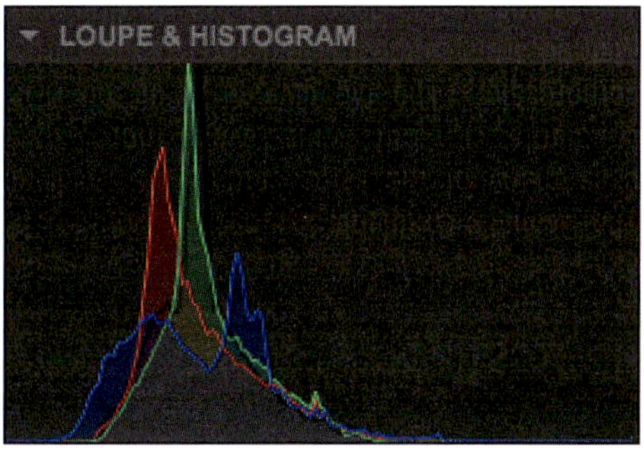

Figure 5.7

Setting tone compression

Given the importance of tone compression it would be great if there were some easy way to set it exactly right.

First rule: Don't rely on the histogram. Although I used it for a visual reference previously, it is at best a relatively crude representation of the tonal values in the HDR image and at worst can lead you totally astray.

HDR Efex Pro is doing its best to display a large amount of image information in the small area available for the histogram. The same is true with the histogram in Levels and Curves of HDR Efex Pro. Software engineers apply algorithms to display the information as meaningfully as possible. And then you try to make decisions based on information that you may not fully understand or which may not be a totally accurate representation of the image data anyway.

This brings us to the second rule: Trust the display. HDR Efex Pro does an excellent job in accurately displaying how the 32-bit HDR image

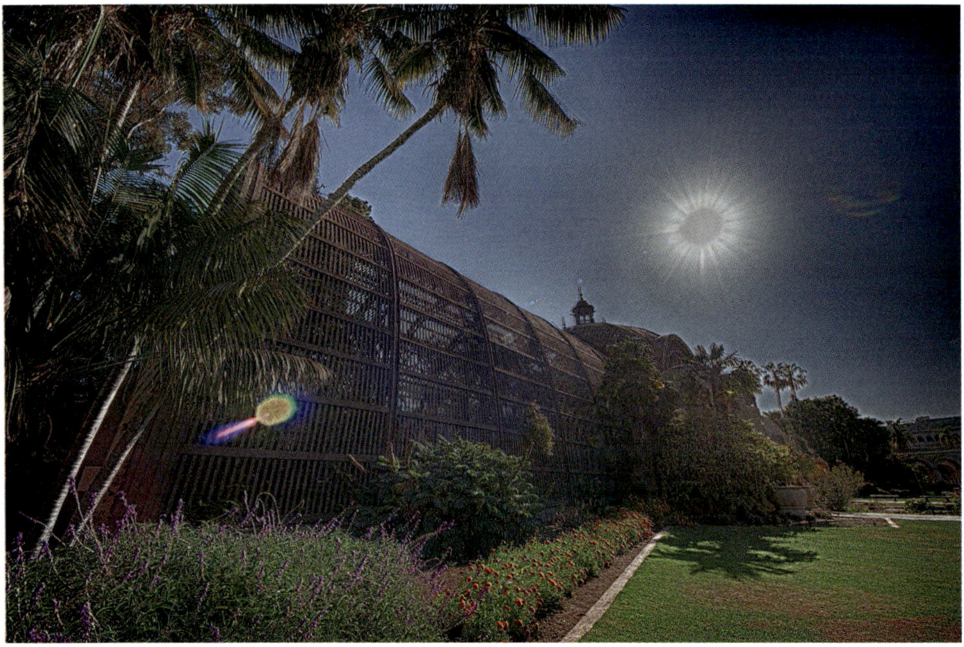

Figure 5.8

in the program looks when saved as an 8- or 16-bit TIFF.

Of course, this means you should employ good color management. Your display needs to be color managed, and if you are making prints your printer needs to be color managed in order to get predictable, repeatable results.

see also

Chapter 7 discusses options that HDR Efex Pro includes to help evaluate the HDR image. These options are useful on a color-managed system, but essential if the system is not color managed.

With tone compression, there is no right or wrong setting. Each preset has a suggested setting for tone compression along with the HDR Method and associated Method Strength. Use the mouse to adjust the Tone Compression slider for more or less compression while watching the image preview. If a setting other than the default setting looks better to you, use it.

tip

Double click on the slider bar to set tone compression to 0. Click the percentage and type a number for a specific Tone Compression setting. Use the arrow keys to increase or decrease tone compression by 1%. Click the preset to return the tone compression to its default value for that preset.

Tone compression works along with the tools in the Global Adjustments section immediately below the Tone Compression slider. Two of these tools are especially important when working with tone compression: the Exposure slider and the HDR Methods.

Many tone compression settings at the higher and lower settings can be greatly improved by relatively minor adjustments to the image using the Exposure slider, which is discussed in detail in Chapter 7.

And there is a very close relationship between tone compression and HDR Method, which is addressed in Chapter 6.

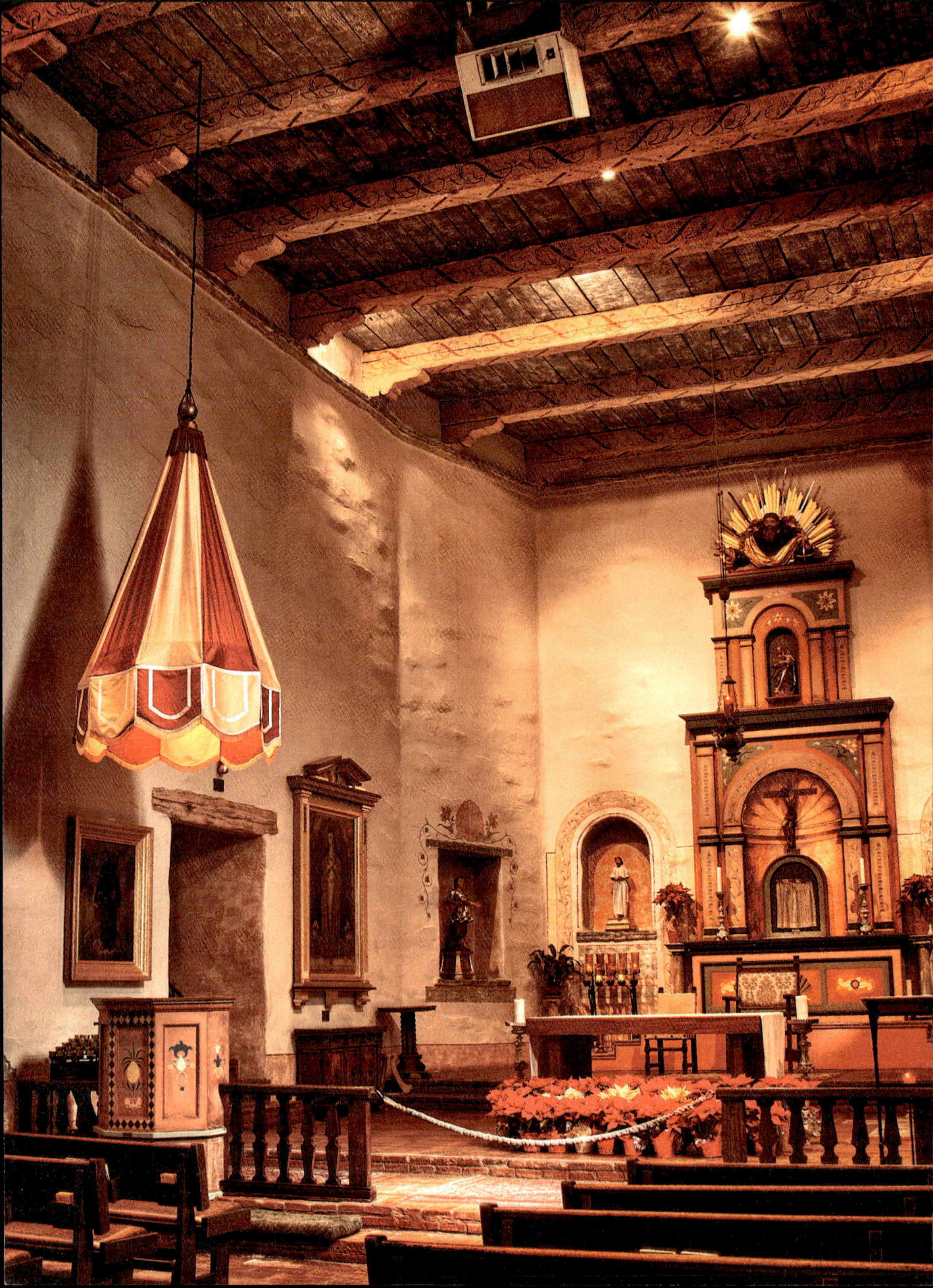

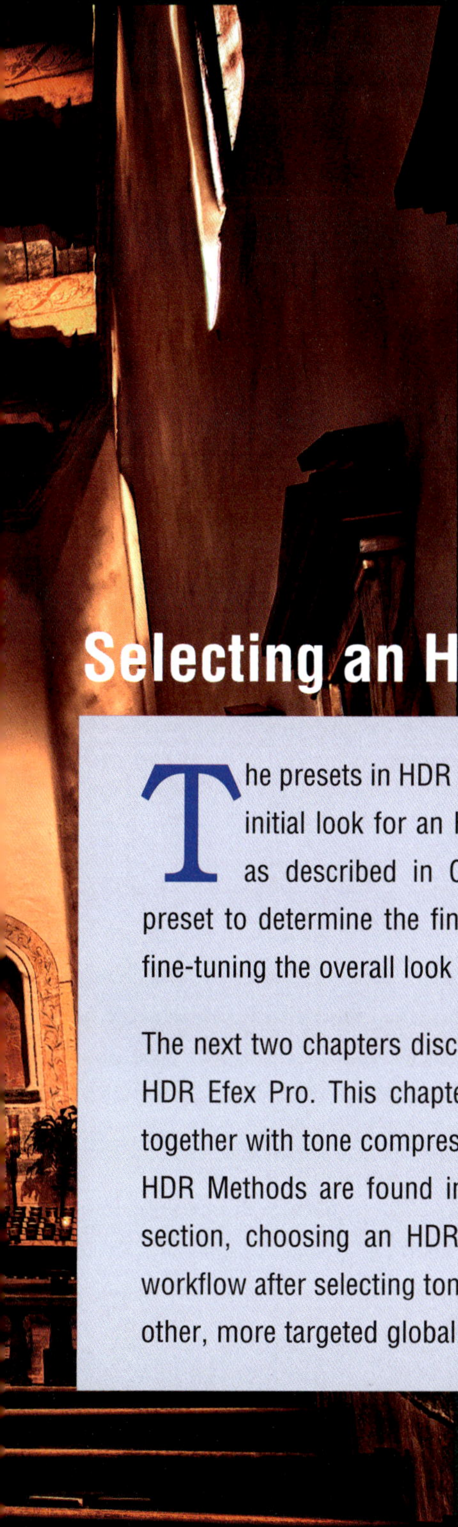

6

Selecting an HDR Method

The presets in HDR Efex Pro are extremely helpful in creating the initial look for an HDR image. Determining tone compression, as described in Chapter 5, begins customizing the chosen preset to determine the final overall feeling of the image. Next comes fine-tuning the overall look of the image.

The next two chapters discuss the Global Adjustment tools available in HDR Efex Pro. This chapter focuses on the HDR Methods that work together with tone compression to customize a preset. Even though the HDR Methods are found in the lower part of the Global Adjustments section, choosing an HDR Method should be the next step in your workflow after selecting tone compression and before going on to make other, more targeted global and local adjustments.

Understanding HDR Methods

Chapter 5 shows that adjusting the Tone Compression slider changes the overall dynamic range of the image. Moving the Tone Compression slider to negative values drives the darker tones and lighter tones to the extremes of the tone curve, while moving the slider to positive values compresses the tones to the center of the tone curve.

With each change in dynamic range, the local contrast in the image also changes. Local contrast is called *microcontrast* in HDR terms and exaggerated amounts of microcontrast are responsible for the "gritty" look in HDR images.

When an HDR image is first created from an image series, the wide dynamic range is tone mapped to values that are presented on your monitor. However, the monitor, and the printer you may eventually use for output, cannot reproduce the full dynamic range of the 32-bit HDR image. The tone mapping that is carried out to display the 32-bit HDR image on your monitor lowers local contrast. By using different HDR Methods along with the Method slider, it is possible to restore, or further compress, local contrast.

HDR Efex Pro includes four tone mapping algorithms. These algorithms are incorporated into the 20 HDR Methods shown In Figure 6.1.

Below the HDR Method drop-down list is the Method Strength slider, which adjusts from 0% (no HDR Method applied) to 100% (the selected HDR Method applied at full strength).

Each preset in HDR Efex Pro uses one of these 20 HDR Methods to achieve its look. But there is no reason why you must stick with the HDR Method in the preset. As with the Tone Compression slider, adjusting the HDR Method and the Method Strength slider can result in a more interesting and distinctive look than simply accepting the default choices.

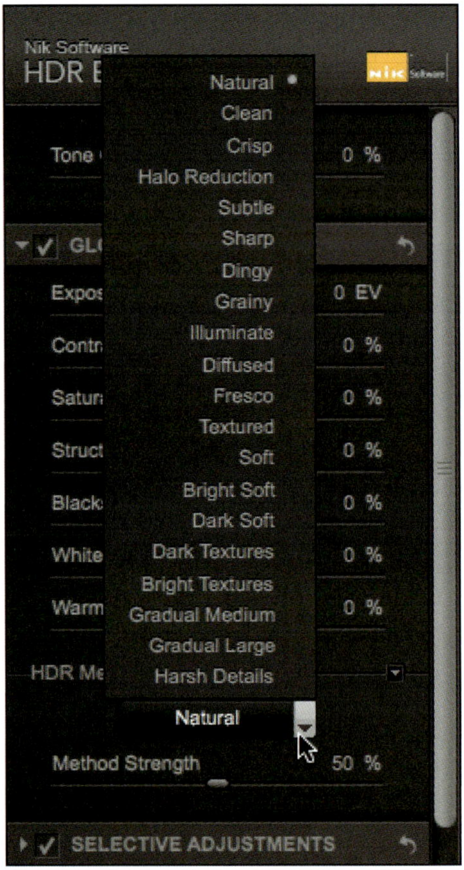

Figure 6.1

tip

Remember that if you come up with a combination of tone compression HDR Method and Method Strength that you think you might use again, save your settings as a new custom preset.

A few of the HDR Methods are not used by any of the presets. These include Halo Reduction, Dingy, Grainy, Illuminate, and Dark Textures. Unless you investigate the HDR Methods drop-down list, you never see the looks that these Methods provide.

see also

Appendix B lists which HDR Method is used by each of the presets.

Having 20 HDR Methods from which to choose may seem like far too many choices. But HDR Methods, like presets, fall into what I see as rough categories, although HDR Efex Pro doesn't group them that way.

I think of these groups in terms of the degree of HDR effect they have on the original image: Naturalistic, Artistic, and Extreme. These lines become blurred when you adjust the Method Strength to low settings, but I find it convenient to think of them in these groups. It is a great help in organizing my workflow.

When I look at an image series and previsualize it as an HDR image, I decide if I'm going to create the resulting image as a natural or fairly natural rendition of the original subject, or whether I want to push it to the artistic side of natural, or whether it might work as a totally unnatural, surrealistic rendition of the reality of the original scene. This gives me a starting point in choosing a preset and in choosing both the tone compression adjustment and an alternate HDR Method to investigate.

The HDR Methods fall into my three groups as follows.

When I think of a realistic rendition, I think of one of the HDR Methods that I categorize as Naturalistic:

- Natural
- Clean
- Crisp
- Halo Reduction
- Subtle
- Sharp
- Gradual Medium
- Gradual Large

To adjust the HDR image for a little edgier look, I think of the HDR Methods that I categorize as Artistic:

- Illuminate
- Diffused
- Textured
- Soft
- Bright Soft
- Dark Soft
- Harsh Details

And if I think I'm after a really edgy look, I look at the HDR image with one of the HDR Methods that I think of as Extreme:

- Dingy
- Grainy
- Fresco
- Dark Textures
- Bright Textures

You can group them somewhat differently and that's fine. What's important to an efficient workflow is to group the HDR Methods in some way as the presets are grouped in order to save time when investigating possible global HDR looks for your images.

HDR Method Types

The rest of this chapter looks at each of the HDR Methods, showing the result of applying that Method to an image at Method Strength of 25%, 50%, 75%, and 100%. Each Method Strength is applied with the Tone Compression slider set to 0%. It will be valuable for you to do this same exercise with one of your own image series and also to adjust the tone compression to see the interactivity between tone compression, HDR Method, and HDR Method Strength.

The HDR image I am using is created from six exposures of a seven-exposure bracket, where each step was 1 EV from its neighbors. It looks pretty good with all the HDR Methods, although in a few cases I have made an exposure adjustment when the HDR Method produced an image that is simply too dark to give any meaningful information. Other than the possibility of this small exposure adjustment, each of the images is made with all of the adjustment sliders, including the Tone Compression slider set to 0.

The full image is shown in each case. However, to truly evaluate the look of each Method and Method Strength, you should pan through your image at 100% magnification. With the HDR Methods I think of as in the Extreme category, and with any other Method that is used with a high Method Strength setting, noise and sensor dust are enhanced, and artifacts can be created that will only be visible at 100% magnification.

Natural HDR Method

Figure 6.2 shows the Natural HDR Method at Method Strengths of 25%, 50%, 75% and 100%. I became interested in HDR imaging as a means of creating images that more closely matched the scene that I was photographing. While HDR Efex Pro has expanded my horizons with the possibilities it presents for creative and artistic expression, I still come back constantly to my original HDR interest with my landscape and close-up photography.

Because I'm looking for a realistic result, I use the Natural HDR Method a lot. Generally, I prefer the Method Strength around the 70% point. This adds microcontrast to the medium-sized shapes that are found in landscape photos without adding any noise to the blue sky or the clouds.

The same holds true in HDR close-up images. Medium-sized structures and edges are enhanced, but smooth surfaces such as flower petals don't gain in noise or digital artifacts.

The Natural Method includes a moderate amount of tone compression along with the microcontrast. You can enhance this tone compression further with the Tone Compression slider.

The Natural Method is an excellent choice if your goal is to create realistic HDR landscape and close-up images.

Clean HDR Method

The Clean Method in Figure 6.3 is another in my group of Naturalistic HDR Methods and, at low Method Strengths, up to about 50%, looks very much like the Natural Method.

Above 50%, however, the Clean Method uses more tone compression in the highlights. This is helpful in creating separation in the clouds, as shown in the 100% image of the Clean Method versus the 100% image of the Natural Method, but the rest of the image falls apart.

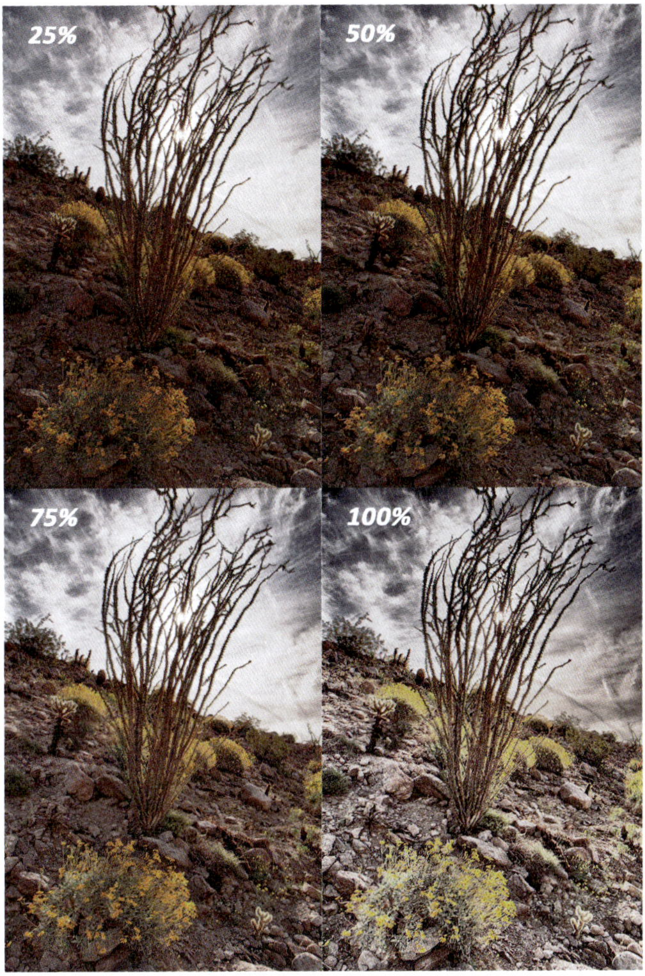

Figure 6.2

With lower-contrast HDR landscape images where a lot of compression is wanted in the light areas, the Clean Method could be a good choice. The Clean Method finds its way into three of the Architecture category presets. Its ability to enhance smaller details as well as the medium-sized details of the Natural Method makes it a good candidate for architectural images and cityscapes.

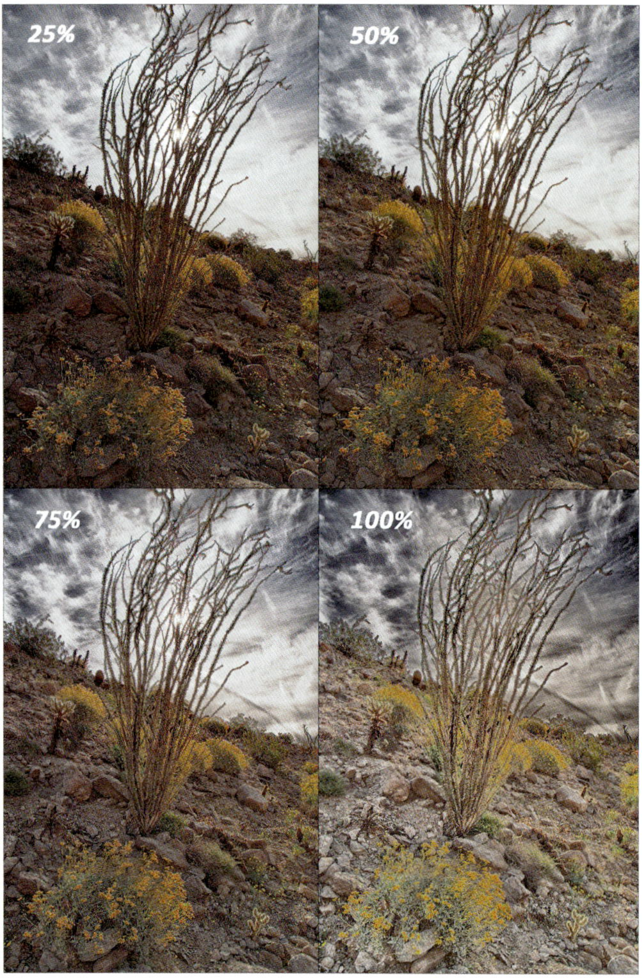

Figure 6.3

However, it can create artifacts at high Method Strengths as you may be able to see in the ocotillo branches against the sky.

tip

Remember to examine each image at 100% zoom when adjusting the Method and Method Strength.

Crisp HDR Method

At Method Strength settings up to about 25%, the Crisp Method (Figure 6.4) produces results similar to the Natural Method, but with slightly more tone compression in the highlights.

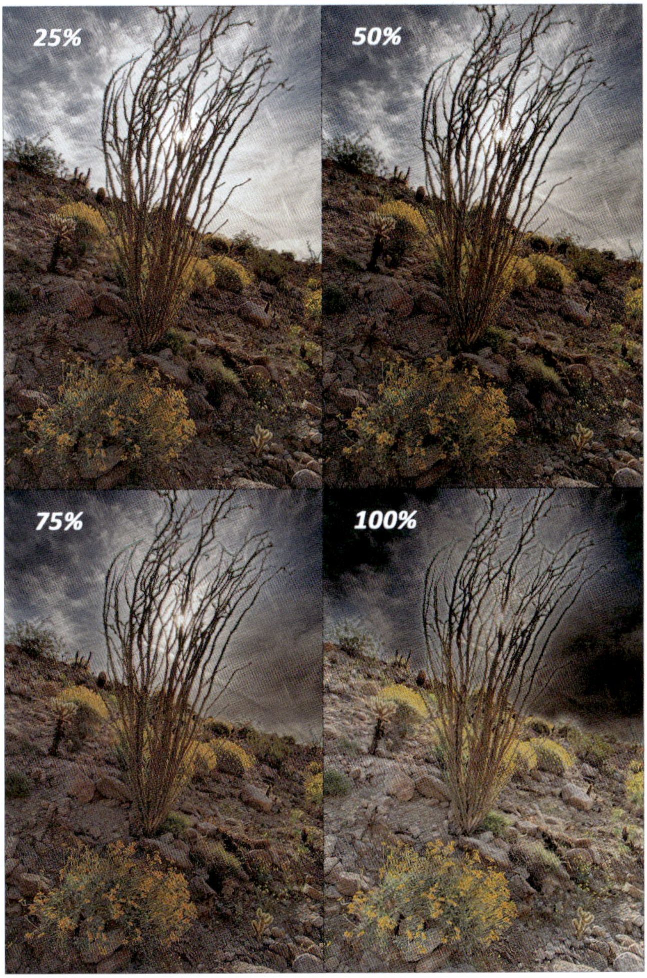

Figure 6.4

Above 25%, highlight tone compression increases rapidly and the entire tonal curve shifts to the darker values. Above 75% Method Strength, haloing around areas of high contrast becomes obvious. A gray halo surrounds the ocotillo cactus against the sky and the halo continues between the top of the ridge and the sky. I have lightened the exposure slightly of the 100% image to make this more obvious.

At lower Method Strengths it is still possible to achieve natural-looking results with the Crisp Method, and I consider the Crisp Method to be part of my Naturalistic grouping. Microcontrast is similar to the Clean Method, enhancing small and medium-sized details with no noise enhancement or artifacts at any settings.

Halo Reduction HDR Method

The Halo Reduction Method illustrated in Figure 6.5 strives to minimize the halos that HDR Methods such as Crisp can create. Halo Reduction accomplishes this by minimizing highlight as well as shadow compression. Even with a Method Strength of 100%, the highlight and shadow image tones are not compressed together into midtones.

When used at Method Strengths between 25% and 75%, Halo Reduction produces one of the most natural looking HDR effects. Microcontrast enhances medium-sized detail. Halo Reduction is similar to the Natural HDR Method, but with somewhat lower overall contrast, especially throughout the midrange tones.

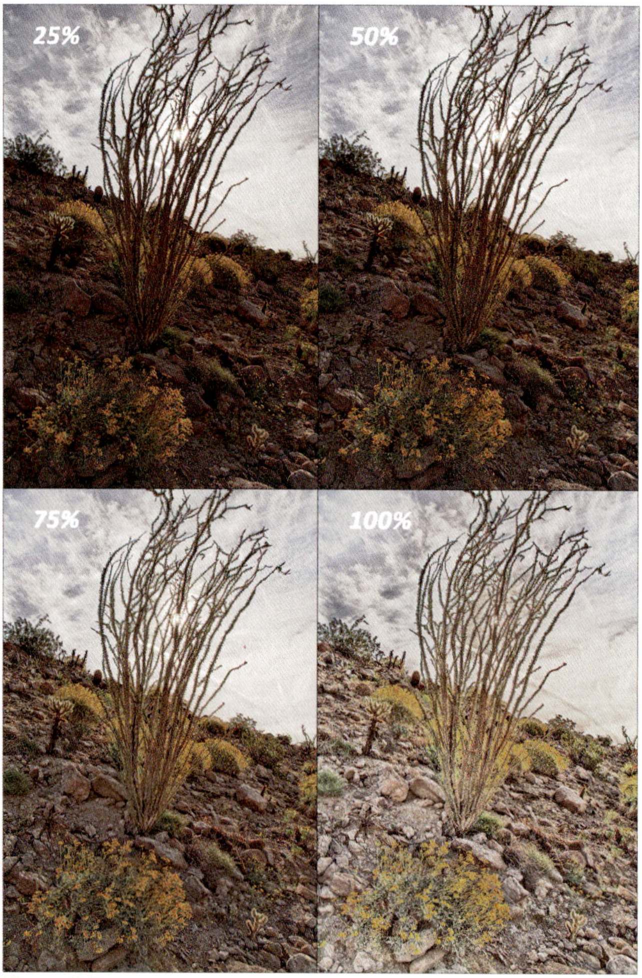

Figure 6.5

Subtle HDR Method

Figure 6.6 shows four strengths of the Subtle HDR Method. Of all the HDR Methods I group in my Naturalistic category, Subtle produces the most obvious compression at higher Method Strengths. This makes it most appropriate for high-contrast subjects.

Strongly backlit subjects and single-exposure Extended Dynamic Range (EDR) images that have higher contrast than true HDR images benefit from the Subtle Method, and it is employed in the Strong Counterlight and Single Exposure 1 presets.

Microcontrast enhances small and medium-sized details, but not to the point where details look artificial.

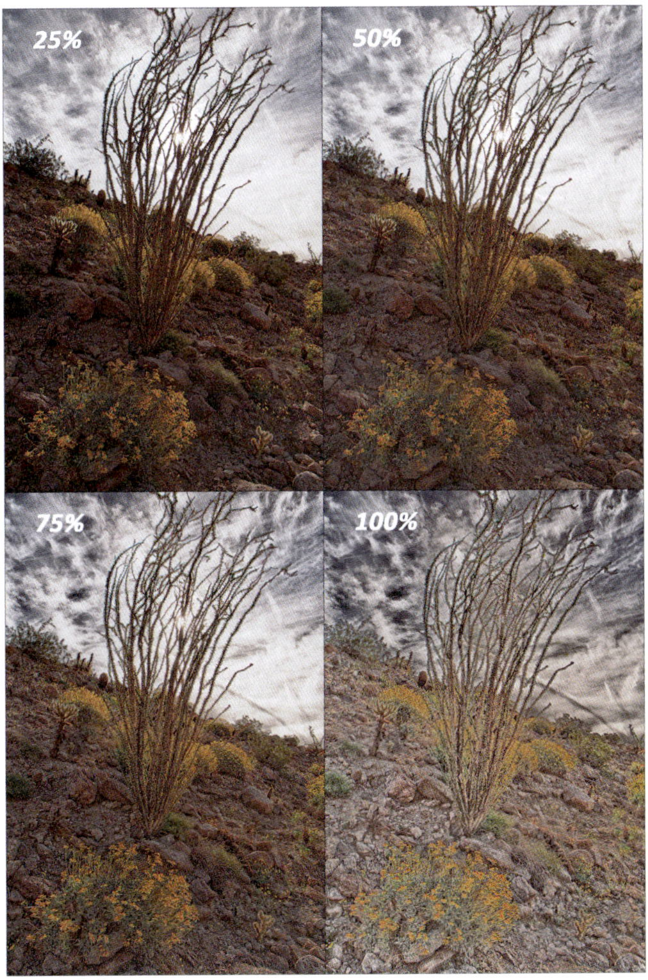

Figure 6.6

Sharp HDR Method

The Sharp Method shown in Figure 6.7 is essentially the Natural Method with higher microcontrast. This produces higher local contrast throughout the image, giving the impression of greater sharpness. This effect is similar to that produced with an unsharp mask filter or using a high pass filter.

The Sharp HDR Method is used in the Realistic (Strong) preset, which is one that I will always look at when I am interested in a realistic rendition. I find that Realistic (Strong) is an excellent starting place for landscapes that have interesting clouds. The preset uses a low setting of Method Strength that results in a very natural result with excellent apparent sharpness.

Landscapes aren't the only images that look good with the Sharp Method. Practically any image with a lot of texture that you want to render realistically deserves a preview in HDR Efex Pro with the Sharp Method.

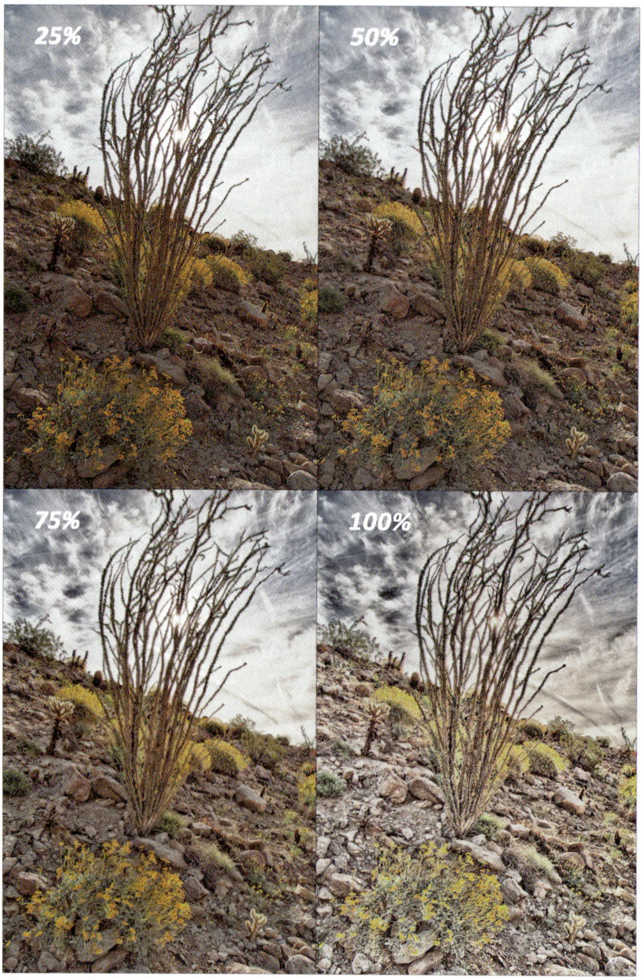

Figure 6.7

Dingy HDR Method

The Dingy HDR Method shown in Figure 6.8 is about as far as you can get from a realistic rendition of a scene, and there is no doubt that it belongs in my Extreme category. It is so extreme that it isn't found in any of the presets.

The Dingy Method really needs to be examined zoomed in at 100% to gauge the full impact. Image tones are strongly compressed to darker values. I added a +0.5 EV exposure correction to the 100% Method Strength image because I was afraid it would print too dark. With the Dingy Method, Method Strength settings greater that 90% result in clipping of dark tones.

Microcontrast is pushed to the limit or close to it. Small details are strongly enhanced along with larger structures. Any noise present in the originals or dust on your sensor is strongly emphasized. Even at low strengths, the Dingy Method produces black dots that look something like film grain in the image. There will be no doubt in anyone's mind that the image was created with HDR software if you process it with the Dingy Method.

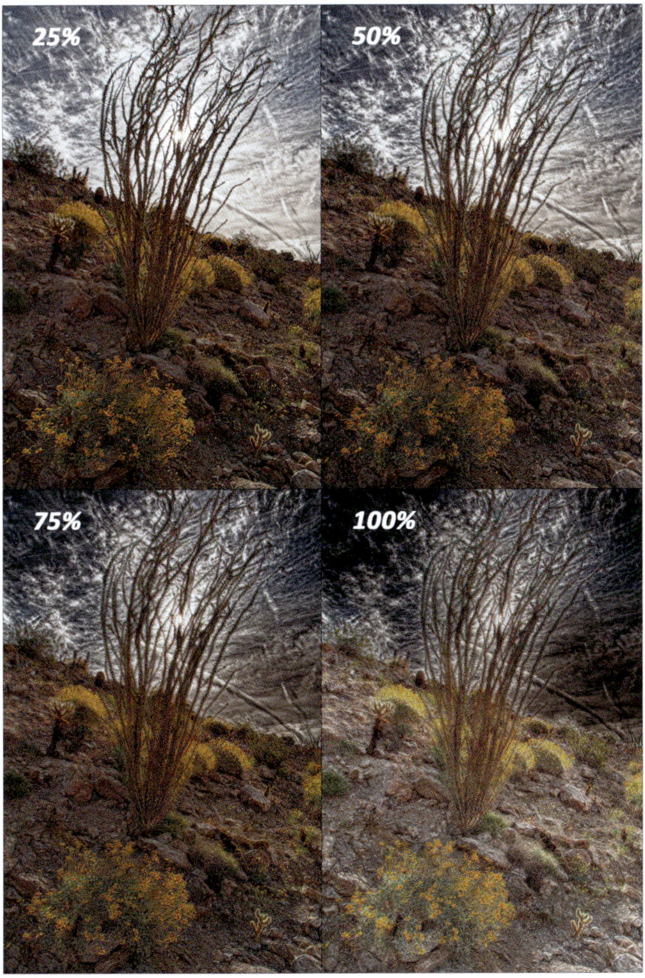

Figure 6.8

Grainy HDR Method

The Grainy Method (Figure 6.9) is a very close relative to the Dingy Method and like Dingy, the Grainy HDR Method is not used in any of the presets. Tone compression is very strong, microcontrast settings are very high to reveal small and medium-sized details, and grain and noise are enhanced. Those same black dots found in the Dingy Method images appear throughout the Grainy images also.

However, the Grainy Method doesn't compress tones as far to the darker values as the Dingy Method does. I didn't experience any clipping of dark tones with the Grainy Method and didn't need to add any exposure correction to the 100% Method Strength image so that the image would print.

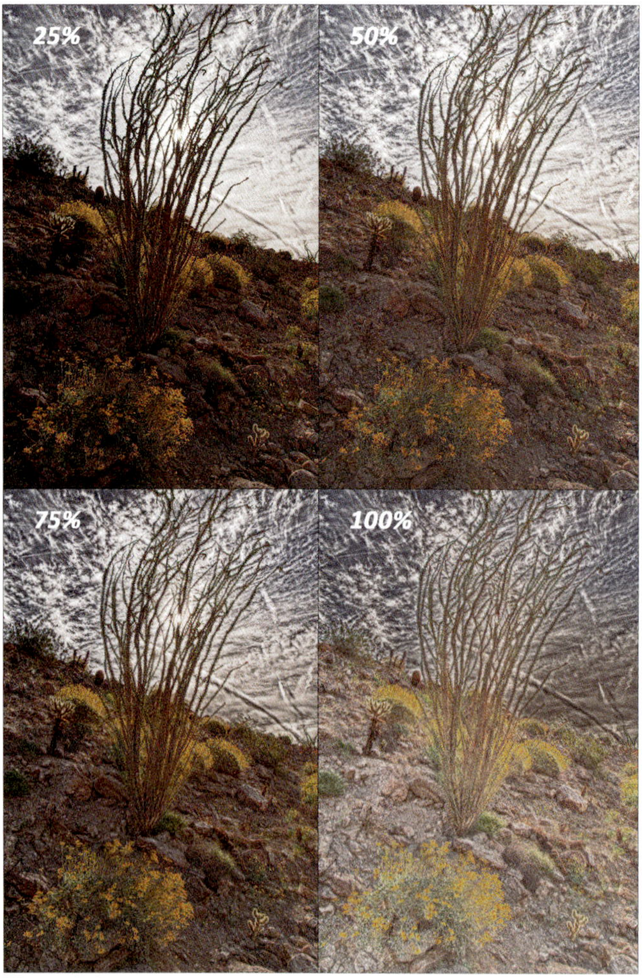

Figure 6.9

Illuminate HDR Method

The Illuminate Method in Figure 6.10 is another of the HDR Methods that isn't used by one of the presets. It is similar in tone compression to the Halo Reduction Method, so the HDR effect is rather subtle.

However, contrast is lower with the Illuminate Method than with Halo Reduction, and the resulting image is brighter. It also appears softer, with a dreamier quality than a Halo Reduction image, but still realistic.

This lower-contrast, dreamier look takes Illuminate out of my Naturalistic category and into my Artistic category.

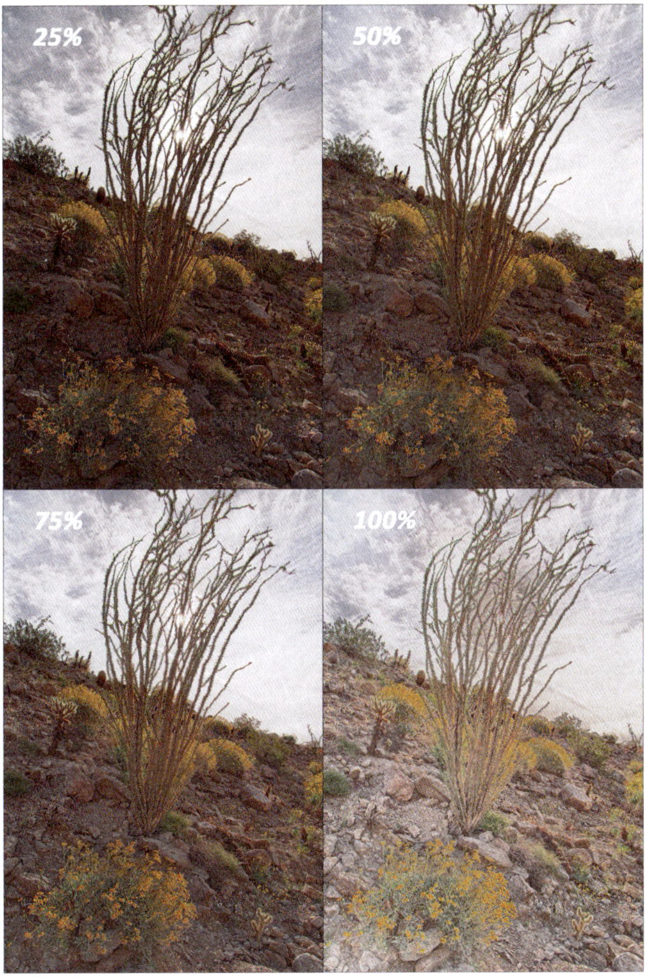

Figure 6.10

Diffused HDR Method

Figure 6.11 shows the Diffused HDR Method. Throughout the full range of Method Strengths, compression is very similar to the Subtle Method, but with lower local contrast that gives the Diffused Method a softer look. Again, this softness is what takes the Method from my Naturalistic category to my Artistic category.

As with the Subtle Method, tone compression is low, making the Diffused Method another good candidate for high-contrast single exposures or backlit HDR images. The only preset in which it is used is Monochrome (Soft), but I find it too soft and low contrast for my taste in a monochrome image. If you choose the Monochrome (Soft) preset, be sure to look at the Subtle Method for the image also.

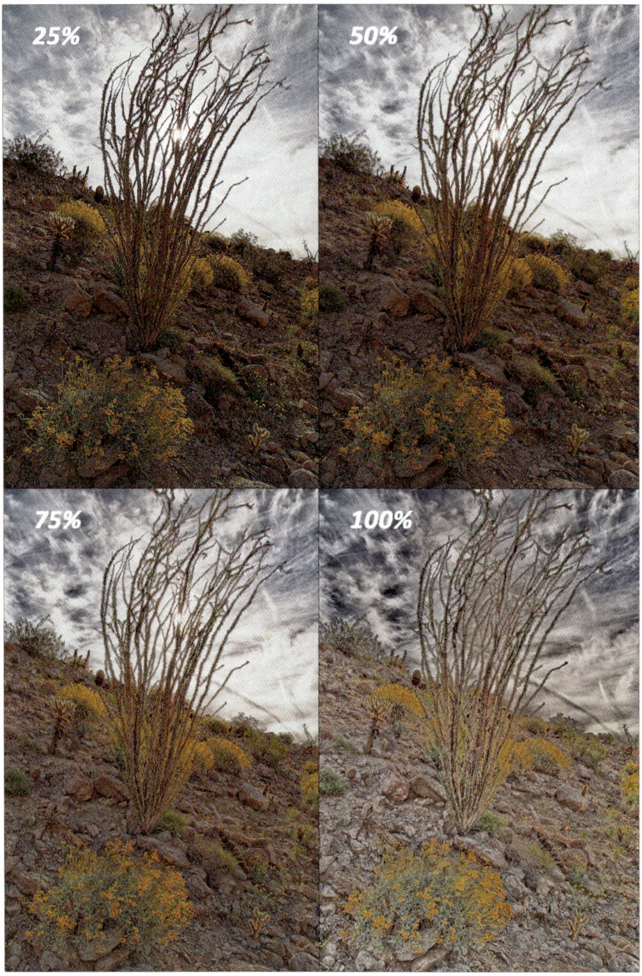

Figure 6.11

Fresco HDR Method

At high Method Strengths, the Fresco Method in Figure 6.12 displays why it earned a place in my Extreme category. Microcontrast emphasizes small details, but also emphasizes noise, and creates the same black dots found in the Dingy and Grainy Methods.

Fresco compresses the highlights toward the midtones of the image, but leaves strong midtones as the Method Strength increases. At high strength settings, both the shadows and highlights are compressed to those midtone values.

The Fresco Method is a good choice when you want an HDR look and you want to add a lot of structure in the brightest areas, such as clouds, while keeping contrast under control in the midtones and shadow areas.

Fresco is another Method that you really need to examine zoomed in at 100% to gauge the effect.

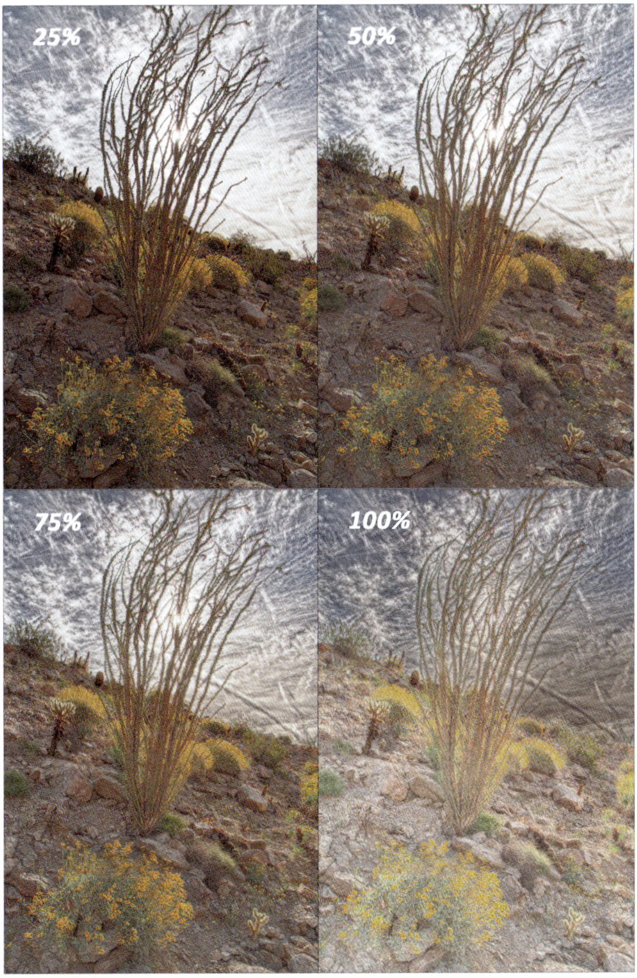

Figure 6.12

Textured HDR Method

The Textured HDR Method is appropriately named. As shown in Figure 6.13, local contrast is fairly strong, but it is uniformly applied to fine, medium, and large details. While the contrast is high, noise is not emphasized and no black dots appear in the midtones or highlights.

If the tone compression weren't so great and the highlights and midtones weren't pushed so far to the darker tones, the result might turn out to be fairly natural. As it is, the HDR effect of the Textured Method at all but the highest strengths lies between natural and surreal, so I place it in my Artistic category.

I found that the Textured Method works very well with many wood products, especially if there is a lot of grain in the product. It is also a good method to experiment with if you photograph old weathered objects such as barns or rusted-out cars. The results can be very interesting without the grunge look usually applied to these subjects.

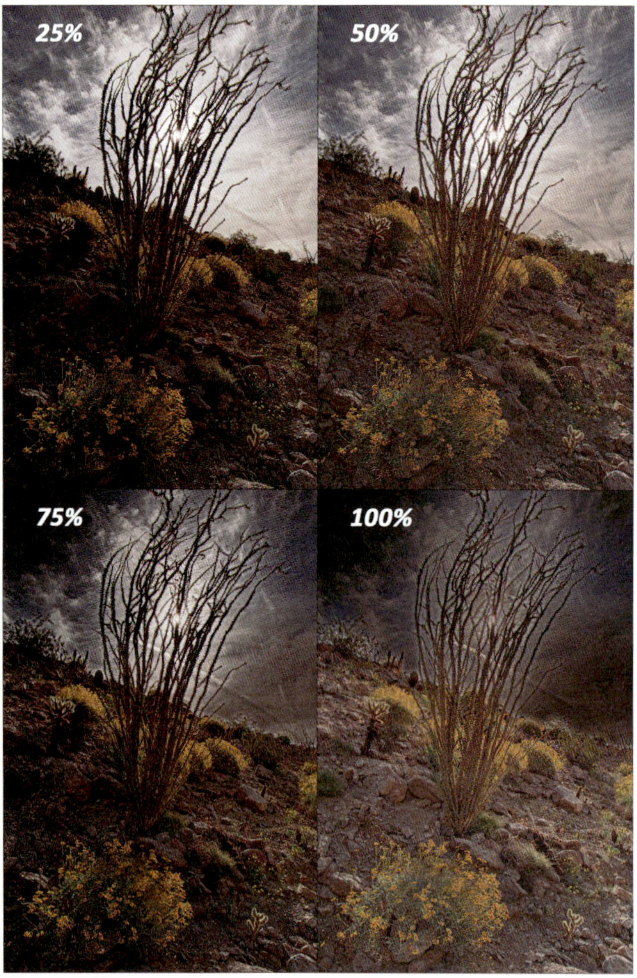

Figure 6.13

Soft HDR Method

The Soft Method in Figure 6.14 uses moderately strong tone compression similar to the Fresco Method, but with far less microcontrast. Highlight values are compressed to the midtones that remain strong until both the highlights and low tones merge with the midtones.

The low microcontrast brings out less structure in the clouds than other HDR Methods, but the low setting does not emphasize noise or add black dots. The resulting image is very smooth with a softness resulting from lowered local contrast rather than diffusion.

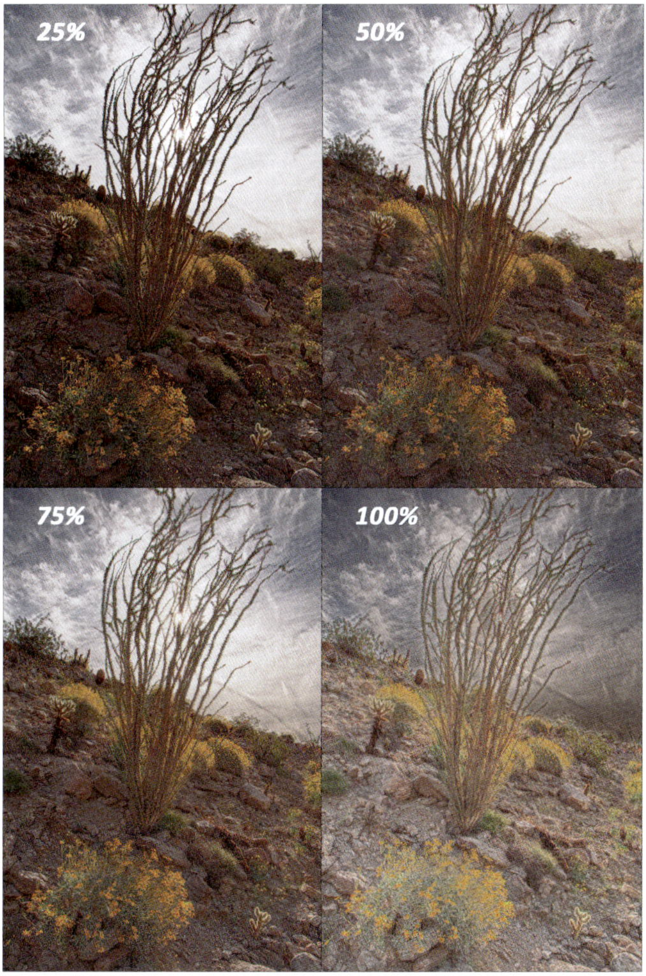

Figure 6.14

Bright Soft HDR Method

When you want a bright, airy feeling for your HDR image, the Bright Soft HDR Method shown in Figure 6.15 is an excellent starting point. Microcontrast is set very low, resulting in little local contrast of small and medium-sized details. The effect is an overall softness that is especially attractive if there are large shapes of strong color in the image.

The tone compression that is applied shifts the tones to the highlights, merging the midtones into the highlights as the Method Strength is increased. Darker tones remain, but they too are shifted to the lighter tones. At high Method Strength, the image is very bright with smooth, soft tonality.

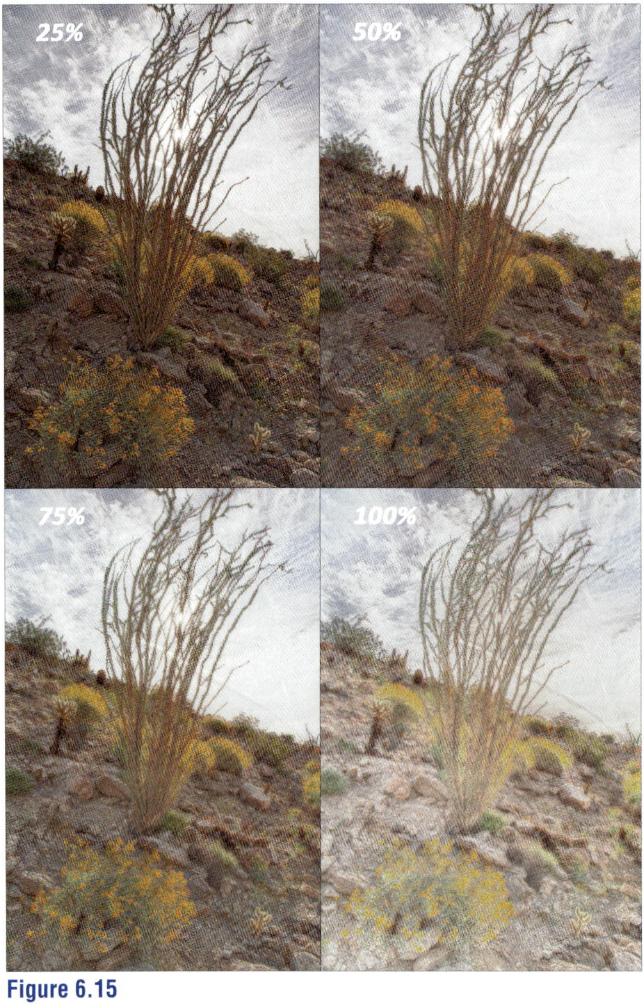

Figure 6.15

Dark Soft HDR Method

The Dark Soft Method (Figure 6.16) is similar to the Bright Soft Method, but with the tones compressed to darker rather than lighter values. Tone compression is somewhat stronger with the Dark Soft Method than the Bright Soft Method. Lighter tones and midtones are compressed fairly quickly to darker values.

Local contrast is very similar to that in the Bright Soft Method, and much less than in the Soft Method. The result, like the result with the Bright Soft Method, is a pleasing overall softness. The Dark Soft HDR Method is also well suited to scenes with large areas of color.

Even though the resulting look is far from natural, it isn't as extreme as some of the other HDR Methods, so I place it in my Artistic category. The Dark Soft Method is used in the Postcard Paradise and Night on Earth presets, but with other major global adjustments applied. Because Dark Soft compresses tones to the darker values, I did lighten the 75% and 100% images by +0.3 EV so they would reproduce better here.

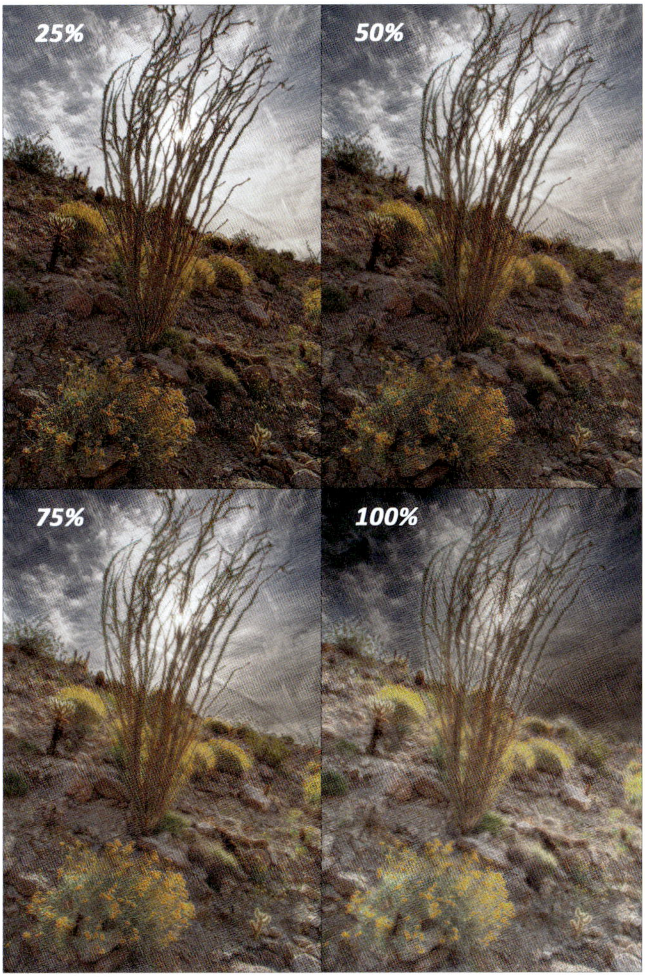

Figure 6.16

Dark Textures HDR Method

Tone compression with the Dark Textures HDR Method (Figure 6.17) is very similar to that of the Dark Soft Method, but local contrast is maximized rather than minimized. This enhances small details, creating a gritty look. For me, this places Dark Textures into my Extreme group. As you have seen with a few others in the Extreme group, Dark Textures is not used in any of the presets. Because of the gritty look, there is no mistaking an image created with Dark Textures as anything but an HDR image.

Tonal values are strongly compressed to the dark side. The result is not as extreme as the Dingy HDR Method, but increasing the Tone Compression slider in the Dark Textures Method creates a similar look to the Dingy Method. As with the Dark Soft Method, I increased the exposure of the 75% and 100% Dark Textures images by +0.3 EV to make the results more visible.

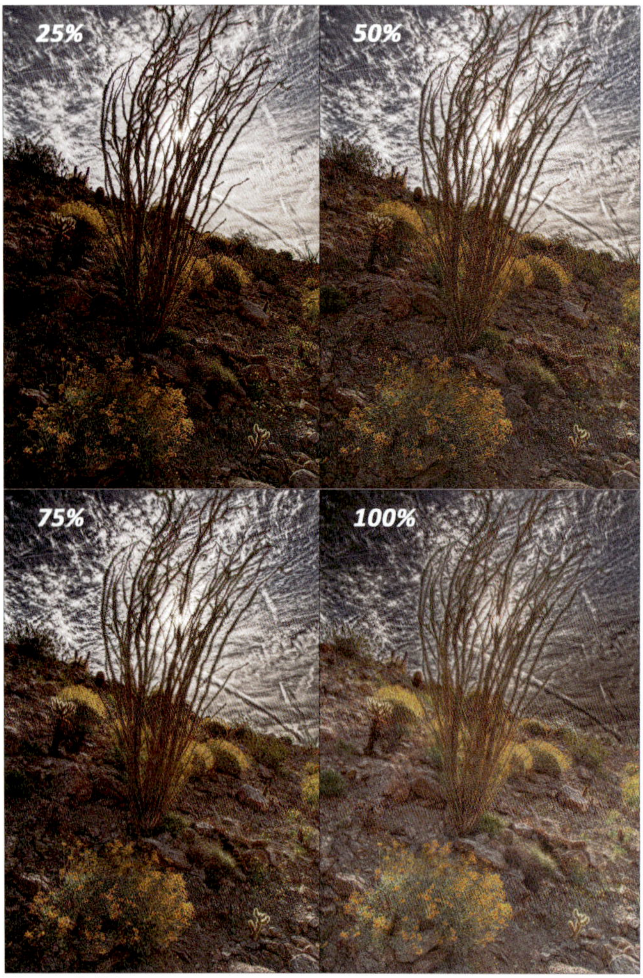

Figure 6.17

Bright Textures HDR Method

While I find the result of the strong microcontrast built into the Bright Textures HDR Method shown in Figure 6.18 enough of an effect to place it into the Extreme group, Bright Textures finds its way into three presets, although at fairly low Method Strengths. Each of these presets — Fine Structures, Vibrant Details & Colors, and Vintage Colors — has a unique look that I have used as a basis for some of my favorite HDR creations.

The Bright Textures Method is pretty much on its own in comparison with the other HDR Methods. Tone compression is less, particularly at high Method Strengths, but microcontrast is much greater overall than the Bright Soft Method. And while the microcontrast is similar between Bright Textures and Dark Textures, they aren't mirror images of one another.

I find Bright Textures particularly good for strongly enhancing the texture of clouds while still keeping the brightest cloud tones bright.

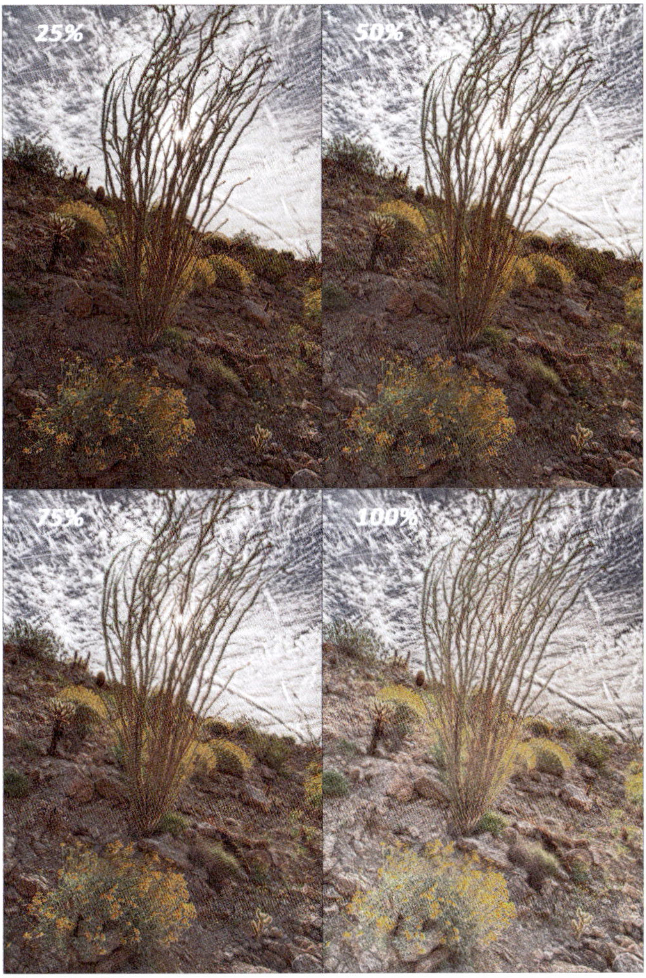

Figure 6.18

Gradual Medium HDR Method

Figure 6.19 shows the Gradual Medium HDR Method. The Gradual Medium Method, along with the next Method, Gradual Large, bears a strong family resemblance to the Natural Method. All three are capable of producing realistic looking images and are particularly good with landscapes.

The differences between them have mostly to do with microcontrast. The Natural HDR Method distributes a small amount of local contrast throughout the image, just enough to recover detail lost to the overall gentle tone compression.

Tone compression with the Gradual Medium HDR Method is very similar to the Natural Method, but local contrast of small and medium-sized objects in the scene is enhanced. This is evident in the sample images by the increased detail in the clouds and in the plants and rocks in the foreground.

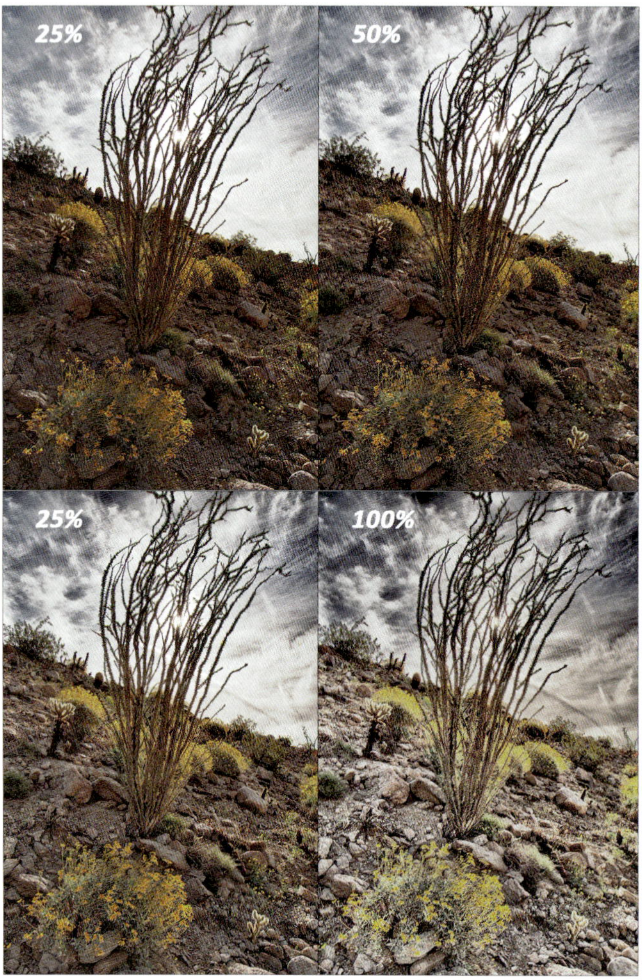

Figure 6.19

Gradual Large HDR Method

For comparison with the Natural and Gradual Medium Methods, Figure 6.20 shows the Gradual Large HDR Method. As I mentioned previously, tone compression is very similar to the Natural and the Gradual Medium Methods. With the Gradual Large Method, however, microcontrast primarily enhances large structures. The decrease in emphasis on small and medium-sized structures is evident by the decrease in contrast in the rocks, but especially in the fine structure of the clouds.

All three of these HDR Methods will produce realistic looking results, particularly when other global adjustments are used, as discussed in Chapter 7. Choosing between them is entirely dependent on the original scene and your interpretation of it. Making these decisions while being aware of the subtle differences between the HDR Methods is part of the joy and pain of HDR imaging.

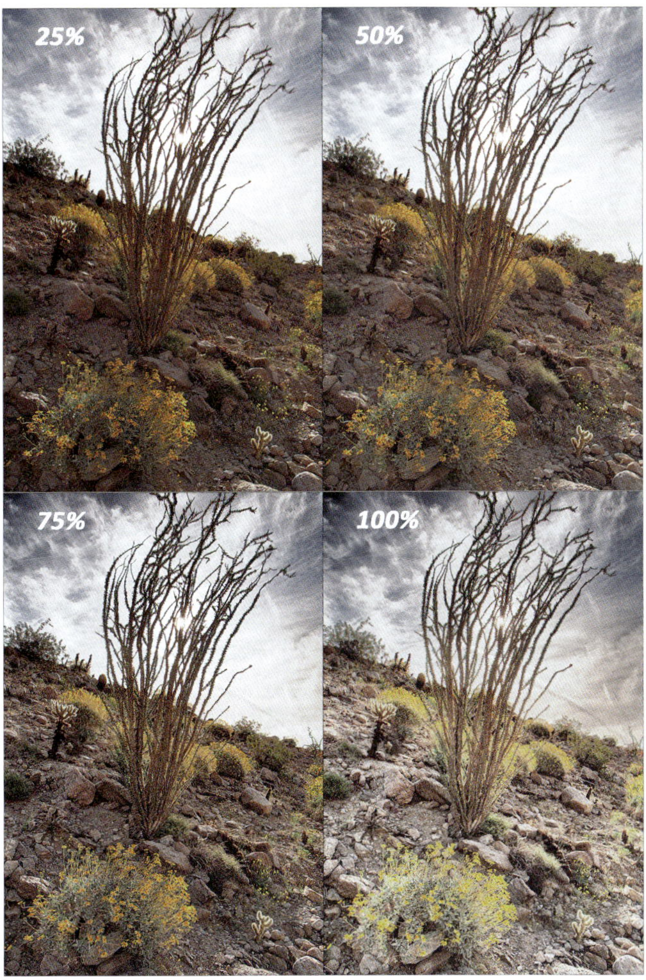

Figure 6.20

Harsh Details HDR Method

I think that the creators of HDR Efex Pro must have been running out of naming ideas by the time they got to this last HDR Method because I don't see the Harsh Details Method, shown in Figure 6.21, as an appropriate name at all. In tone compression, Harsh Details is very closely related to the Illuminate and Halo Reduction Methods. Microcontrast is slightly greater and fine details are enhanced slightly more, but not to the point of being "harsh." I don't find the resulting image, even at the highest Method Strength, abstract enough even to classify Harsh Details as an Extreme effect. While not totally realistic, it falls into my Artistic category.

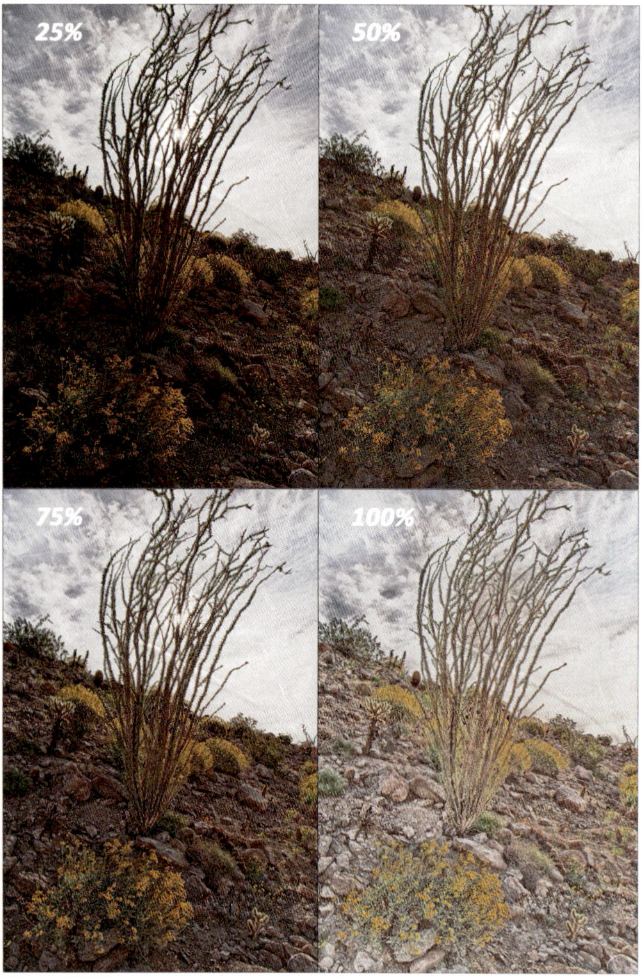

Figure 6.21

However, the Harsh Details HDR Method finds its place in the presets as a component in the Bleach Bypass Look. The Bleach Bypass Look is definitely in the Surreal category of presets, but more as a result of the way in which other global adjustments are used along with the particular settings for tone compression and the Harsh Details HDR Method.

The Chapter 7 discusses customizing the sliders in the Global Adjustments section to create unique effects once you have selected a tone compression setting and an HDR Method and Method Strength.

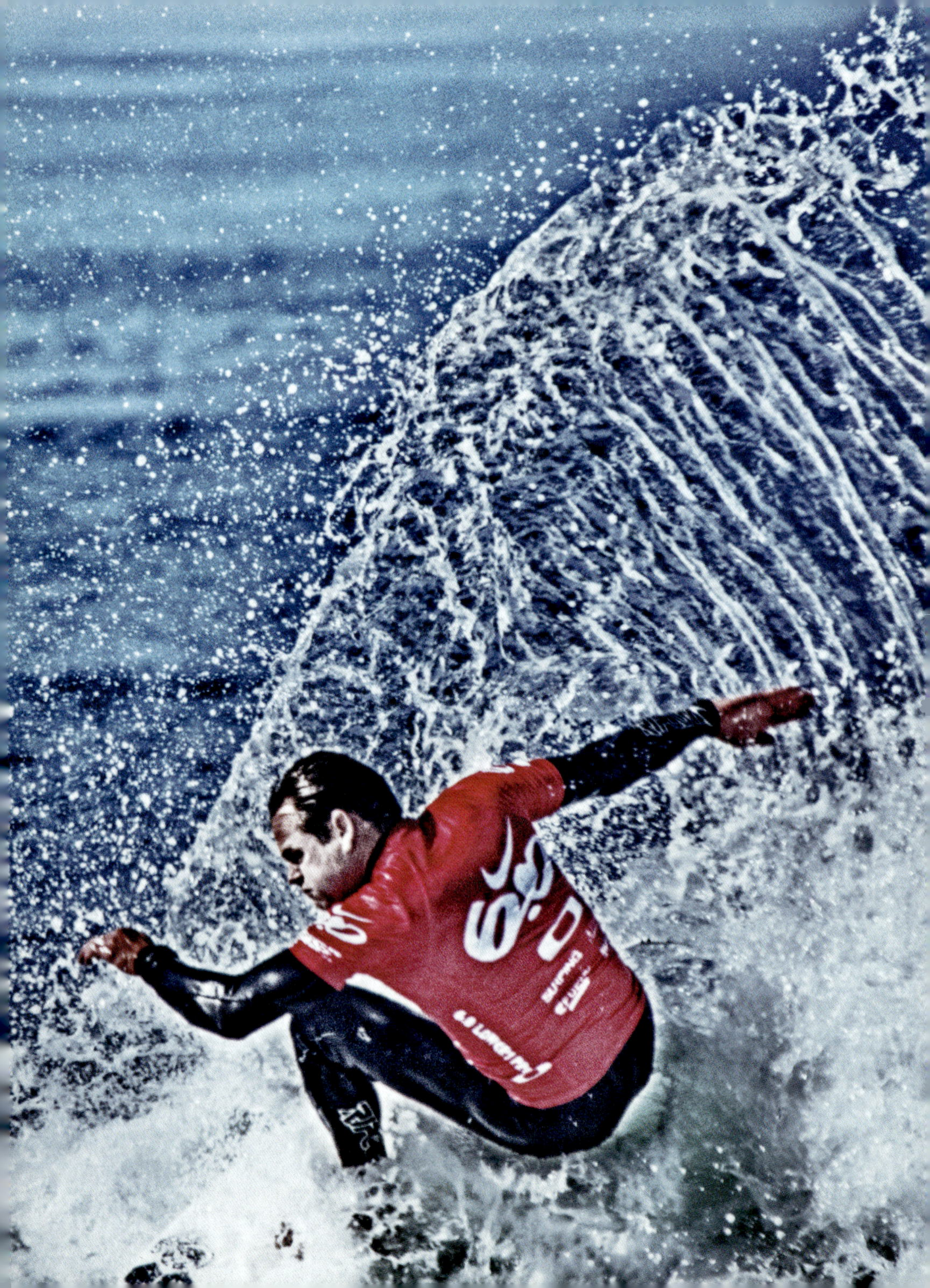

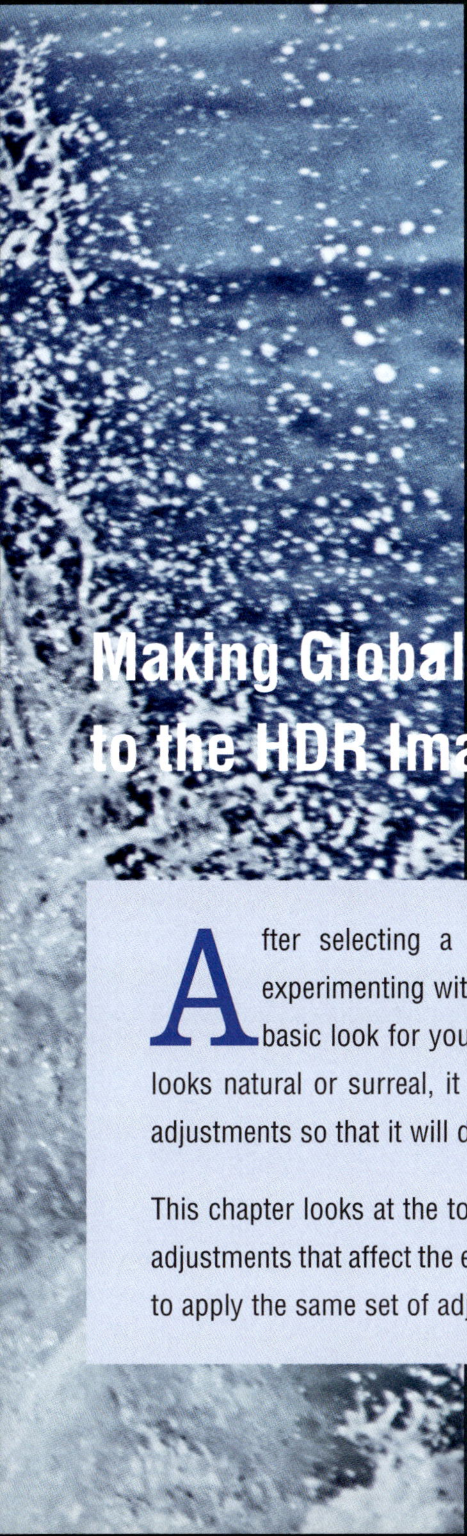

7

Making Global Adjustments to the HDR Image

After selecting a preset, adjusting tone compression, and experimenting with various HDR Methods, you have created a basic look for your HDR image. No matter whether the image looks natural or surreal, it is likely that you need to make some tonal adjustments so that it will display the way you want it.

This chapter looks at the tools provided in HDR Efex Pro to make tonal adjustments that affect the entire image. Chapters 8 and 9 show you how to apply the same set of adjustments to local areas of the image.

The Global Adjustments Section

Just as the name implies, the Global Adjustments section (see Figure 7.1) contains tools that affect all the pixels in an image, hence the term global adjustments. The section contains the following tools:

- Exposure
- Contrast
- Saturation
- Structure
- Blacks
- Whites
- Warmth

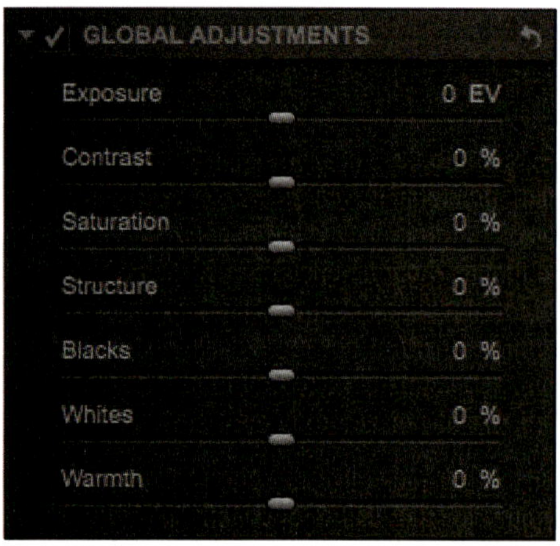

Figure 7.1

see also

Chapter 2 discusses the layout and use of the sliders in detail.

In the optimum workflow, you use the tools from top to bottom as they are arranged in the Global Adjustments section. Doing so minimizes the time you might need to spend readjusting a tool lower in the order if you later adjust one higher in the list.

note

When you use the global adjustments, it is important that you view them on a color-calibrated monitor. HDR Efex Pro uses sophisticated algorithms to map the tones of the 32-bit HDR image to your monitor, but if you have not calibrated the monitor, there is a good chance that the changes you see when you make adjustments may not be what you get when you print the image or when the image is viewed on another monitor.

With 8-bit images, global controls are not as useful as they are with HDR images. Global tools don't work as well with lower-bit-depth images because of the limited amount of image information on which to work.

The game changes with an HDR image. With the enormous amount of tonal information available, global adjustments are usable over a wide range without the banding and other artifacts that often result when they are used with lower-bit-depth images.

The following sections look at each of these tools and show the effect each one has on an image.

Adjusting Exposure

The Exposure slider is used to adjust the midtone values in the image. Because the adjustment is global, all pixels are adjusted uniformly by the same amount. This causes the lighter values and the darker values to change by the same amount. Adjusting the Exposure slider to the right makes all the pixels uniformly brighter, while adjusting it to the left causes all image pixels to become darker.

note

There are four ways to adjust any of the sliders: Drag the slider with your mouse; type numbers into the dialog box to the upper right of the slider; tap the right or left arrow keys; use the mouse to click on a position on the slider. If you want to reset a slider to 0, double-click anywhere on the slider.

Exposure adjustments are available from –3 EV to +3 EV in steps of 0.1 EV. An adjustment of 1 EV is the equivalent of opening or closing your camera aperture by 1 stop, so with the Exposure slider set at 0, there are 3 stops of brightening available and 3 stops of darkening.

You need to be careful when adjusting the slider, however, because all the pixels in the image are affected by the adjustment. You can see this graphically by opening the histogram by choosing Levels and Curves→Detail, or the histogram in Loupe & Histogram at the bottom of the Control Palette.

As you adjust the Exposure slider, the histogram shifts in the same direction. If your image histogram looks like the one in Figure 7.2, any

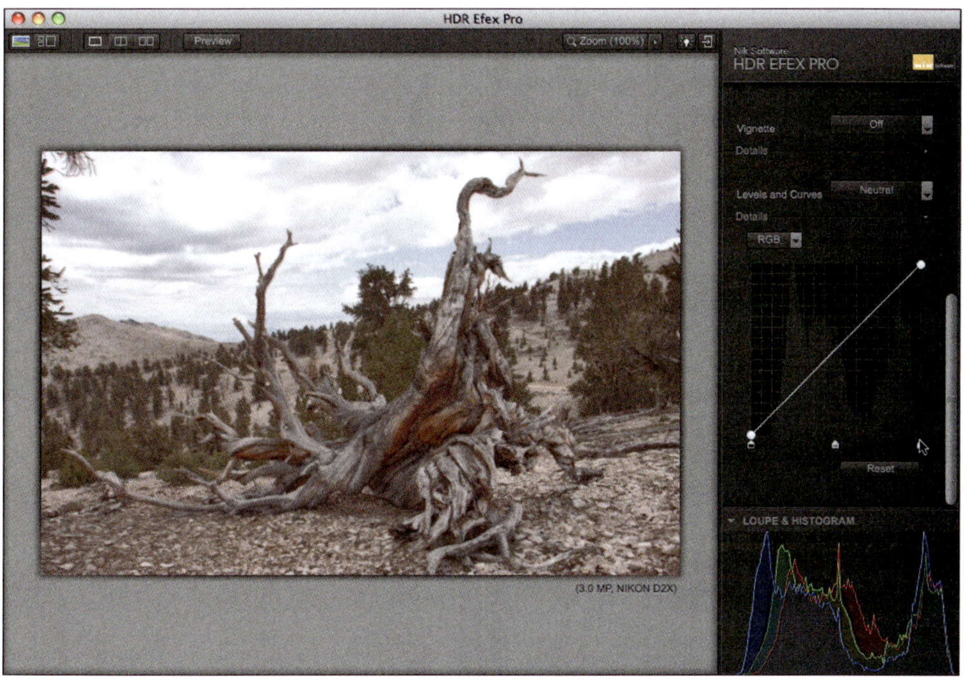

Figure 7.2

adjustment to increase exposure will quickly result in clipping the highlights.

note

Even if you feel comfortable interpreting a histogram in Photoshop, use it only for guidance in HDR Efex Pro. I use it here as a visual aid, not as a tool on which I make final judgment. I base those judgments on the way the image looks on my calibrated monitor.

Throughout the rest of this chapter, I demonstrate global adjustments with an image series I shot in the Ancient Bristlecone Pines Forest, which is part of the Inyo National Forest in the White Mountains of the Eastern Sierras in California.

For this series, I expose a bracket of three RAW captures, 1 stop apart. With the sun behind the cloud directly in front of me, I know the contrast will be low enough that three exposures will capture the full dynamic range with my dSLR. I create the HDR image through Adobe Bridge so that I can save it as a Smart Object. I know I want the final image to be realistic, but with more contrast to reflect the stark terrain. And, of course, I want to enhance the structure and tonality I see in the clouds that I know won't be present in any exposure that has any decent detail in the fallen bristlecone pine.

After HDR Efex Pro creates the HDR image, I choose the Realistic (Strong) preset as a starting point. I feel that the preset's default tone compression of +50% is too strong, so I lower it to +25%. I do the opposite with the Method Strength, which I feel is not strong enough, raising it from the default +22% to +55%. Figure 7.3 shows the adjusted image and my adjusted settings.

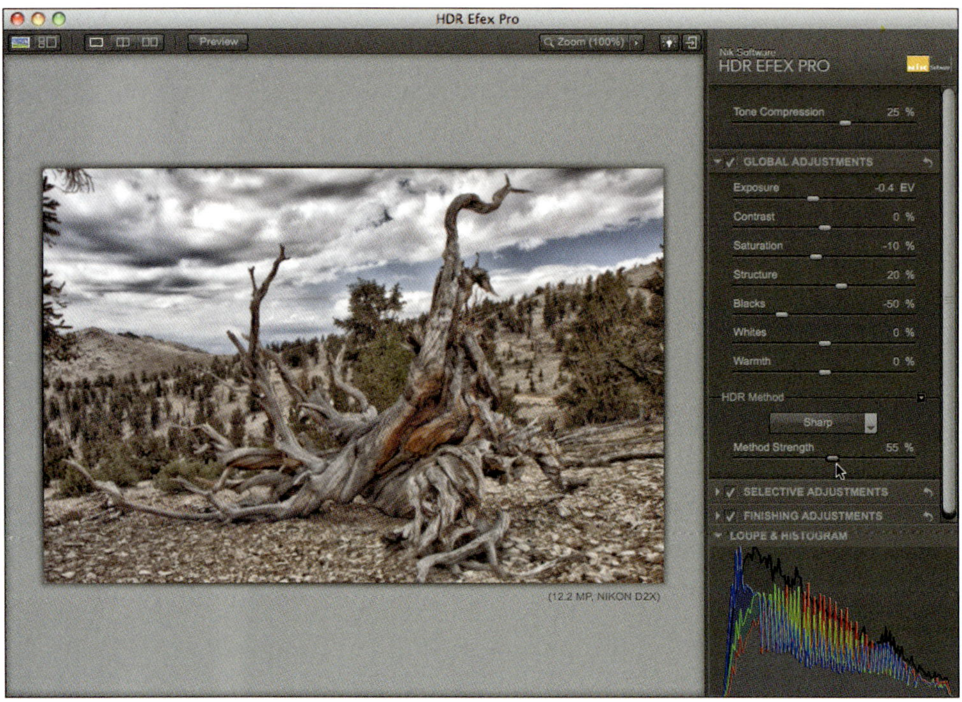

Figure 7.3

Not a bad start, but there is a lot of room for improvement. The image is still darker and lower in contrast than I want. There may be a good white value in the sky, but there certainly is no good black value to anchor the scene. This is typical in HDR imaging, especially if the image series is properly exposed and does not extend beyond the highlight and shadow clipping points.

You can see from Figure 7.3 that the default setting for the Exposure slider with the Realistic (Strong) preset is –0.4 EV. Each preset achieves its effect by a combination of factors, and certain global adjustments contribute to each preset along with specific HDR Methods, Method Strength settings, and Tone Compression settings.

My first step in adjusting this image is to see if the –0.4 EV exposure setting is giving me a good midtone. To do this, I zoom to 50% and navigate to an area of the HDR image that contains midtones, as shown in Figure 7.4.

Because the sun isn't lighting the scene, I want the image to be on the dark side, but the –0.4 EV setting is just a little too dark. I tap the right arrow key once to adjust the Exposure slider to –0.3 EV. That looks about right, so I zoom out to view the entire image and then use the light bulb icon to change the background behind the image to white (see Figure 7.5). Comparing the brightest areas in the clouds to the white background, the clouds haven't gained that much in brightness, so I'm happy with the exposure adjustment.

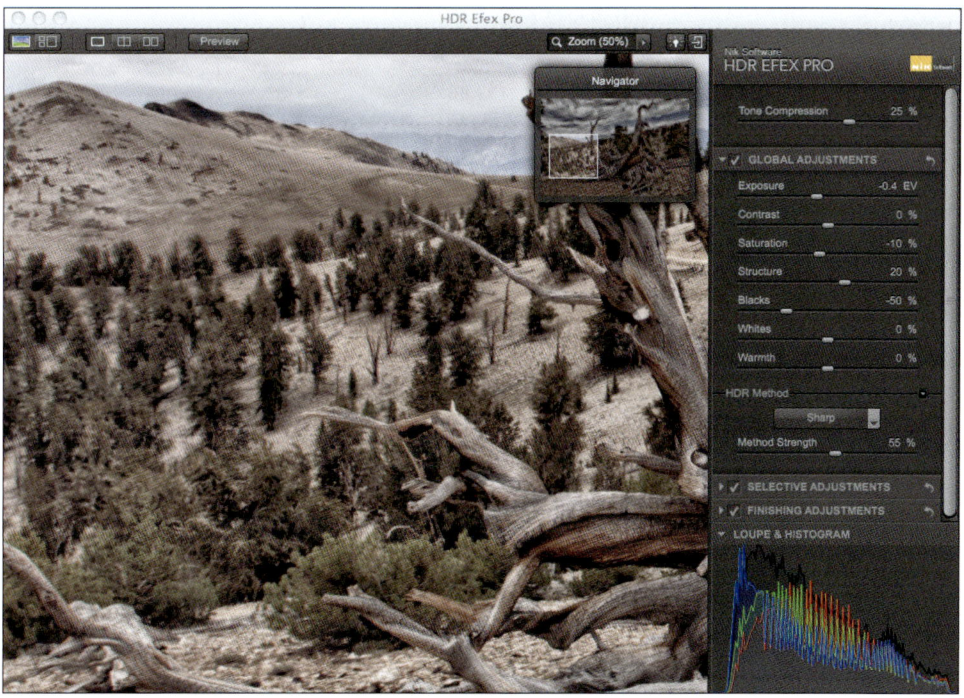

Figure 7.4

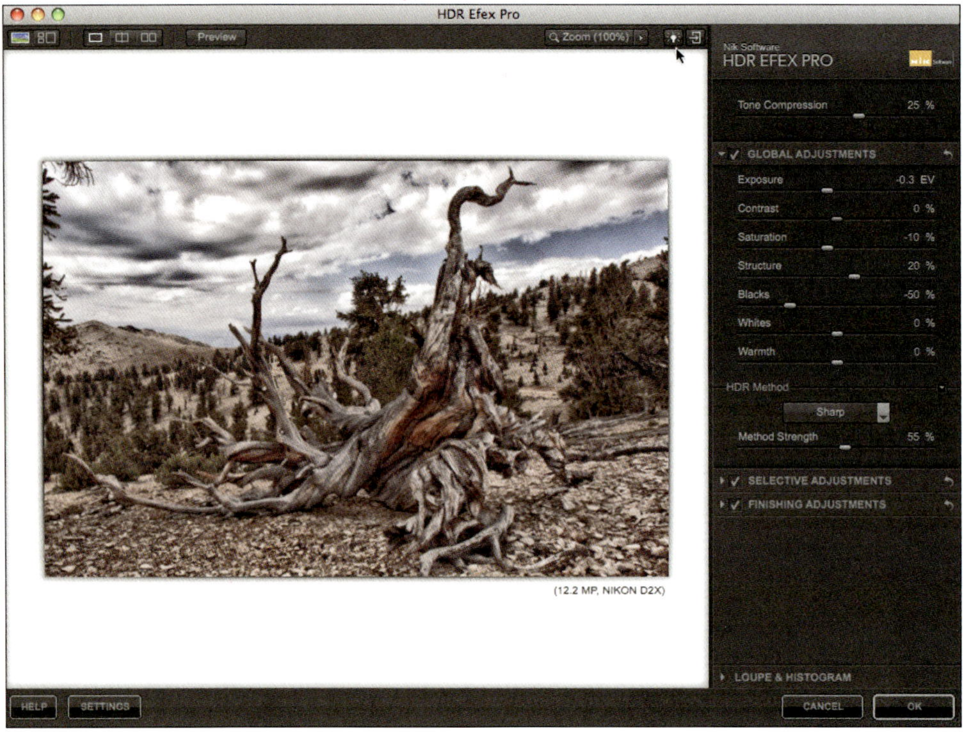

Figure 7.5

note

If the amount of adjustment you make with the Exposure slider causes the shadows to become too black (or too gray) or the highlights to become too light (or too gray), the Blacks and Whites global adjustments will bring them back in line.

At times you will find that you need to make significant adjustments to the Exposure slider, while at other times, such as this one, the adjustments are minor. The degree of adjustment required with any of the Global Adjustments sliders is entirely dependent on the decisions you make regarding the choice of preset, and any adjustments you make to the preset's tone compression, HDR Method, or HDR Method Strength.

In particular, the relationship between exposure and tone compression requires a balancing act in adjusting the two sliders. For positive values of exposure adjustment, increasing tone compression subtly lightens the image while decreasing tone compression subtly darkens the image. For negative values of exposure, increasing tone compression subtly lightens the image and decreasing tone compression darkens it. If you cannot achieve an exposure setting that totally satisfies you, try making a tone compression adjustment.

Adjusting Contrast

The next step is to adjust the contrast of the image. *Contrast* is the difference in brightness between the brightest and darkest parts of the image. A high-contrast image has mostly highlight and shadow tones with few midtones. A low contrast image is lacking in very bright and very dark areas, with most of the tonal values gathered around the midtones.

The contrast of the bristlecone pines image looks pretty good already with the default 0% contrast for the Realistic (Strong) preset. One reason for this is the film-like S-shaped curve (see Figure 7.6) that the Realistic (Strong) preset applies to the image.

An S curve increases upper tonal values and decreases lower tonal values. The result is a steeper curve in the middle than a straight line, from pure black, the lower-left point of the curve, to pure white, the upper-right point. The steeper the middle section, the greater the contrast of the image.

see also

Use of the Levels and Curves tool and other options available for it are discussed in Chapter 10.

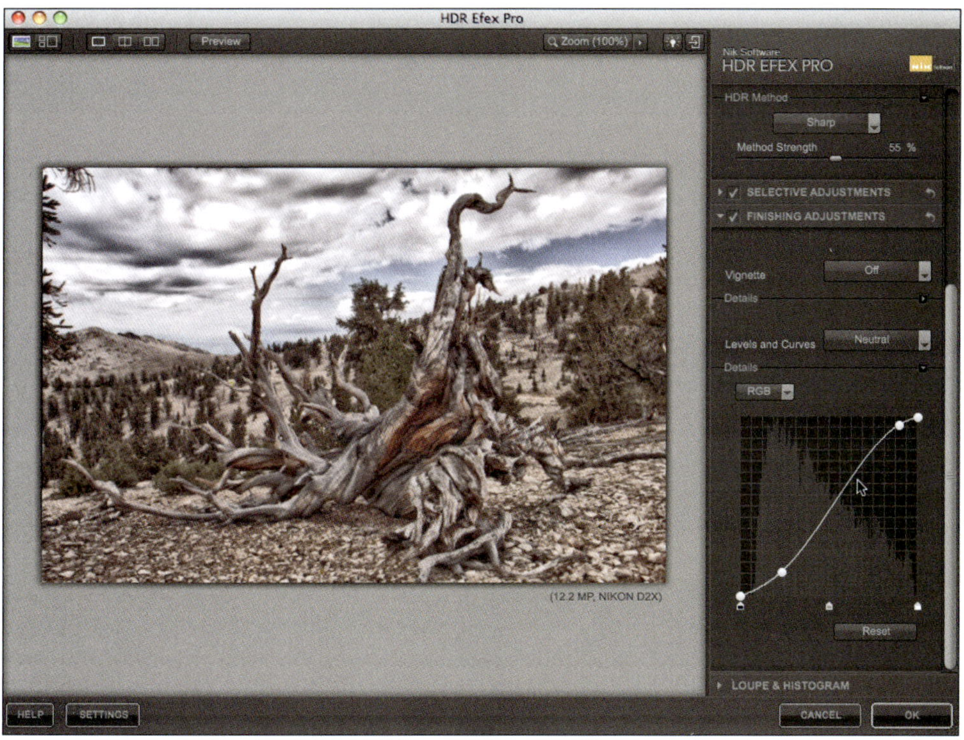

Figure 7.6

Even though the contrast looks pretty good, I adjust the Contrast slider to a couple of other settings to see the effect of decreasing or increasing contrast. Adjusting the slider to a contrast setting of –25% produces the result in Figure 7.7. That result is too flat for me.

Increasing the slider to +25%, as shown in Figure 7.8, is too contrasty for me, but not by a lot. I settle on a contrast setting of +10%, as shown in Figure 7.9.

The range of the Contrast slider is –100% to +100% on some arbitrary scale. While it isn't really obvious from this image or the relatively minor contrast adjustments in Figures 7.8 and 7.9, adjusting contrast also has an effect on image saturation. This is shown in Figure 7.10, where a +75% increase in contrast shows large gains in saturation of the blue sky and the red in the trunk of the fallen bristlecone. Therefore, it is important to make any contrast adjustments before you make any adjustments to the Saturation slider.

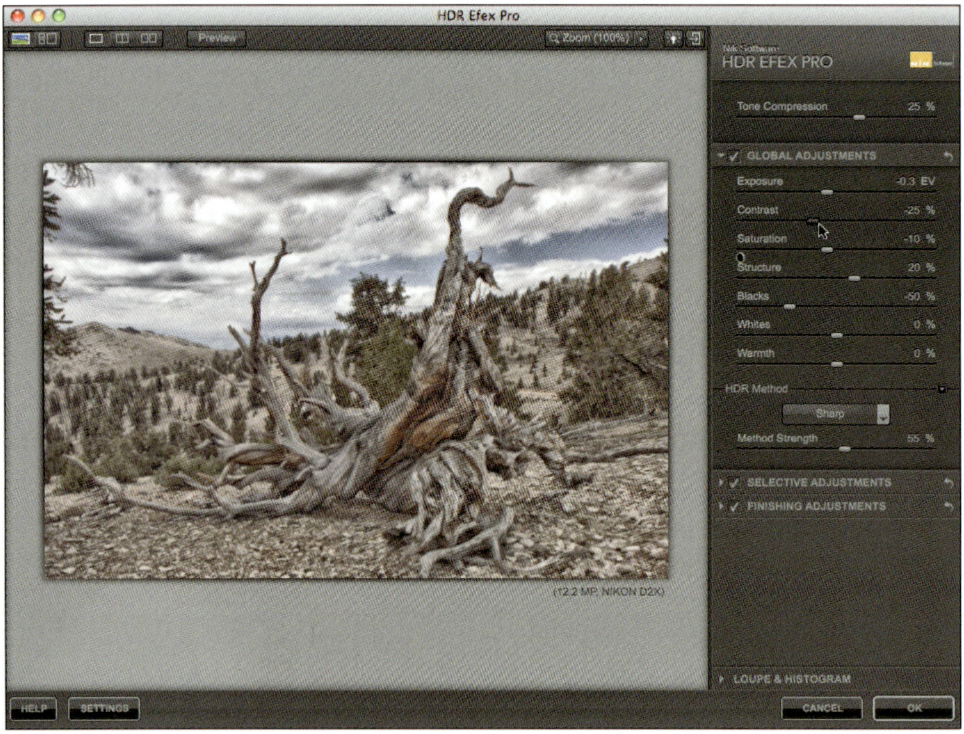

Figure 7.7

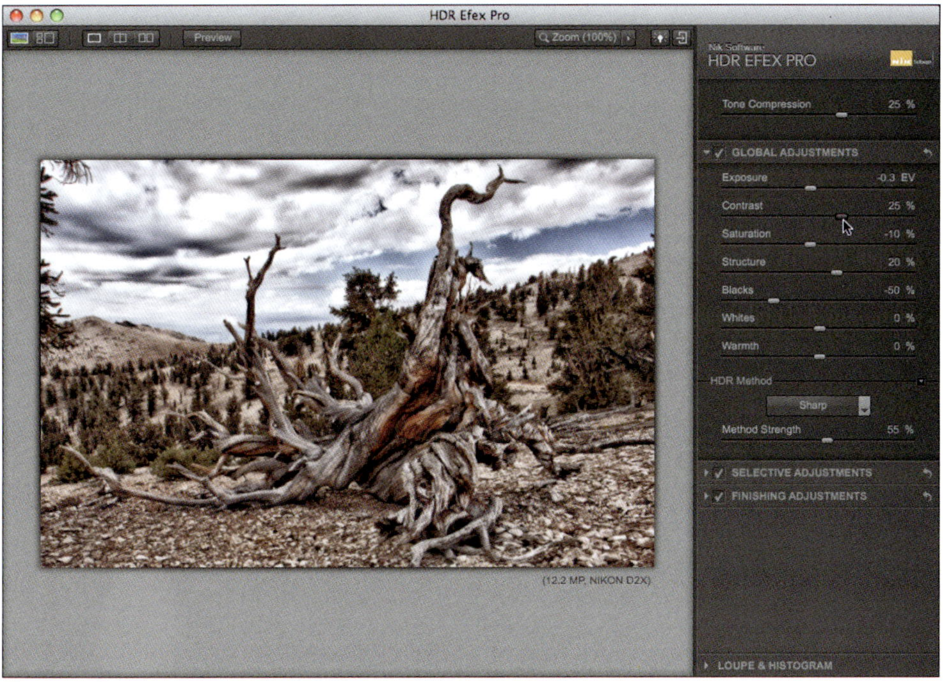

Figure 7.8

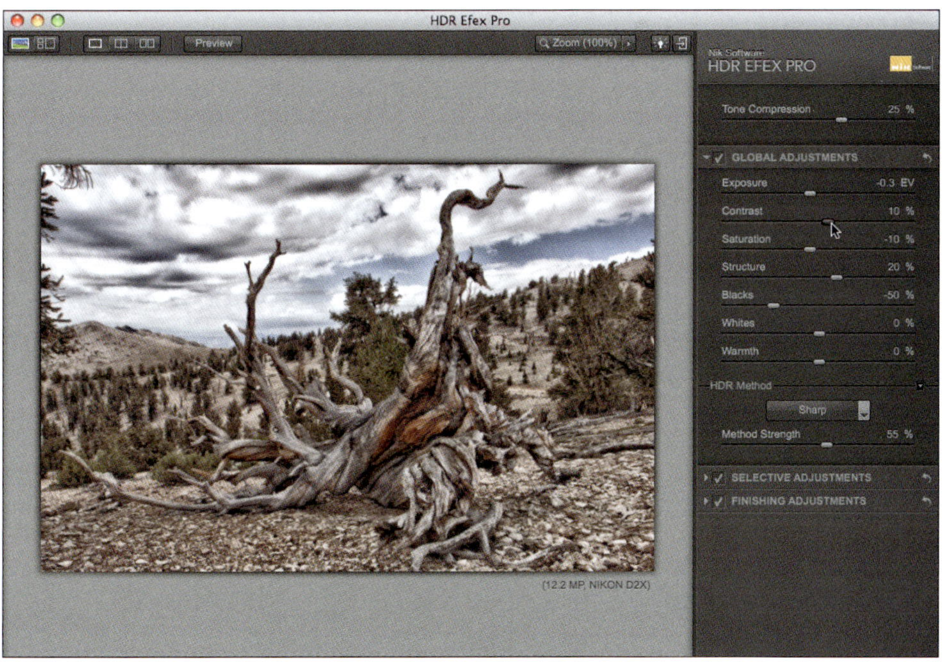

Figure 7.9

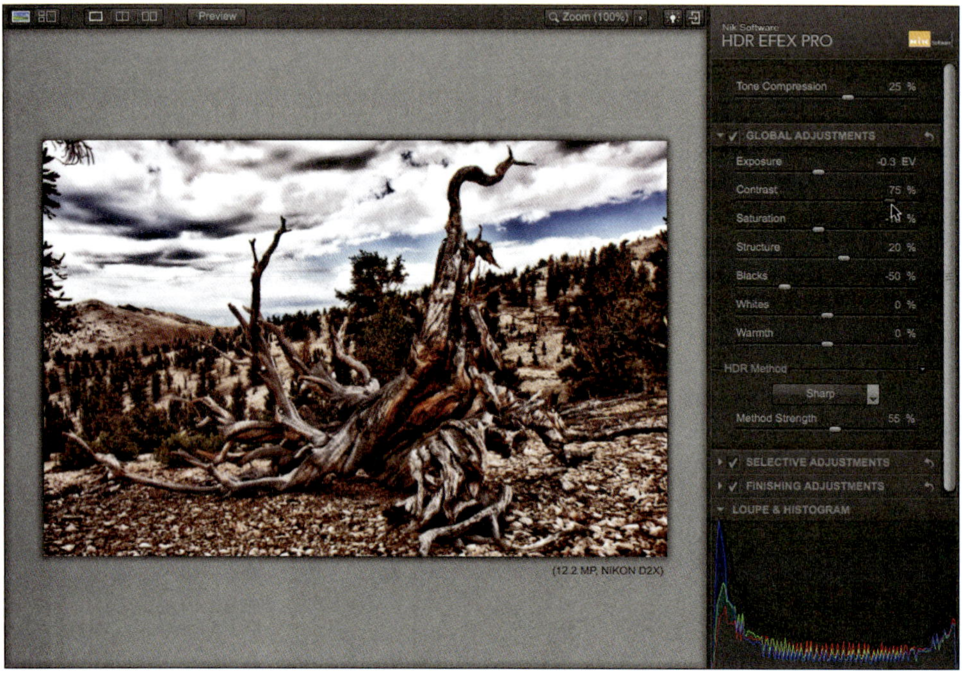

Figure 7.10

Adjusting Saturation

The Saturation slider is the next Global Adjustments tool. *Saturation* is the amount of color in a color. In any color space, a pixel that is fully saturated does not contain any amount of gray. If the pixel is totally unsaturated, then there is no hue in the pixel and only the underlying gray luminance value remains. Chapter 4 describes how HDR Efex Pro achieves its monochrome presets by adjusting the Saturation slider to a value of 0.

With a 32-bit image, a lot of color information is available, so the underlying image can become extremely saturated. However, when this is tone mapped for display on a monitor, it only appears as saturated as the monitor (or printer) can produce.

The bristlecone pines image definitely needs a saturation adjustment. Moving the Saturation slider to –100%, as shown in Figure 7.11, makes me think that, with a few tonal adjustments in Silver Efex Pro 2, it would make an interesting monochrome or toned image.

But as an HDR image, I want to go the other direction and try increasing the saturation to +50%, as shown in Figure 7.12.

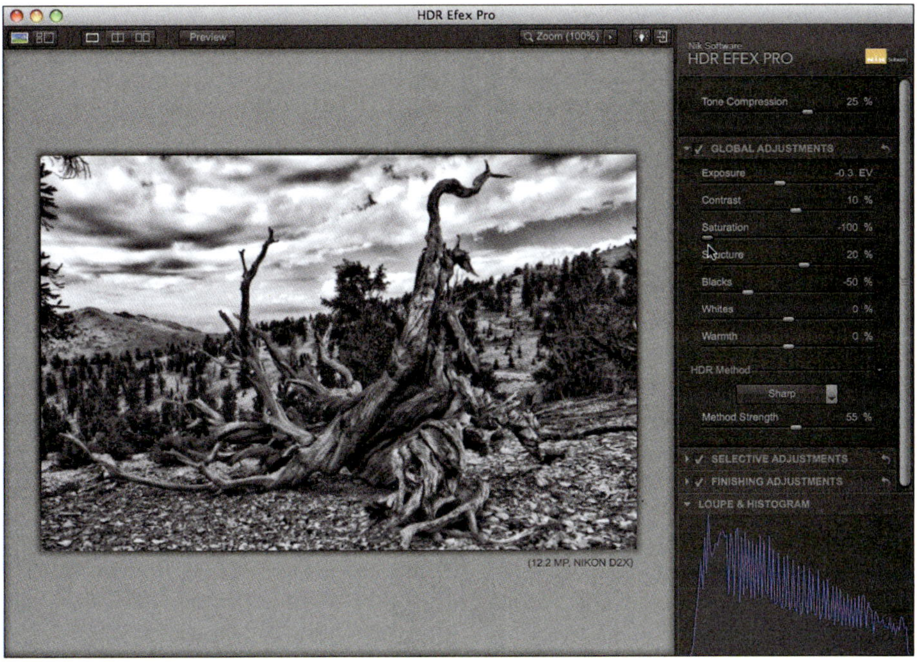

Figure 7.11

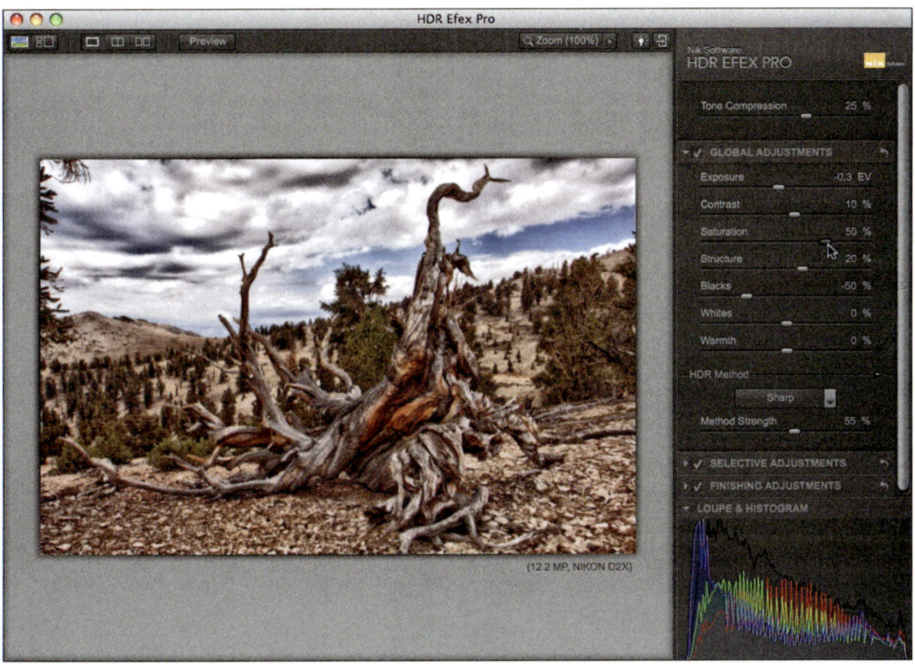

Figure 7.12

Like most photographers, I tend to oversaturate my images while I work on them, and then regret it later after I've lived with them a while. I have a feeling I'm going to think that this much saturation is going to look "cartoony" when I make a print, so I'm going to back off on the adjustment to +35% with the result shown in Figure 7.13.

The scale of the Saturation slider is –100% to +100%. At –100%, all color values are eliminated, resulting in a grayscale (monochrome) image. At +100%, the colors are fully saturated and will display on your monitor with as much saturation as your monitor can produce. Of course, this varies greatly from monitor to monitor, which is another good reason to calibrate your working monitor. Even though the saturation will look different on someone's uncalibrated monitor, at least your results will be consistent and repeatable.

When I'm working in HDR Efex Pro, I periodically like to look back to see how far I've come from the original HDR image created by the Default preset and check to see if I have strayed from my original thoughts on where the image adjustments should go. I do this by clicking Preview above the Main Image Window. Figure 7.14 shows the result of doing this at this point in the global adjustments, before making changes to the image structure. I like what I've done so far.

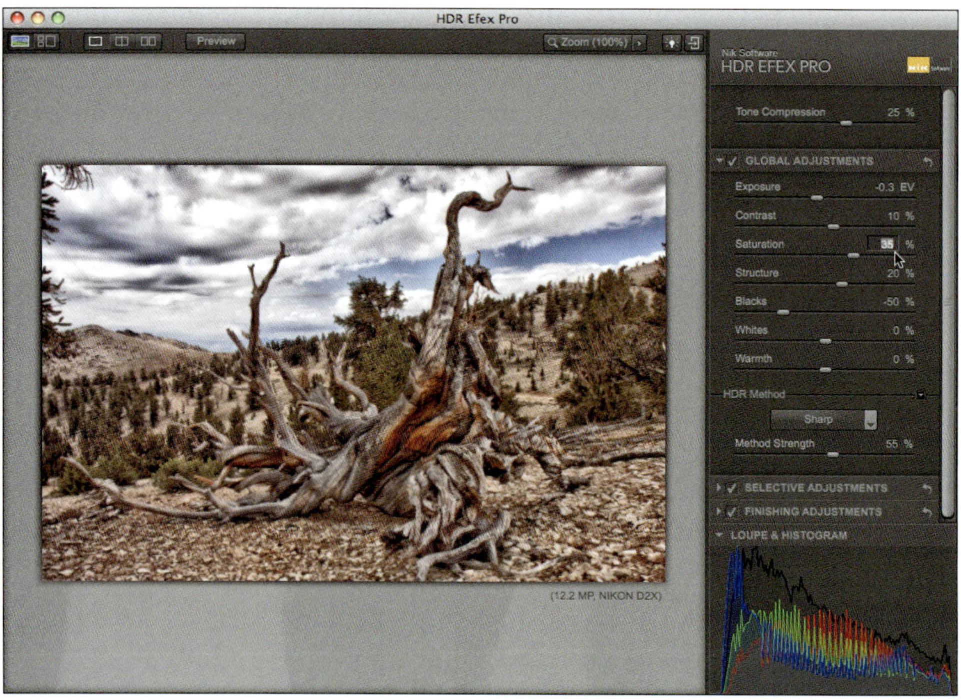

Figure 7.13

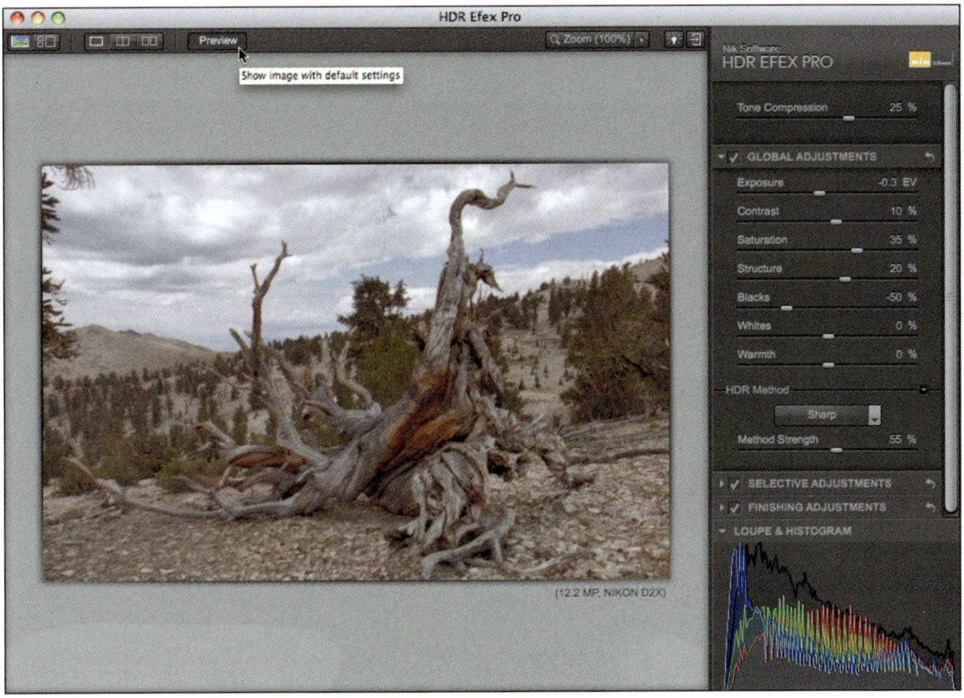

Figure 7.14

Adjusting Structure

To this point, the global adjustments have been the same as those found in non-HDR imaging programs, which all include tools for adjusting exposure, contrast, and saturation. The Structure slider, on the other hand, is a tool unique to HDR imaging, although its effect can look similar to high pass filtering found in Adobe Photoshop and a few other imaging programs.

However, the structure adjustment differs from high pass sharpening in significant ways. For one, the structure adjustment is a simple slider, making it far easier to use, and the result is immediately visible on the monitor. For another, the range of the slider is –100% to +100%. The negative values of the Structure slider provide a means of visually softening the image by lowering image detail, as well as using the positive values of the structure adjustment to increase image detail.

The most important difference is in the way adjustments to the Structure slider affect the image. High pass filters act on all the image information, including the edges of objects. The structure adjustment in HDR Efex Pro applies a unique form of microcontrast only to the image information that is within the edges of the object, but not to the edges themselves. Adjustments made with the Structure slider can provide a significant increase in detail without causing the haloing often seen with high pass filtering.

The Structure slider increases or decreases local contrast. Usually only small adjustments are necessary unless you are looking for a strong HDR look because the effect of the strength adjustment can be quite powerful.

Structure adjustments will also enhance image noise and any dust on the sensor. For this reason it is essential to adjust the Structure slider while viewing the image at a zoom setting of 100%, and then use the Navigator window to see the effect of the structure adjustment in several areas of the image.

The default setting for structure with the Realistic (Strong) preset is +20%. I chose the area in Figure 7.15 to view at 100%. This area contains clouds so I can see any noise buildup, along with a representative sampling of other elements in the HDR image. In Figure 7.15, the structure setting is at the default +20%. Some noise is definitely visible in the clouds and distant mountains.

Setting the Structure slider to –75% in Figure 7.16 eliminates the noise, but both the foreground bristlecone branch and the background mountains have lost contrast and therefore apparent sharpness. Between the two, I prefer to see noise.

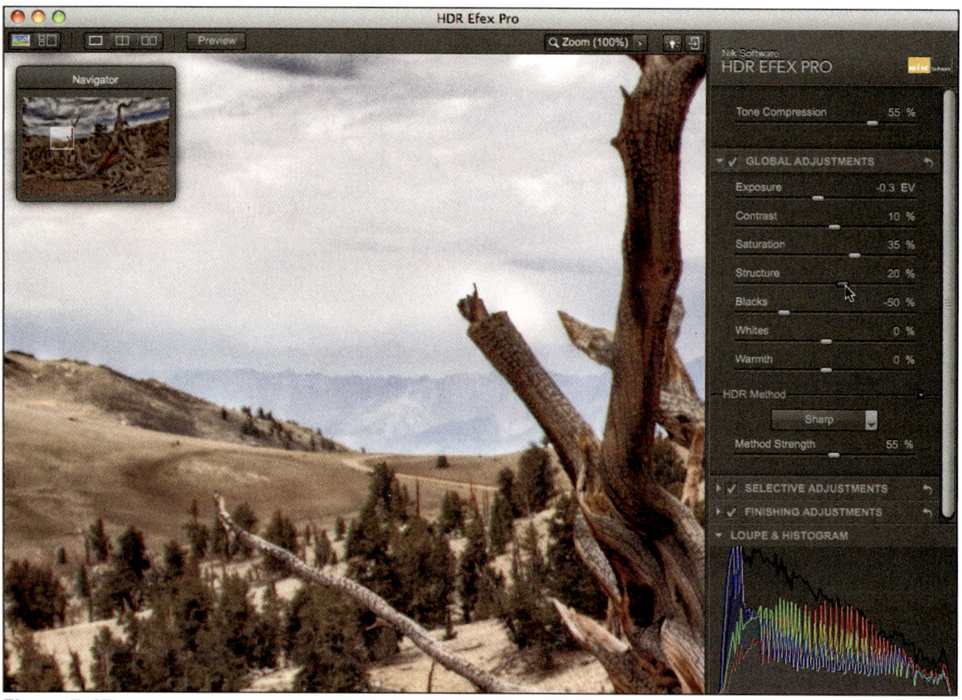

Figure 7.15

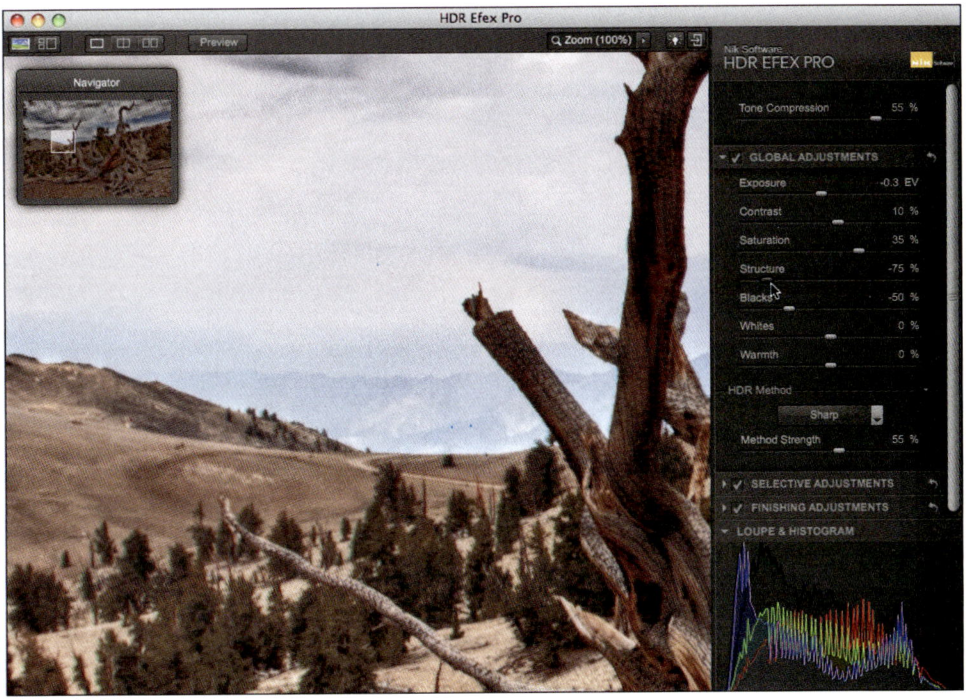

Figure 7.16

see also

When a globally applied structure adjustment creates artifacts in the image, make a local structure adjustment with a Control Point to increase or decrease microcontrast where needed. Chapters 8 and 9 discuss Control Points.

Adjusting the structure to +75%, as shown in Figure 7.17, gives me lots of noise, a nice gain in apparent sharpness, but a big gain in contrast, too. This setting is too high for me.

After trying other settings for the Structure slider and using the Navigator to pan around to see the effects at other parts of the image, I settled on a structure setting of +40%. The +40% setting is shown at 100% magnification in Figure 7.18 and in the full image in Figure 7.19.

note

View the image at 100% magnification when adjusting the Structure slider.

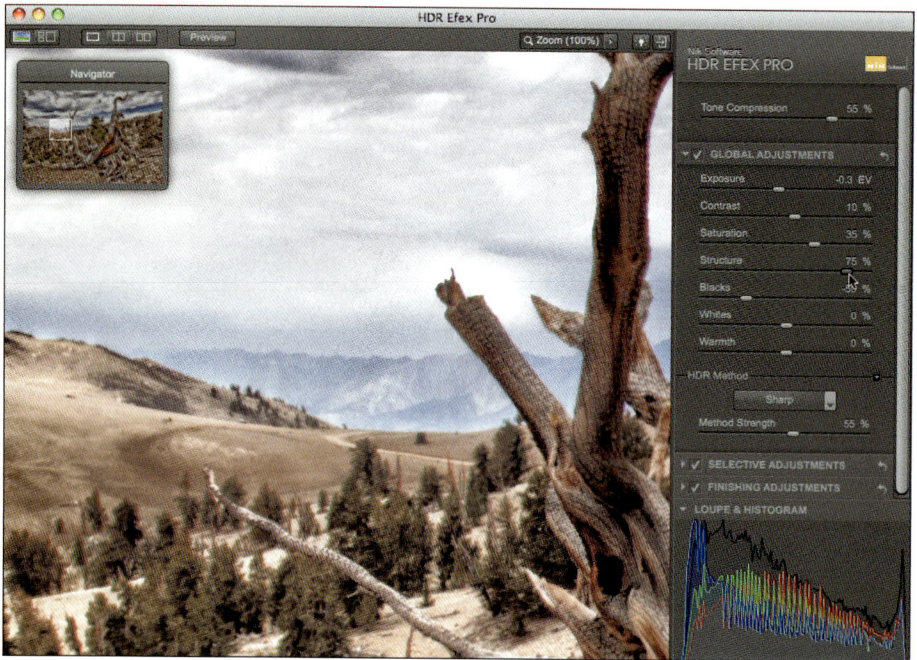

Figure 7.17

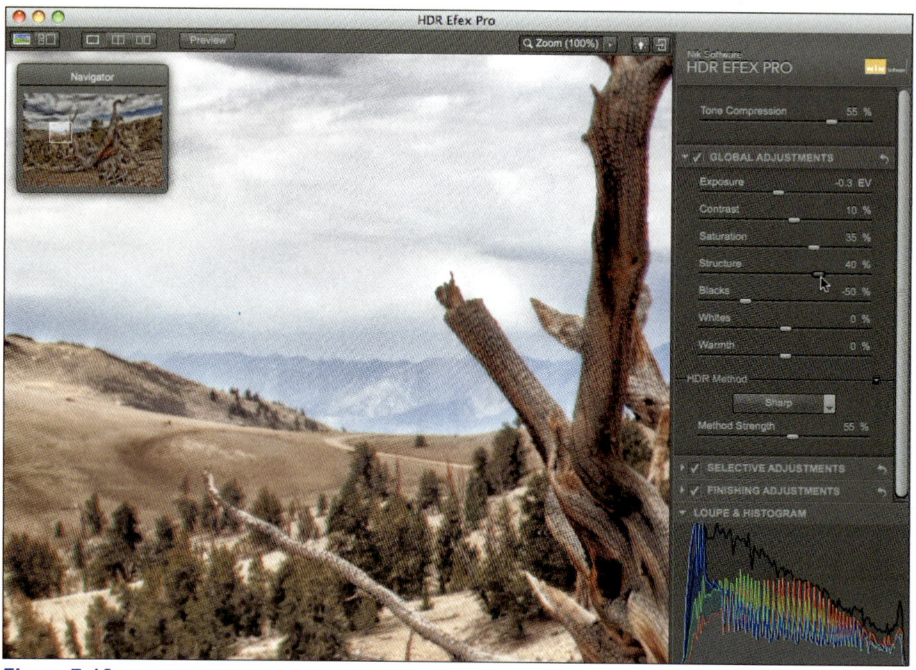

Figure 7.18

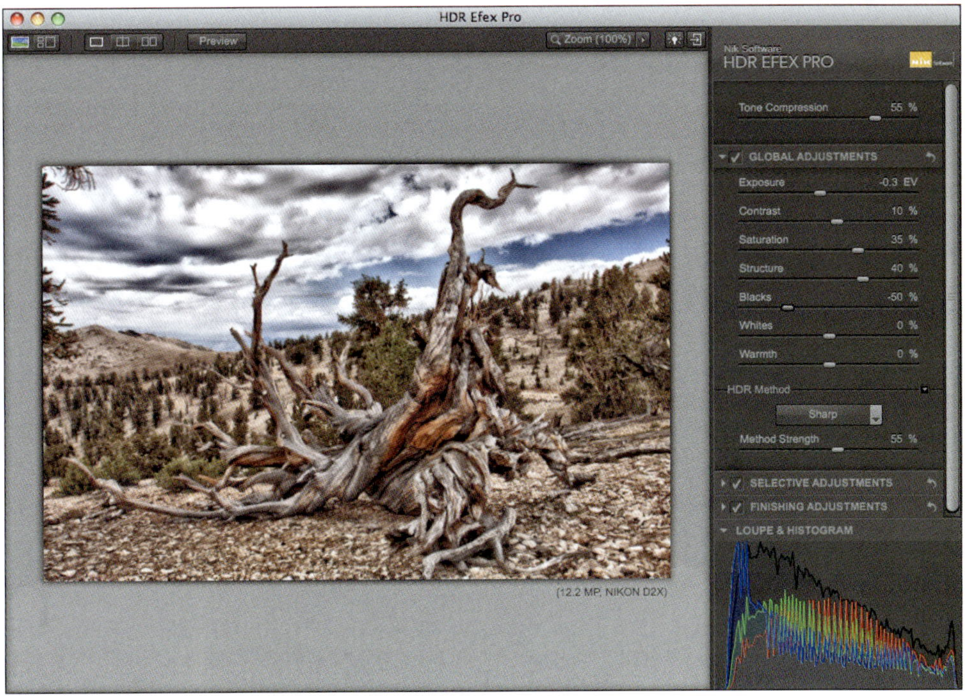

Figure 7.19

Adjusting Blacks

There are certainly times in photography when you don't want a really strong black in your image. But those instances tend to be special cases, such as a high-key portrait or a simulated faded photo effect like that produced by the Vintage Colors or The Old Cottage presets in HDR Efex Pro.

Other than a few special cases, it is important to have a good black in the image to give it tonal depth and to fool the eye into thinking that a full tonal range is present even if it isn't. The Blacks slider in the Global Adjustments section is the tool you use to produce a good black in HDR Efex Pro.

The farther you adjust the slider from its 0 setting, the more black value is added to each pixel. While the brightest whites are unaffected unless the slider adjustment is extreme, all other tones are adjusted. The Blacks slider is an excellent tool to recover information in an overexposed or underexposed HDR image, and even with a properly exposed image series, small adjustments in the Blacks slider go a long way.

The range of the Blacks slider, like many other global adjustments, is –100% to +100%, so you can also use the Blacks slider to recover shadow detail. Most of the time, however, because of the nature of HDR imaging, it is necessary to increase rather than decrease the Blacks slider when making global adjustments to create a good black.

The Blacks slider is also the tool to use if the adjustment made to the midtones with the Exposure slider lightened the shadow values to grays rather than blacks or clipped the shadow values. Moving the Blacks slider to the right adjusts gray shadow values to black, and moving it to the left recovers clipped shadow tones.

The default setting for the Blacks slider in Realistic (Strong) is –50%. With the image at full screen in the Main Image Window and with the background behind the image white or gray, that setting looks good. But with the black background, as shown in Figure 7.20, there isn't any place where the image is obviously as black as the background.

Zooming the image to 50% magnification and navigating to a place where I would want a rich black in Figure 7.21, I see more shadow detail than I would like with the default blacks setting.

However, any move I make with the Blacks slider to the right, even to a setting of –40%, as shown in Figure 7.22, darkens the trees too much for my taste. I'm going to leave the blacks setting at the default –50%. If I'm still bothered by the lack of a good black, I'll deal with it later with a local adjustment.

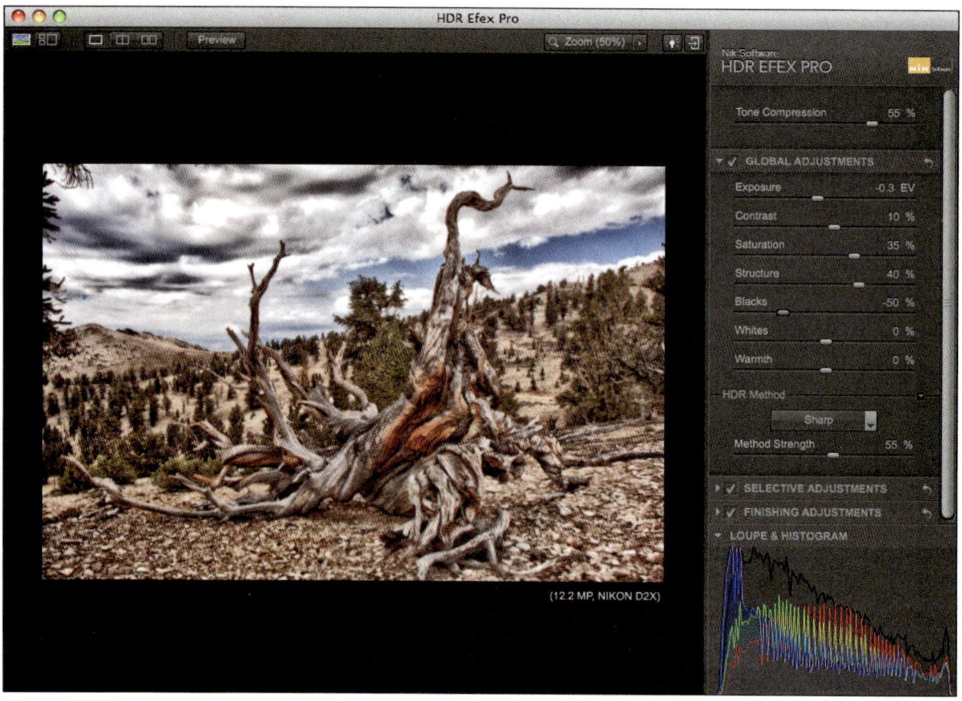

Figure 7.20

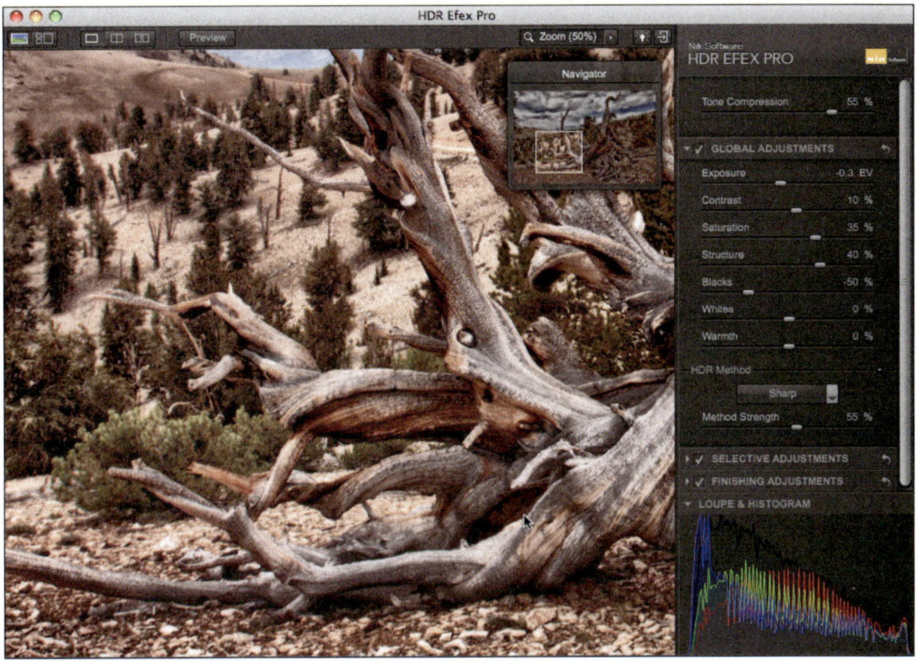

Figure 7.21

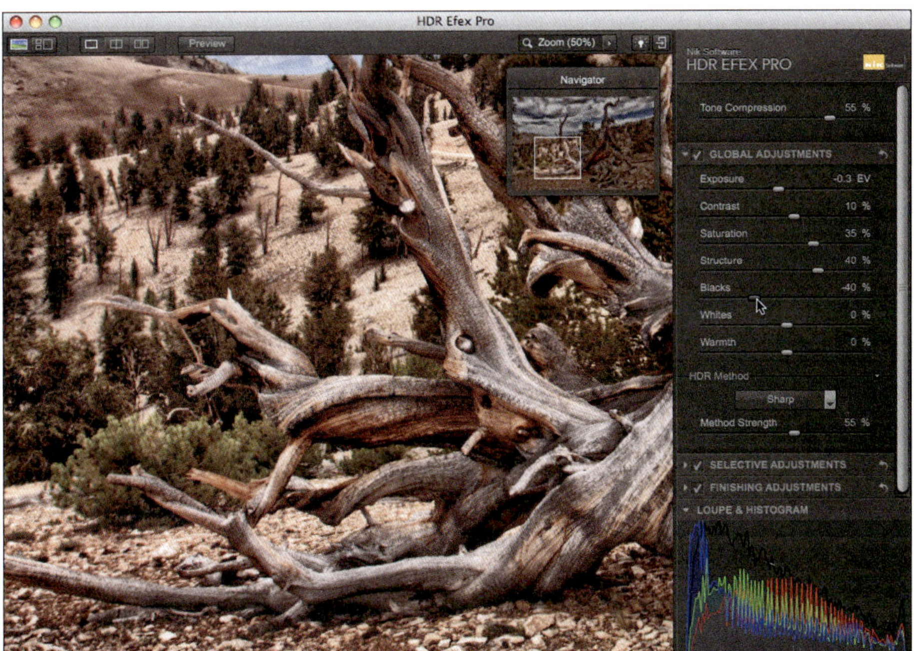

Figure 7.22

see also

Local adjustments are covered in Chapters 8 and 9.

If you're watching the histogram that I've left active at the bottom of the Control Palette while making global adjustments, you see that there is a small gap between the left side of the histogram and the beginning of the histogram tone curve when the Blacks slider is set to –50%. It is still present, although smaller, when the Blacks slider is set to –40%.

To make the curve meet the left side of the histogram to ensure that there are pure black pixels in the image, the Blacks slider must be adjusted to nearly 0%, darkening the image well beyond an acceptable level. It is always better to adjust your image in HDR Efex Pro according to what you see on a calibrated monitor rather than to a setting on a histogram.

Adjusting Whites

Just as the Blacks slider allows you to adjust the darkest tones in the image, the Whites slider allows you to adjust the brightest tones. Moving the slider to the right adds white value to each pixel without affecting the darkest values unless the adjustment is extreme. Moving the slider to the left lowers highlight values and is useful in recovering highlight detail.

The whites adjustment is the tool to use if the initial exposure adjustment to the midtones caused the highlights either to clip or to become gray. Moving the Whites slider to the right brightens gray highlights and moving the slider to the left recovers clipped highlights.

Whereas a good black adds depth to an image, a good white with associated lighter values creates a feeling of openness and airiness. How much of this type of feeling you want in the image will determine the amount of adjustment you make to the Whites slider.

Like the Blacks slider, the Whites slider requires a gentle touch. Moving the slider to the extremes of its –100% to +100% range makes huge changes in tonality, not just for the lighter values. Because most every image should have a bright white with just a hint of tonality as well as a good black, some adjustment to the Whites slider is usually necessary.

The Realistic (Strong) presets use a default whites setting of 0%. As I review the image with the global adjusts made so far against the black, gray, and white backgrounds, I'm thinking that it is a bit more somber than I now want. This is especially true when the image is viewed with the white background and I'm thinking of printing it with a white border or framing it with a white mat (see Figure 7.23).

Adjusting the Whites slider to +10%, as shown in Figure 7.24, is too much, so I split the difference and settle on a whites adjustment of +5%. (see Figure 7.25). Checking the clouds at 100% magnification seems to indicate there might be some clipping of the highlights, but the histogram says that the highlights are under control. If the highlights are clipped, I can adjust them later with a Control Point local adjustment. The image is looking great, although a little bit too cool, but that is the next adjustment.

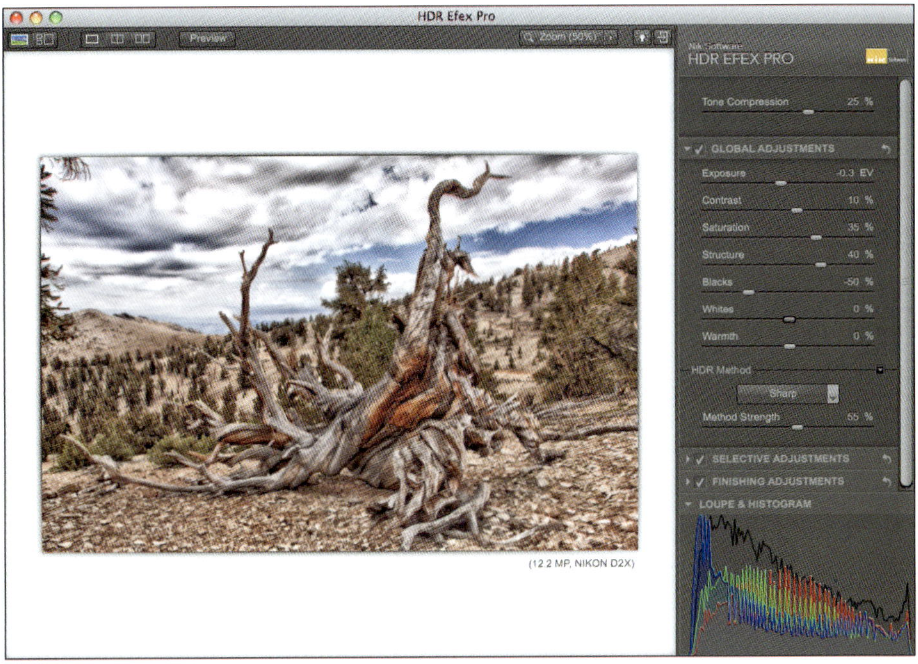

Figure 7.23

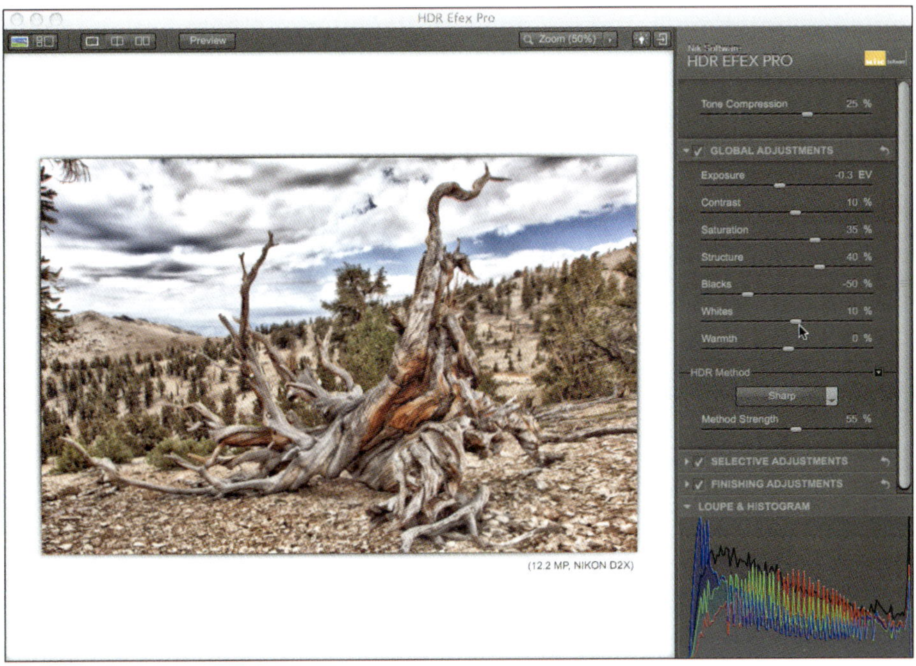

Figure 7.24

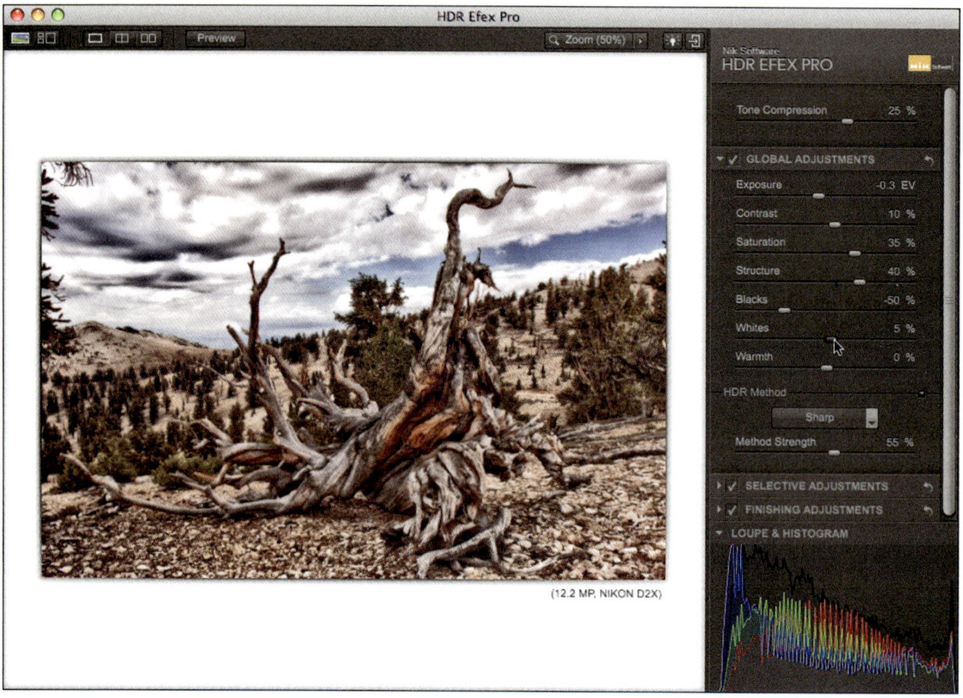

Figure 7.25

Adjusting Warmth

The final global adjustment in HDR Efex Pro controls the warmth (the proportion of yellow or blue) of the HDR image. The result is similar to placing a blue or yellow color conversion filter over your lens or adjusting the white balance in an imaging program.

The range of the Warmth slider is marked as –100% to +100%, but that doesn't help much. Moving the slider all the way to the left adds a strong blue cast (see Figure 7.26). Adjusting it all the way to the right adds a strong yellow cast (see Figure 7.27).

Unless you are creating some sort of special effects image, it is hard to imagine what you would use these extremes for, but they are available in HDR Efex Pro.

The Warmth slider may be the most difficult global adjustment to use. At least it seems that way to me most of the time, especially with images like this one.

Unless I'm shooting products in the studio and require a neutral color balance, I always adjust my camera to a neutral color balance or correct a RAW capture to neutral using a gray step wedge in the scene, and then add warmth to the images.

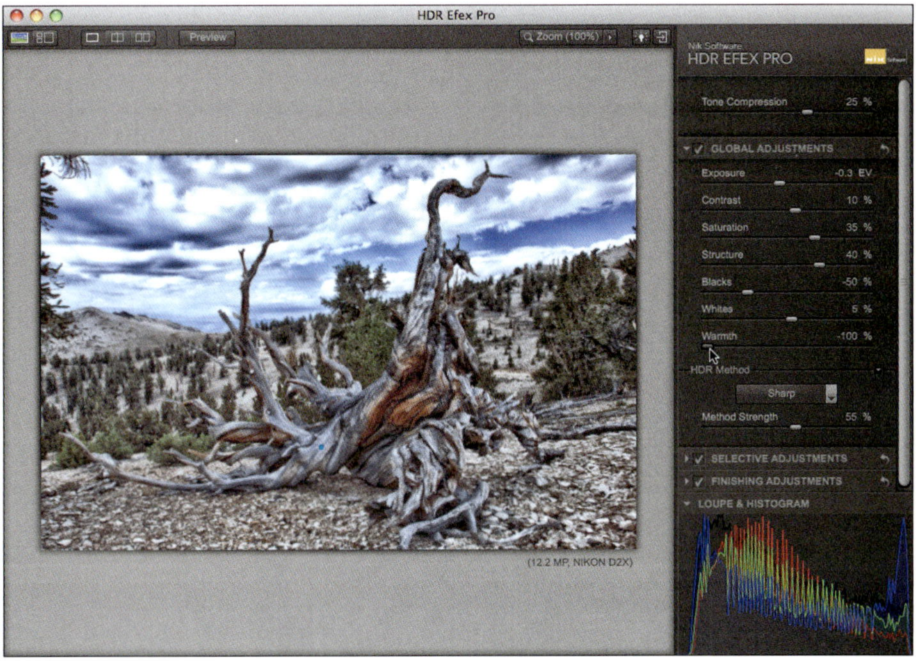

Figure 7.26

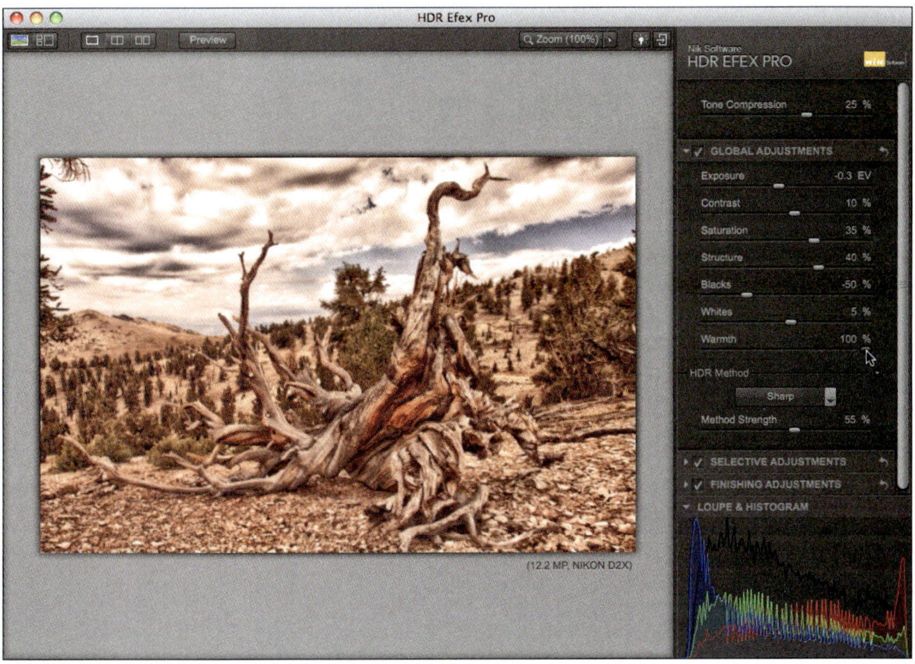

Figure 7.27

Scenes like this one are the most difficult to decide how much warmth to add. So far, the color balance is cooler than the scene I remember. Some of this is the result of the 10,000-foot elevation, but most of it is my feeling that the bristlecone pines are a warmer tone than the image reflects.

I really like the way the fallen bristlecone pine looks in Figure 7.28 with a warmth adjustment of +20%, but the clouds and the living trees are too yellow. The green that we see in trees already has a strong yellow component, and HDR images enhance this, sometimes very strongly. Adding more warmth just compounds the problem.

After trying other warmth adjustments, I decide on a setting of +15%. (see Figure 7.29). The clouds are still too warm, but I can deal with them later with a Control Point local adjustment.

Global adjustments along with adjustments to the default tone compression and HDR Method settings give you tremendous control over the overall look of the final HDR image.

Figure 7.30 shows the bristlecone pine image series with the default preset applied, just as HDR Efex Pro initially layered the three images.

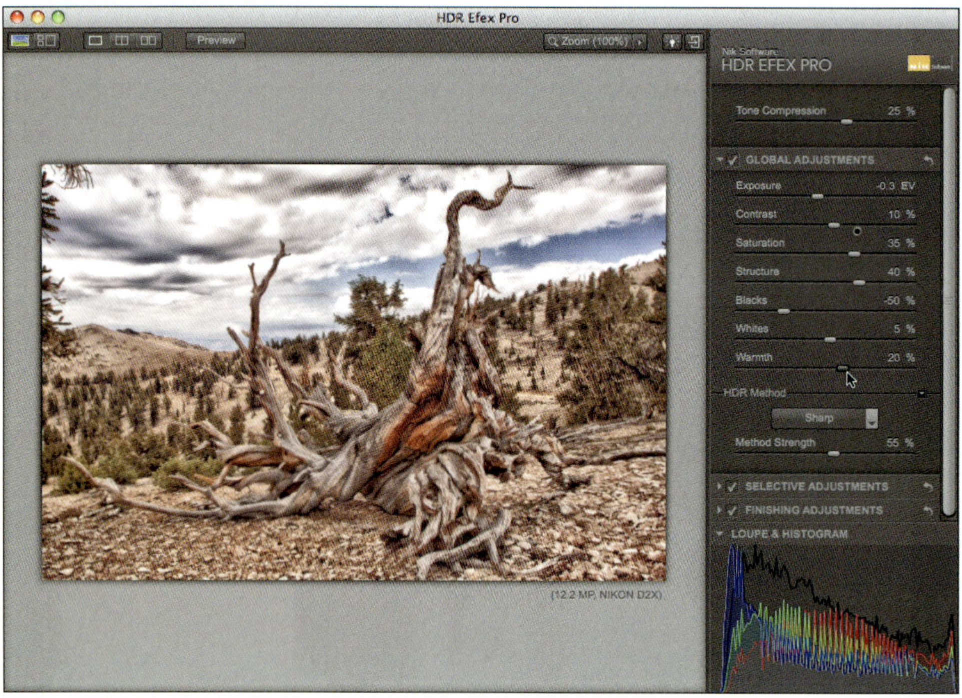

Figure 7.28

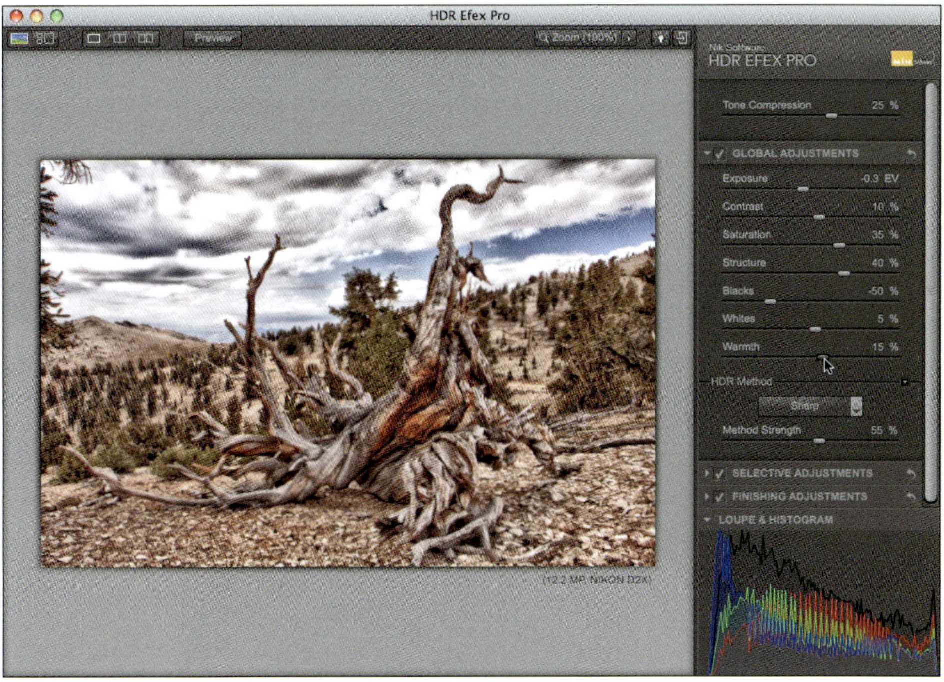

Figure 7.29

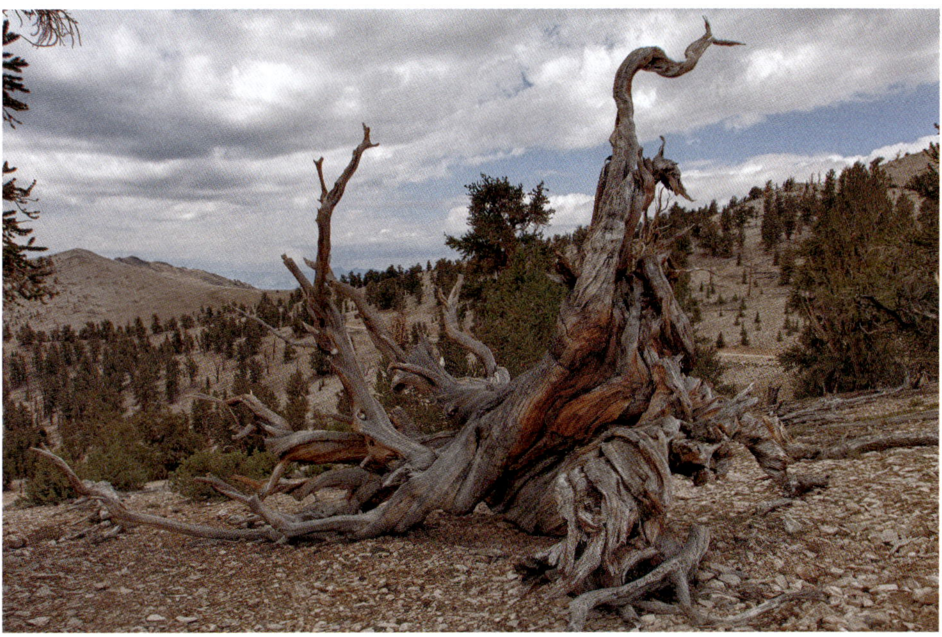

Figure 7.30

The Realistic (Strong) HDR Efex Pro preset that I chose as a starting point for the image creation produced Figure 7.31 with its default settings.

With the global adjustments made in the course of this chapter, the resulting image is shown in Figure 7.32.

While it is possible to accept any of these images as a final HDR output, I hope that you agree the image has undergone a positive transformation from Figure 7.31 to Figure 7.32.

In Chapter 9, there are a few more small tweaks to the image. But before that happens, you need to become familiar with how the tools used in Chapter 9 operate.

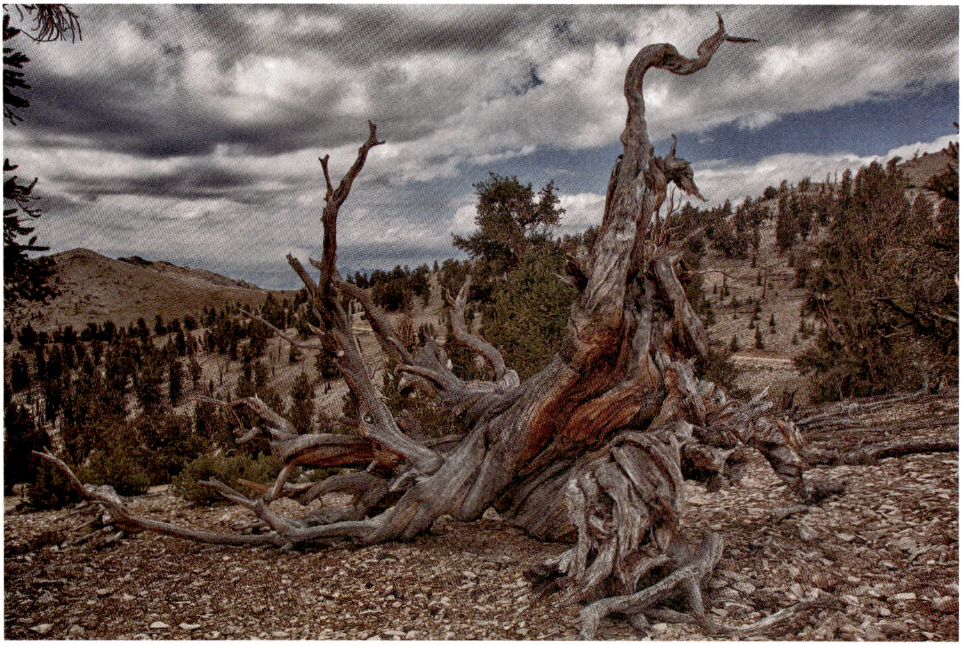

Figure 7.31

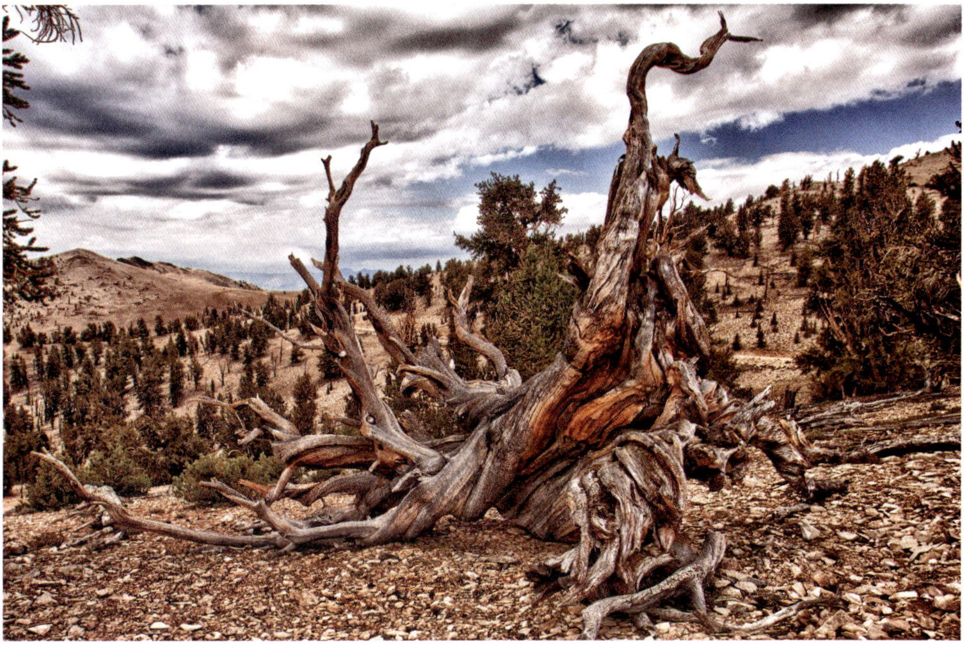

Figure 7.32

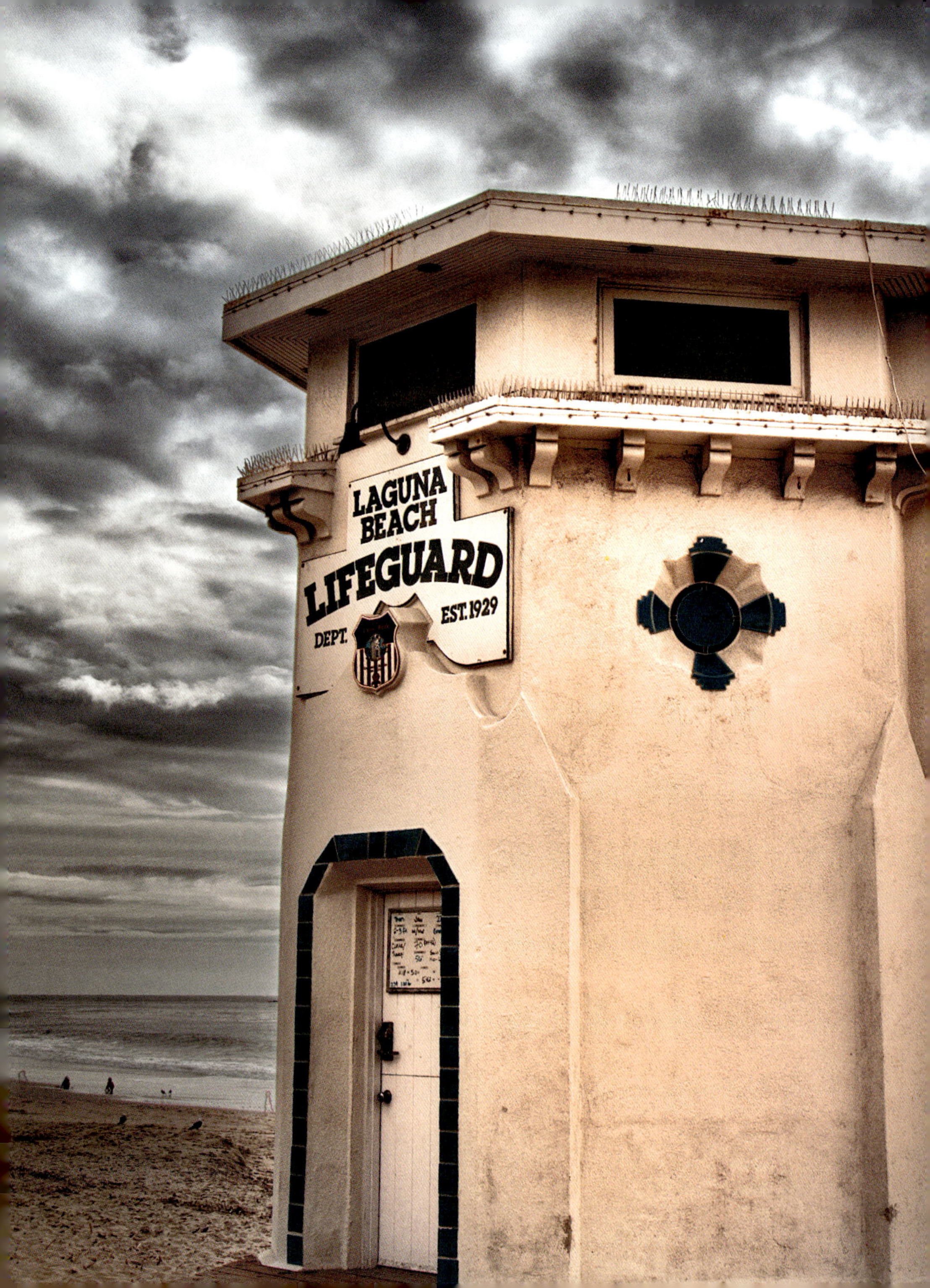
LAGUNA BEACH
LIFEGUARD
DEPT.
EST. 1929

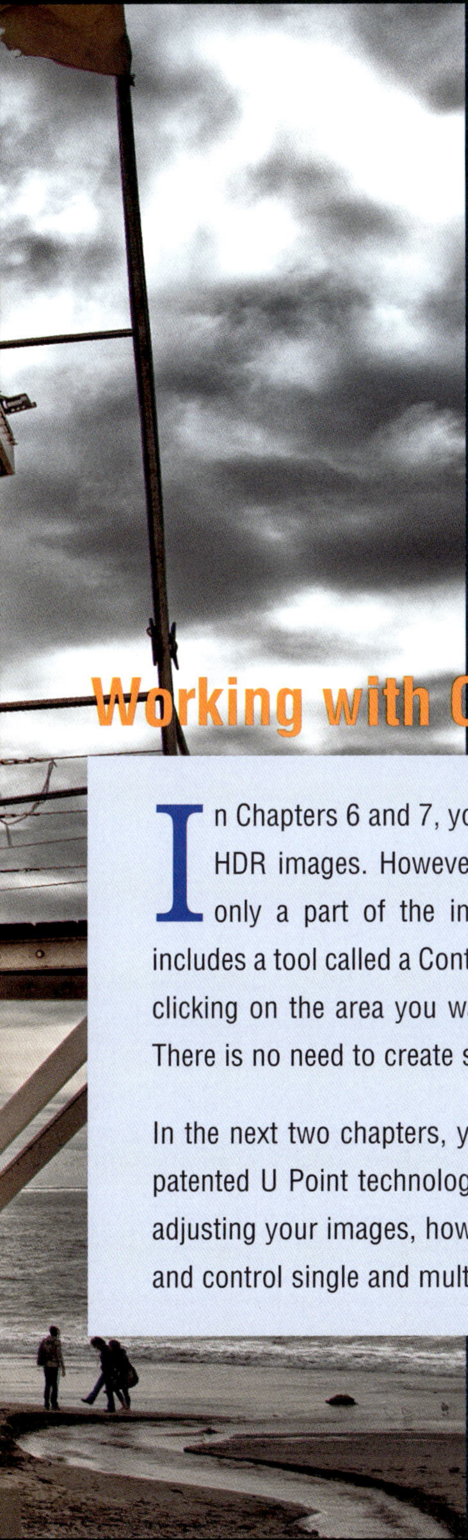

8

Working with Control Points

In Chapters 6 and 7, you learn how to make global changes to your HDR images. However, there are times when you want to adjust only a part of the image, not the entire image. HDR Efex Pro includes a tool called a Control Point that allows you to do this by simply clicking on the area you want to change and making the adjustments. There is no need to create selections or masks.

In the next two chapters, you see how to do this using Nik Software's patented U Point technology to power Control Points. Before you start adjusting your images, however, first look closely at how best to create and control single and multiple Control Points.

Selective Editing with the U Point Tool

If you are familiar with Photoshop or similar image-editing software, you know that a large part of your time during editing can be consumed with creating selections. This is especially true when the area to be selected is complex, has very soft edges, or appears in a number of disconnected areas in the image.

In HDR imaging, you constantly encounter the need to adjust a portion of the image. In Figure 8.1, for example, if you want to change the look of the clouds by adjusting their exposure or change their structure without affecting the sky or the rest of the image, creating a mask for the clouds would be a daunting task in an image-editing program.

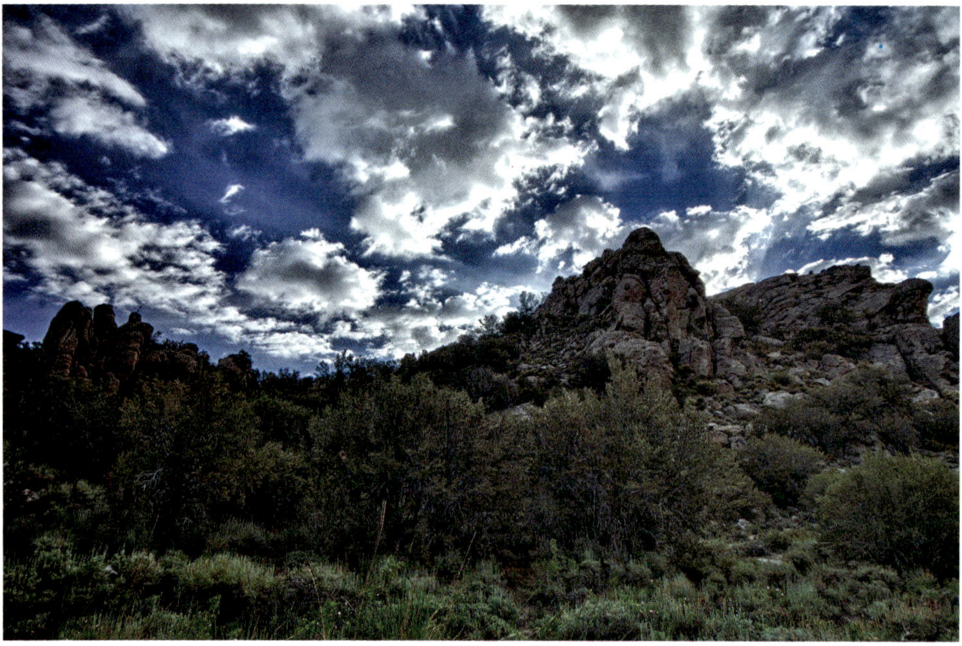

Figure 8.1

Using the U Point-powered Control Points in HDR Efex Pro, however, it is a simple matter of adding a Control Point and adjusting the size of the area you want to control — the selection is done automatically.

Figure 8.2 shows the amount of control you have using Control Points. It took me only a few seconds to make these adjustments.

The other great thing about Control Points is that they work along with the global adjustments you make. By using Control Points, you can increase or decrease the amounts of any of the global adjustments that you make and do this to highly targeted values in your image. The adjustments are all made in the 32-bit color space, so they are smooth and well controlled.

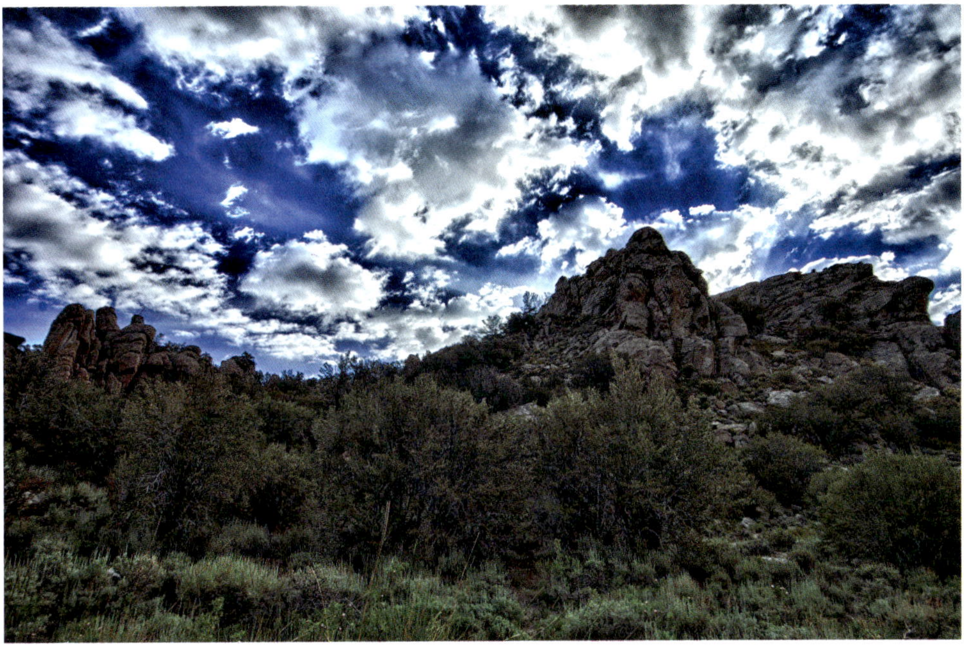

Figure 8.2

The Control Point tool is found in the Control Palette in the Selective Adjustments section below the Global Adjustments, as shown in Figure 8.3.

If the Selective Adjustments section is closed, as it is in Figure 8.4, click on the twirler next to the Selective Adjustments title to open it, as shown in Figure 8.3. If there is no check mark in the box next to the twirler, click in the box to place a check mark there. The check mark indicates that the Selective Adjustments Control Point tool is active.

Now that the section is open, you can see the Add Control Point disc icon next to it. Click the disc icon and you are ready to add your first Control Point.

tip

If the area you are targeting is very small and you want to be accurate with the target placement, before you click the disc, tap the spacebar to zoom to your preset magnification and use the Navigator to find your position. Then click the Add Control Point disc icon, release the mouse, and click in the precise position in the zoomed image.

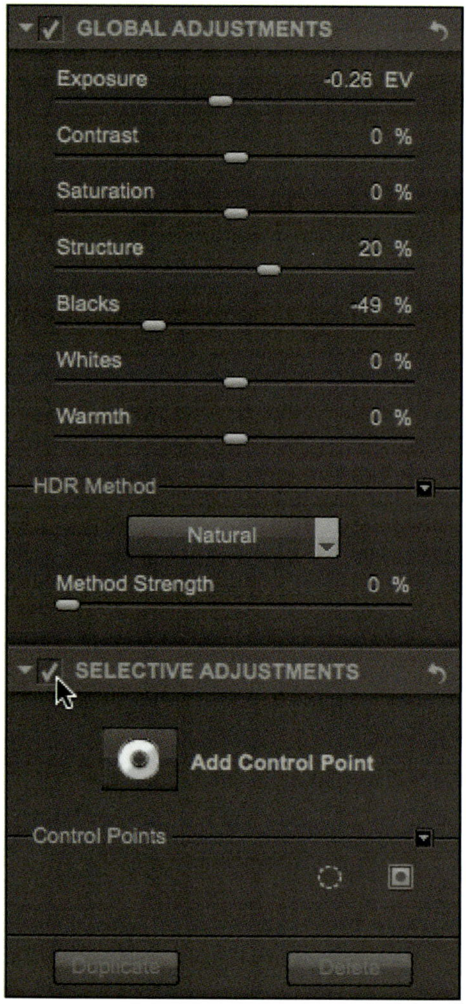

Figure 8.3

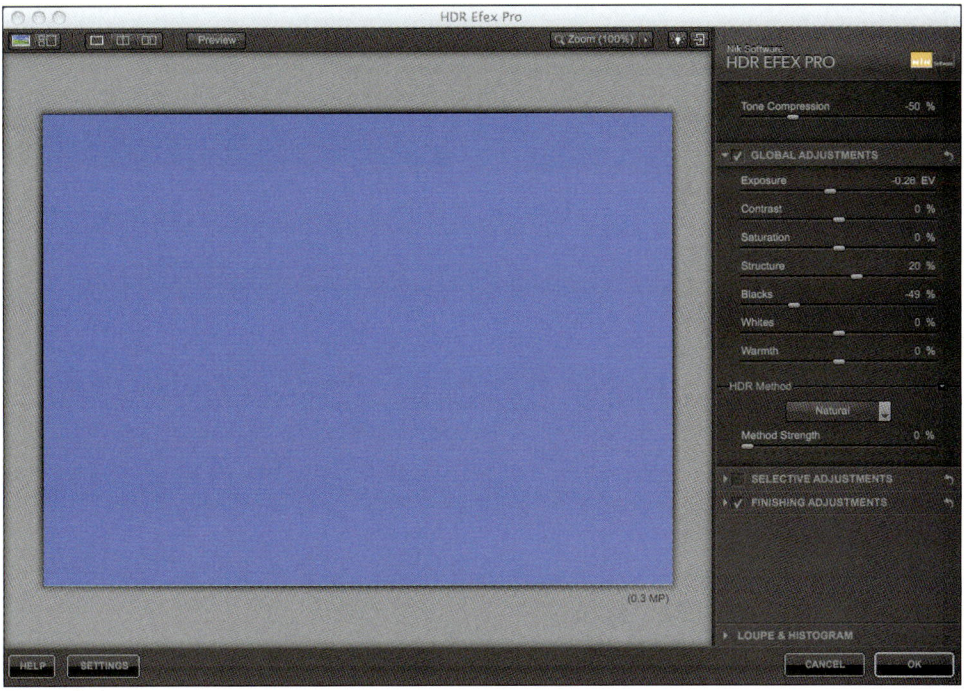

Figure 8.4

Adding a Single Control Point

With the Selective Adjustments section open and the Control Point activation check box selected, you can add a Control Point to your HDR image.

Click the disc icon, and then release your mouse button. Your mouse pointer will turn into a target-looking icon. Position the target over the area of the image to which you want to make the local adjustment and click again to drop the target onto the image. You don't need to be all that precise because it is easy to reposition the center of the Control Point by clicking and dragging it around.

tip

I prefer to use keyboard shortcuts to place Control Points. Press Ctrl/⌘+Shift+A to place a Control Point target on the image. Position the target with your mouse, and click to drop it.

When you first place the Control Point, it will show a minimum of adjustments like the ones in Figure 8.5. These are the adjustments you will use most often.

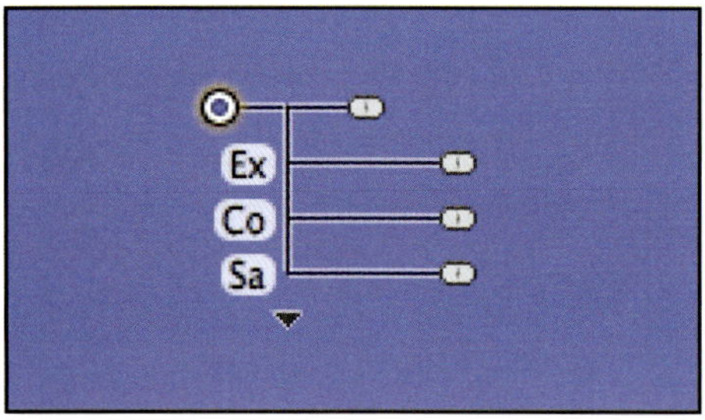

Figure 8.5

In summary, here are the steps to add a single Control Point:

1. **Make sure that the Selective Adjustments section is open.** If not, click the twirler to open it.
2. **Make sure there is a check mark in the box next to the twirler.** If not, click in the box to activate the Selective Adjustments tool.
3. **If the spot on which you want to place the Control Point isn't large enough, tap the spacebar on your keyboard to zoom to your preset magnification.**
4. **Use the keyboard shortcut Ctrl/⌘ +Shift+A to add a Control Point target to the image.**
5. **Using your mouse, drag the target to the position you want it and click to drop it in place.**

Expanding and Collapsing a Control Point

At the end of the vertical line in the Control Point is a twirler. It could be above or below the abbreviation for the third adjustment, depending on how close to the top or bottom edge of the image you have positioned the Control Point. To see all the possible adjustments, you need to click on the twirler and the other five appear, as shown in Figure 8.6. If you don't want to use them, you can collapse the last five by clicking on the twirler again.

see also

Chapter 9 discusses in detail the eight adjustments and how to use them.

tip

Press E to expand or contract any active Control Point.

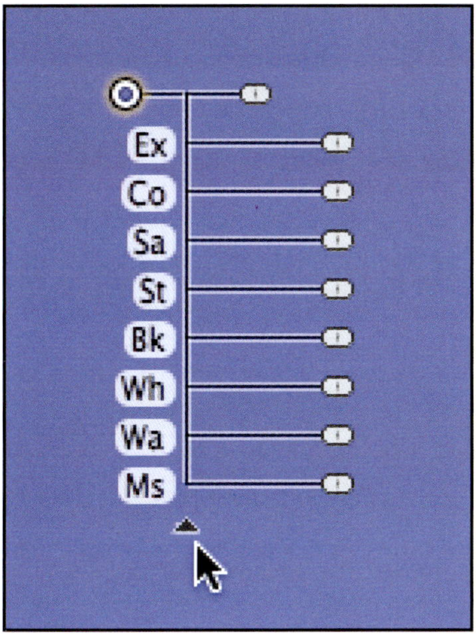

Figure 8.6

Depending on where in the image you place the Control Point, the adjustment sliders may be arranged vertically above or below the point itself, or horizontally to the left or right of the vertical line, as shown in Figure 8.7.

This can be confusing at first, but you see in Chapter 9 that moving away from the vertical line increases the adjustment and moving toward the line decreases it.

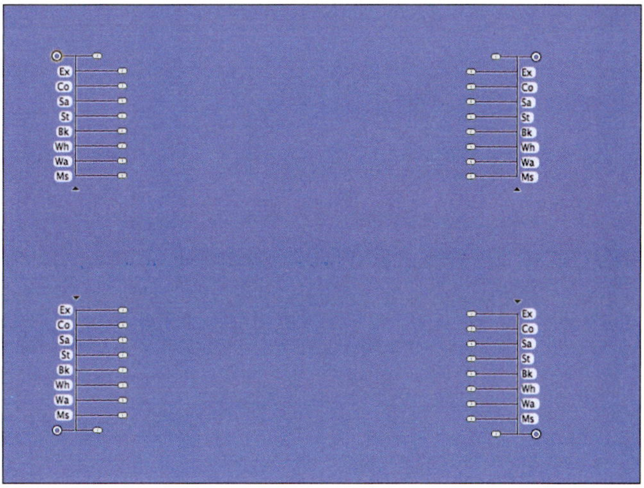
Figure 8.7

Previewing a Control Point

If you look back in the Selective Adjustments section after you have added a Control Point, you will see the entry Control Point 1 under the heading Control Points, as shown in Figure 8.8.

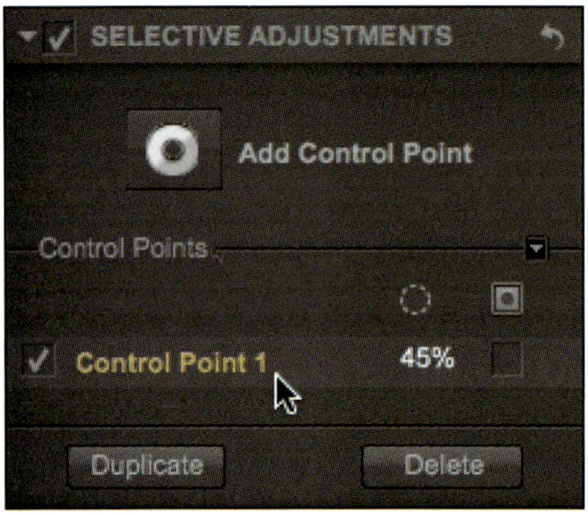

Figure 8.8

If your palette looks like Figure 8.9, click the twirler in the Control Points line and it will open to show your Control Point.

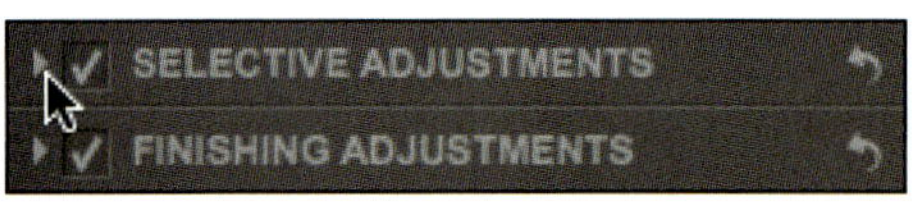

Figure 8.9

To the left of your Control Point 1 is a box with a check mark in it. This indicates that the adjustments you made using Control Point 1 are visible in the image in the Main Image Window. If you had made an adjustment to the default settings of the Control Point after you had placed it, you could deselect this check box for a look at the image without the Control Point adjustment.

tip

You can also see before and after views by clicking and holding the Preview button in the View Modes menu bar. This temporarily removes all the Control Point adjustments as well as all the global adjustments.

When you first place the Control Point, its name in the palette is highlighted in gold. This indicates that it is the active Control Point.

To the right of the Control Point 1 entry in Figure 8.8 is a number and an empty check box. The number indicates the percentage of the image that the Control Point is affecting.

The check box to the right of the percentage is one of the coolest things about U Point technology. When you click in it, a check mark appears. In the Main Image Window, your HDR image changes to a contrasty monochrome version.

What you are seeing in the Main Image Window is the mask that HDR Efex Pro created when you placed the Control Point. The white areas are where the Control Point adjustments act at 100%, while the black areas indicate where the adjustments have no effect. Areas of gray show the relative effect that the adjustments have on those areas.

Figure 8.10 shows what the selection area looks like when I place a Control Point in the sky.

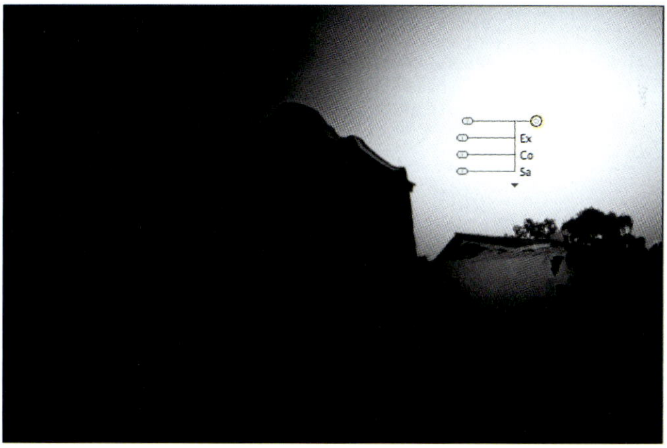

Figure 8.10

Adding Multiple Control Points

Once you see how easy it is to add Control Points for local adjustments, you will find it difficult to limit yourself to a single Control Point. I rarely complete an HDR image without multiple Control Points.

You can add up to 64 Control Points to the image. And if you choose to open your HDR image as a Smart Object and you save it as a Smart Object, all of your Control Points and their settings are also saved.

see also

Information about opening your HDR image as a Photoshop Smart Object is in Chapter 3. More information on saving the final HDR image as a Smart Object is in Chapter 10.

Using multiple Control Points gives you extremely precise control over your image. Each Control Point you add is "smarter" than the previous ones. This is because they "learn" what precise image information you are trying to adjust from the Control Points that you placed previously.

This learning occurs because the U Point technology looks at all the information in the image at the point that you select. This information includes brightness, contrast, RGB values, and more. This information is then used to precisely target other areas within the range you have set for the Control Point.

When multiple Control Points are close together or overlap, the U Point technology is able to target the image values even more precisely. The interaction is so precise that overlapping Control Points add or remove enhancements from nearby or overlapping Control Points just as a single Control Point does with global adjustments.

Figure 8.11 illustrates this interaction. I added a Control Point to increase the exposure in the upper left of the sky. Because of the feathered edge of the Control Point and the reflection of the sky in the building, the upper left of the building also becomes lighter.

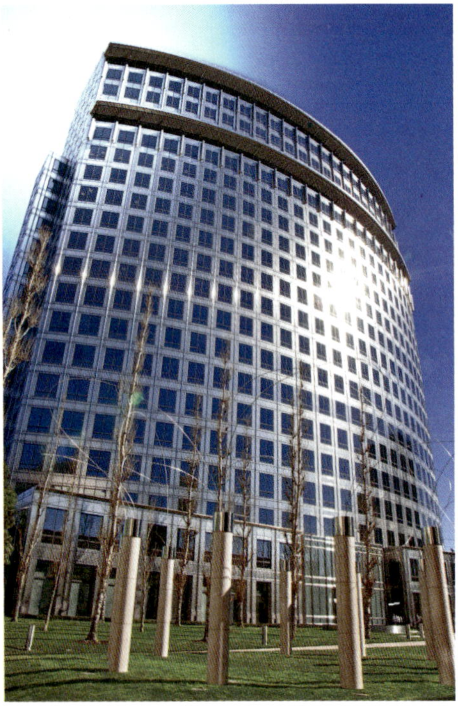

Figure 8.11

By adding multiple Control Points in the building at their default settings, which is no adjustments, I removed the exposure from the building, as shown in Figure 8.12.

For comparison with Figure 8.12, the original photo of the building without the exposure adjustment is shown in Figure 8.13.

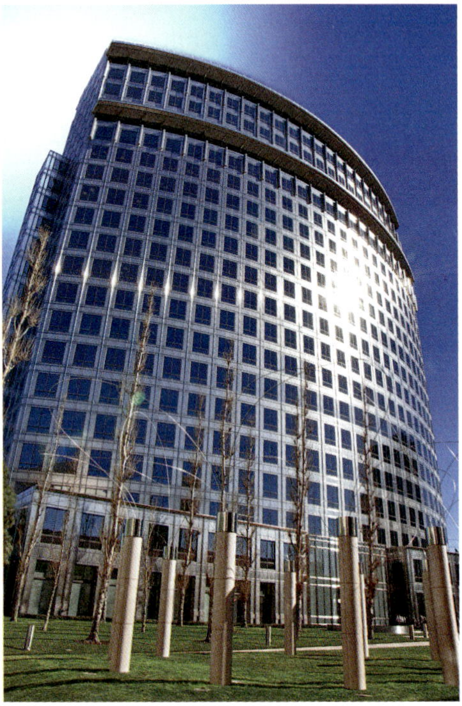

Figure 8.12

But I'm getting ahead of myself. In the next chapter, you put all this information about Control Points to practical use.

Creating multiple Control Points

Creating multiple Control Points is as simple as repeating the steps you used to create a single Control Point. But when you do, some additional things happen in the Selective Adjustments section, and some additional possibilities open up to control them.

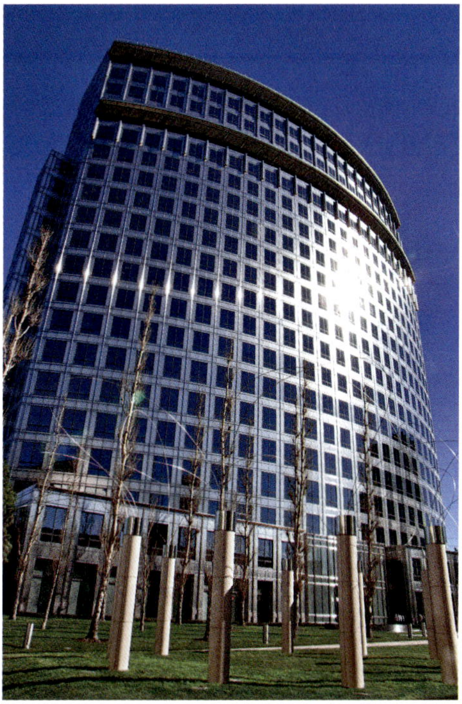

Figure 8.13

Using the keyboard shortcut Ctrl/⌘+Shift+A, I added two Control Points in Figure 8.14, placing one in the right area of the sky and the other in the left. The first is shown by a dot in the sky while the second is shown in its default state of adjustment.

tip

To show the default or expanded adjustments for multiple Control Points, Shift+click on each one.

In the Selective Adjustments section shown in Figure 8.15 you can see that both Control Points are listed.

You can also see that Control Point 2 is highlighted in gold, indicating that it is the active Control Point. The last one you add is always the active one until you select or add another.

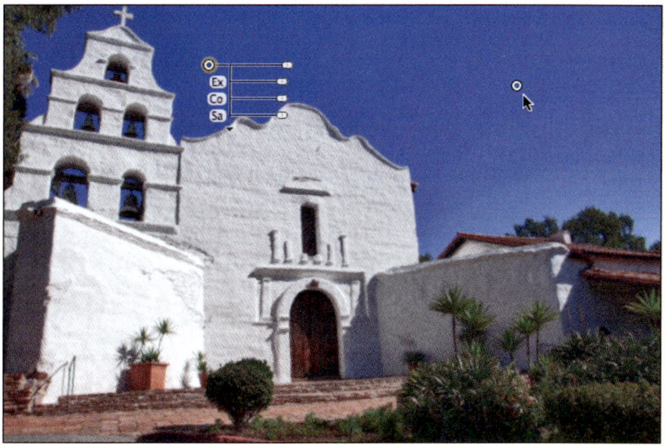

Figure 8.14

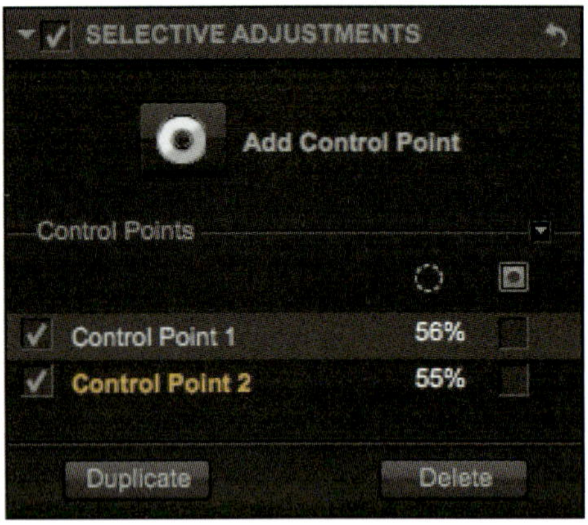

Figure 8.15

It often makes sense to use multiple Control Points rather than one large one. This minimizes the influence of your adjustments in areas that you don't want adjusted. This also saves you from adding Control Points to remove adjustments where they spill over into areas that didn't need adjustment.

Figure 8.16 shows three Control Points I placed in an image with a large area of blue sky in order to select all of the sky. The accompanying mask view in Figure 8.17 illustrates how precise this technique really is. You can even see that the slivers of sky visible around the bells in the mission bell tower are selected.

There are four ways to add multiple Control Points. My least favorite way is using the standard keyboard Copy and Paste commands Ctrl/⌘+C and Ctrl/⌘+V. By this technique, once you copy the Control Point, you don't know that you have it until you paste it. When you do paste it using the keyboard shortcut Ctrl/⌘+V, you still can't see it until you click to drop it into its new position. Too many steps for me. However, this technique is fast if you need to add the same Control Point to many locations in the image.

A second technique is to select either the Control Point in the image or its name in the palette and click Duplicate in the palette. This creates a

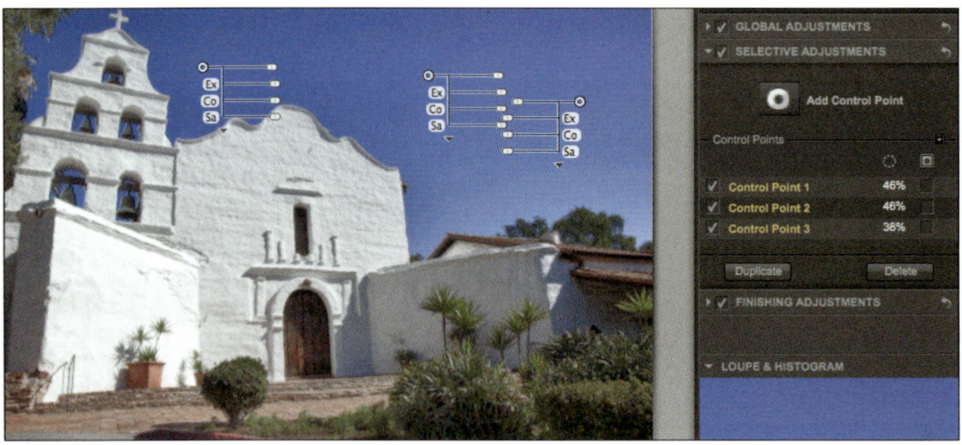

Figure 8.16

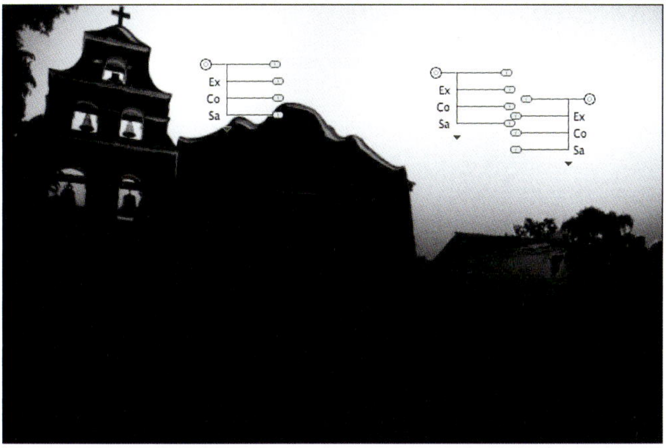

Figure 8.17

Control Point icon right next to the original Control Point. Then all you need to do is use your mouse to drag it to its new position.

Another way to duplicate a Control Point is with a keyboard command. After clicking the Control Point in the image, press Ctrl/⌘+D. This method places the new Control Point icon next to the original (and next to your mouse pointer), making it easy to drag it to its new position.

The fourth and quickest way to duplicate a Control Point is press and hold Alt/Option, click on the Control Point, and drag to the new position. The original Control Point remains and the duplicate appears at the new location.

see also

Appendix A has a list of keyboard shortcuts.

Now that you have multiple Control Points, it would be nice to be able to preview the areas that they cover. Fortunately, you can.

One way is to treat each Control Point individually and click on the box to the right of its name to show the monochrome mask. But there is an easier way.

Above and in line with the boxes that you select to show individual mask previews is a small square icon. Clicking it selects all the check boxes below it and a monochrome image appears in the Main Image Window showing all the areas of the image covered by Control Points. Your image will look like the one shown in Figure 8.18. If you have so many Control Points that the entire image looks white, clicking check marks on and off shows you the area covered by those particular Control Points.

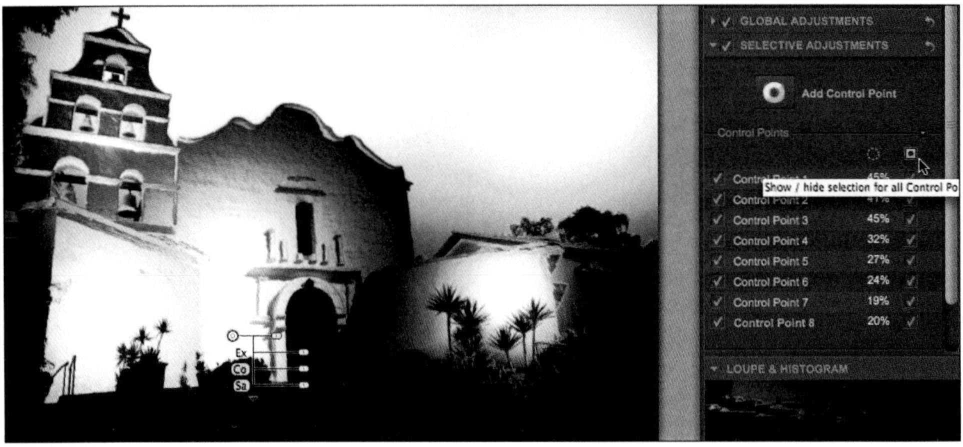

Figure 8.18

To see the adjustment settings for a Control Point if they aren't visible, click on its name. To see the adjustment settings for more than one Control Point, Ctrl/⌘+click the names in the palette or the icons in the image. To select consecutive Control Points in the palette, click the first and Shift+click the last.

Synchronizing Control Points

When you have an image such as the one in Figure 8.13, where you are using multiple Control Points to adjust the blue sky or other continuous areas, you usually want those continuous areas to look exactly alike. This means you must set all the Control Point adjustments exactly alike. HDR Efex Pro makes it easy to do this.

One way is to duplicate a Control Point as many times as you need to and place these clones by using the mask view until the continuous area is evenly toned in the monochrome mask. If you never need to make any further adjustments to the Control Points, you're done.

But I'm typically trying different tweaks and adjustments all the time on every image. HDR Efex Pro makes it easy and quick to try different approaches and, with its accurate preview of the final results, it lends itself to experimentation. So you can synchronize Control Points when they cover a continuous area.

As you have seen in other cases with Control Points, there are multiple ways to do this. You can Shift+click or Ctrl/⌘+click their icons or names in the palette to make all of them active. Then you can make your adjustments to all of them at once and move on to your next step.

But if you want to perform other adjustments on all of them later, you need to repeat the process each time. A better way to proceed is to gather them into one Control Point group. When you do this they are linked together for the entire session or forever if the HDR image is a Smart Object.

To group multiple Control Points, you need to select the Control Points so that they are all active, and then press Ctrl/⌘+G to group them. Rather than being listed individually in the palette, they are listed as Group 1 (or Group 2, and so on), as shown in Figure 8.19.

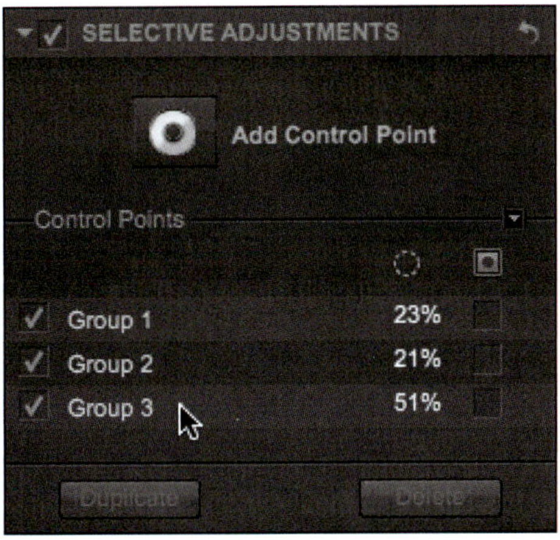

Figure 8.19

There is an even easier way to group Control Points in many images. Because they are almost always in a line, or closely gathered together, you can hold down your mouse button and draw a bounding box around them, as shown in Figure 8.20. After you select them, press Ctrl/⌘+G to group them together.

If you ever need to ungroup the Control Points, select the group icon in the image or the group name in the palette, and press Ctrl/⌘+Shift+G.

In summary, here are the steps to add and synchronize multiple Control Points:

1. **Make sure that the Selective Adjustments section is open.** If not, click on the twirler to open it.
2. **Make sure there is a check mark in the box next to the twirler.** If not, click in the box to activate the Selective Adjustments tool.
3. **If the spot on which you want to place the first Control Point isn't large enough, tap the spacebar to zoom to your preset magnification.**
4. **Press Ctrl/⌘+Shift+A to add your first Control Point target to the image.**

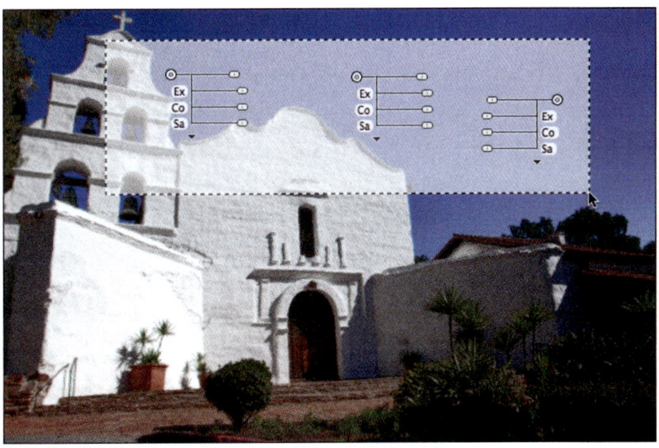

Figure 8.20

5 **If you need additional Control Points to synchronize with this first one, press Ctrl/⌘+D to create as many clones of the first Control Point as you need.**

6 **Drag these clones to the positions where they are needed.** If you are zoomed to 100% in the image, use the Navigator to move the image to each position.

7 **Make sure that you have positioned the clones correctly by selecting the mask check box and looking at the mask in the Main Image Window.**

8 **If everything is good, draw a bounding box around them with your mouse, release the mouse button, and press Ctrl/⌘+G to group them.**

9 **If you need additional uncloned Control Points when you finish your adjustments with these, repeat Steps 1 through 4 to place them.**

Deleting a Control Point

I don't often find that I need to delete a Control Point. I'm usually adding them, or, if I'm not happy with one, dragging it to a new position to adjust something else.

But there are times when you might need to delete one, and again, there are several ways. In the Selective Adjustments section, there is a Delete button, as shown Figure 8.21. Click the Control Point name in the palette until it turns gold and then click Delete to permanently remove that Control Point. The same technique works with a Group.

My technique is even quicker. Select the Control Point or Points or the Group you want to delete in the Main Image Window and press Delete or Backspace.

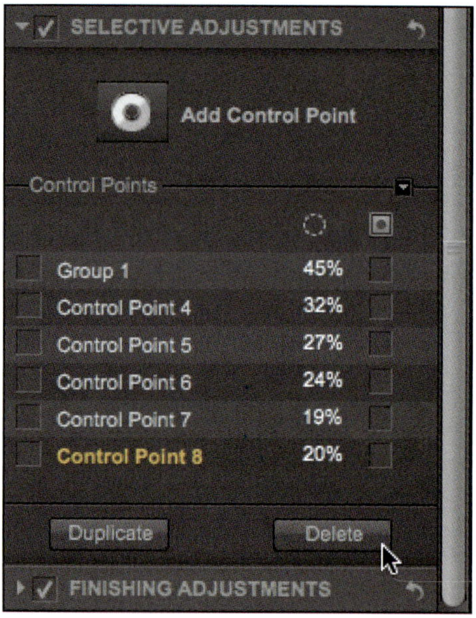

Figure 8.21

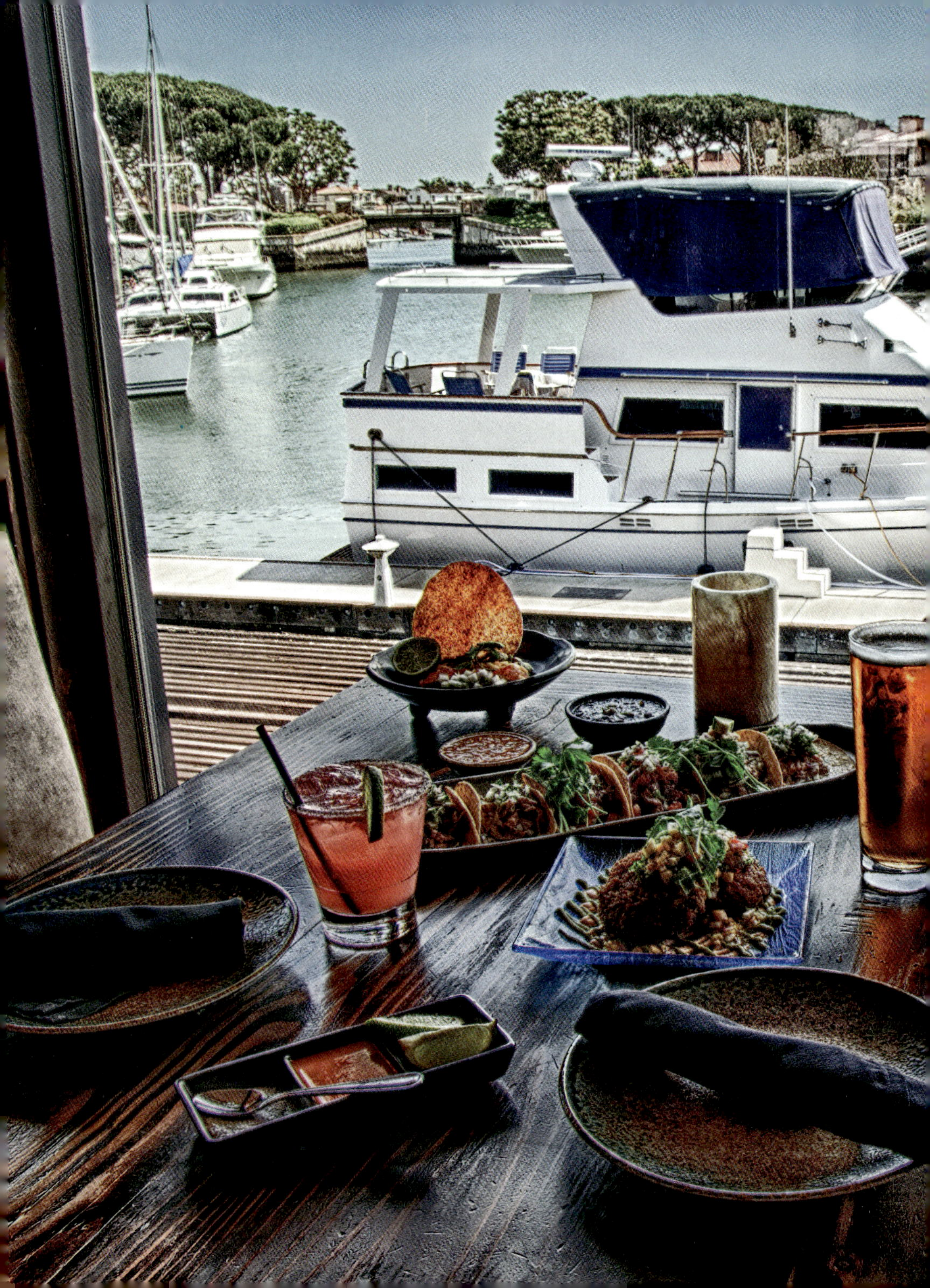

9

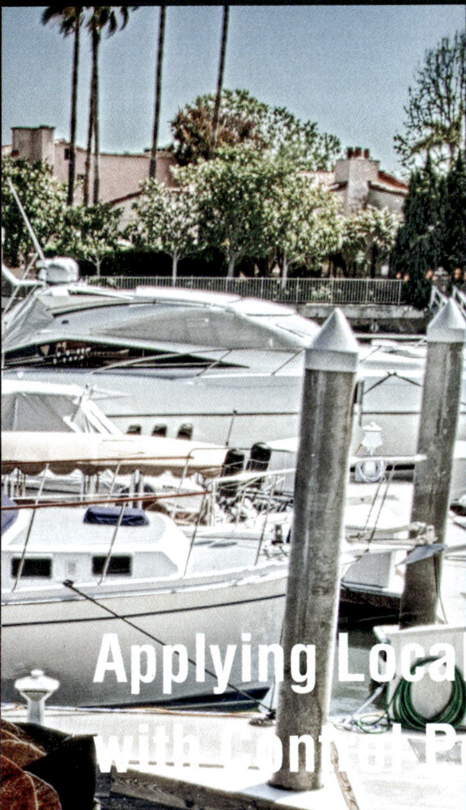

Applying Local Corrections with Control Points

Unlike the global adjustments in Chapters 6 and 7, local, or selective, corrections are changes that affect only a portion of the HDR image. As effective as the global adjustments are in HDR Efex Pro, every HDR image can benefit from additional corrections to local areas.

Nik Software's patented U Point technology changed the entire process of applying local corrections with the introduction of Control Points. Control Points provide the same adjustments that are available globally, but with the ability to apply or remove the global adjustments in selective areas. This is as simple as clicking on an area of the image and making the adjustment.

Local Corrections Overview

After you adjust tone compression, select the HDR Method Strength, and make global adjustments, it is quite common that there are areas in the image that would benefit from additional adjustment.

Using a tool in the Global Adjustments section to adjust these local areas would result in the adjustment being applied to the entire image rather than to the local area. For situations where local adjustments are needed, Control Points provide an easy way to make highly localized changes.

The need for local changes can arise for many reasons. For example, the global controls in HDR Efex Pro, while creating an interesting overall effect, can have unwanted results locally. At very high and very low tone compression settings, for example, local contrast is decreased. While the overall look may be what you are after, the image may need more contrast in some areas to avoid looking flat.

Similarly, many combinations of tone compression and Method Strength blend the exposure of the center of interest into the rest of the image when you want the center of interest to be brighter. The human eye is naturally drawn to the brightest point in the image.

HDR image processing also affects color saturation, but not equally for all colors. Reds in particular tend to become oversaturated far more quickly than other colors. For some subjects this is appropriate, but when there are small areas of red in the image away from the center of interest, their saturation can draw the eye away from where you want it.

Greens have a slightly different problem, but this problem too can be minimized with a local adjustment in saturation. What our eyes see as green actually has a lot more yellow in it than green. When an HDR image is created, a green forest often has an unsightly yellow cast. While there are no global or local adjustments for specific colors in HDR Efex Pro, the yellow cast can be minimized by decreasing the local saturation or warmth setting where the yellow cast is too strong.

Creating Control Points in the image makes it easy to perform local corrections for these and other adjustments without leaving HDR Efex Pro. Control Points provide the same adjustments available in the Global Adjustments section. Additionally, each Control Point includes an adjustment for HDR Method Strength along with the Size slider that controls the diameter of the area affected by the Control Point.

The following adjustments are available in every Control Point:

- Exposure
- Contrast
- Saturation
- Structure
- Blacks
- Whites
- Warmth
- Method Strength

The best approach for using Control Points is generally to use them in the order in which HDR Efex Pro presents them, always beginning with the Size slider. It won't be necessary to use all the adjustments for every Control Point, but applying them in the correct order saves time going back and forth to readjust sliders.

Moving the Control Point sliders in the proper direction with your initial adjustment is a time-saver also. Depending on the position of the Control Point, the adjustments appear in four possible orientations along the vertical line. In some orientations, moving a slider to the left increases the adjustment. In other orientations, moving the same slider to the left decreases the adjustment. But in all orientations, moving the slider *away* from the vertical line increases the adjustment and moving the slider *toward* the vertical line decreases the adjustment.

Adjusting Exposure

Changing exposure is the most common local adjustment. HDR Efex Pro tone maps the image series according to the mathematical rules that are incorporated in the program and based on the exposure information in the images. The result, even in the default HDR preset that maps tones most widely across the tonal values, may not match your interpretation of the scene.

The exposure adjustment may be very simple. Figure 9.1 is an HDR image created in HDR Efex Pro with the Default preset.

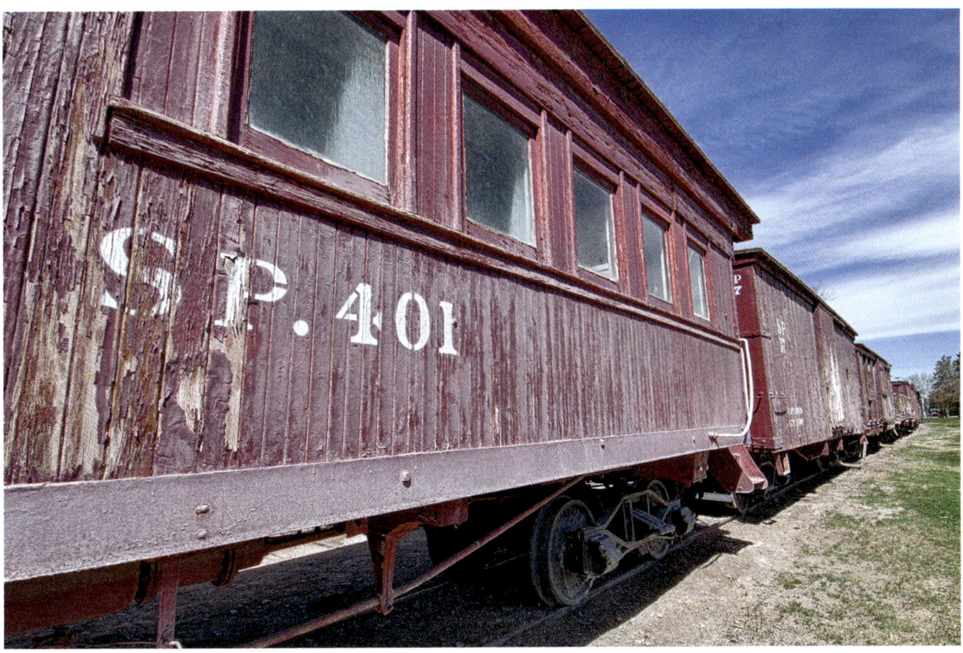

Figure 9.1

After making a tone compression adjustment and global adjustments to exposure and contrast, the image looks good overall, but the undercarriage of the train is too dark, as shown in Figure 9.2.

Adding the Control Points shown in Figure 9.3 brings out the detail that is lost with the global adjustments I made. Control Point 5, which is not highlighted in gold in the Control Points list, is one that I added in the shadow area next to the wheels. It has no adjustment applied and serves to prevent the exposure adjustments to the undercarriage from opening up the shadow on the ground.

tip

The quickest way to add a Control Point is to press Ctrl/⌘+Shift+A, the keyboard shortcut to add a Control Point, rather than clicking the Control Point disc icon.

With all the tonal information available in an HDR image, it is easy to overdo exposure adjustments. I easily could have made the undercarriage so light that it would look totally unnatural, as if it were not in shadow at all. While doing so will create wild effects, it wouldn't be right for where I wanted to go with this image. Figure 9.4 shows the final processed result.

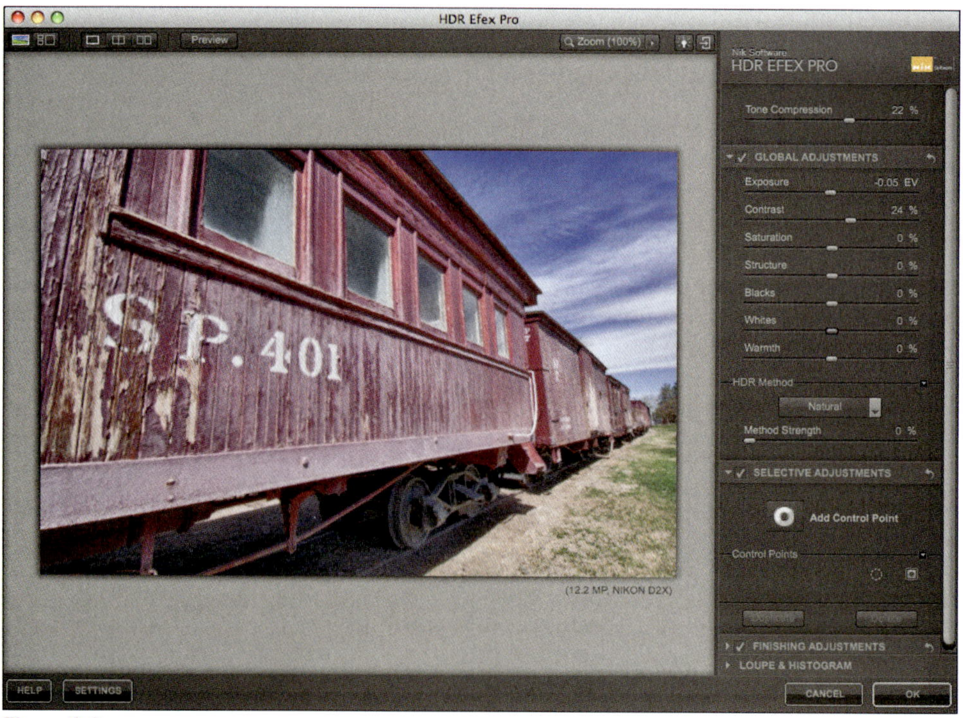

Figure 9.2

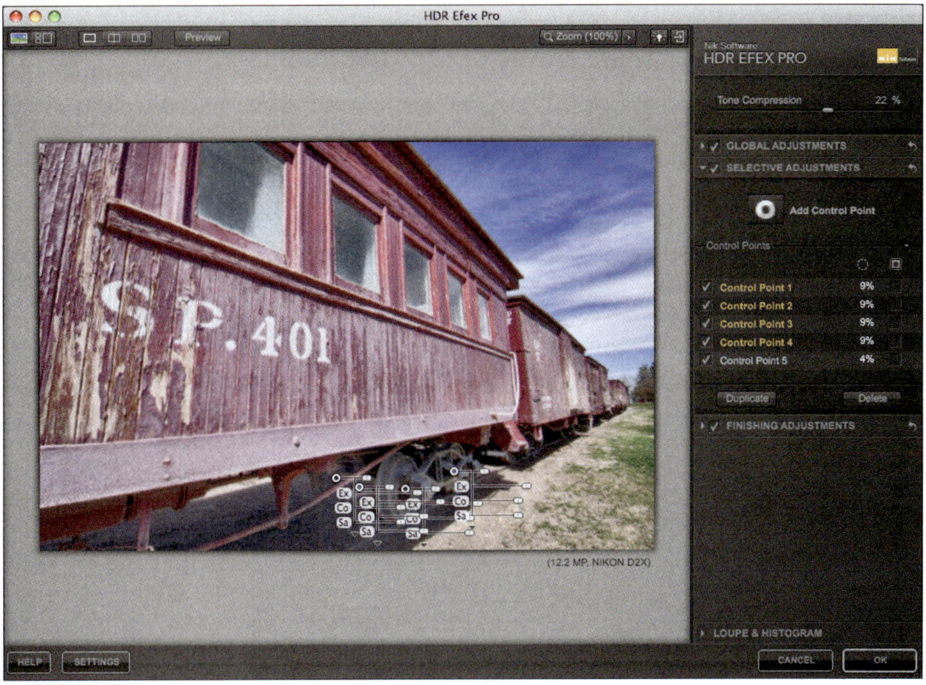

Figure 9.3

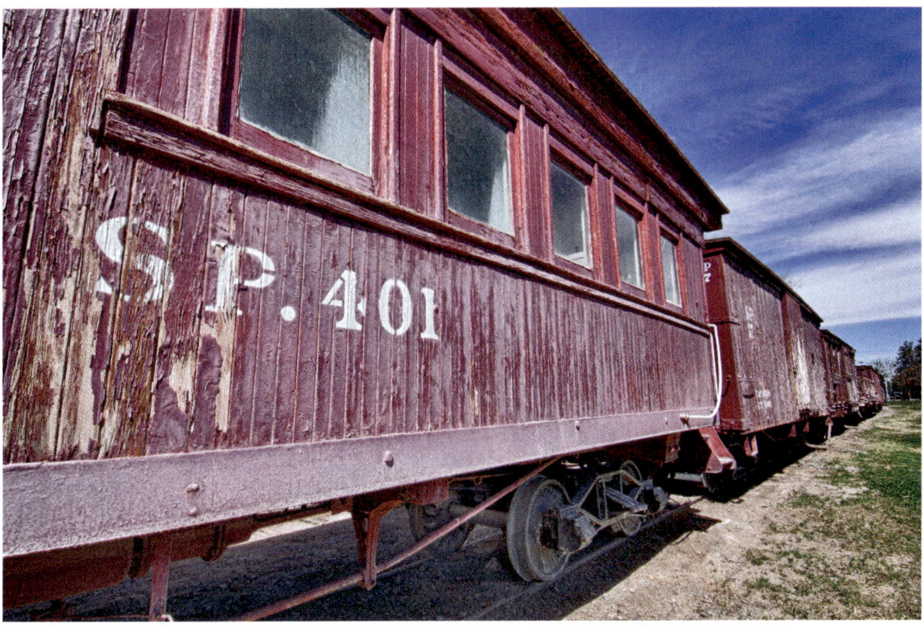

Figure 9.4

Sometimes you come up against an image where the exposure adjustment is far more complex. Figure 9.5 is the final processed HDR image of a church interior where I wanted to have detail in the old church pews and walls as well as in the stained glass window.

I shot the interior in the afternoon with the sun shining in through the window. I could have made my work easier by shooting it in the morning when the contrast is lower, but I wanted the feeling of the stained glass window lighting the interior.

The HDR is the result of a nine-exposure image series with each exposure separated by 1 EV, a 9-stop bracket. I was after a realistic look, so I chose the Realistic (Balanced) preset as a starting point. This first step is shown in Figure 9.6.

With global adjustments, I knew I could make the walls, ceiling, and pews look the way I wanted, but the stained glass window needed a lot of local adjustment. If I had chosen a preset that used lots of tone compression, such as Friendly Scenery or Strong Counterlight, I would have less need for local exposure adjustments, but the realistic look would be lost.

Figure 9.7 shows the Control Points I used to bring back detail in the stained glass window. Those Control Points in the window all have negative exposure values, but the exact values vary because different areas of the window required different adjustments. Many of the exposure adjustments in this image use the full –3 EV range of the Control Point Exposure slider.

To make all the adjustments I wanted, I used all 64 of the available Control Points. If there were more, I would have used them to darken the wall to the left of the stained glass window as you look at it.

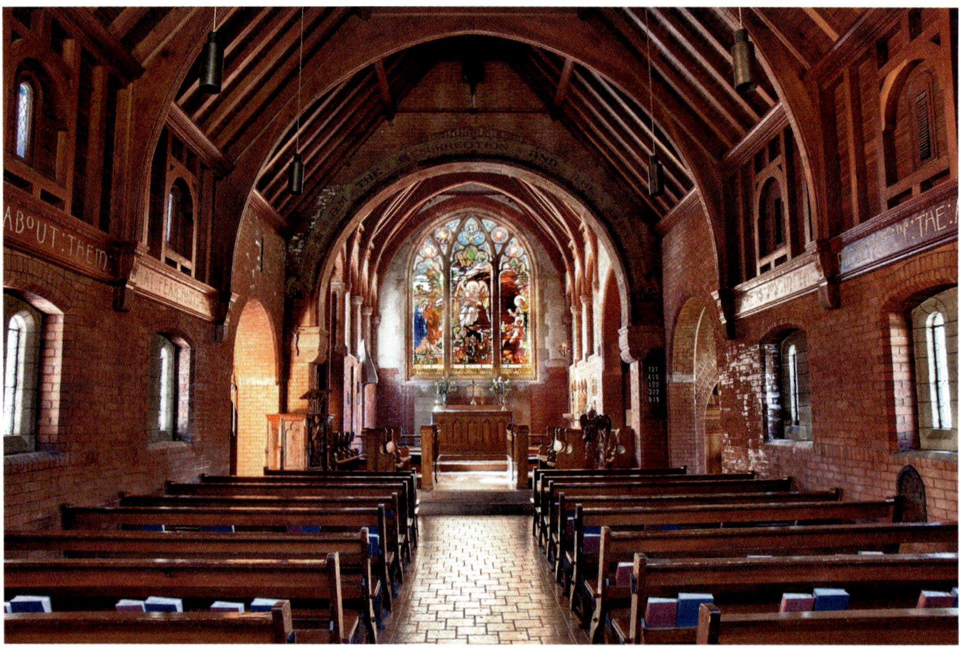

Figure 9.5

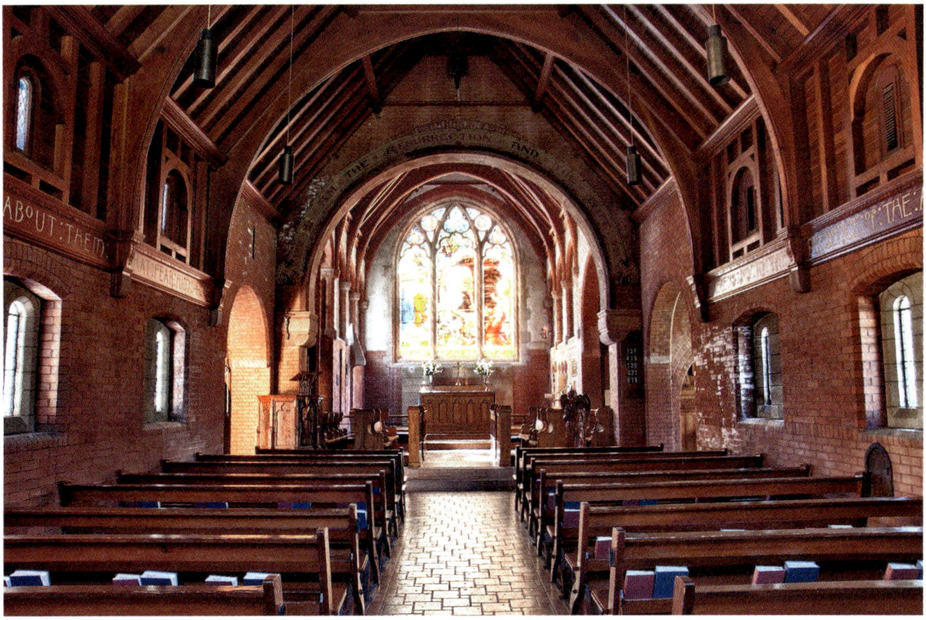

Figure 9.6

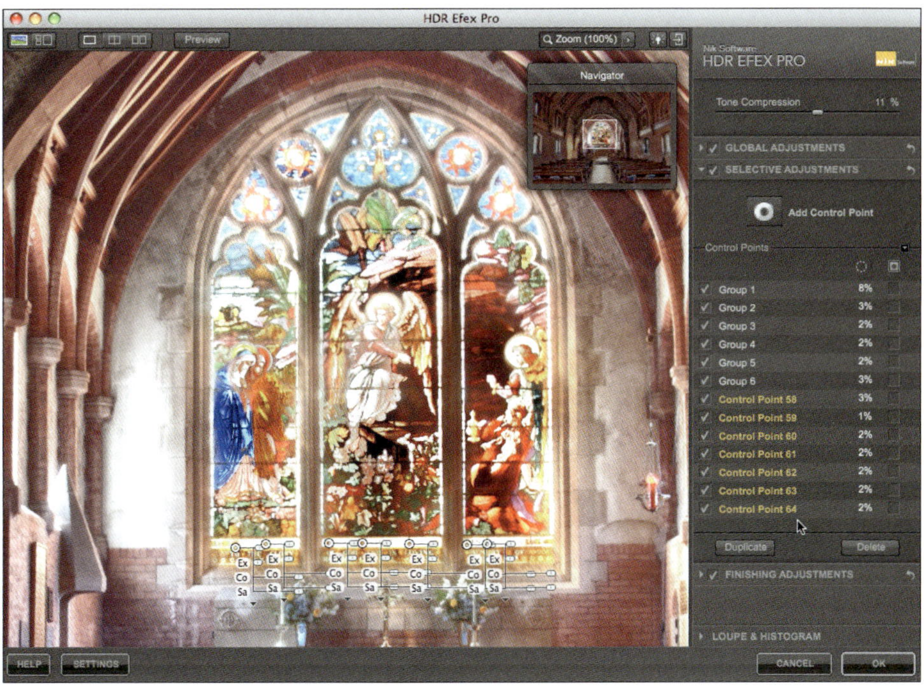

Figure 9.7

Adjusting Contrast

Control Point contrast adjustments are often used along with an exposure adjustment. The combination is very effective if you want to draw the viewer's eye to the center of interest. This is the case with the processed HDR image in Figure 9.8.

I like the potential sense of depth in the photo with the foreground tree and the distant mountain with the sun behind it. But the default processed HDR image in Figure 9.8 lacks contrast and depth, due in large part to the snowstorm that is creating the interesting clouds.

Selecting the Postcard Paradise preset rather than the Default preset and adjusting tone compression, Method Strength, and a few global adjustments helps the contrast, as shown in Figure 9.9, but the image still lacks depth.

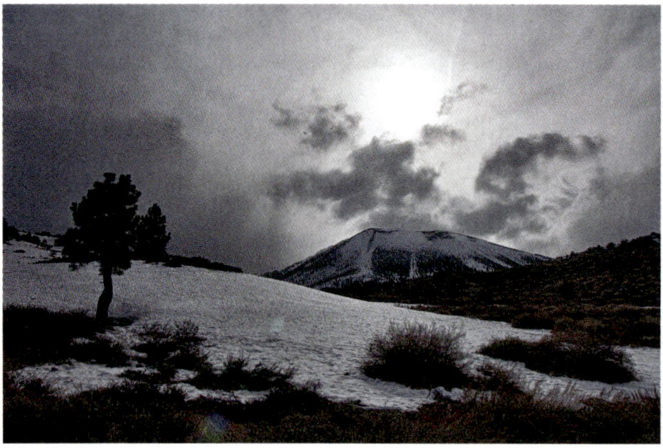

Figure 9.8

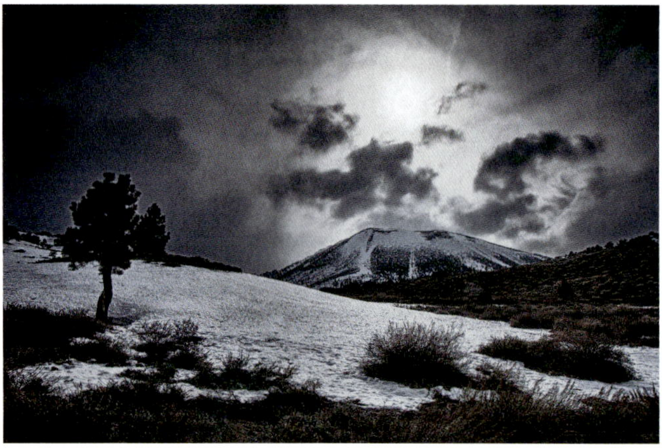

Figure 9.9

To draw the eye to the mountain, I added two groups of Control Points. Group 1 added exposure and contrast to the snow on the mountain. I didn't add any Control Points to the sky to subtract these adjustments because I like the "glow" that the adjustments create above the mountain. This glow is a result of the soft, feathered edge of every Control Point. Adding a new Control Point with no adjustment creates a harder edge and minimizes the glow.

see also

Using a Control Point to control other Control Points is discussed in Chapter 8.

I placed the Control Points in Group 2 on the dark areas of the mountain and gave them all a –1 EV exposure adjustment and a +25% contrast adjustment. The combination of these two groups lowered local brightness in the dark rock areas and added contrast to the mountain.

With this accomplished, I added a Control Point with a +1.5 EV adjustment to brighten the foreground tree relative to the rest of the scene. Again, I let the Control Point adjustment feather off naturally so there is a little glow around the tree. The Control Points are shown in Figure 9.10 and the final processed result in Figure 9.11.

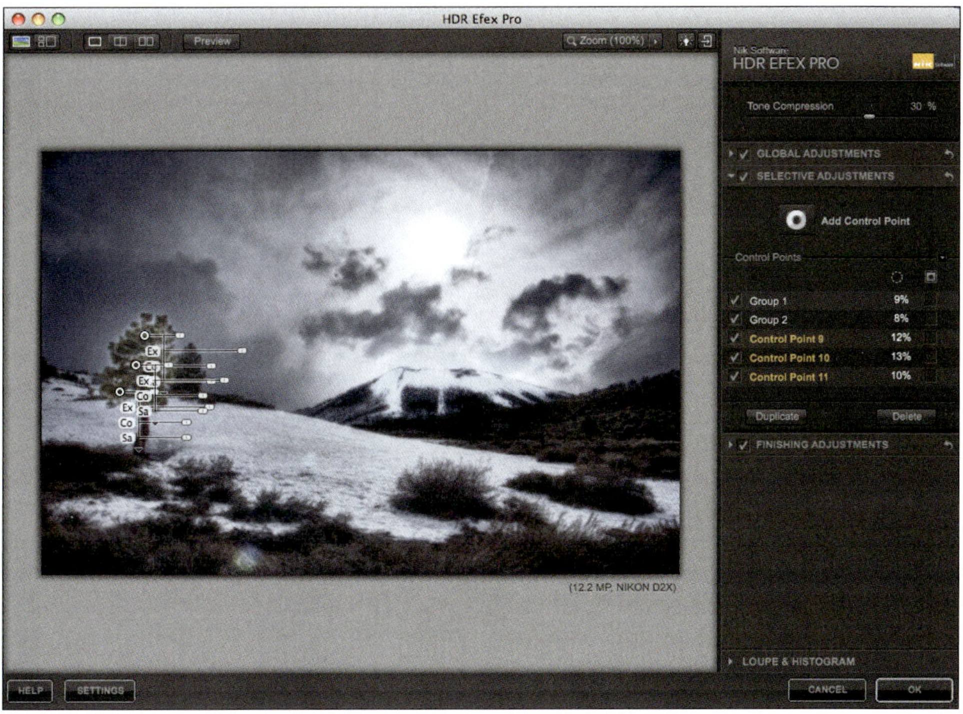

Figure 9.10

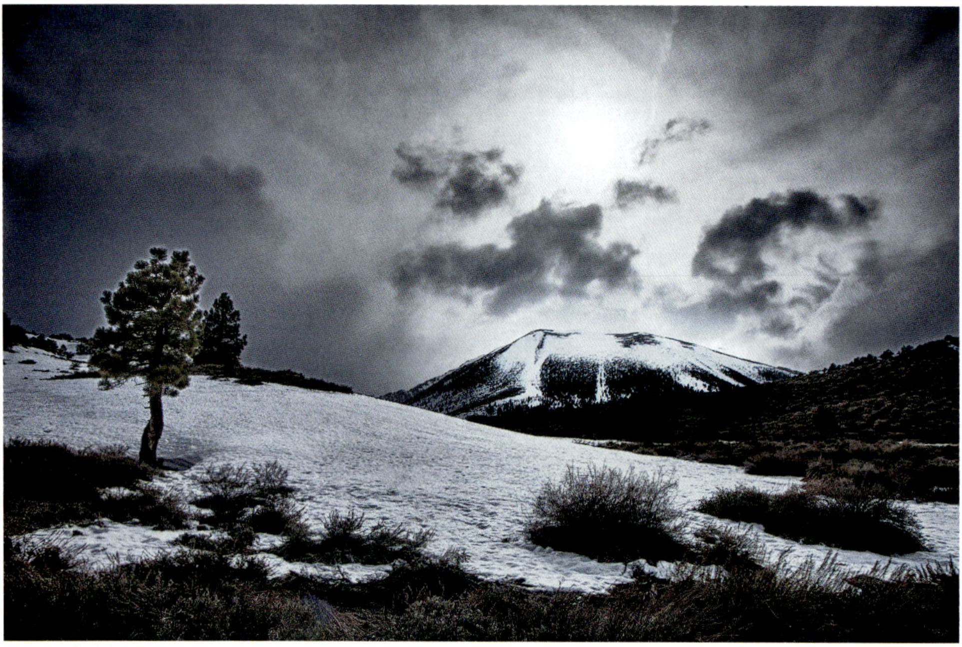

Figure 9.11

Adjusting Saturation

Depending on the preset you choose, the color saturation in different areas of the image may be too high or not high enough for your taste. Adjusting saturation globally to correct this can result in other areas of the image becoming over- or undersaturated. Adjusting saturation locally is often the better solution.

The Saturation slider in a Control Point is used to increase or decrease saturation in selective areas. If the preset and the global adjustments in your image result in most of the image looking good but some areas being undersaturated, a positive adjustment is needed. On the other hand, if some areas are oversaturated, a negative adjustment in saturation is called for.

I find myself using the Saturation slider in a Control Point most often to increase the saturation of a blue sky. You don't always have amazing cloud structures when you shoot image series for HDR imaging — sometimes you just have a flat blue sky.

When HDR Efex Pro processes the image series with a range of blue sky from deep blue to white or nearly white, the result is a midtone blue. Not unattractive, just boring, as the sky is in Figure 9.12. Even after I chose the Vibrant Details and Colors preset and adjusted tone compression, Method Strength and global adjustments, the sky didn't look good.

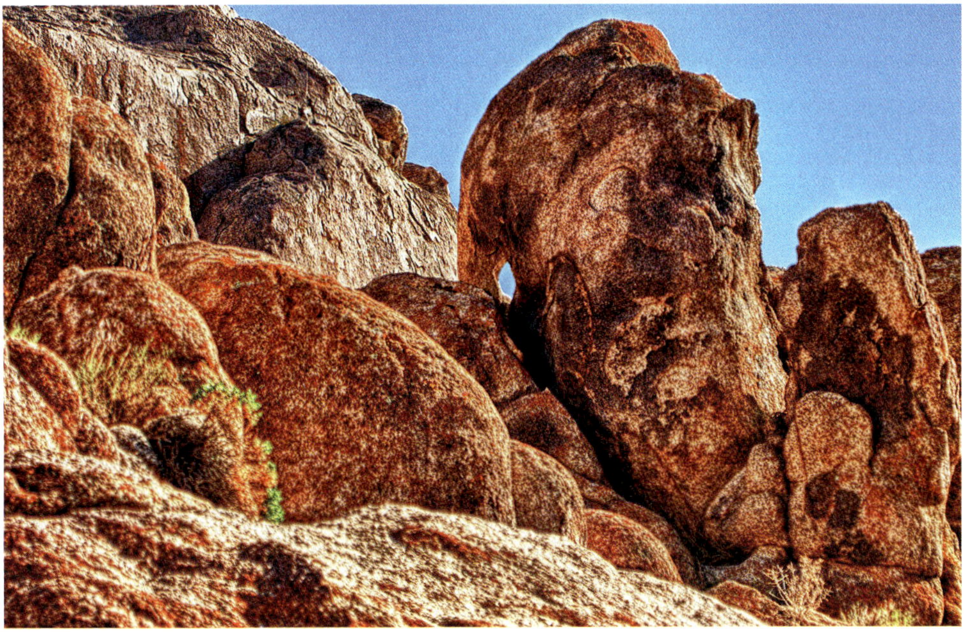

Figure 9.12

I added my first Control Point to the right area of the sky and lowered the exposure by –0.6 EV. Adjusting the Contrast slider had no effect because there is no contrast to speak of. Increasing the Saturation slider to +45% created a good strong blue to complement the warm rocks produced by the Vibrant Details and Colors preset.

I duplicated the first Control Point using the keyboard shortcut Ctrl/⌘+D and added another Control Point to the left part of the sky. I thought I would be finished at this point, but I noticed that the sliver of sky between the two areas was lighter than the two sides even though the control areas of the two Control Points overlapped there. So I duplicated the second Control Point and added a third one, as shown in Figure 9.13.

Figure 9.14 shows the final processed HDR image.

tip

If you duplicate a Control Point, you can adjust the sliders for the original and the clones simultaneously if they are all highlighted in the Control Points palette or if you have grouped them with the keyboard shortcut Ctrl/⌘+G.

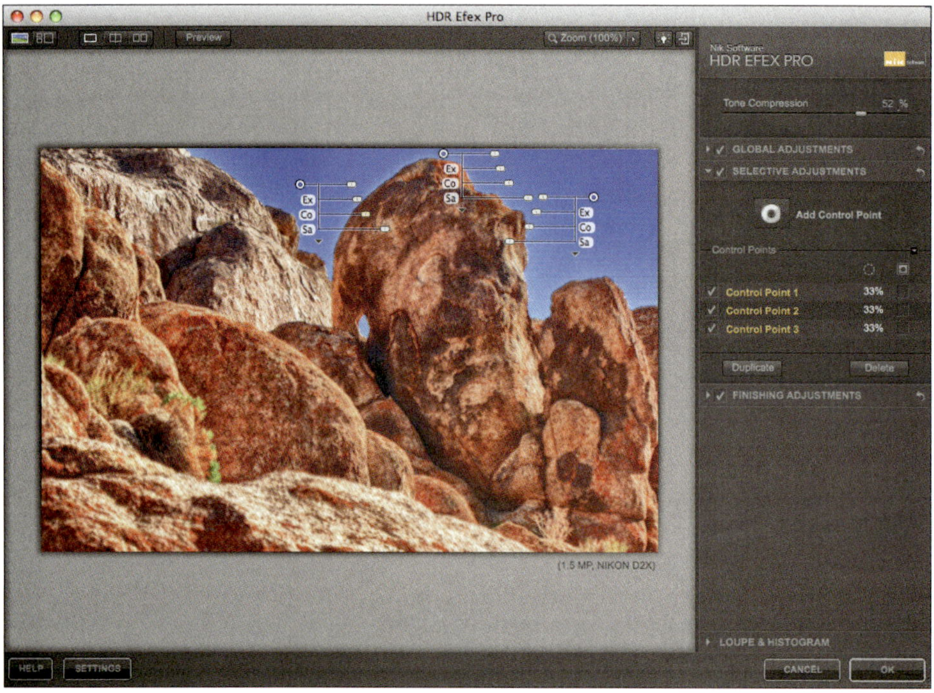

Figure 9.13

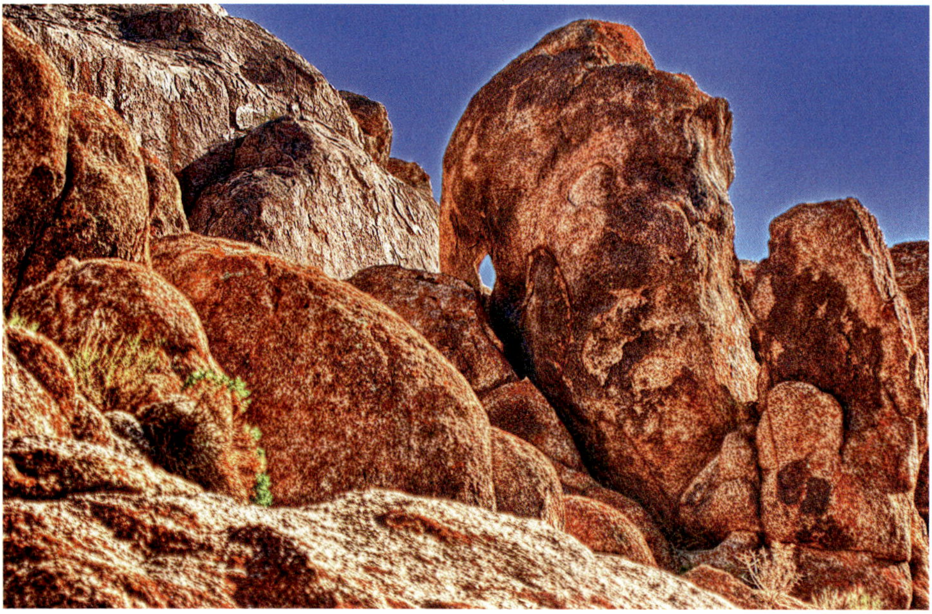

Figure 9.14

I have just the opposite problem with the image in Figure 9.15. The Subdued Contrasts preset that I chose makes the water look great, but the surfer's face and shirt are oversaturated. For me, this draws too much attention to those areas when I want the viewers attention focused on the spray that the surfer made in the wave.

Placing Control Points on the shirt and on the surfer's face, and adjusting saturation along with exposure and contrast, produced the result I wanted in Figure 9.16.

There is another, entirely different, way to use the Saturation slider in a Control Point. While you can't make a global adjustment to totally desaturate an image and then bring back color in an image, it is possible to use the Saturation slider in a Control Point to achieve a similar effect. Figure 9.17 shows the result of doing this.

It required a lot of Control Points to achieve this result. When you desaturate a local area using a Control Point, the effect tends to spill over into areas that you don't want to desaturate. Once

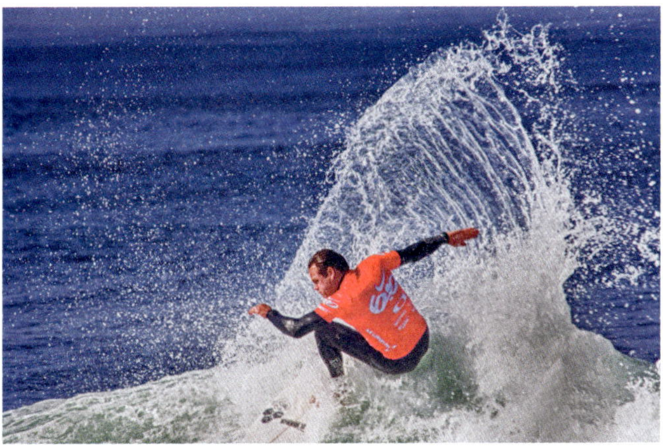

Figure 9.15

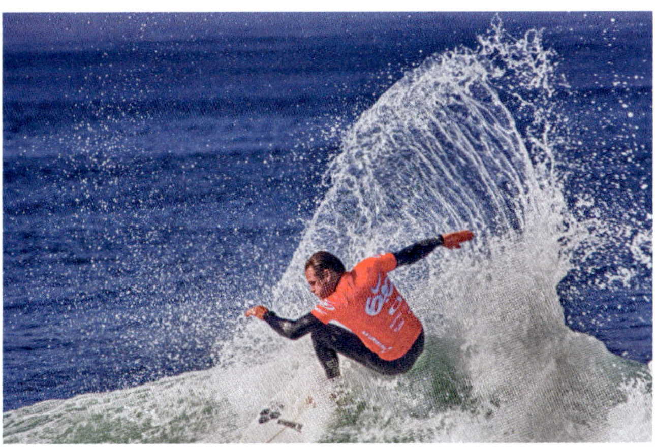

Figure 9.16

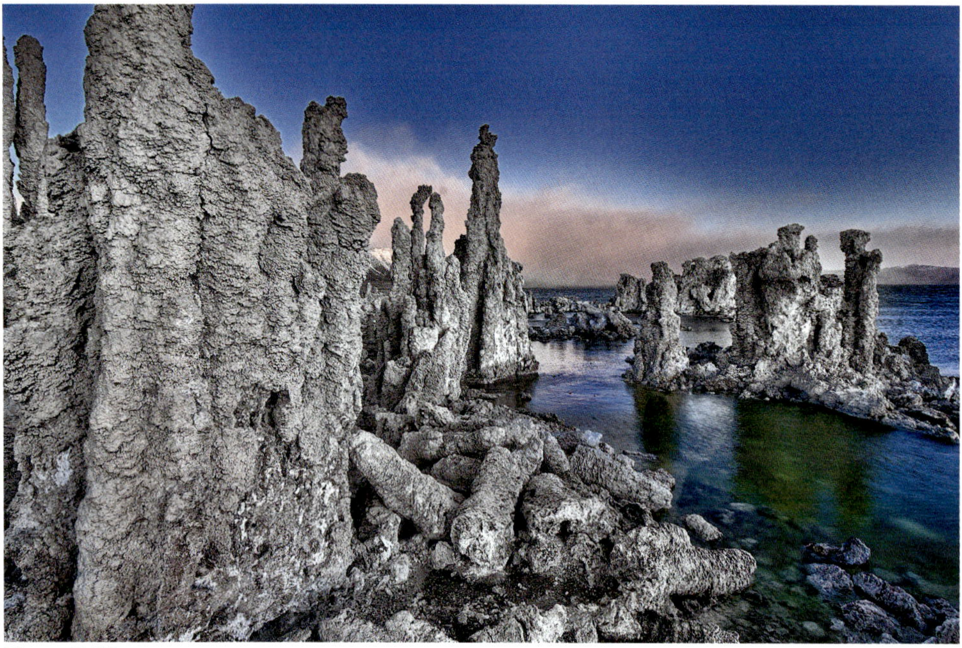

Figure 9.17

you have desaturated the areas you want, you must go back and surround them with other Control Points where the Saturation slider is set to 0. These other Control Points can have other adjustments, but no adjustment in the Saturation slider.

Figure 9.18 shows the HDR Efex Pro screen for the adjustments I made to create Figure 9.17. The Control Points I used to desaturate the tufa towers are shown and their names highlighted. The larger circles indicate the four Control Point groups, each with multiple individual Control Points to confine the desaturation to the tufa towers.

The image almost works for me because the tufa towers are pretty much a dirty gray in real life.

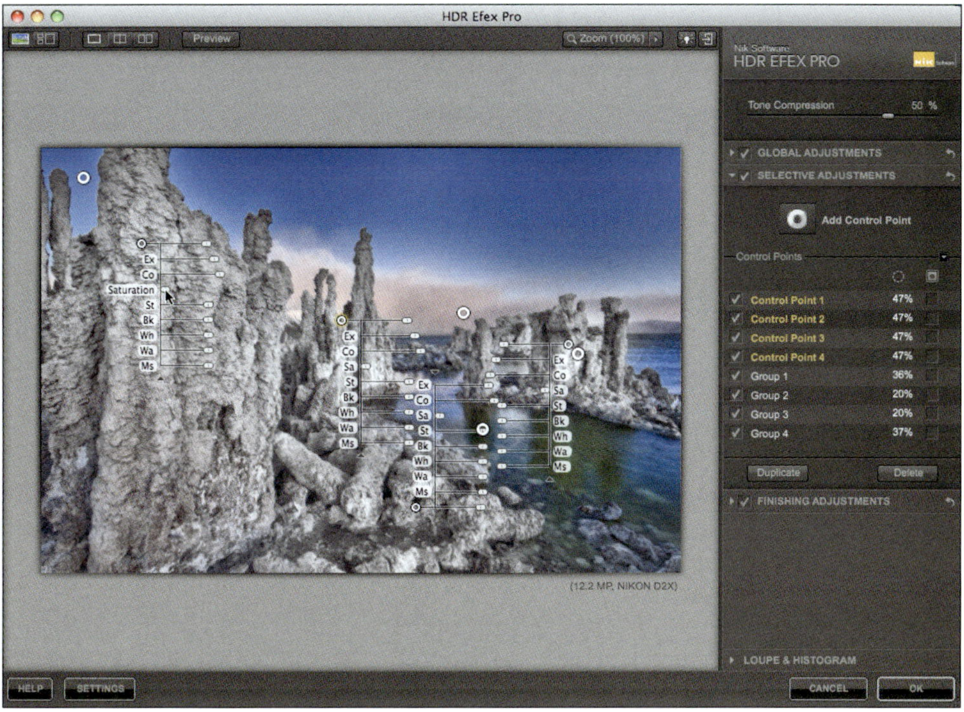

Figure 9.18

Adjusting Structure

I say that the processed HDR image in Figure 9.17 almost works for me because the towers lack the detail that they have when you are close to them. I had increased the contrast of the Control Points that I used to desaturate the towers, but that didn't help enough.

A lot more local contrast is needed, and that is what the Structure slider provides. With all the tower Control Points selected, I adjusted the Structure slider to +100%. When I did this, I noticed that the base of the closest tower didn't receive enough of the effect. I added another duplicate of the tower Control Points there. The Control Points and structure adjustments that I used are shown in Figure 9.19.

Figure 9.20 is the resulting processed HDR image. The additional finely detailed structure adds much needed texture to the towers.

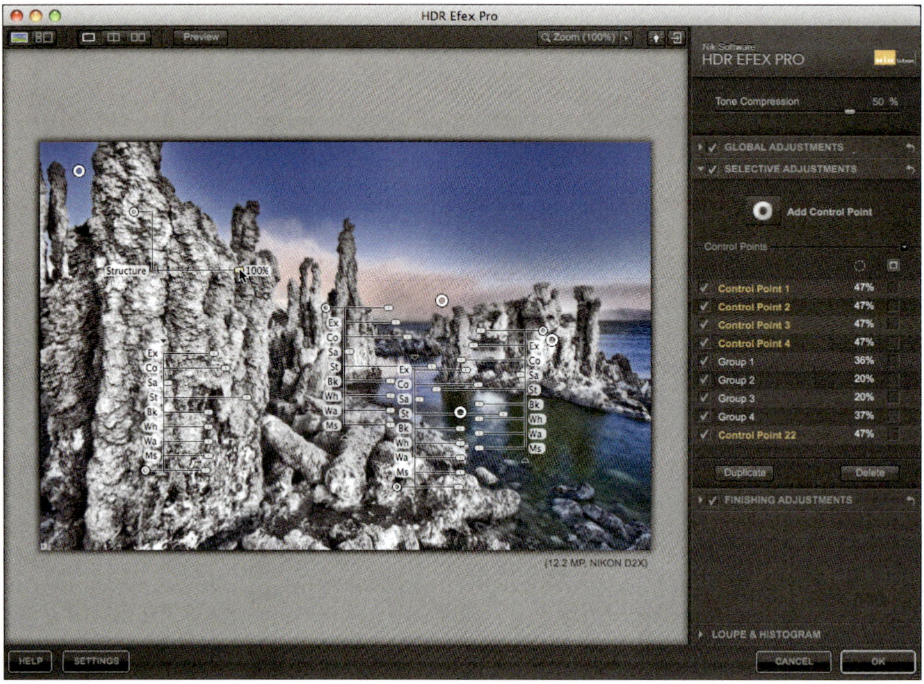

Figure 9.19

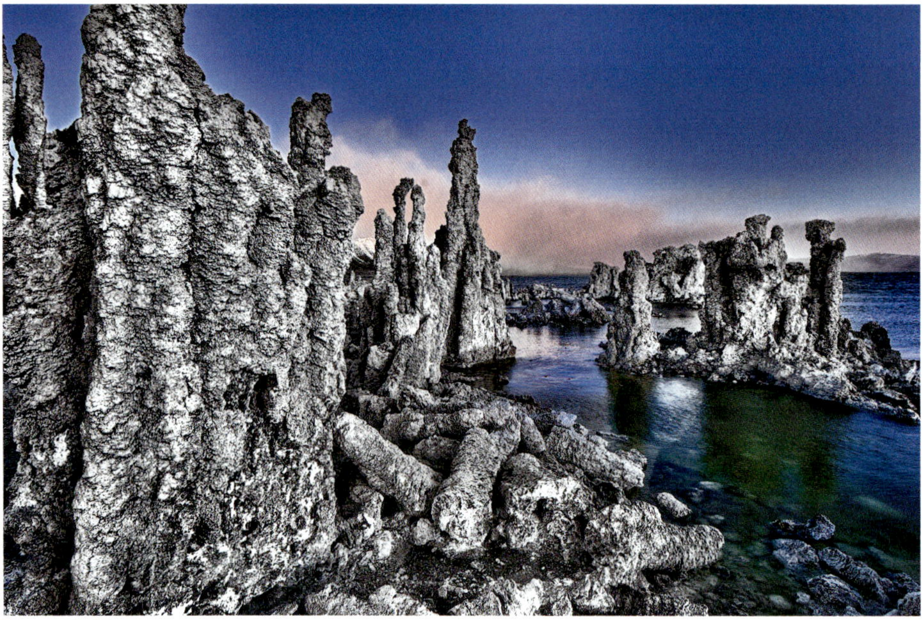

Figure 9.20

Another place to use a Control Point with a structure adjustment is when you need to add texture to clouds. Figure 9.20 looks good to me everywhere except in the sky and in the cloudbank in the distance.

The sky needs to be more even in tone. That's easy with an exposure adjustment in a few Control Points.

The cloudbank will benefit from the additional texture that a structure adjustment provides. After placing a Control Point in the largest area of the cloudbank, I adjusted the Structure slider to +100%. Then I duplicated this Control Point twice more for the rest of the clouds. The final processed HDR image is shown in Figure 9.21.

Despite my success with this image, I don't find myself using the Structure slider in the Control Points very often other than to remove artifacts caused by using the global structure adjustment. It works so well in this case because the conversion to monochrome by a simple desaturation causes such a huge loss of contrast, globally as well as locally. I often adjust the Structure slider in the global adjustments, however. With the additional structure in the towers, it just seemed right to build more texture in the cloudbank, also.

I find that the farther I go down the list in the Control Points adjustments, the less I use them. The designers of HDR Efex Pro must have seen this coming because the default list when you place a Control Point only shows the Exposure, Contrast, and Saturation sliders. To reach the others that I find less need for requires you to click to access them.

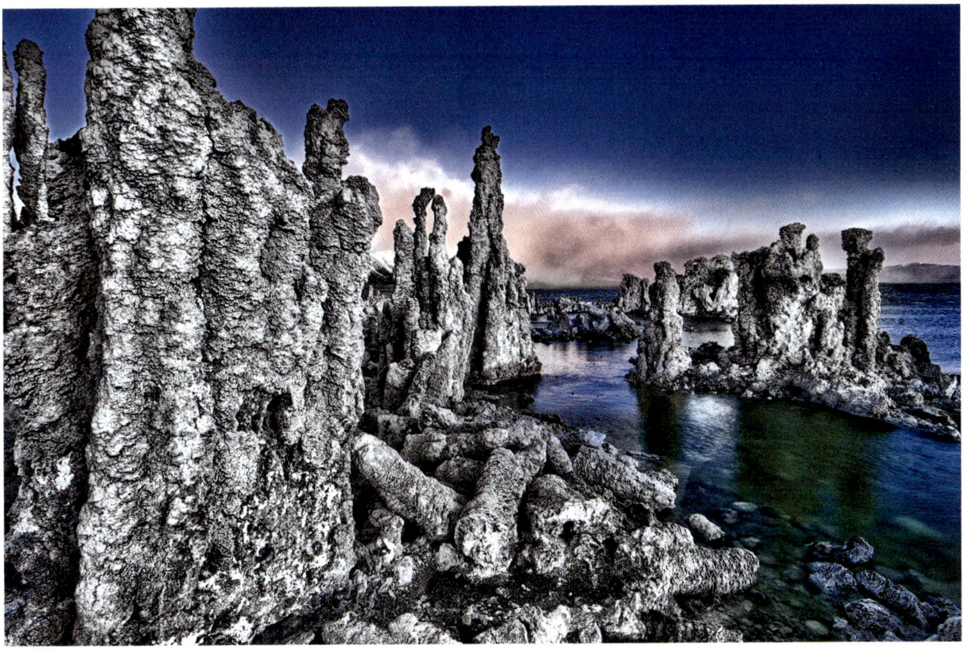

Figure 9.21

Adjusting Blacks

After you use the Blacks slider in the Global Adjustments section to achieve a good black in your HDR image, you can use the blacks adjustment in the Control Point to lighten shadows or areas that have gone too dark. It is also effective, along with an exposure and contrast adjustment in the Control Point, in darkening shadows.

Like the Control Point Exposure slider that adjusts the full tonal range of the image area controlled by the Control Point, the Blacks slider adds black value to all pixels controlled by the Control Point. Small adjustments primarily affect the darkest tones. It adjusts some of the lower midrange values that fall within the effective area of the Control Point, but far less than an exposure adjustment does. This spill is not really a bad thing — it creates a smooth transition without *banding* (abrupt tonal changes) to the affected pixels.

I find that I don't use a blacks adjustment in a Control Point that often, but when I create HDR images at dusk it is very effective in both lightening and darkening low tonal values, as in Figure 9.22.

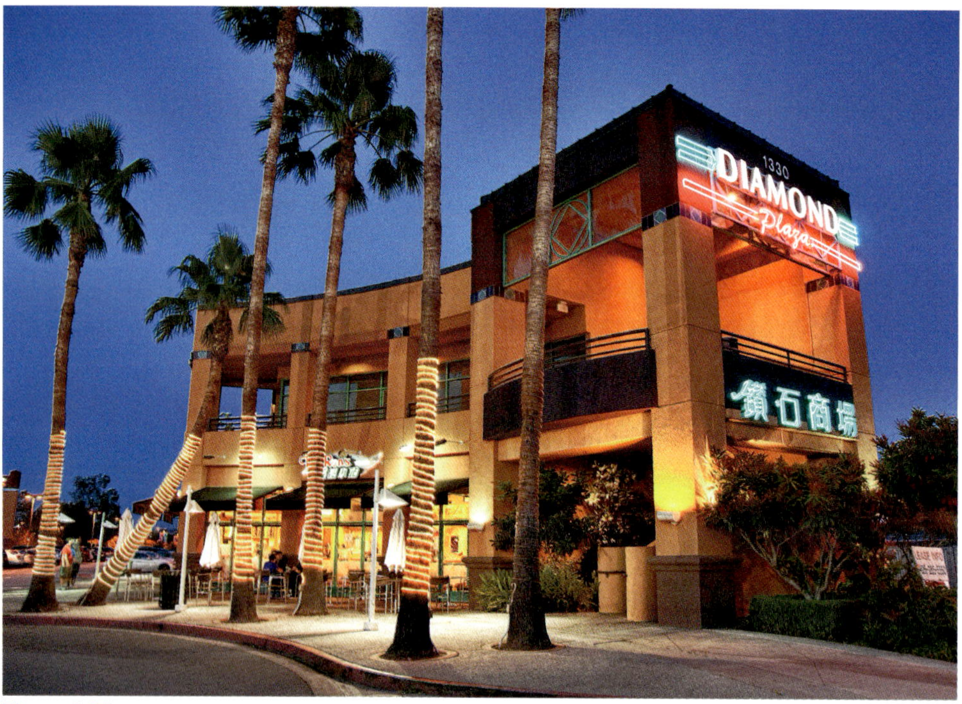

Figure 9.22

Dusk is a wonderful time to shoot image series for HDR processing. The contrast range of most scenes will be far greater than you can capture in one exposure and there is something magical about the interplay of light just after sunset that HDR photos successfully capture.

I shot the images for Figure 9.22 on assignment for a shopping center that had just been purchased by one of my clients. There were a lot of empty spaces and much of the shopping center was undergoing renovation, yet photos were needed to promote the location and attract new tenants. I decided to shoot most of the overall photos at dusk for the drama of the time of day and to mask the shortcomings of the site.

For this image I used the Clean City 2 preset, which works really well for architectural subjects, as a starting point. The Clean City 2 preset uses a negative adjustment of the global adjustments Blacks slider. I changed this to give a good black, and then made other global adjustments to arrive at Figure 9.22.

The adjustments make the trim along the top and the balcony of the building as well as the plants close to the building too dark. The leasing sign in the plants is too light, and so is the roadway and sidewalk along the bottom. Local exposure, contrast, and blacks adjustments in Control Points, as shown in Figure 9.23, correct all these issues.

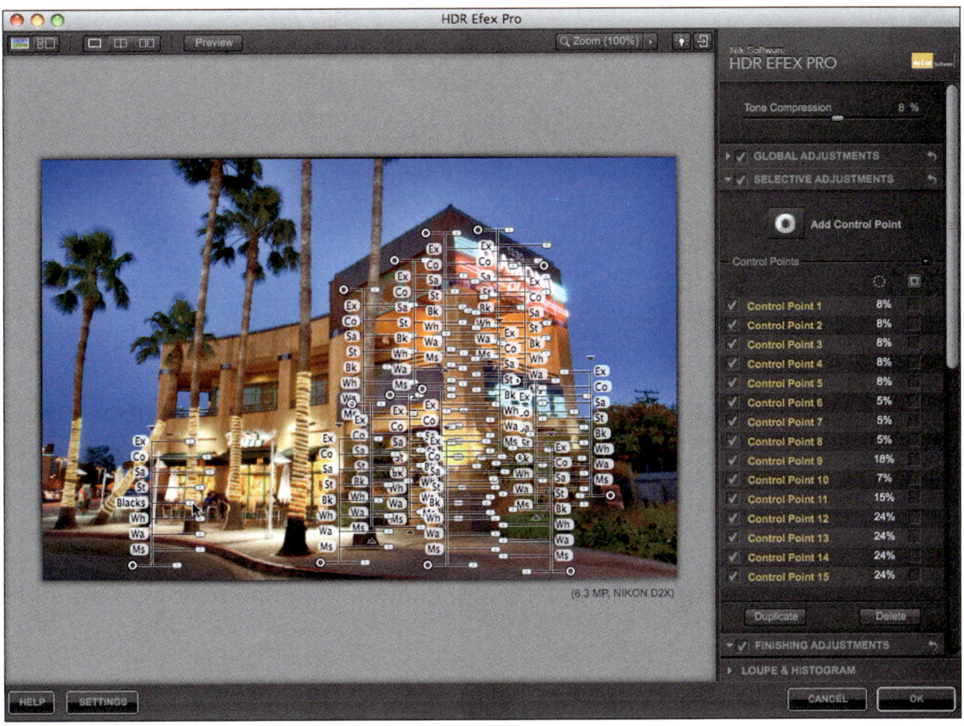

Figure 9.23

Figure 9.24 shows the final processed HDR image. Without HDR imaging technology it might be possible to create an image with this range of tonality with an imaging program. But there would have been no way to shoot the eight different views that I did in one evening to complete the job within the client's budget.

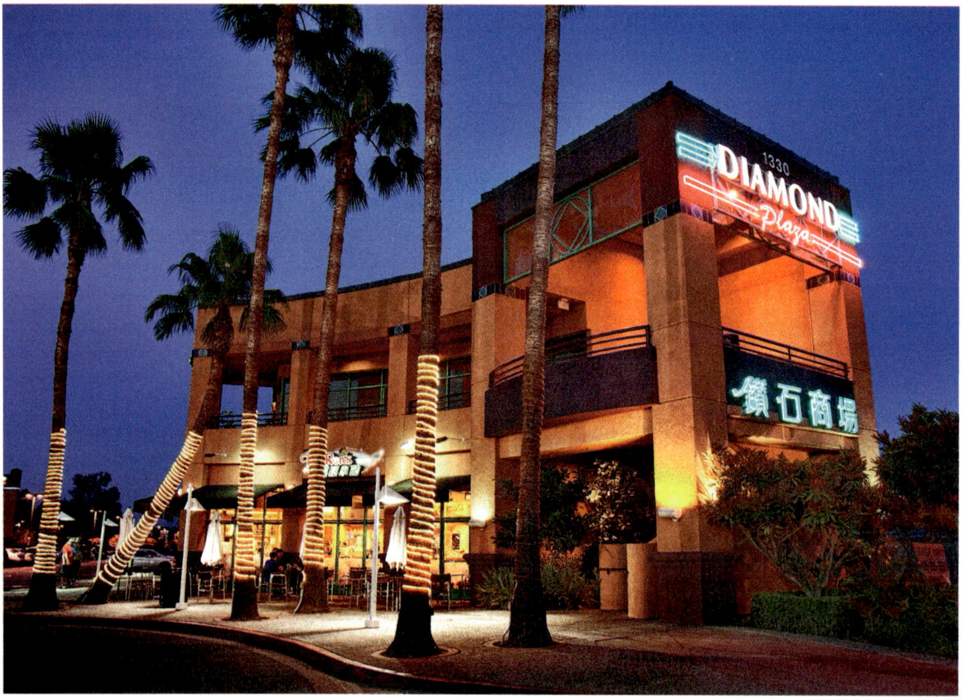

Figure 9.24

Adjusting Whites

The Whites slider in a Control Point, like the Blacks slider, is used to lighten or darken the selected area of the image. Whereas the Blacks slider adds black to all pixels, the Whites slider adds white to all pixels. With a small adjustment to the Whites slider, there is some spill of the effect into the midtones, this time into the upper-midrange tonal values. Again, this gradual application of the effect eliminates the possibility of banding in the affected area.

I found an old railroad caboose at a railroad museum. Because it had reached the end of its road, it seems appropriate to use the End of the Road preset along with some tone compression, Method Strength, and global adjustments to create the processed HDR in Figure 9.25.

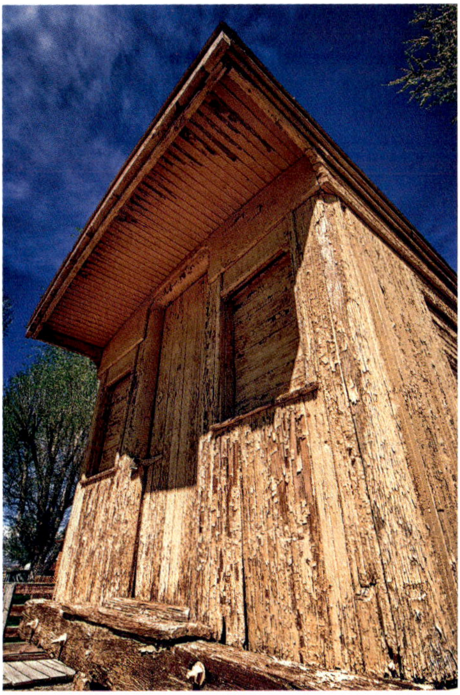

Figure 9.25

End of the Road uses a dark vignette as part of the preset. I like the effect of the vignette to draw your eye into the photo, but the vignette, along with the other adjustments that I made, darkens the clouds in the upper left too much for me. I feel the photo has more depth if there is a relatively light object in the distance.

see also

Chapter 10 discusses the vignette tool and its use.

I placed a Control Point with a large diameter in the white part of the clouds. I tried using the Exposure slider in the Control Point, but it lightened the blue sky, also. Using the Contrast slider, I darkened the blue sky that was affected, but then part of the clouds lost detail and became too white. I set the Exposure and Contrast sliders to 0 and opened the Whites slider.

tip

To set a Control Point slider to 0, double-click anywhere on the slider bar or on the slider itself. To move the slider one adjustment increment at a time, use the left or right arrow key.

Adjusting the Whites slider to +40% produced just the result I wanted, as shown in Figure 9.26.

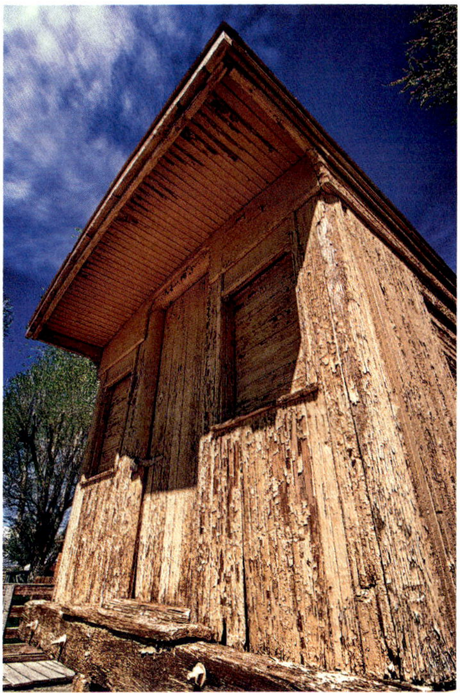

Figure 9.26

The Whites slider is also an effective tool when the HDR image has a white subject and white values in other areas of the image that compete with the subject for attention. Figure 9.27 is an example.

I used the Postcard Paradise preset to create the processed HDR in Figure 9.27. The Dark Soft HDR Method used in Postcard Paradise along with +30% tone compression has rendered the whites in the building and the clouds to almost equal tones of gray. I want the building to be the center of interest. I can achieve this by making it brighter than the foreground cannon and the background sky.

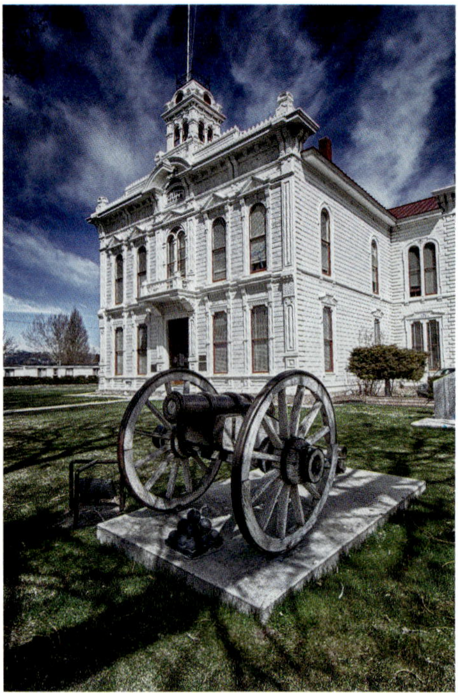

Figure 9.27

Increasing the Whites slider in the global adjustments from –41% to –20% brightens the building and separates it from the foreground nicely. But the adjustment also brightens the clouds too much for my taste.

To tone back the clouds, I added a Control Point with a –50% setting for the Whites slider and a +65% setting for the Structure slider. The adjustment to the Whites slider lowers the tonality of the clouds. The adjustment to the Structure slider brings through more of the blue sky behind the clouds.

I duplicated this Control Point six times using Ctrl/⌘+D and placed these cloned Control Points on other cloud areas. The result looked good, so I selected Save and processed the image back to Photoshop, and it is shown in Figure 9.28.

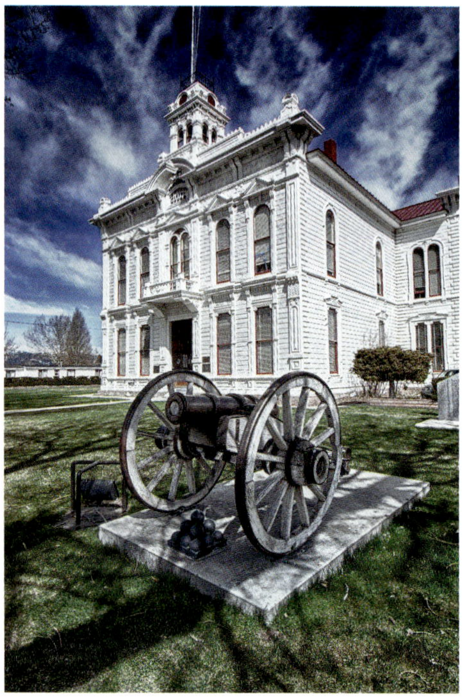

Figure 9.28

Once I saw the result in Photoshop, I realized that all the planes of the building were approximately the same shade of white, making the building look more two-dimensional than I wanted. Fortunately, I had opened the image series through Adobe Bridge in Photoshop as a Smart Object. I reopened the image in HDR Efex Pro again by clicking the HDR Efex Pro layer in the Smart Object stack and all of my previous settings were still available to me.

see also

Opening an image series as a Smart Object is discussed in Chapter 3.

Back in HDR Efex Pro, I added a Control Point to the front of the building and adjusted the Whites slider to brighten the façade. When I was satisfied with the adjustment, I duplicated the Control Point and placed the duplicates to brighten the front of the building and the far right of the building that is facing in the same direction as the front. I grouped them as Group 2. I grouped the cloud adjustments as Group 1.

Because these Control Points overlapped the side wall, I added three Control Points on the side wall with just a slight –10% Whites slider adjustment and grouped these as Group 3. These groups and the relative slider settings for the first Control Point in each group are shown in Figure 9.29.

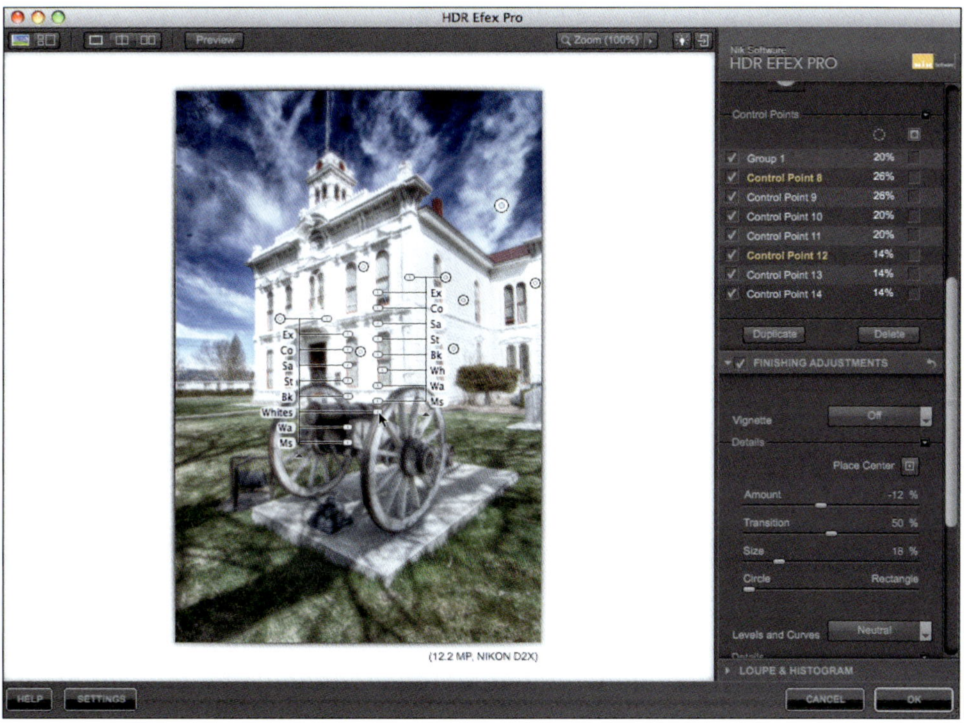

Figure 9.29

Figure 9.30 shows the final processed HDR image.

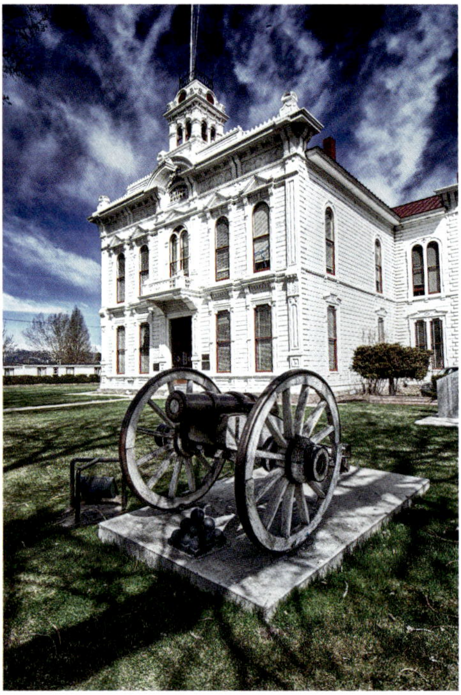

Figure 9.30

Adjusting Warmth

The Warmth slider in a Control Point is used to add or subtract warmth from local areas of the image. In HDR Efex Pro, positive warmth adjustments enhance the yellow tones that are present, and negative adjustments decrease the yellow tones, making the area bluer, or "cooler."

In general, I like my images on the warm side overall, so I usually add warmth with a global adjustment. Only occasionally do I add or remove warmth locally.

When I do use a local warmth adjustment it is usually to remove blue from shadow areas in sunlit scenes. HDR Efex Pro balances the lighting between sunlit and shadow areas, resulting in a mixed color balance in the HDR image. Adding a Control Point to the shadow area and a positive adjustment to the Warmth slider balances the color of the two areas. But as I was working on the snow scene that appears in this chapter as Figure 9.11, I thought that the bushes in the foreground could use some color to add interest and to make the image less monochromatic. It was too early in the chapter to add warmth then, so I will do it now.

Because I opened and saved this HDR as a Photoshop Smart Object, I reopened the image and added a Control Point in one of the bushes in the foreground. After adjusting the diameter of the Control Point to cover the bush, I added +1 EV of exposure, –15% contrast, +30% saturation and +100% warmth.

The global adjustments I had originally applied to the image included a –22% warmth adjustment, so that my local adjustments simply recovered some of the warmth that I had removed. I duplicated this first Control Point nine times and cloned it to the other bushes. Some of these clones were adjusted to different diameters to match the bushes to which they were attached.

When I was done, I intended to add a Control Point without an adjustment in the middle ground on the right where one of my Control Points was lightening and warming the bushes, but I decided I like the spill into those bushes and I let it remain.

Figure 9.31 shows the new Control Points. I grouped them before I saved the image as a Smart Object.

The final processed image with the warmer bushes is shown in Figure 9.32.

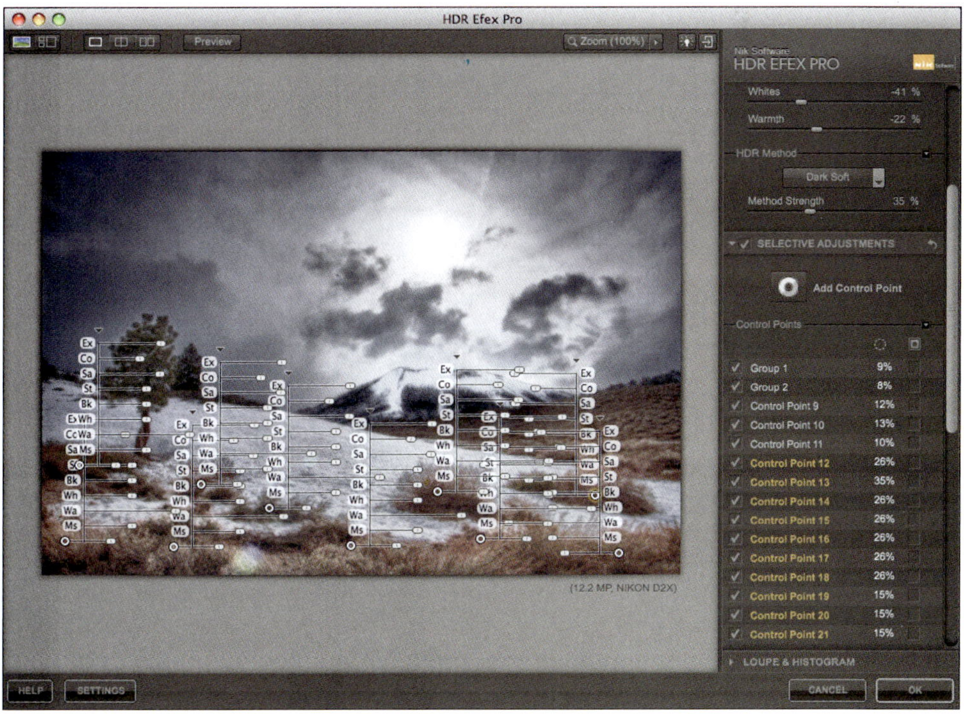

Figure 9.31

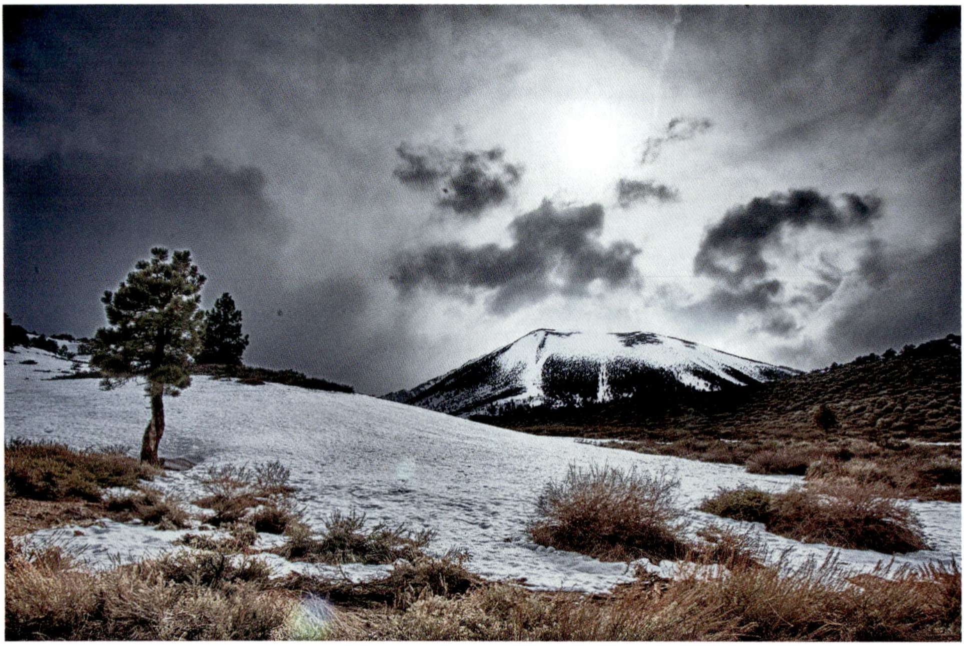

Figure 9.32

The Warmth slider in a Control Point differs from all the other Control Point sliders in one important way — it requires there be a certain range of colors within the diameter of the warmth Control Point. All the other sliders perform their functions regardless of the colors present. Even the Blacks and Whites sliders darken and lighten tones even if there is no black or white within the diameter of their Control Point.

A warmth adjustment requires warm tones, yellows especially, in the selection area for a positive warmth adjustment. It requires cool tones, especially blues, for a negative warmth adjustment. This is illustrated in Figure 9.33.

The roof of this old steam locomotive is painted a cream color. I adjusted the left half of the roof with a +100% warmth adjustment Control Point and the right half with a –100% adjustment Control Point. Because there are yellow values in the roof, the adjustments are visible.

However, when I add a Control Point to the blue engine and adjust the Warmth slider to +100%, as shown in Figure 9.34, there is no increase in warmth within the Control Point, which covers the entire engine.

So if you want to use a warmth adjustment, make sure there are warm tones present on which the slider can work.

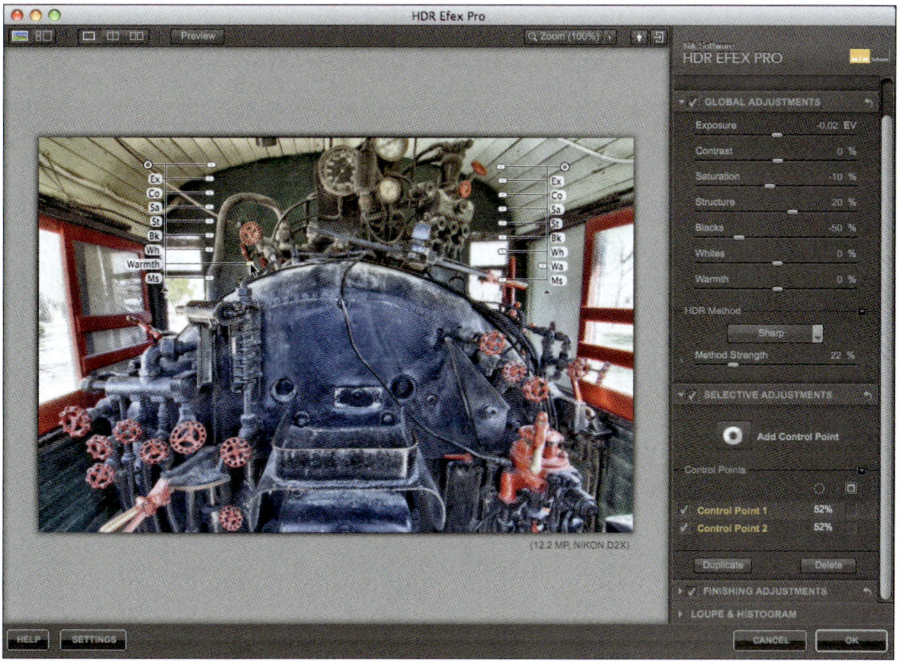

Figure 9.33

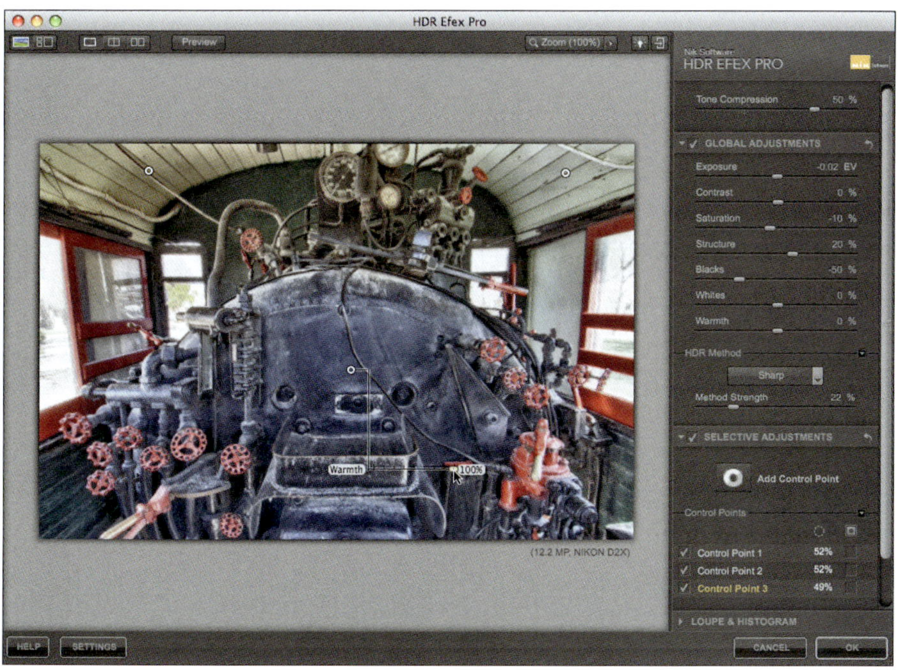

Figure 9.34

Adjusting Method Strength

The Method Strength slider in a Control Point is the adjustment to use to add local contrast and texture in the HDR image. Zoom the Main Image Window to 100% magnification to accurately view the effect of the adjustment.

The old locomotive serves as a good example of what can be done with the Method Strength slider in a Control Point.

I first deleted the Control Points I created previously. Next I opened the Preset Browser and chose the Single Exposure 2 preset as a starting point. Even though the HDR image is a result of a nine-exposure image series bracketed at 1 EV steps and not a single exposure, the Single Exposure 2 preset gives me the look I prefer.

After making changes to the tone compression setting and some global adjustments, the processed HDR image without Control Points is shown in Figure 9.35.

It looks good, but more can be done to add interest to the engine compartment by adding just a single Control Point with a Method Strength adjustment. Figure 9.36 shows the Control Point in the center of the engine and the effect of a +100% Method Strength adjustment. This is too much for me, so I ended up with a +75% adjustment.

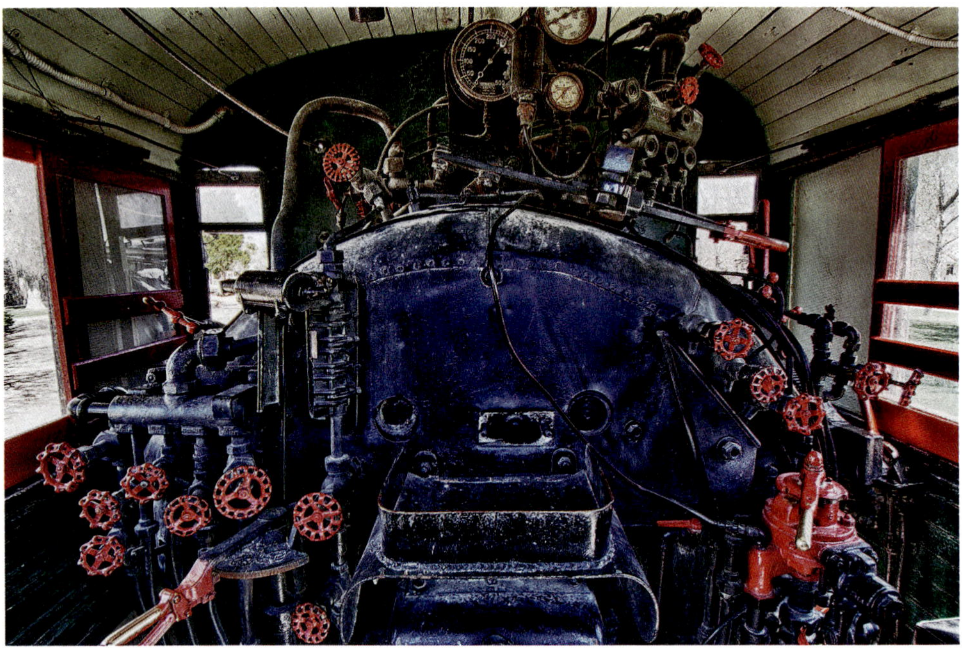

Figure 9.35

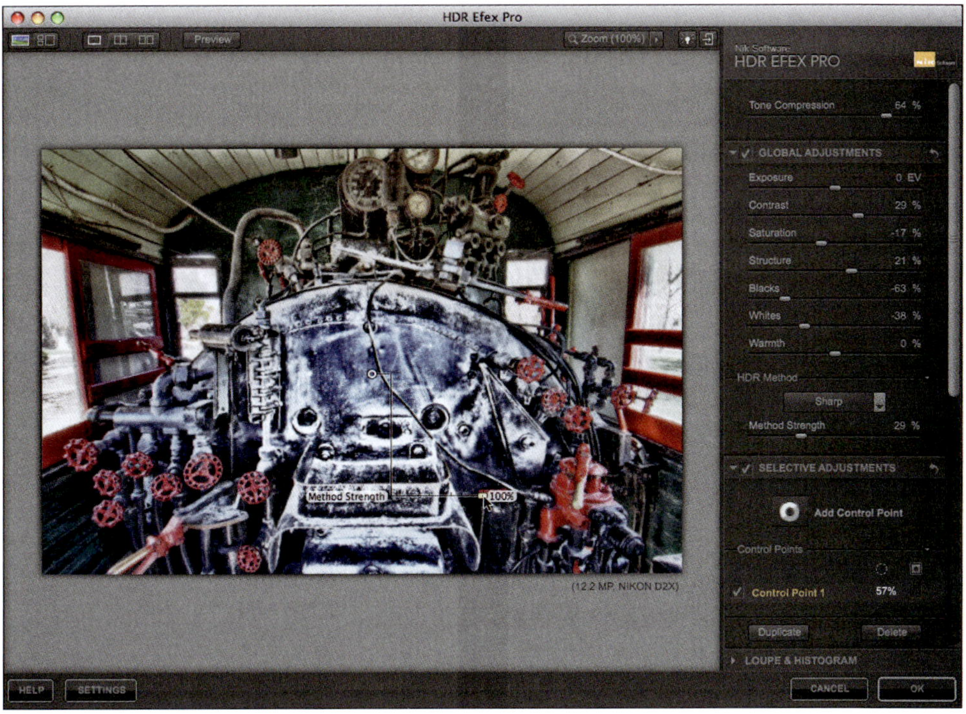

Figure 9.36

Now that the engine itself is looking good, I'm bothered that the windows are so bright. They keep drawing my eye away from the engine. Even though I know there is information in the three darkest exposures of the bracket about the outside scene, it didn't end up in the HDR image. But a negative Method Strength adjustment to reduce local contrast often brings this information back without creating haloing artifacts at the edges.

I began with a new Control Point, Control Point 2, in the upper part of the left window, shown in Figure 9.37. The Method Strength slider is adjusted to –30%, but note also the Structure slider that is set to –70%. I did this to keep the scene outside the window out of focus to add to the feeling of depth.

I then duplicated this Control Point six times and added it to the other windows, as shown in Figure 9.38. Because these Control Points spilled over into the interior, I added a number of Control Points with no adjustments in the ceiling and along the interior walls. The final processed HDR image is shown in Figure 9.39.

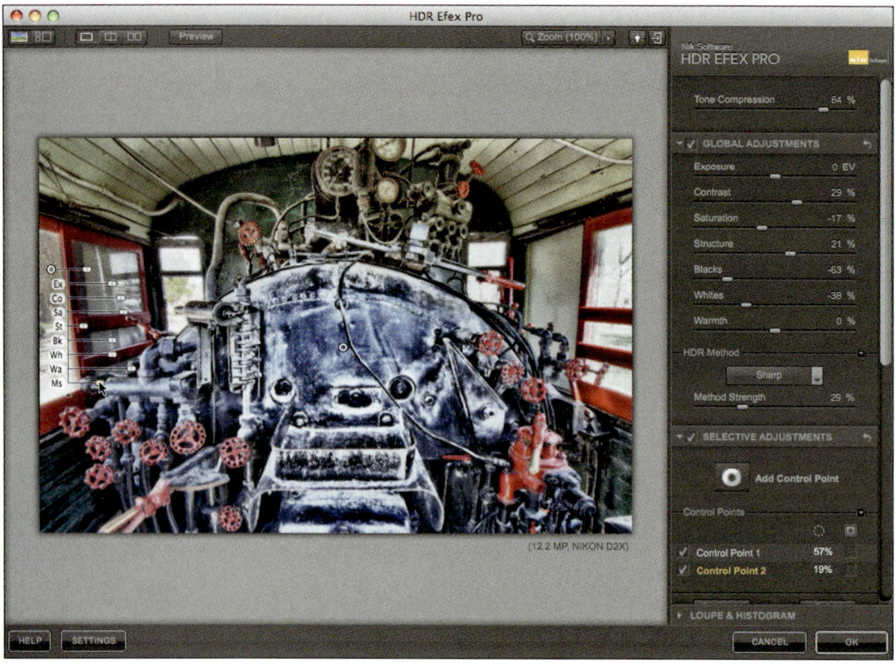

Figure 9.37

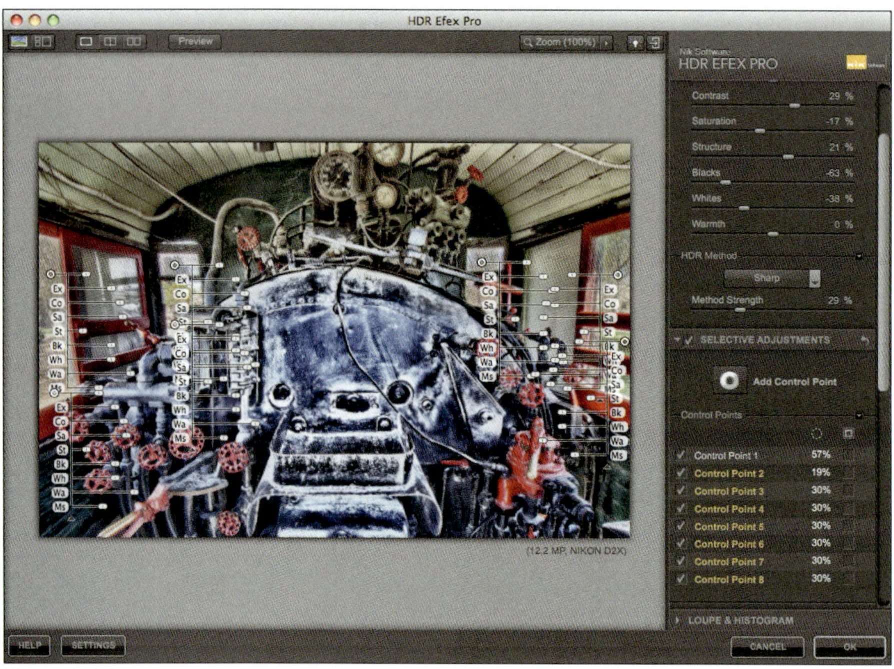

Figure 9.38

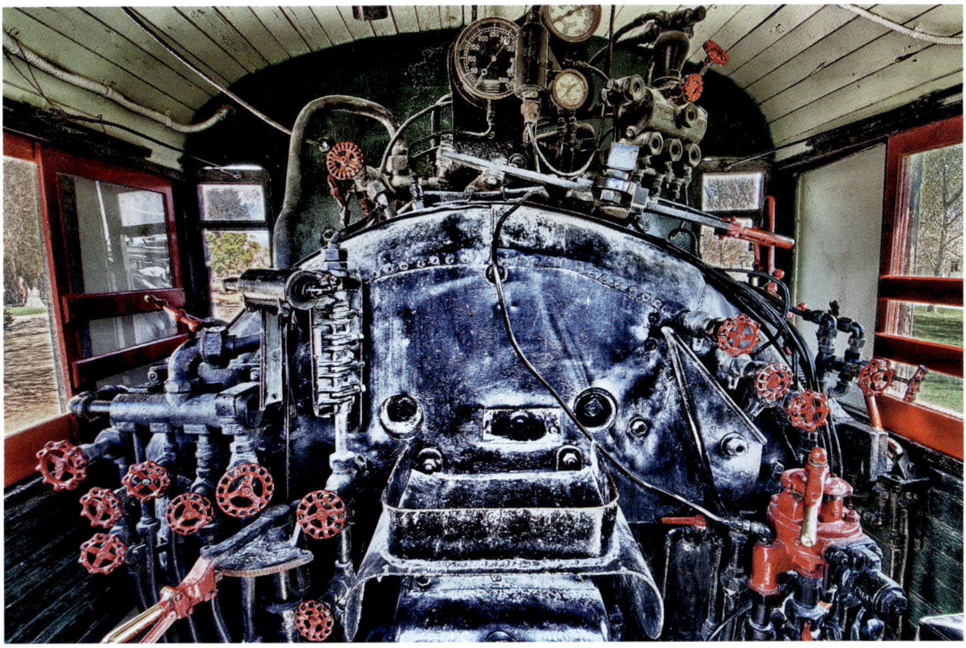

Figure 9.39

Putting It All Together

Before I close this chapter, I want to revisit an image to apply some local corrections. It is the final image in Chapter 7, reproduced here as Figure 9.40.

I mentioned at the close of Chapter 7 that there were some small adjustments that I wanted to make to finalize the image. One was to remove some of the warmth in the clouds.

Figure 9.41 shows the four Control Points that I used to select all the clouds and apply a –25% warmth adjustment to remove the yellow tint.

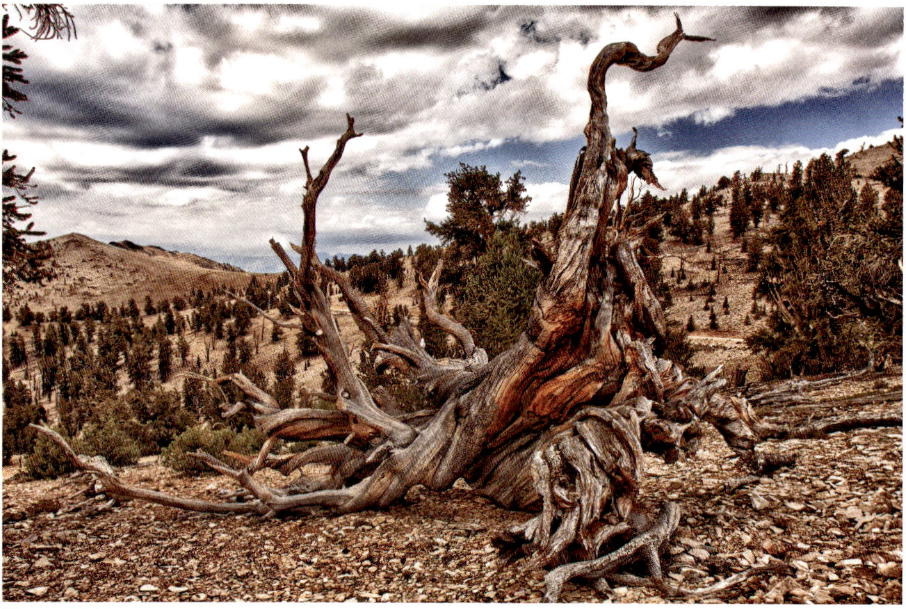

Figure 9.40

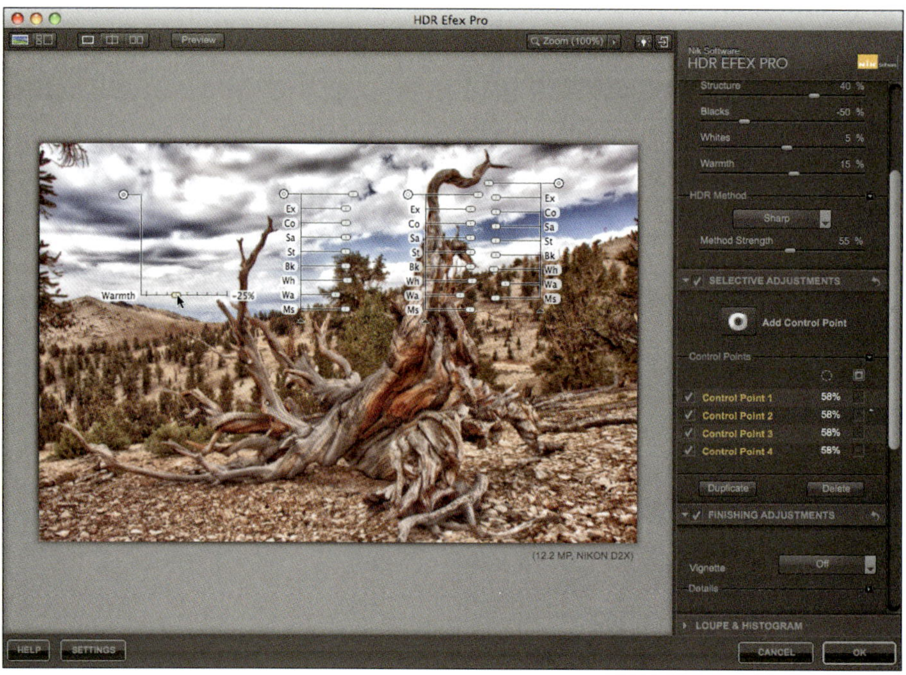

Figure 9.41

I quickly checked the Control Point mask view, as shown in Figure 9.42, to ensure that I had selected all the clouds. When I checked this with only three Control Points, I found that the clouds at the far edges weren't totally selected. After this check, I added the fourth Control Point.

Next, I wanted to remove some of the yellow cast in the trees. As I mentioned earlier, this is a common problem with greens in HDR images, and it is easily corrected with a negative warmth adjustment or a decrease in local saturation. For this image, a negative warmth adjustment works best.

After grouping the cloud Control Points as Group 1, I added a few additional Control Points on important trees, as shown in Figure 9.43. The warmth adjustments were all different, but all were very close to –30%.

Now there is just one final Control Point adjustment to make. The area of warm wood in the fallen bristlecone pine, which is my center of

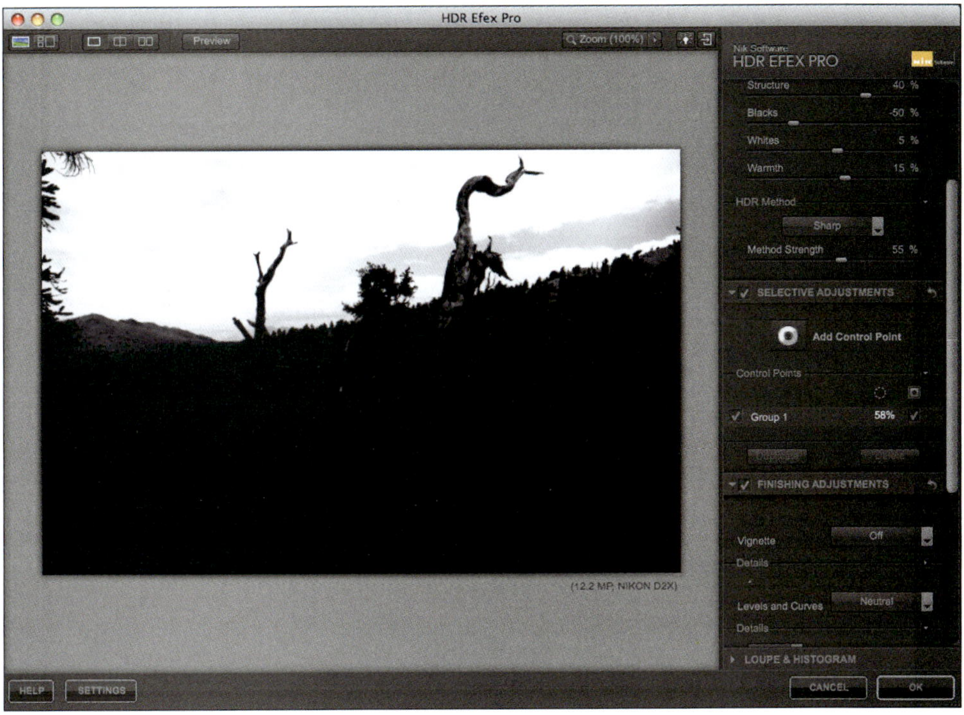

Figure 9.42

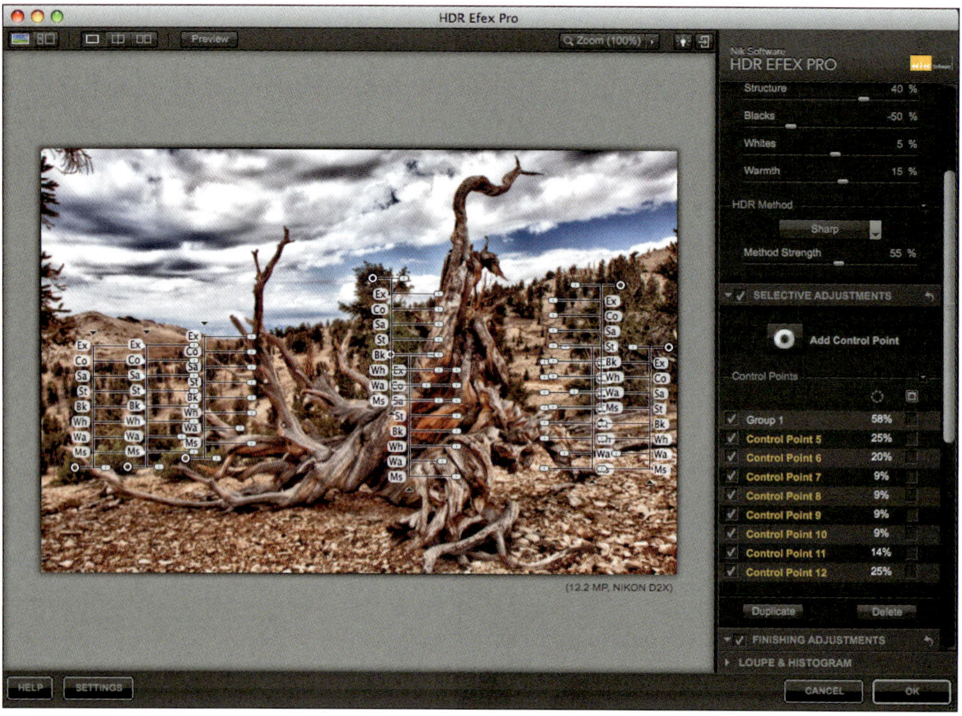

Figure 9.43

interest, needs to be a little more interesting. A Control Point there with exposure, contrast, saturation, structure, warmth, and Method Strength adjustments gives the final adjusted and processed image in Figure 9.44.

In Chapter 10 I make one final enhancement to this image.

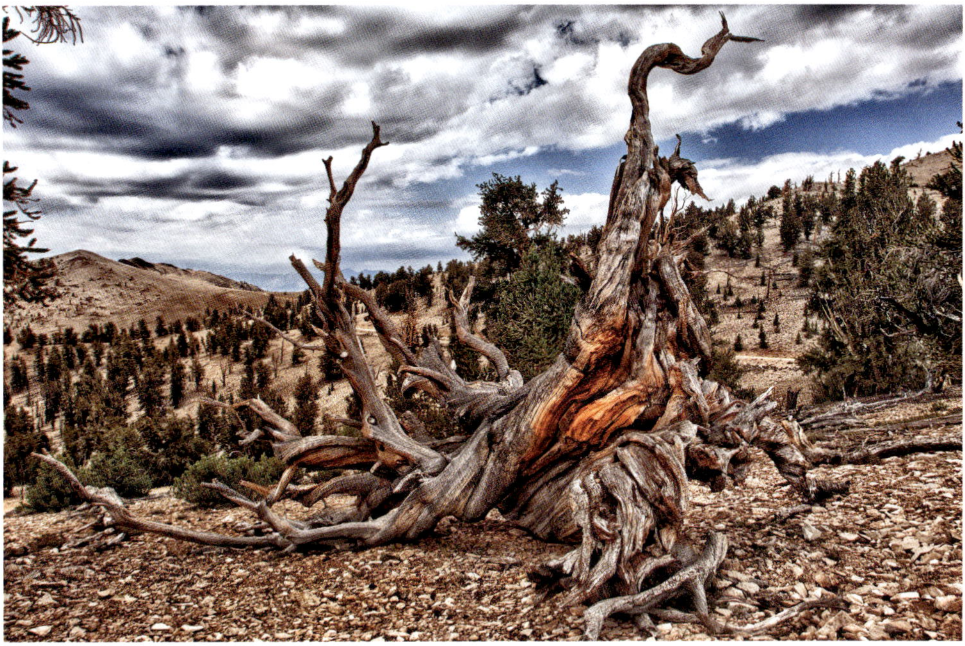

Figure 9.44

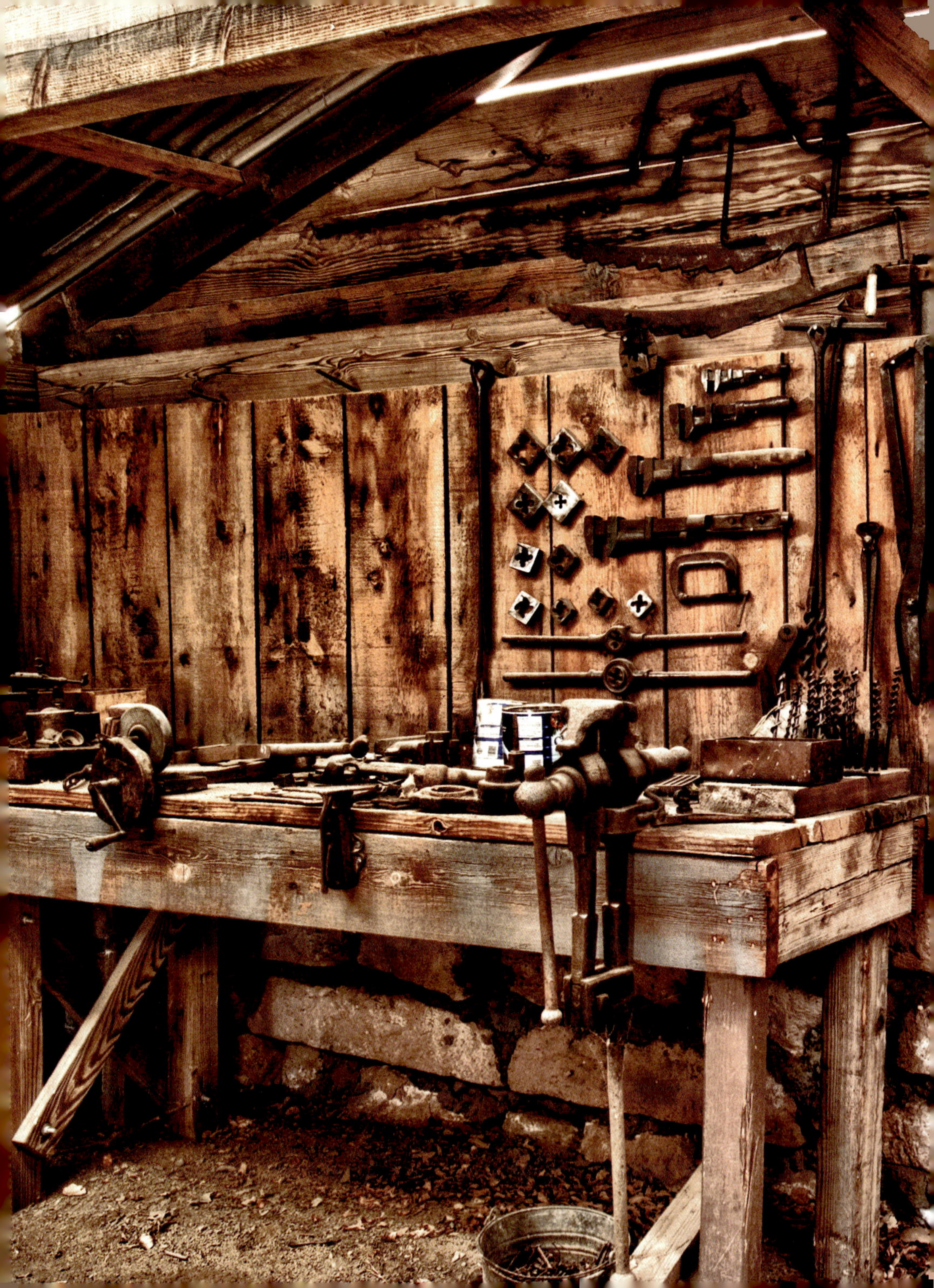

10

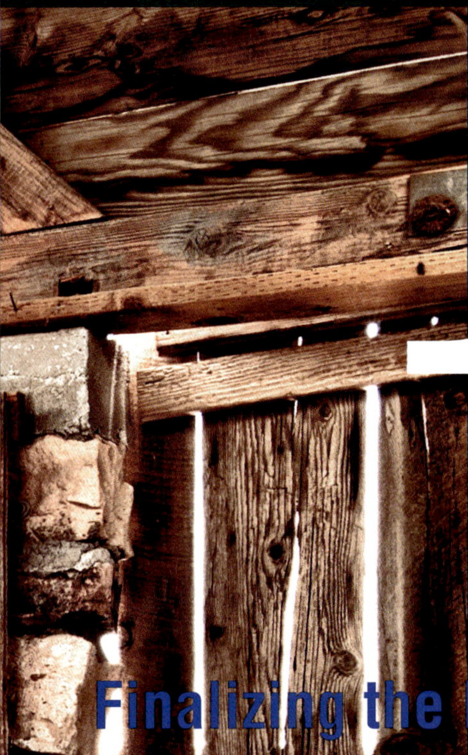

Finalizing the Image

HDR Efex Pro doesn't abandon you once you create an HDR image and adjust it globally and locally to your liking. The program includes additional tools to aid in further refining the image. Using these tools is by no means necessary because you can use similar Photoshop tools, but having them available in HDR Efex Pro is more convenient and with some tools produces a higher-quality result by using the greater bit depth of the HDR image.

This chapter discusses the tools in the Finishing Adjustments section of HDR Efex Pro, which includes one of the most versatile tools for creating vignettes available in any photographic software. The chapter closes with a discussion of the options available when you are ready to save the final HDR image.

Adding a Vignette

In photography, a *vignette* is the loss of clarity or resolution at the edges of an image compared to that in the center. Vignettes are most often thought of as a darkening of the edges relative to the center. However, the edges could just as well be lighter than the center and the effect would still be called a vignette. In fact, the edges could be the same tonal values as the image but simply be more out of focus, although not simply from depth of field effects, and these softer edges would also be considered a vignette.

The presence of a vignette in a photograph is as old as photography itself. Historical photographic techniques from the pinhole camera to the early multiple-element camera lenses all produced images with edge vignettes.

Modern toy cameras with plastic lenses such as the Holga produce images with strong vignetting, but the digital camera trend seems to have taken the opposite tack and aimed to eliminate vignetting in images. The current popularity of toy cameras and software tools to simulate the effects of toy cameras indicates a trend among some photographers away from the sometimes sterile look that digital cameras produce.

The appeal of vignettes has had its ups and downs throughout history. Early in the history of photography, a portrait was expected to have darkened edges. This was followed by a period when high-key portraiture became the rage and a baby or child's portrait was expected to have soft edges that were lighter than the light background. Photo lab darkroom technicians developed their own secret techniques to produce soft, even vignettes in prints.

At the present, anything goes, but the trend seems to be away from vignettes. Photoshop and various Photoshop plug-ins include tools to remove the natural vignetting in almost all photographic lenses. It has come to the point where lenses are tested by DxO Labs and Adobe for vignetting and optical aberrations and these are automatically removed when the software reads that a particular lens is used to capture the image. Lightroom, Camera Raw, and DxO Optics Pro include these tools. Adobe offers a free utility, Adobe Lens Profile Creator, allowing users to profile their own lenses.

Personally, I'm from the old school and a big fan of vignetting. I'm happy to see that HDR Efex Pro has included a very sophisticated set of tools to create vignettes in images.

The most common purpose for adding a vignette, especially in portraiture or wedding photography, is to draw the viewer's eyes to the subject of the photo. The effect is less commonly used in landscape photography because it seems overly fake to have an obvious dark (or worse, light) vignette in an even blue sky. However, with the vignette controls in HDR Efex Pro and because the program operates in 32-bit color space, it is possible to create vignettes that look more like graduated filters than a traditional vignette.

Vignettes are also employed as a means of enhancing the mood of a photo. A strong dark vignette in a low-key photo will heighten the mood of foreboding and mystery. A light vignette suggests a feeling of airiness and openness. But a light vignette can also suggest a feeling of fading and age, and HDR Efex Pro uses this in a few of the presets.

It is possible to create a vignette by adding black or white to the edges of an image. Many plug-ins and vignette techniques use this method. But simply painting black or white results in a false-looking effect.

HDR Efex Pro uses a more sophisticated method. Because there is so much image information available in the HDR image, HDR Efex Pro uses that information to create the vignette in a manner similar to adjusting the Blacks and Whites sliders in global adjustments or a Control Point. The result is not unlike that produced in a traditional darkroom, and its effect is far more subtle and believable than simply painting the image edges with black or white.

Selecting a vignette type

There are eight prebuilt vignettes in the Finishing Adjustments section in HDR Efex Pro, as shown in Figure 10.1. There is also an Off preset, which is the default unless a vignette is programmed into the preset that is selected. Six of the presets add differing amounts of darkening to the edges while the other two lighten the edges.

The Lens 1 vignette preset is a very subtle darkening of the edges, as illustrated using the solid blue background in Figure 10.2. It is typical of the slight vignetting that might be found in a fast telephoto zoom lens at wide aperture.

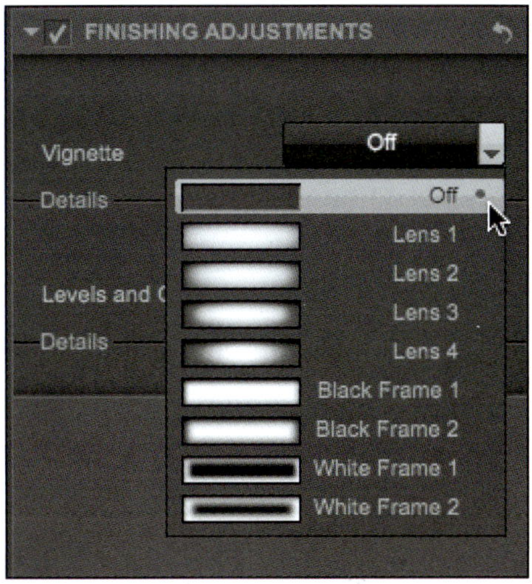

Figure 10.1

A somewhat stronger darkening vignette is Lens 2, shown in Figure 10.3. It is still fairly subtle, but more pronounced than Lens 1.

With the Lens 3 vignette, the darkening effect is quite obvious and intrudes farther into the image area, as shown in Figure 10.4. It is similar to the vignetting of an extremely wide-angle rectilinear camera lens. It is also fairly typical of the vignette effect applied by portrait labs to portraits of individual sitters.

The strongest of the lens vignettes is Lens 4, shown in Figure 10.5. There is more than 1.5 EV of exposure variation from the center of the image to a corner, the type of vignetting found in older design, extreme wide-angle lenses for view cameras, which required a center filter to equalize exposure across the image. The effect is very strong, but not out of place for some HDR images.

Figure 10.2

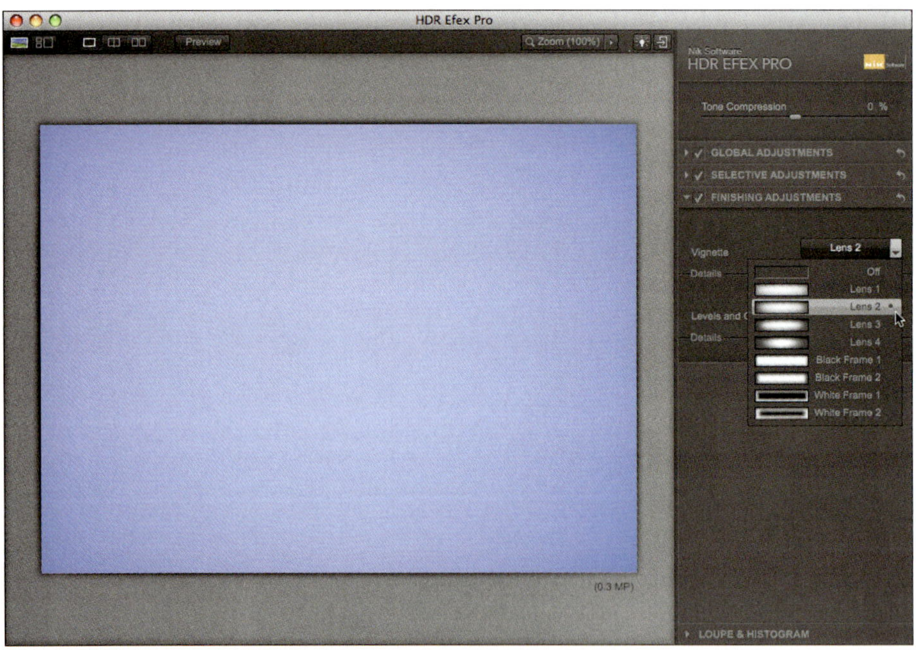

Figure 10.3

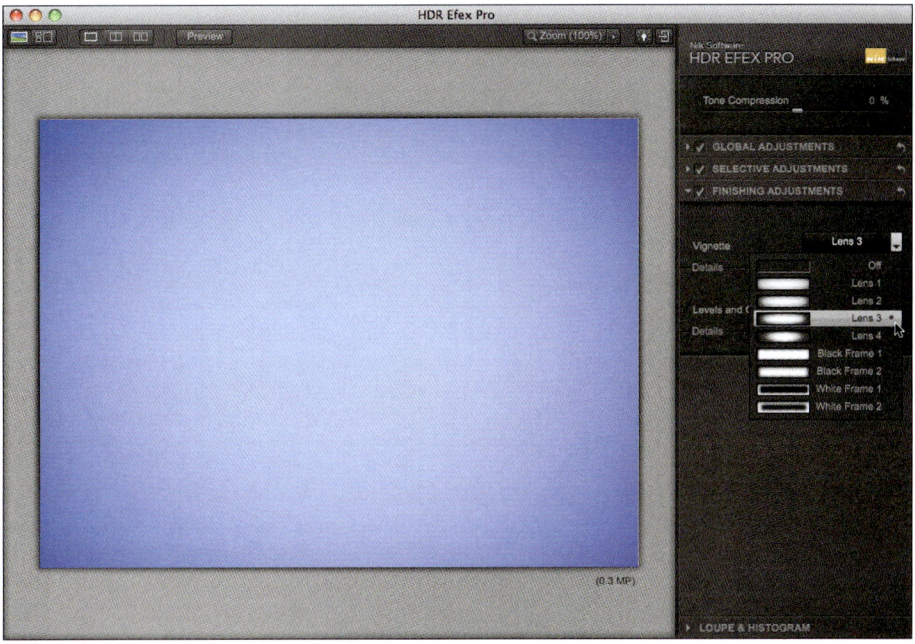

Figure 10.4

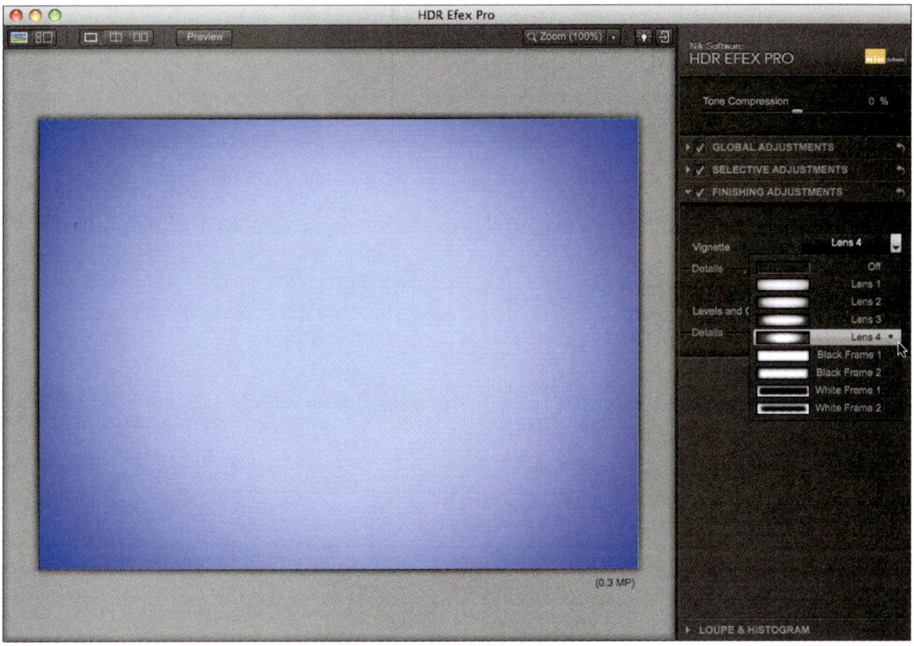

Figure 10.5

The four lens vignettes mimic to some extent the vignetting created by optical lenses. They generate a circular effect with the least vignetted area in the center of the image. Selecting the Black Frame 1 vignette results in edge darkening, but with the vignetted areas parallel to the image edges. The effect is roughly rectangular, as shown in Figure 10.6, rather than the roughly circular effects of the lens vignettes.

Black Frame 2 generates the same type of rectangular vignette as Black Frame 1, but over a larger area and with a larger transition area from the center of the image to the edges. Black Frame 2 is shown in Figure 10.7. The rectangular effect of using Black Frame 1 and Black Frame 2 creates a "picture frame" around the image to draw the viewer's eyes in.

The final two vignette presets, White Frame 1 and White Frame 2, produce the same vignette looks as Black Frame 1 and Black Frame 2, but the edges are lightened rather than darkened. White Frame 1 is shown in Figure 10.8 and White Frame 2 in Figure 10.9.

As with the HDR presets, you can use the vignette presets just as they are designed or as a starting point to create a custom vignette for your image.

Customizing the vignette

If one of the prebuilt presets doesn't exactly fit your image, HDR Efex Pro includes tools to customize the preset to your liking. To access the vignette tools, click on the Details twirler to open the Details palette, as shown in Figure 10.10.

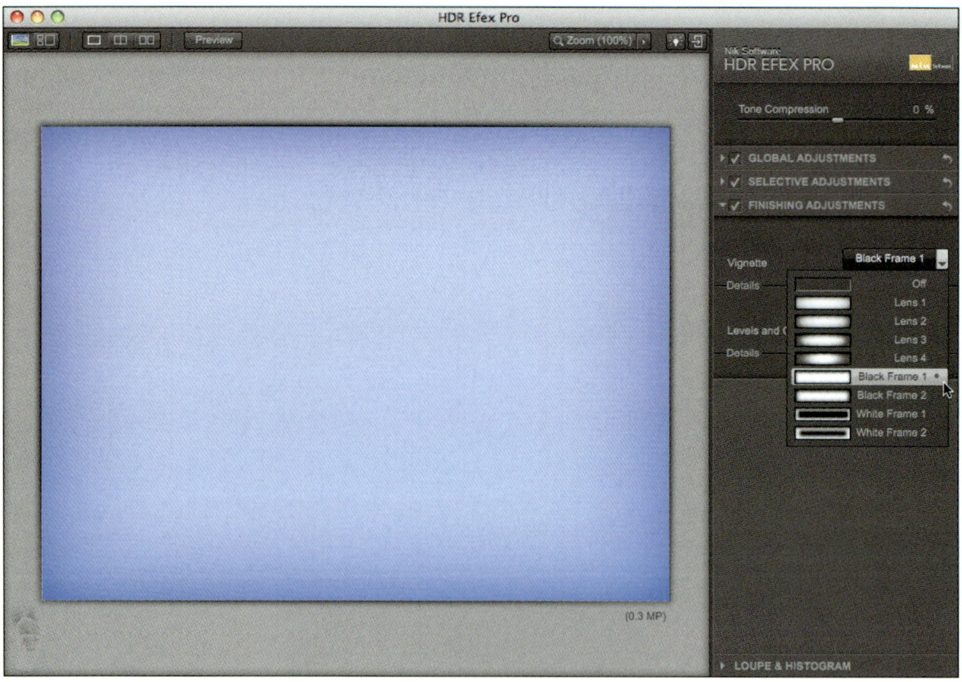

Figure 10.6

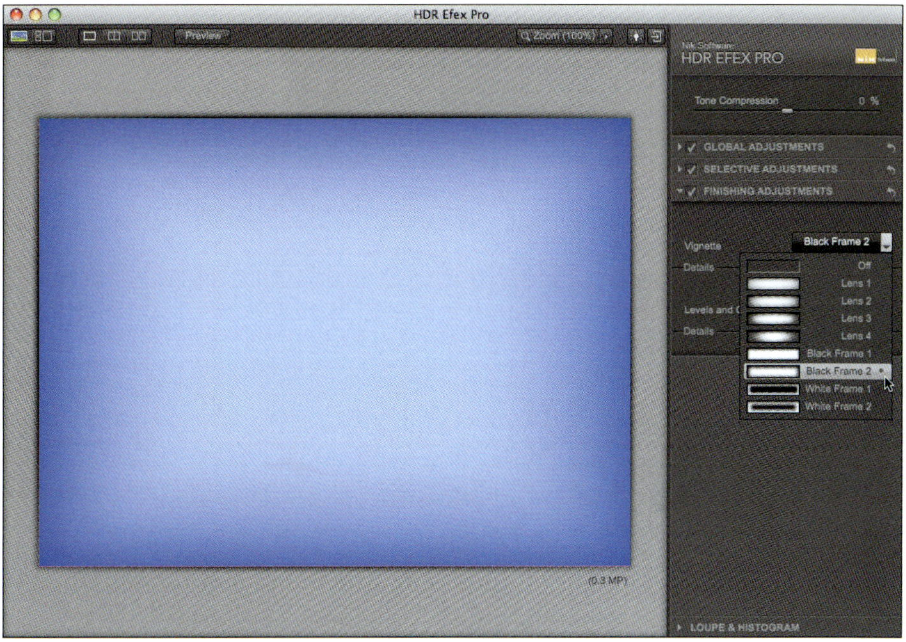

Figure 10.7

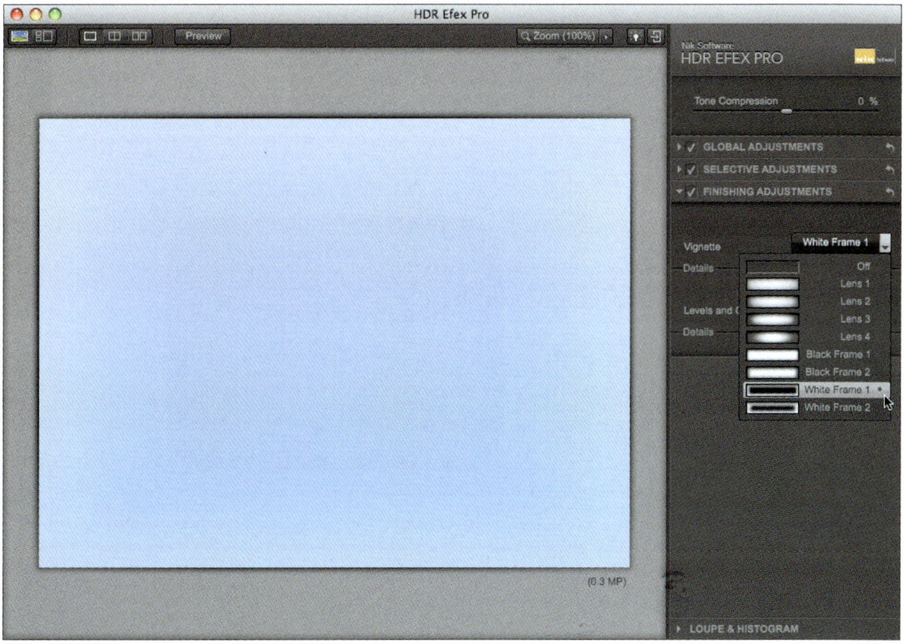

Figure 10.8

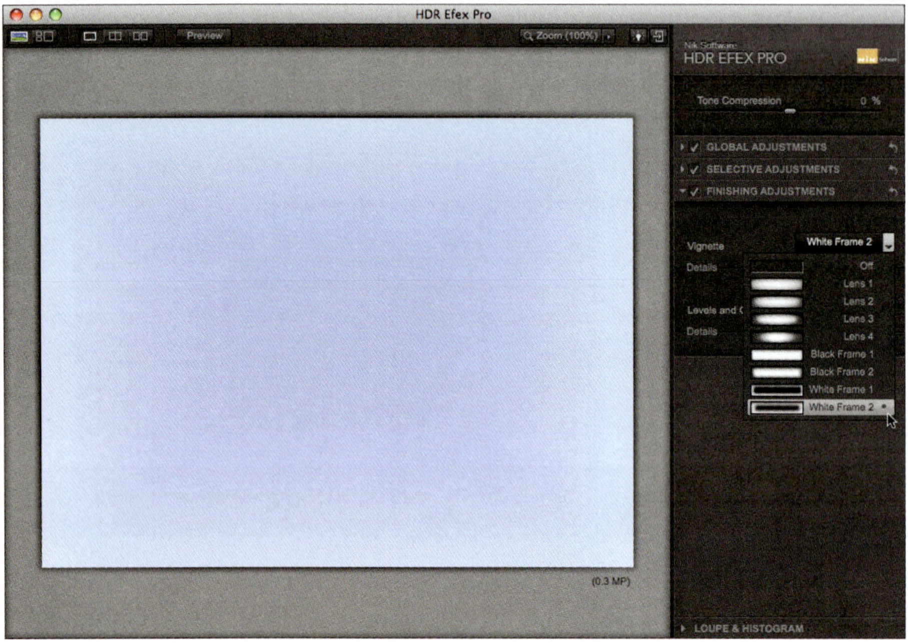

Figure 10.9

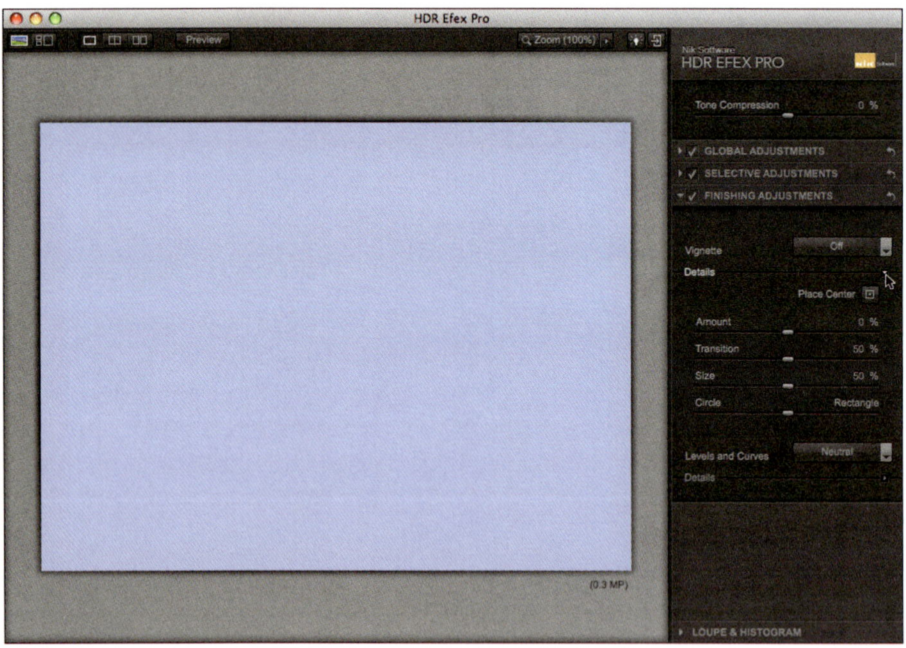

Figure 10.10

There is a Place Center button and four sliders:

- Amount
- Transition
- Size
- Circle—Rectangle

With enough experience working with the vignette tool it is possible to ignore the presets and work directly with these customizing tools. However, I recommend starting with a preset and then using the custom adjustments to fine-tune the vignette.

Adjusting the amount

The Amount slider controls the strength and tonal value adjustment of the vignette. The default is 0%, which produces no vignette at all. Moving the Amount slider to the left produces a gradually darker vignette, as shown in Figure 10.11. Moving the Amounts slider to the right produces a gradually lighter vignette, as shown in Figure 10.12.

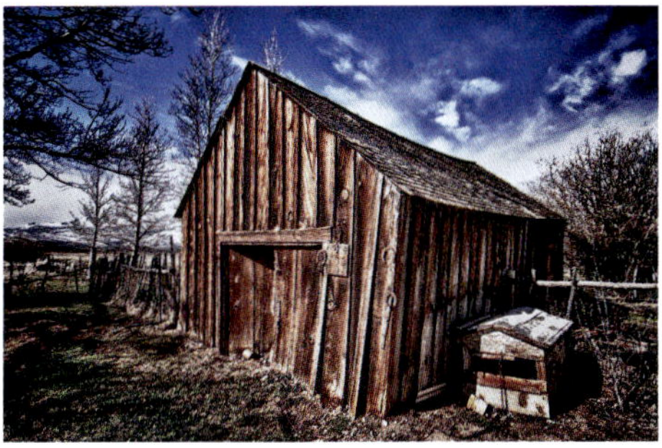

Figure 10.11

tip

To adjust the sliders in increments of 1%, position the cursor over the slider, click to highlight the slider and use the left and right arrow keys to adjust the slider.

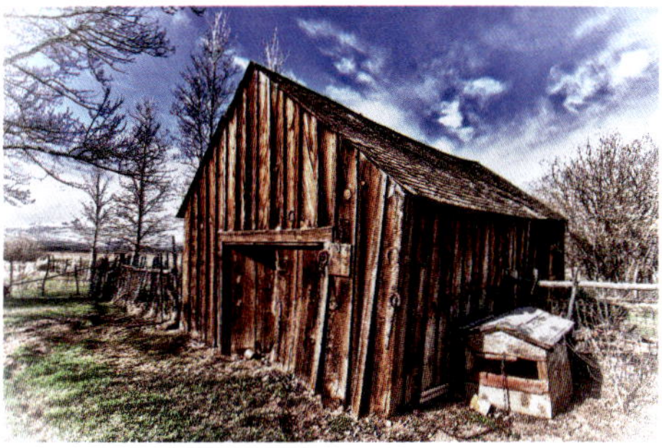

Figure 10.12

Adjusting the size and edge softness

The next two sliders, Transition and Size, work together to determine the relative degree of vignetting that is present in the image. With both of these sliders set to 0%, the other sliders and the Place Center button have no effect. At least one of these sliders must be set to an amount greater than 0% for the vignette to be active.

The Transition slider adjusts the softness of the edge of the vignette. With the Transition slider set to 0% and the Size slider set to 100%, the vignette has a fast transition from vignette to image and a relatively sharp edge, as shown in Figure 10.13.

Adjusting the Transition slider to the right from the 0% position gradually softens the edge of the transition. At 100% with the Size slider still set to 100%, as shown in Figure 10.14, the vignette transitions far into the image.

Leaving the Transition slider at 100% and adjusting the Size slider to 25% creates a very soft transition while keeping the lightening vignette from intruding very far into the center of the image. Figure 10.15 shows the result of these settings.

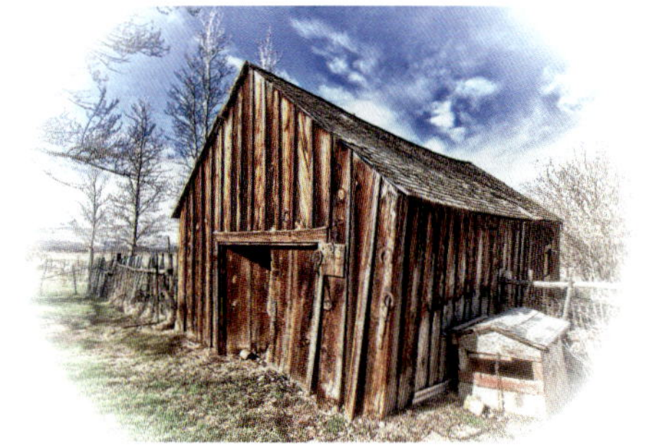

Figure 10.13

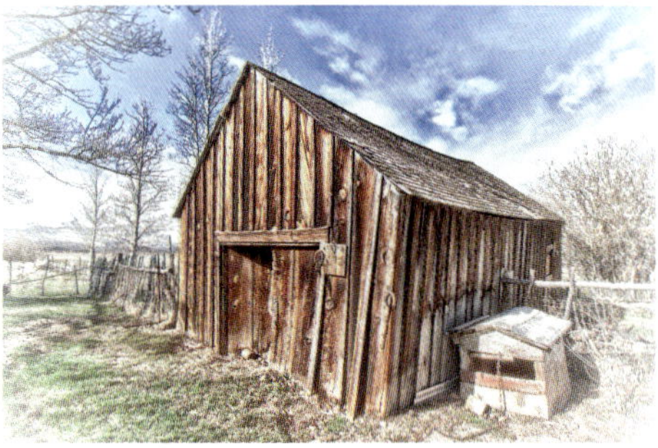

Figure 10.14

Because these two sliders are so intimately connected, adjusting them can be confusing. Small changes can be difficult to see, especially when the edges of the image contain a lot of detail rather than a smooth tone, like a blue sky.

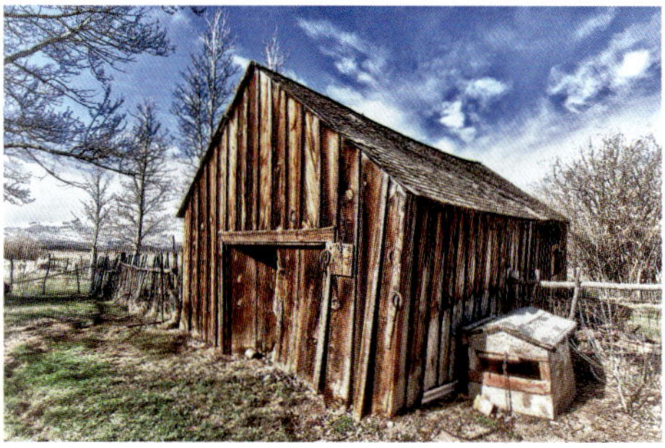

Figure 10.15

I have found the most efficient way to adjust the size and edge softness is by double-clicking the Size slider to set it to 50%, its default position, then adjusting the Transition slider to produce the edge softness that I want. Then I adjust the Size slider to the left to make the vignette smaller, or to the right to make it larger. Once you are familiar with these two sliders you only need to make these adjustments once to achieve the result you want.

Adjusting the shape

The final slider is labeled Circle on the left end and Rectangle on the right end. This slider controls the shape of the vignette from circular to elliptical to rectangular. Figure 10.16 shows the result of setting the slider all the way to the Circle position on the far left of the slider. I have exaggerated the vignette to make the shape more obvious by setting the amount to 100%, the transition to 0%, and the size to 80%.

With all the other sliders at the same settings that are used for Figure 10.16, moving the shape slider halfway between the Circle and Rectangle positions produces the elliptical vignette shown in Figure 10.17.

With the shape slider all the way to the right Rectangle setting, the vignette looks like Figure 10.18.

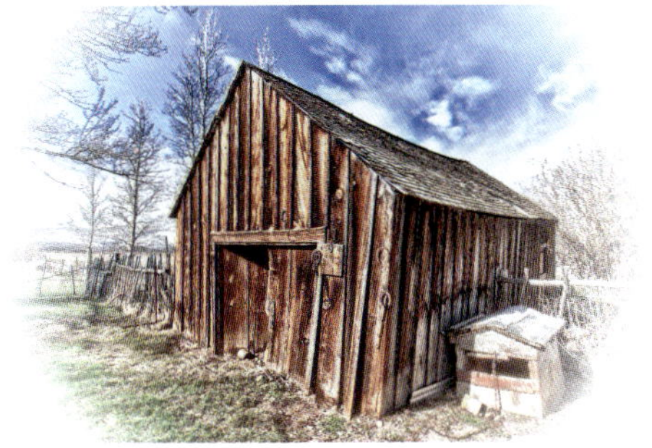

Figure 10.16

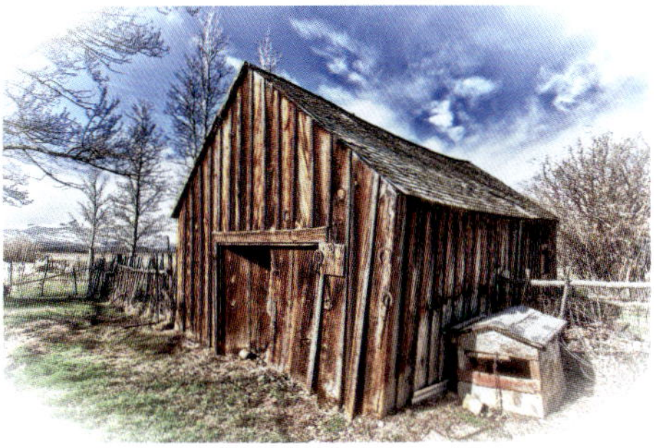

Figure 10.17

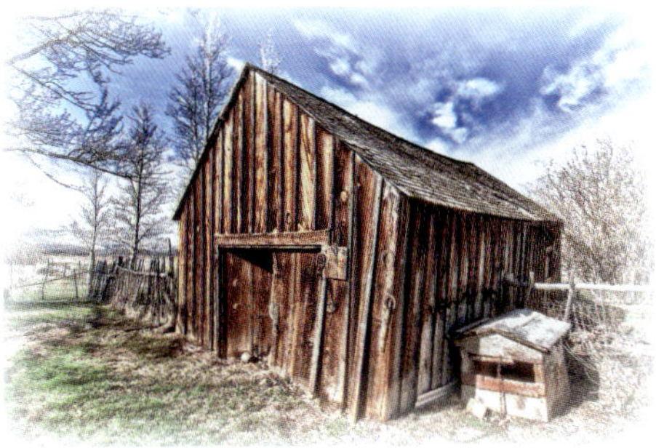

Figure 10.18

The transformations from circular through elliptical to rectangular are smooth, so there are many possibilities.

Adjusting the center

Adding to the possibilities is an option that is not often found in a vignette tool. HDR Efex Pro allows you to position the center of the vignette anywhere in the image.

Adjusting the position of the vignette is done with the Place Center button found just above the vignette sliders and shown in Figure 10.19.

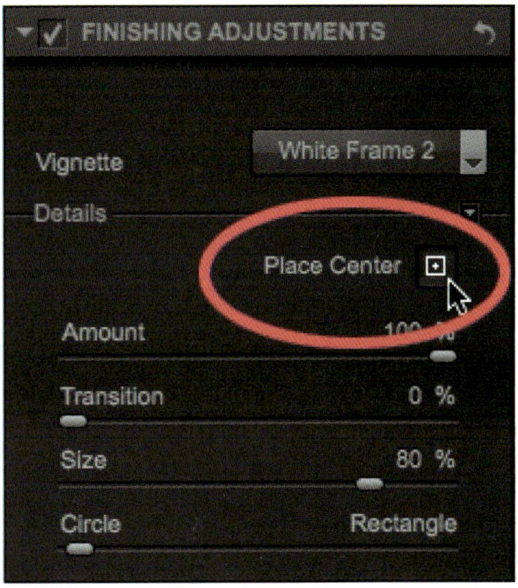

Figure 10.19

Figure 10.20 shows the result of clicking the Place Center button, which turns into a cross-shaped cursor when you roll your mouse over the image, and clicking the cursor at the center of the lower edge of the barn. Again, I am using the same exaggerated vignette to illustrate the resulting change in position.

You may not want an obvious vignette around your subject, but rather just a little something to add a gradation to the sky. The ability to reposition the vignette in this way allows you to add a

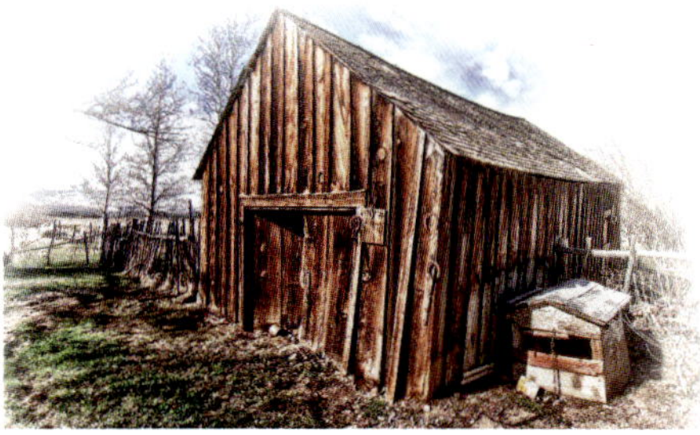

Figure 10.20

graduated neutral density filter or polarizer effect to darken the blue sky while having minimal effect on the rest of the image. The final result of applying these changes is shown in Figure 10.21.

With all the tone compression and global adjustments I made to the HDR image, the sky was still a flat tone of blue. I played around with adding Control Points, but couldn't get the sky to darken evenly from one side to the other.

Using the vignette tools, I chose the Lens 4 preset and adjusted the Amount slider to a high negative amount so I could easily see the effect. Then I

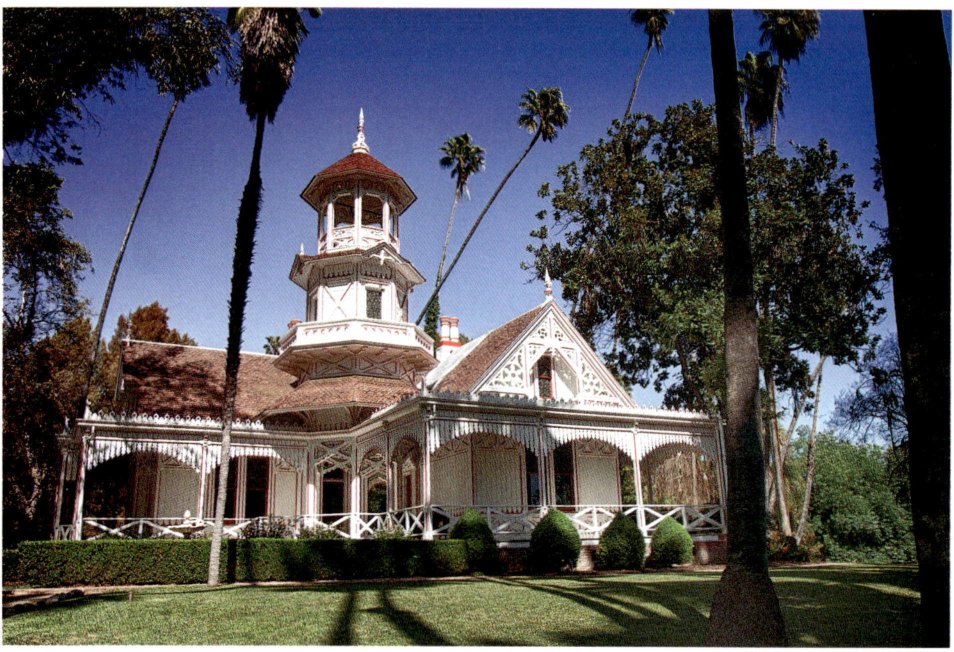

Figure 10.21

moved the Transition slider to a soft transition and adjusted the Size slider to give a small vignette. The vignette I created was still visible at the top, bottom, and a little on the sides.

Using the Place Center button, I set the center to a place on the foreground grass. It took a couple of tries to find just the right place. Then I went back and lowered the Amount slider setting and ended up with a nicely gradated blue sky and nothing in the image to give it away that I had created the gradation using a vignette.

At the close of the last chapter, I mentioned there was one more enhancement that I wanted to make to the bristlecone pines image, Figure 9.44. That enhancement is to add a soft vignette to darken the edges and draw the viewer further into the image. Figure 9.44 is reproduced again here as Figure 10.22.

I saved the image again as a Photoshop Smart Object, so I was able to open it in HDR Efex Pro with all the previous settings intact. I chose the Lens 2 preset as a starting point and adjusted the Amount slider to –100% to better view the vignette, as shown in Figure 10.23.

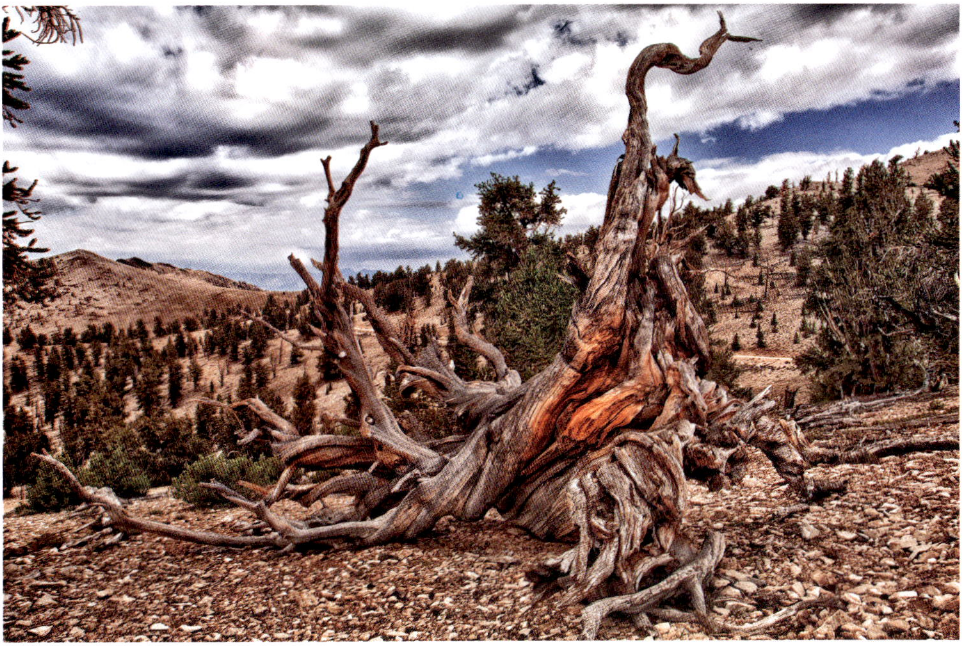

Figure 10.22

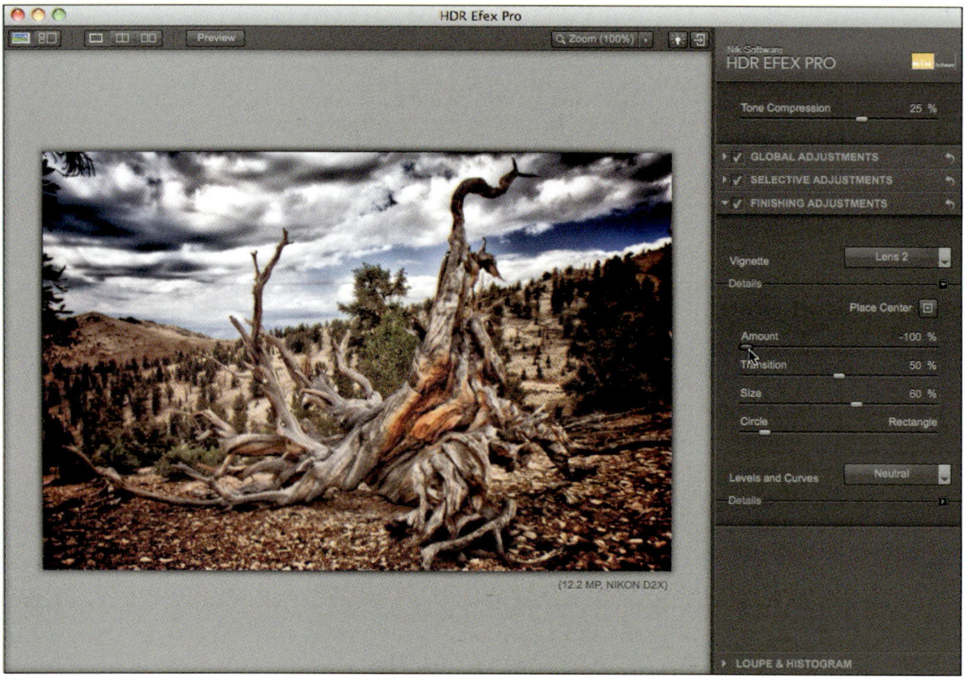

Figure 10.23

I wanted mostly just to darken the corners of the image. I did this by decreasing the Transition slider to make the transition more abrupt, and decreasing the size of the vignette to make the vignette itself smaller. The last step was to move the Amount slider from –100% to –20%. These settings are shown in Figure 10.24 and the final image is in Figure 10.25.

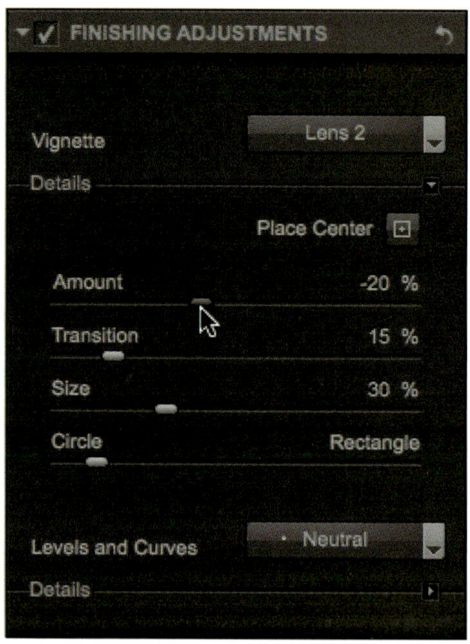

Figure 10.24

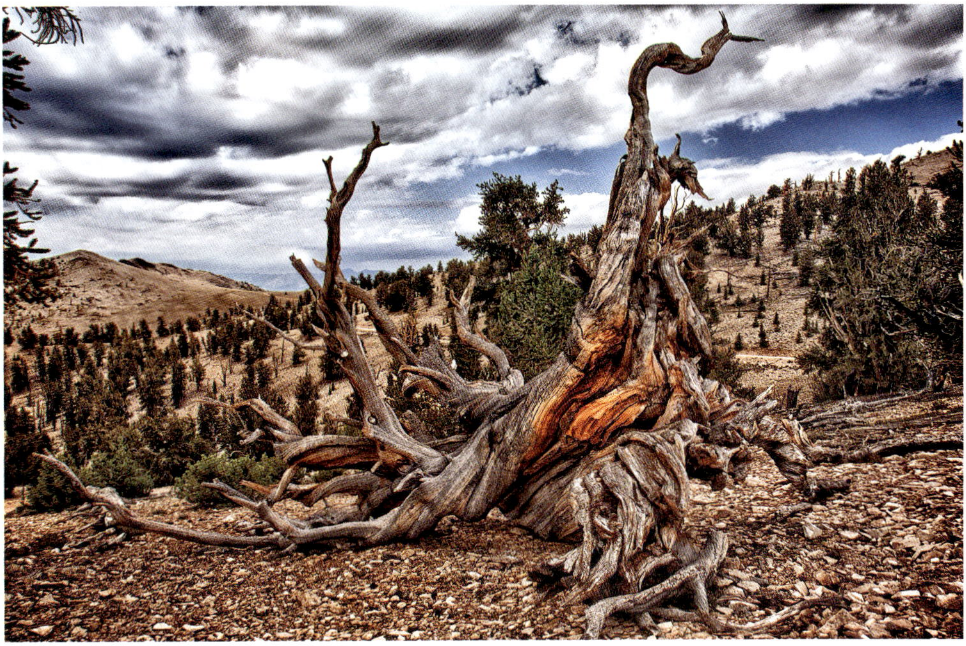

Figure 10.25

Adjusting Levels and Curves

I have previously cautioned against judging and adjusting your image based on the way it looks in the histogram in the Levels and Curves palette of the Finishing Adjustments. I repeat that caution here. It is far easier to work with a color-managed monitor and use the white, gray, and black backgrounds in HDR Efex Pro when adjusting your images than to adjust your image based on the histogram approximation.

If you aren't completely comfortable using the Curves tool in Photoshop, you will likely have a difficult time with Levels and Curves in HDR Efex Pro. Depending on the speed of your computer, any change made to the curve will take some time to appear in the image and in the histogram itself. This can lead you to making another change before the first change completely takes effect. And small changes in the histogram can result in large changes in the look of the HDR image.

Fortunately, HDR Efex Pro has a Reset button in the Levels and Curves palette that resets any adjustments to the Neutral Levels and Curves setting. However, clicking Reset can be unfortunate if the preset you have chosen uses a curves adjustment. If the Reset button changes your preset curve to Neutral, you need to choose the preset again, and in doing so, you lose all the other adjustments you have made. When you adjust the curve of a preset containing a curves adjustment and want to return to the original preset curve, use the Ctrl/⌘+Z keyboard shortcut rather than the Reset button.

Levels and Curves is a powerful but dangerous tool. Many of the manual adjustments you can make to the curve are the same adjustments you can make with global adjustments such as exposure and contrast. Many of the preset curves are far too strong to apply unless the image is very low in contrast. You will miss very little and you may save yourself some time and frustration if you simply skip over this section of the chapter. However, if you feel adventurous, read on.

The Levels and Curves tool (Figure 10.26), is found below the Vignette tools in the Finishing Adjustments section.

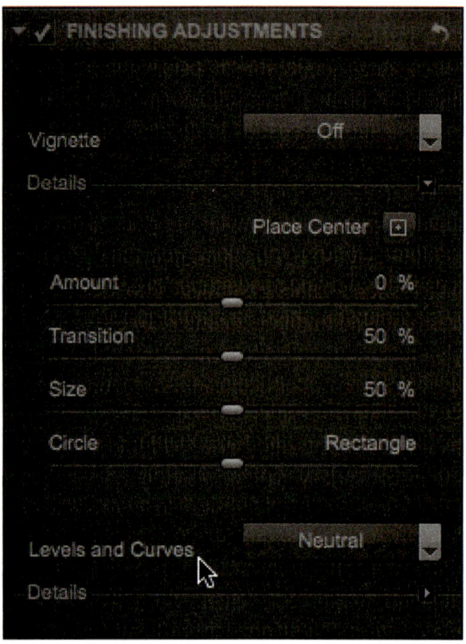

Figure 10.26

The Levels and Curves tool consists of two parts: a set of presets shown in Figure 10.27 and a curves diagram shown in Figure 10.28. If the diagram is not open, click on the twirler opposite the Details name.

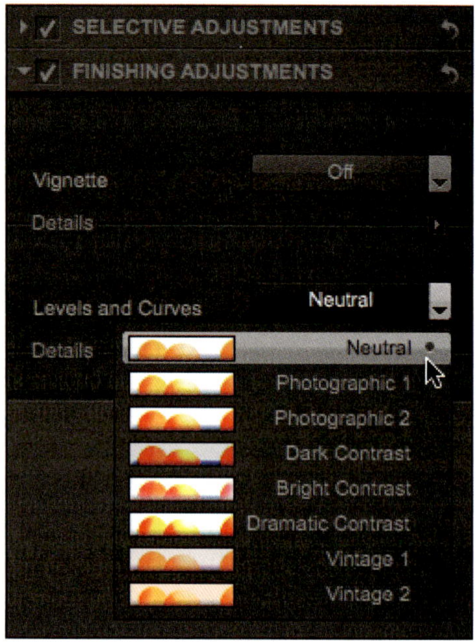

Figure 10.27

Understanding the curves diagram

Before looking at the eight presets, it is important to understand the curves diagram in Figure 10.28, because each of the presets is represented by different settings on the diagram.

The horizontal axis of the diagram represents the tonal range of the HDR image before any adjustments are made to it. The point farthest to the left represents an RGB value of 0, pure black, and the point farthest to the right represents an RGB value of 255, pure white. The midpoint of the horizontal axis represents a neutral gray tone.

The vertical axis of the diagram represents the tonal range of the adjusted image. The lowest point represents pure black and the highest point represents pure white. The midpoint again represents a neutral gray.

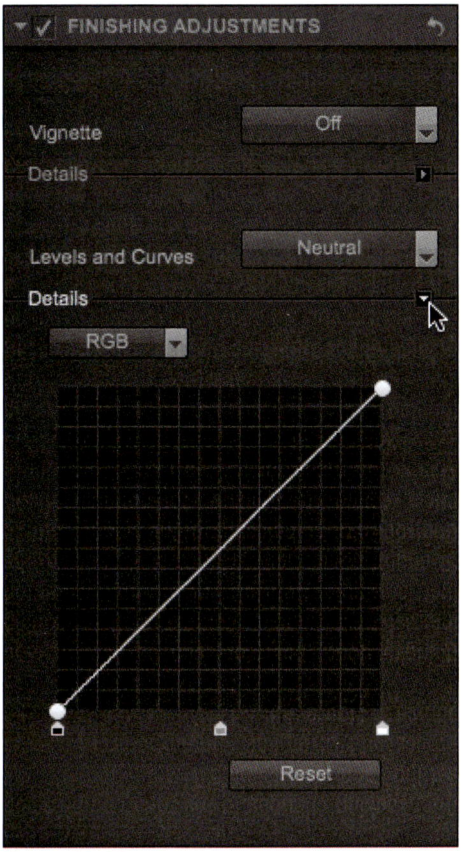

Figure 10.28

The diagram consists of a grid of 256 squares. As shown in Figure 10.28, there is a diagonal line from the lower left to the upper right. This line is the "curve" of the Curves tool. It represents the relationship between the unadjusted tones in the default image and the modified tones in the adjusted image. When it is straight and diagonal as shown, the adjusted tonal values are identical to the unadjusted tonal values.

When the curve is no longer straight but is actually curved, as it is in most of the presets in the Preset Browser, the shape represents a nonlinear relationship between the unadjusted and the adjusted tonal values. In the unadjusted image when the curve is a straight line, adjacent tonal values are separated by an equal amount. In the adjusted image, tonal values that were adjacent no longer are separated by equal amounts. Light tones could be lighter or darker than they were in the unadjusted image and separated from neighboring tones by a different amount than they were in the unadjusted image. The same could hold true for midtones or dark values, also. Each of the Levels and Curves presets is based on a curve of a different shape. It is also possible to change the shape of the curve manually, which is discussed later in the chapter.

Above the diagram is a drop-down menu. The default position is RGB and the diagram represents the relationship between all the primary colors in the image. Clicking on the drop-down menu opens it as shown in Figure 10.29. With Red, Green, or Blue selected, the diagram shows the relationship between the unadjusted and adjusted tonal values for each of these colors.

With an image open, as shown in Figure 10.30, a histogram of the image tones is overlaid on the diagram. Figure 10.30 shows how the unadjusted image is represented when the Default preset is selected.

There is another change to the diagram when an image is open that is shown in Figure 10.30. Three small icons appear below the horizontal axis. These icons are, from left to right, the black-point slider, the midtone slider, and the white-point slider. These three sliders are the Levels tool for the image. For all the presets, these sliders remain in the positions shown in Figure 10.30. Later in the chapter I discuss making manual adjustments to the Levels sliders.

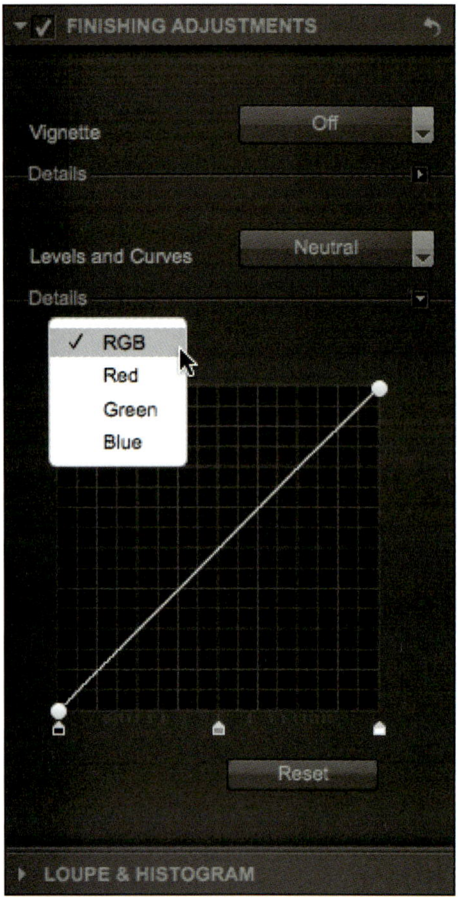

Figure 10.29

Selecting a preset adjustment

Eight preset curve adjustments are available in HDR Efex Pro. Access these by clicking on the Levels and Curves drop-down menu. The program uses the preset curve adjustments to create the different looks produced by the HDR presets. The curve presets can also be used as initial adjustments for manually changing the curve of the image.

The Neutral preset illustrated in Figure 10.31 is used by the Default preset and is represented by a straight line on the diagram. Input tonal values are not adjusted with the Neutral preset.

The Photographic 1 preset modifies the tonal relationship with a gentle S curve, as shown in Figure 10.32. This curve is similar to the way a lower-contrast photographic film would have captured the scene. Both lighter and darker tones are modified slightly. Contrast, represented by how steeply the middle portion of the curve rises, is increased, but only slightly over the straight-line steepness of the Neutral preset.

The Photographic 2 preset in Figure 10.33 presents a steeper curve than the Photographic 1 preset, and the increased contrast is visible in the image. The result is still very photographic, like a contrasty color slide film. The increased contrast results from moving the two points on the curve between the endpoints closer together. These points are called *anchor points,* and they represent points on the curve where the shape of the curve is modified.

The remaining presets move further and further from photographic representations. The Dark Contrast preset shown in Figure 10.34 adds an additional anchor point in the dark values, and both of the anchor points in the dark values are lower than the anchors in the two Photographic presets. Their lower position in the vertical axis means that the adjusted tones are darker and this is obvious in the image.

The Bright Contrast preset shown in Figure 10.35 has an additional anchor point in the lighter tones of the curve. This anchor point is raised along the vertical axis, so the tones are brighter. The steepness of the straighter portion of the curve is about the same as the previous two presets, which is greater than the Photographic presets, but the result is not overly contrasty.

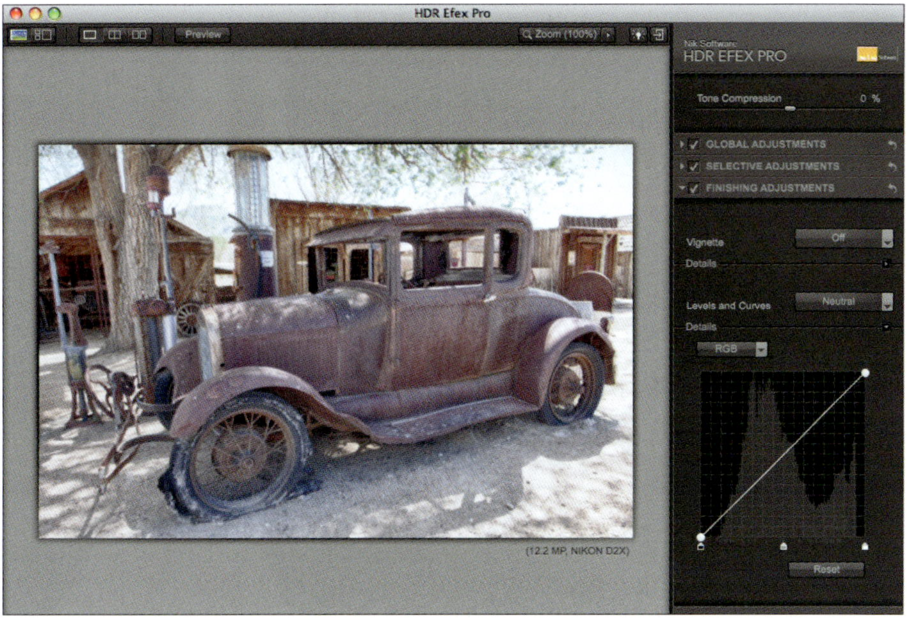

Figure 10.30

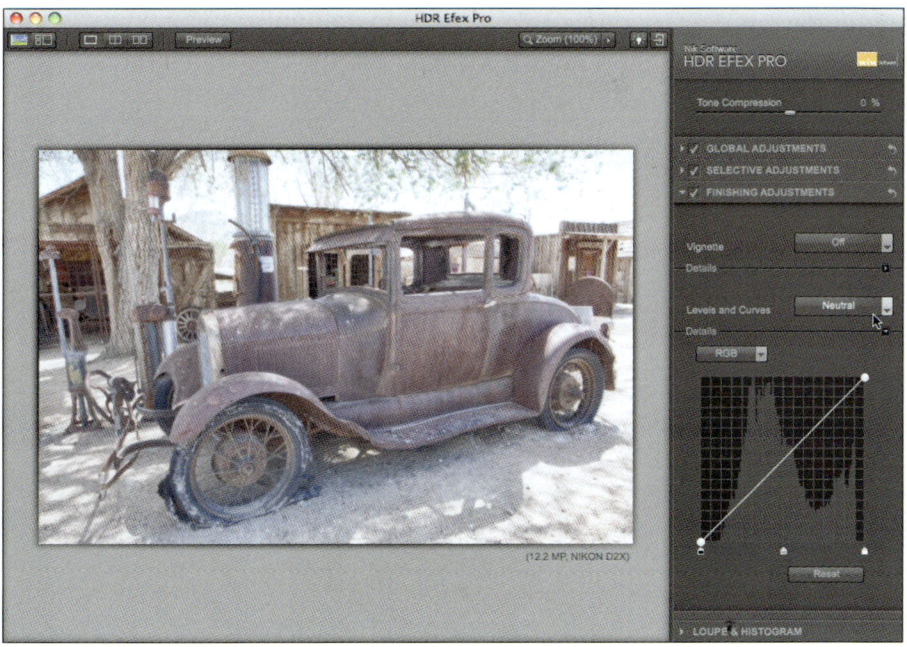

Figure 10.31

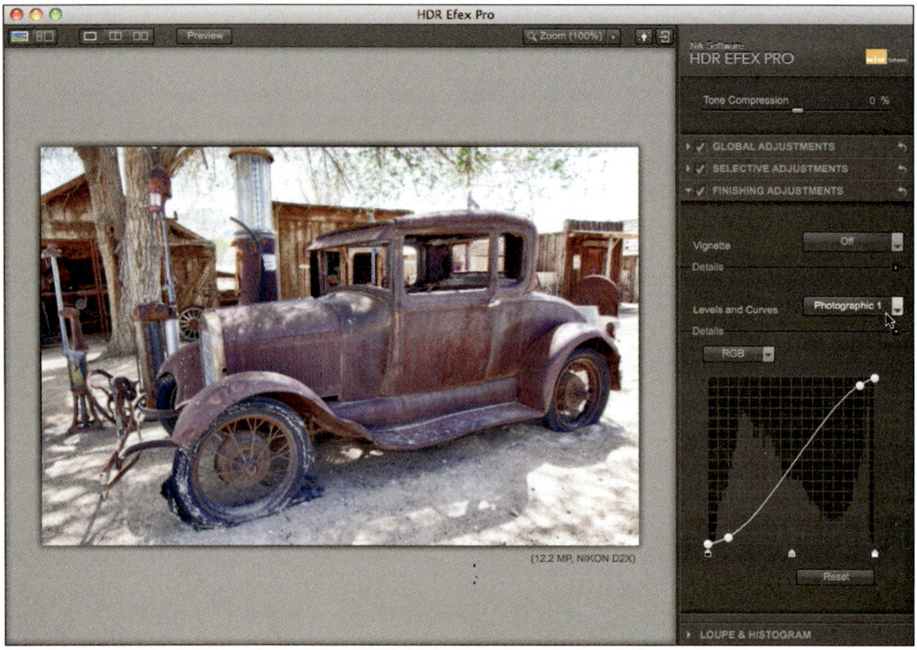

Figure 10.32

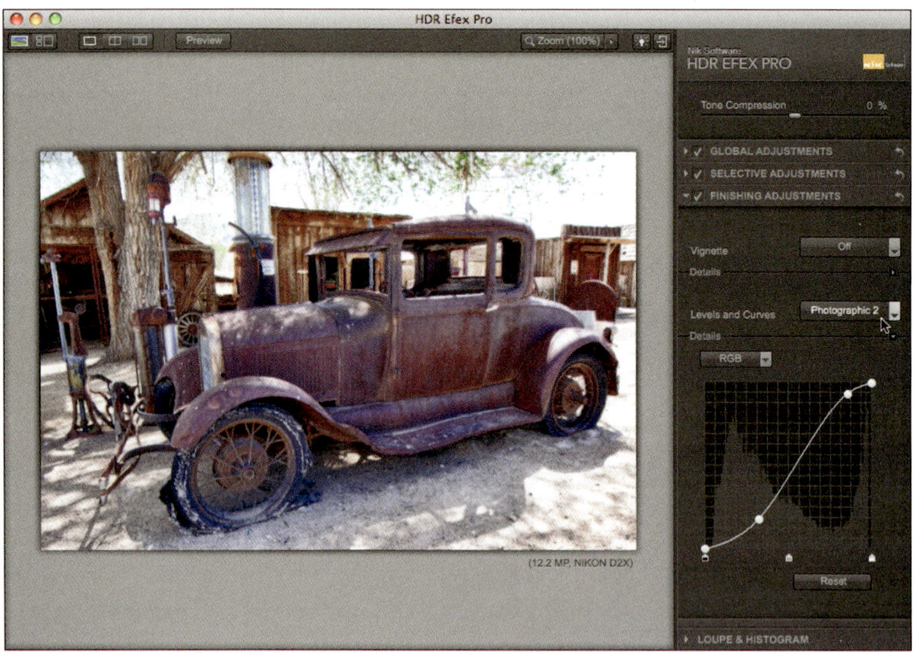

Figure 10.33

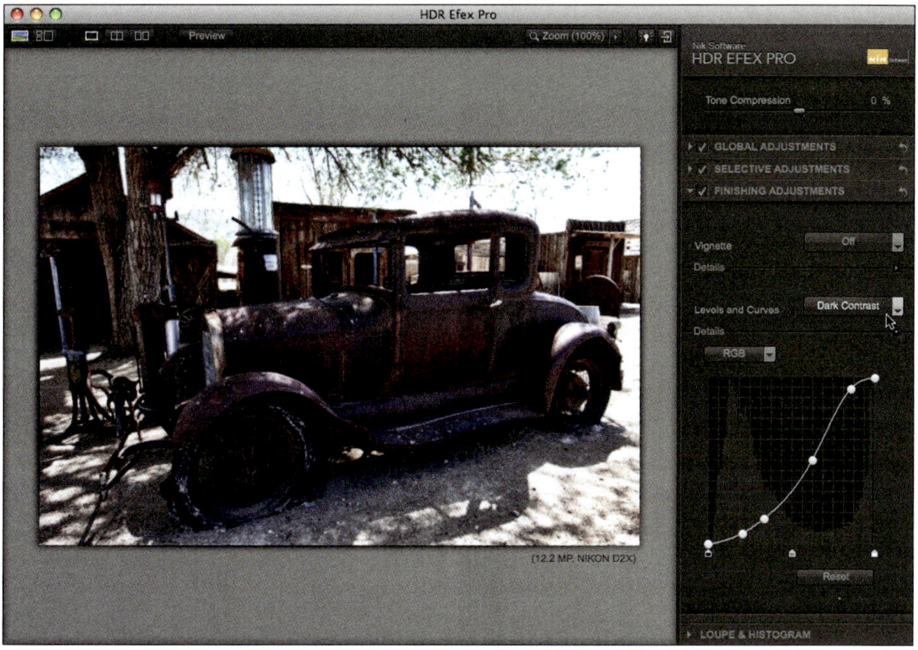

Figure 10.34

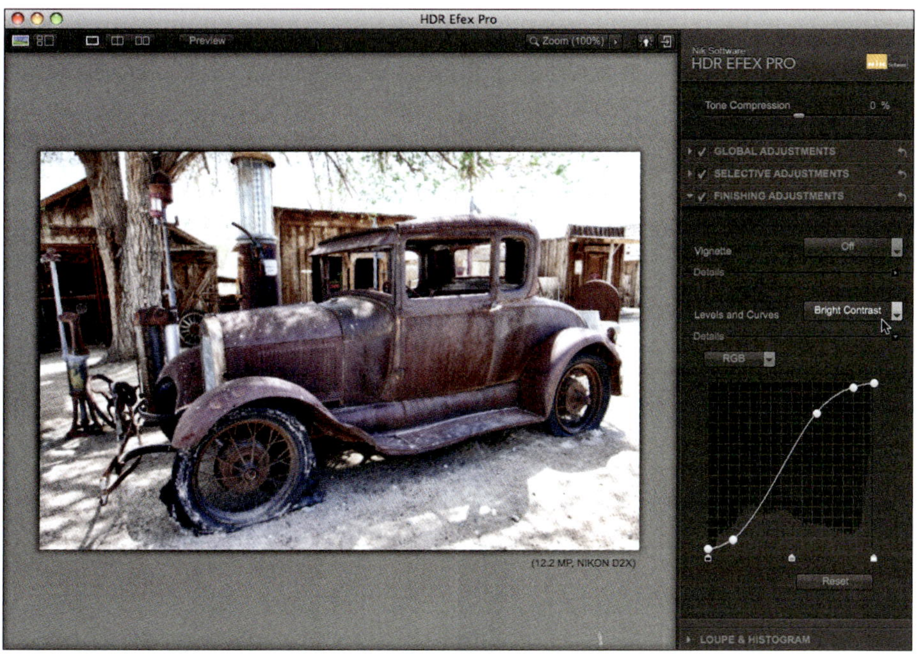

Figure 10.35

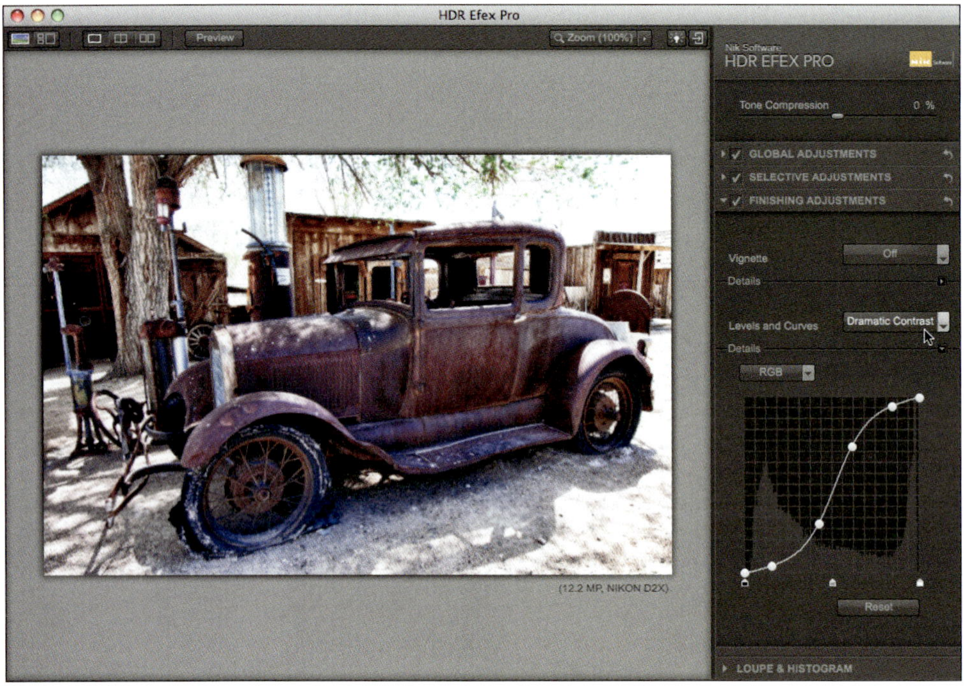

Figure 10.36

The Dramatic Contrast preset in Figure 10.36 is probably over the top for all but the lowest-contrast HDR images. The additional anchor points lower the dark tones and raise the light tones. The center section of the curve is approaching vertical, resulting in very high contrast in the image. This extreme adjustment could only be made in an HDR image with its enormous tonal range. With a lower bit-depth image, tones would be dropping out and large gaps would appear in the histogram. I have yet to find one of my images on which I would use this preset unmodified.

The final two presets are Vintage 1 and Vintage 2. They use the same RGB curve as the Photographic 1 preset, but produce far different results. The Vintage presets differ from all the previous presets because they include adjustments to individual RGB curves. These adjustments to the separate color curves change the color balance of the image.

Figure 10.37 shows the Vintage 1 preset with the adjustment that is present in the Blue curve. The inverse S curve lowers the contrast in the blues. That effect turns out to be helpful for this image because most of it is in shadow and lit by blue sky rather than the sun. There are other adjustments to the other colors, but the change to the blues is the most dramatic.

The Vintage 2 preset is shown in Figure 10.38. Again, I am showing the adjustment made to the Blue curve, as it is the most dramatic. While the curve is nearly a diagonal, thc cndpoints for both the dark and light values have been changed from the lower and upper limits. The effect of these changes is to remove the blue from the darkest and lightest values of the image. Combined with small changes to the Red and Green curves, the result is a purple tone in the image.

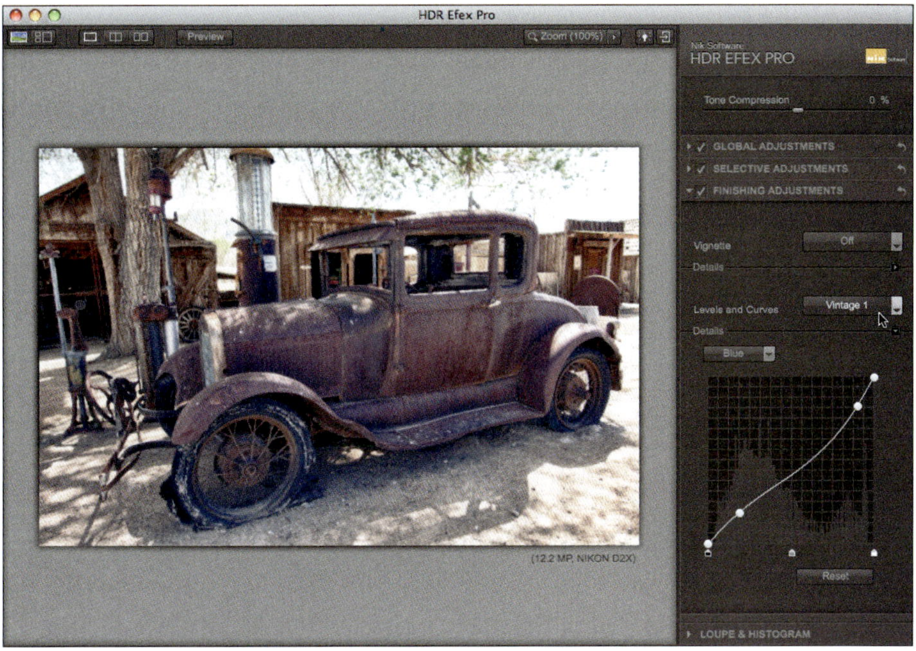

Figure 10.37

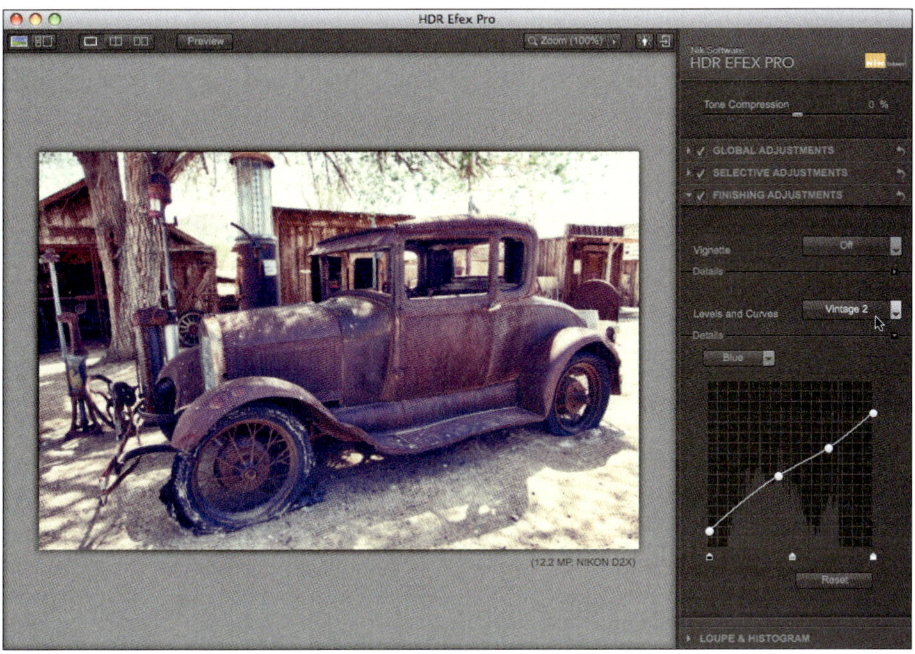

Figure 10.38

It is possible to use these Curves presets to replace any of the Curves presets used by the HDR presets from the Preset Browser. However, the Curves presets are pretty heavy handed with most images. I deliberately chose a low-contrast HDR image to use as an example, and most of the presets are still too strong. But, like the HDR presets in the Preset Browser, the Curves presets can be changed manually.

Adjusting Levels and Curves manually

As I have said several times, I recommend using the Global Adjustments sliders along with the black and white backgrounds in HDR Efex Pro to adjust the black and white points of the image. However, it is possible to obtain the same result by adjusting the Levels icons.

Moving the black-point slider to the right darkens the dark tones, just as adjusting the Global Adjustments Blacks slider to the right does. Moving the white-point slider to the left brightens the lightest values, the same as adjusting the Global Adjustments Whites slider to the right does. As these sliders move, the curve and histogram readjust to display the new relationships.

Adjusting the midtone slider also changes the curve and histogram. Moving it to the left, toward the darker tones, shifts the histogram to the left and lightens the midtones. Moving the midtone slider to the right shifts the histogram to the left and darkens the midtones.

tip

Double-click a Levels slider to return it to the default position.

Adjusting Curves rather than Levels can produce far more dramatic changes to the image. The shape of the curve can be modified in any conceivable way. This is done by clicking on the curve at any point to add an anchor point. Dragging an anchor point upward creates a peak in the curve and makes the corresponding tone and those close to it lighter. Dragging an anchor point downward creates a valley and the associated tones become darker. Increasing the steepness of the curve adds contrast to the image. Flattening the curve decreases contrast.

Dragging the curve in bizarre ways, as I have done in Figure 10.39, creates bizarre results, like solarized-looking highlights.

If you are truly adventurous, try making changes to the individual RGB curves to change the color balance of the image. Dragging down the dark tones of the Blue curve adds warmth to shadow areas. Increasing the midtones and lighter tones in the Red channel adds warmth to a sunset or makes an old truck look more rusted as in Figure 10.40.

After making adjustments to the individual color channels of the HDR image in Figure 10.39, my final rather conservative result is shown in Figure 10.41. In the process of deciding that this would be my final image, I created bizarre solarized colors and cross-processed-looking images. The range of possibilities is only limited by your patience and your artistic taste.

It only takes a small change to the curve to make a dramatic change to the image, particularly in the RGB color curves. And it is difficult to make small changes. Even with a very fast computer, the change to the shape of the curve and the redraw of the image is slow. You can be tempted to think your change was too small and drag the anchor point higher, and then find that the first adjustment hadn't completed and now you have overdone the change. Unfortunately, the anchor points don't respond to tapping the arrow keys or any other way to make accurate small

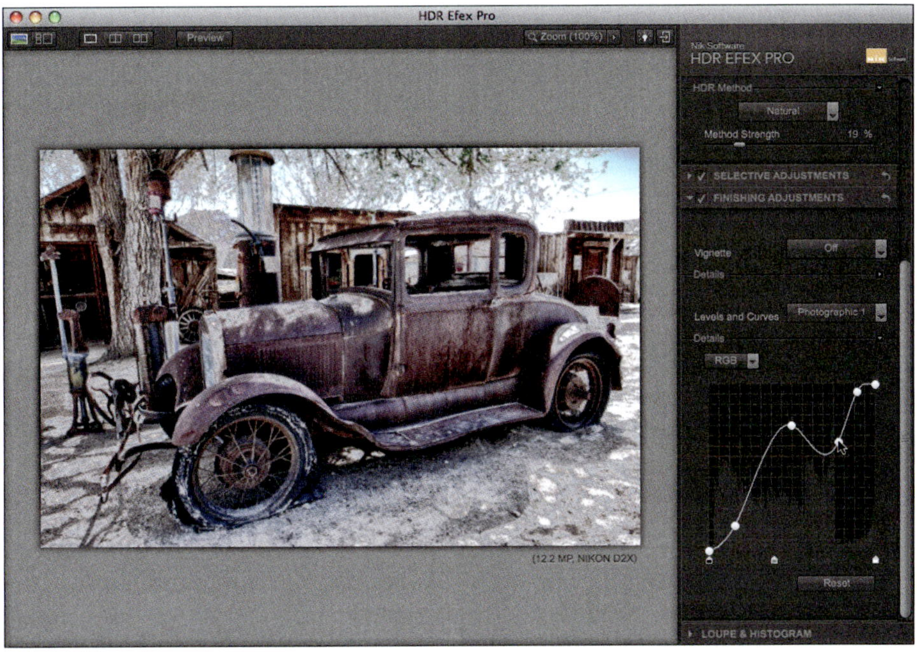

Figure 10.39

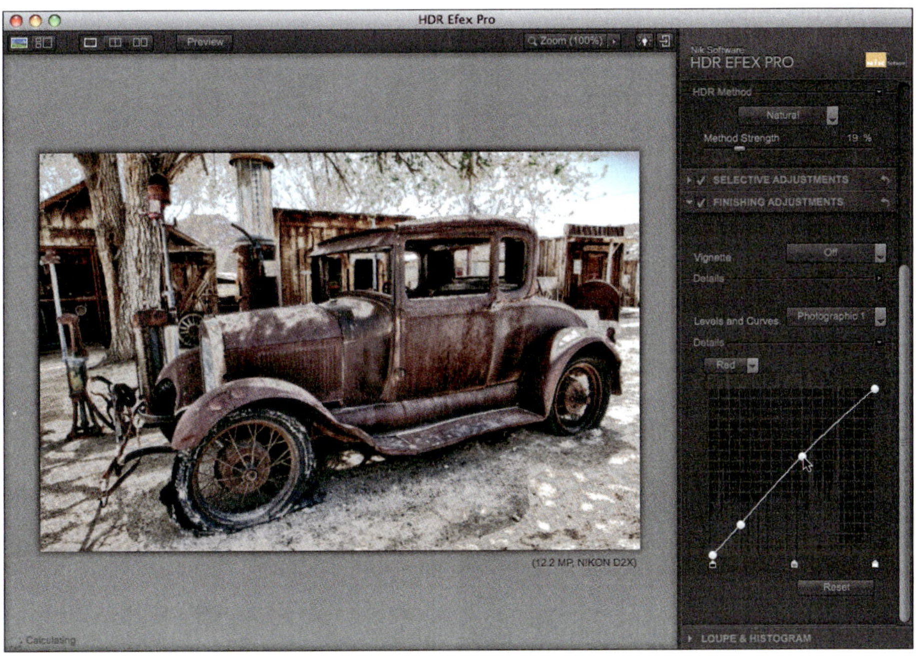

Figure 10.40

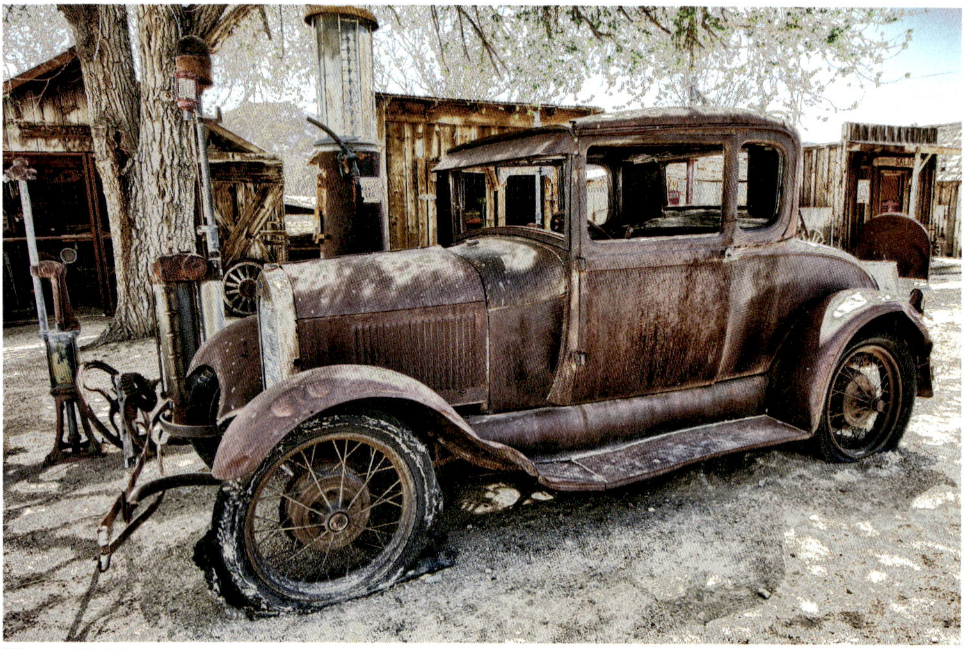

Figure 10.41

adjustments. So be patient if you have adventured into Curves adjustments. And remember that clicking Reset takes everything back to the Neutral Curve preset, which may save you, or force you to begin all your adjustments again.

tip

To remove an anchor point, double-click it.

tip

If you create a custom curve with a result you really like, open the Preset Browser if it is not already open and save the image as a Custom Preset. The adjustment curve changes become part of the preset and can be recalled in the future.

Checking the Image Before Saving

HDR Efex Pro contains two more displays that seem almost an afterthought on the part of the program designers. These displays are the Loupe and the Histogram, and they share a window at the very bottom of the Control Palette, as shown in Figure 10.42. If the window is closed, click the twirler to open it.

The Loupe & Histogram window is locked in position and can't be unlocked and docked anywhere else on the screen. I don't find myself consulting it very often, but you may.

Figure 10.42

Using the Loupe

Clicking Loupe opens the Loupe view if it isn't already active. The Loupe view displays the area of the image beneath the cursor at 100% with all the image adjustments applied. With the Loupe view open you can drag the cursor around the image and preview any part of it at 100%.

This is the same view that is available using the Zoom tool at 100%. The difference is that with the Loupe window open, it is always possible to make a quick check of the image at 100% without selecting the Zoom tool. And because it is a small area, as you move your cursor around the image the Loupe view updates almost instantaneously, even after you have made a large set of global and local adjustments, or if your computer isn't very fast.

The Loupe view is also useful if you want to preview the effect of making an adjustment on a specific area of the image. In Figure 10.42, there is a pushpin icon at the right side of the Loupe & Histogram title bar.

Its default position is shown in Figure 10.43, with the tip of the pushpin pointing slightly to the right. This is the unlocked position, and the Loupe view changes as the cursor moves over the screen image.

Click the pushpin and it becomes your cursor icon. Move it around the image until the area of interest is displayed in the Loupe window, and then click the left mouse button to lock that view in the Loupe window. The pushpin icon is now vertical in the Loupe & Histogram title bar as shown in Figure 10.42, and the view is locked in the window. Any adjustments you make to the area in the view are instantaneously displayed in the Loupe window.

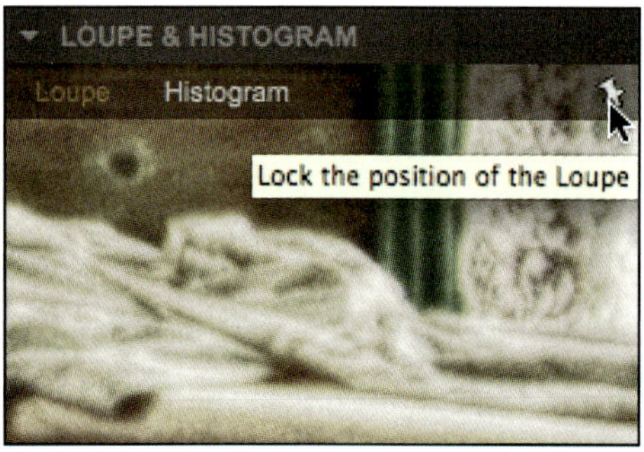

Figure 10.43

tip

With the Loupe window open, clicking the right mouse button activates and deactivates the pushpin, respectively locking and unlocking the view.

Understanding the Histogram

Click Histogram in the Loupe & Histogram title bar and the Histogram window opens, as shown in Figure 10.44. The general shape of the histogram is the same as that of the histogram in the Curves display, but this histogram shows the relative distribution of RGB values. The color channels are displayed in their respective colors. There is also a black line that shows the composite histogram.

As with the histogram in the Curves display, dark values are on the left and light values to the right. For Figure 10.44, the histogram shows that there is a lot of Blue and Green information and very little Red information in the darkest areas of the image. Very quickly, the Green values fall off and track the Red values through the remainder of the dark tones, midtones, and highlights. Blue values remain below the Red, and Green values for much of the image until the lightest tones.

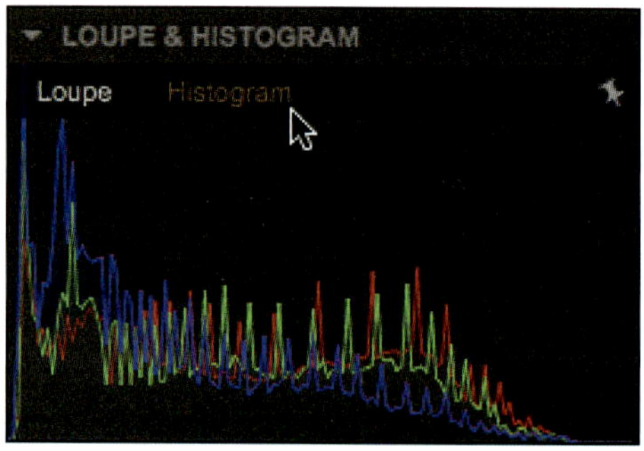

Figure 10.44

This is even more clearly shown when you click in the Histogram window. The view changes with each click, from the composite view in Figure 10.44 to views of the individual color channels. The Red channel is shown in Figure 10.45, the Green channel in Figure 10.46, and the Blue channel in Figure 10.47.

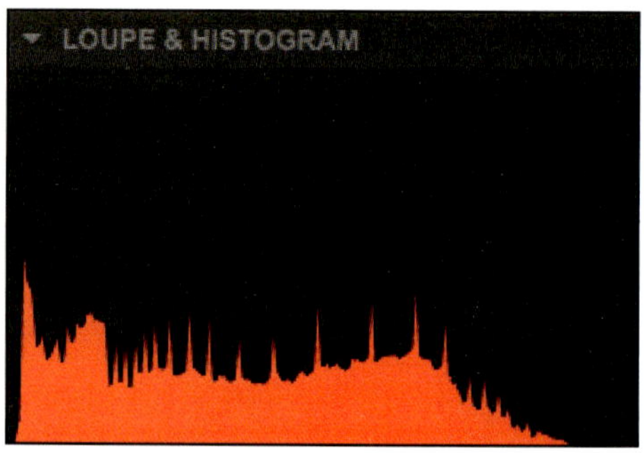

Figure 10.45

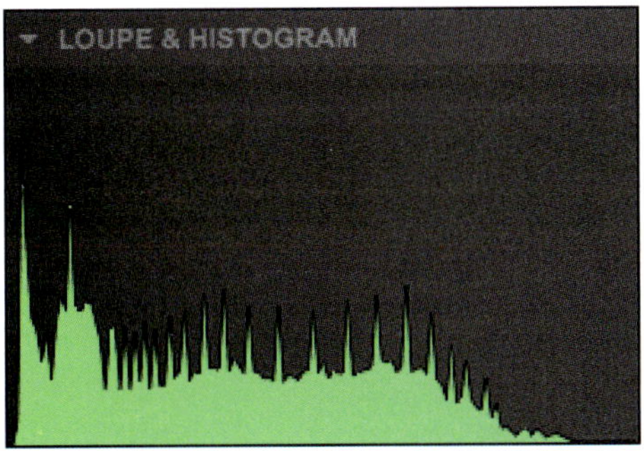

Figure 10.46

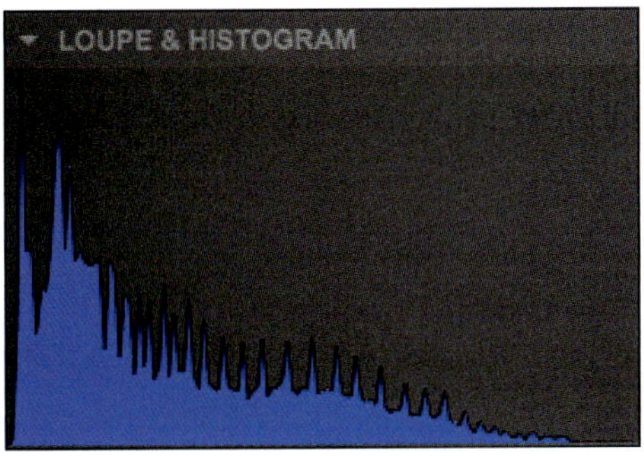

Figure 10.47

For me, this is all very nice, but I just don't ever find myself using the information. I judge the image by the way it looks in the Main Image Window, against the white, gray, and black backgrounds. I use global and local adjustments to warm or cool the image. And if I'm really feeling brave, I open the color channels in the Curves display and make a small change to the curve. I encourage you to also make your decisions based on the look of the image preview on a color-managed monitor, not on its graphical representation on a histogram.

Saving Your HDR Image

With your image adjusted and finalized, it is time to save it. How you save it depends on the preferences you select in HDR Efex Pro and on the imaging program you use to open the image or image series. The remainder of this chapter looks at each of the imaging programs and the ways in which it is possible to save the image.

see also

Chapter 2 discusses HDR Efex Pro preferences available through the Settings button and suggests settings to use when the final HDR image is saved. Chapter 3 discusses opening images through the imaging programs.

When opened from Lightroom

The default file format and bit depth of the HDR output image are determined by the initial choices made in the drop-down menu in the Image Output Settings palette of the Settings palette in HDR Efex Pro. In Chapter 2, I recommend making the default setting TIFF 16 unless the HDR images are primarily created only for the web where JPEG is the correct choice.

However, if you decide you prefer a different file format or bit depth than the one you selected when you initially set the preferences, click

Settings in HDR Efex Pro, open the Image Output Settings palette, as shown in Figure 10.48, and change the setting before you click Save to save the image. For example, if your default is TIFF 16, but you created a quick HDR image to e-mail, you can change the setting to JPEG. This change now becomes your new default setting.

Once you save an image that you opened in Lightroom, the location of the file is determined by the setting in the Stacking palette. I recommended using the HDR Efex Pro default settings. These settings automatically reimport the image to Lightroom with "_HDR" added to the name of the first image in the image series and with the HDR image "stacked" next to the first image in the series. This is shown in Figure 10.49.

If you originally chose to automatically reimport but not to stack the image, the final HDR is saved to the original folder in Lightroom with "_HDR" appended to the filename, but with no indication that it is associated (stacked) with another image.

If you choose not to automatically reimport, HDR Efex Pro presents you with the standard Save As dialog box for your operating system.

And if you decide that the default setting you originally made in the Settings palette is not appropriate for this image you are saving, click Settings and change the Stacking setting. HDR Efex Pro remembers this change and the change becomes your new default.

When opened from Aperture

When saving images that began with an image series in Apple Aperture, HDR Efex Pro treats the image in the same way it treats an image series opened in Lightroom. The file format and bit depth of the HDR output image are determined by the choices in the drop-down menu in the Image Output Settings palette of the Settings palette, as shown in Figure 10.48. If you decide to use a different file format or bit depth for a particular image, click Settings, open the Image Output Setting palette, and change the settings. These become your new default settings.

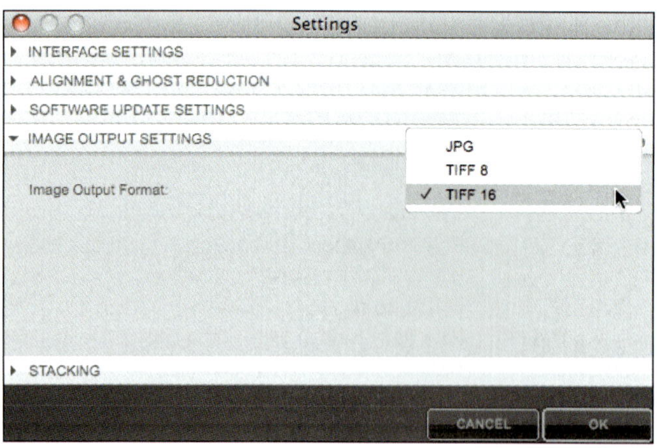

Figure 10.48

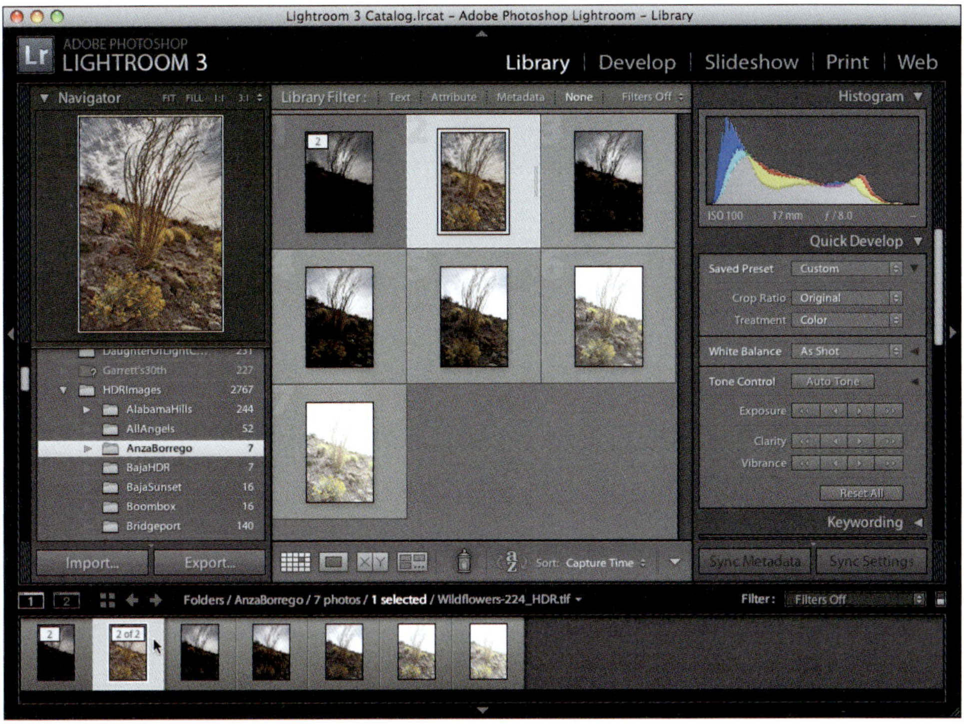

Figure 10.49

The file location where the image is saved is determined, as it is with Lightroom, by the settings in the Stacking palette. If both "Automatically Re-import" and "Stack with first image" are selected, the HDR image is saved in the same folder as the image series with "_HDR" appended to the image filename and placed in the browser next to the first image in the image series. Aperture adds a number in the upper-left corner of the thumbnail. The number is one greater than the number of images in the series. If the image series has seven brackets, the number is 8, as shown in Figure 10.50.

If you decide you want to save the image in a location other than the location of the image series, open the Stacking palette and deselect the check box for automatically reimporting the image. The Stack with first image check box is automatically deselected and when you click Save in HDR Efex Pro, the standard Save as dialog box appears.

As with Lightroom, leaving the Automatically Re-import check box selected but deselecting Stack with first image saves the HDR image in the same directory as the image series, but the HDR image is not stacked with the first image in the series and the thumbnail in Aperture has no number associated with it.

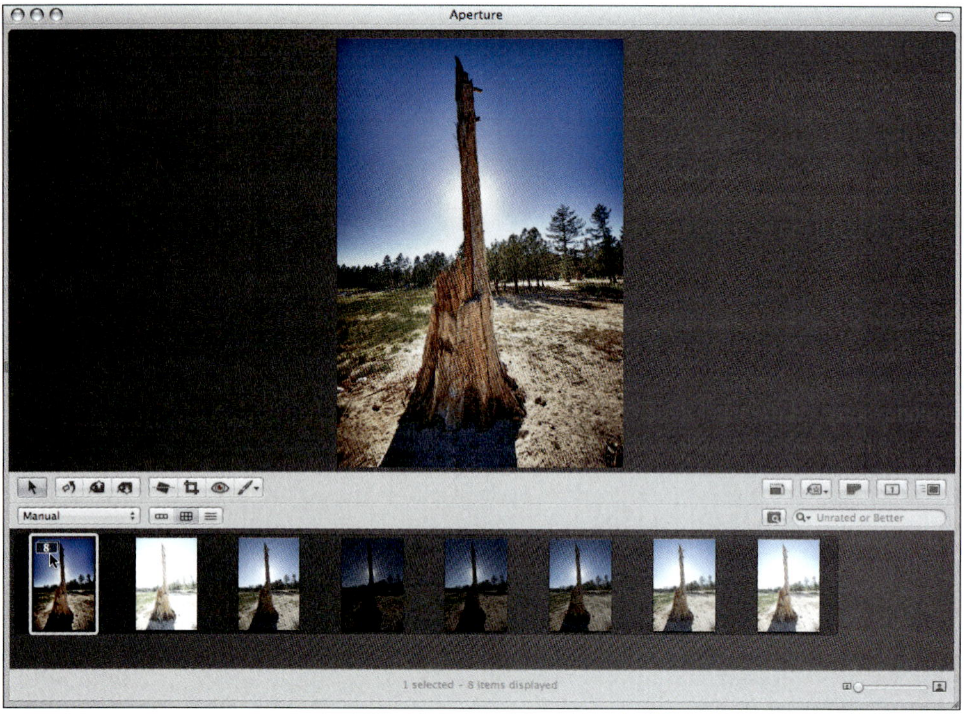

Figure 10.50

When opened from Bridge or Photoshop

When the image series is exported to HDR Efex Pro from Bridge or Photoshop, Photoshop controls RAW file conversion and image aligning. HDR Efex Pro loses a small amount of flexibility because of this, and that loss is most apparent when it comes to saving the final HDR image.

As shown in Figure 10.51, the Image Output Settings and the Stacking palettes are no longer available in the Settings palette. When an image or image series is exported to HDR Efex Pro from Bridge or Photoshop and the Open as Smart Object check box is not selected, the final HDR image is sent back to Photoshop as a 16-bit TIFF in the AdobeRGB color space when you click Save. This is true even if the original image or image series is in JPEG format and the sRGB color space. Back in Photoshop, the HDR image is treated no differently than any other 16-bit TIFF.

When opened as a Smart Object

If the image or image series is opened through Bridge or Photoshop as a Smart Object, once you click Save in HDR Efex Pro, the situation is a bit more complicated.

The HDR image opens in Photoshop CS5 Extended with HDR Efex Pro named as a Smart Filter in the Layers palette, as shown in Figure 10.52.

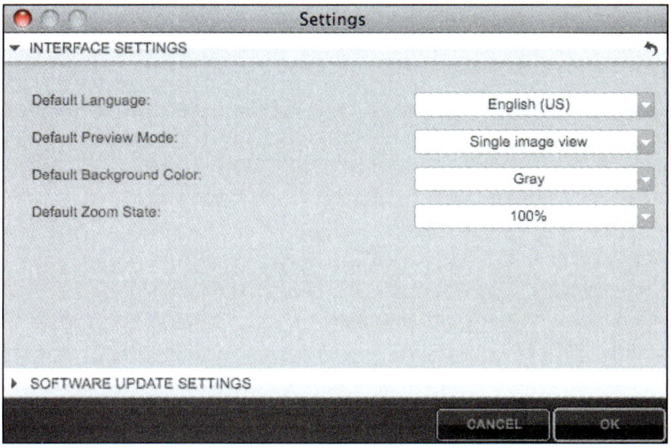

Figure 10.51

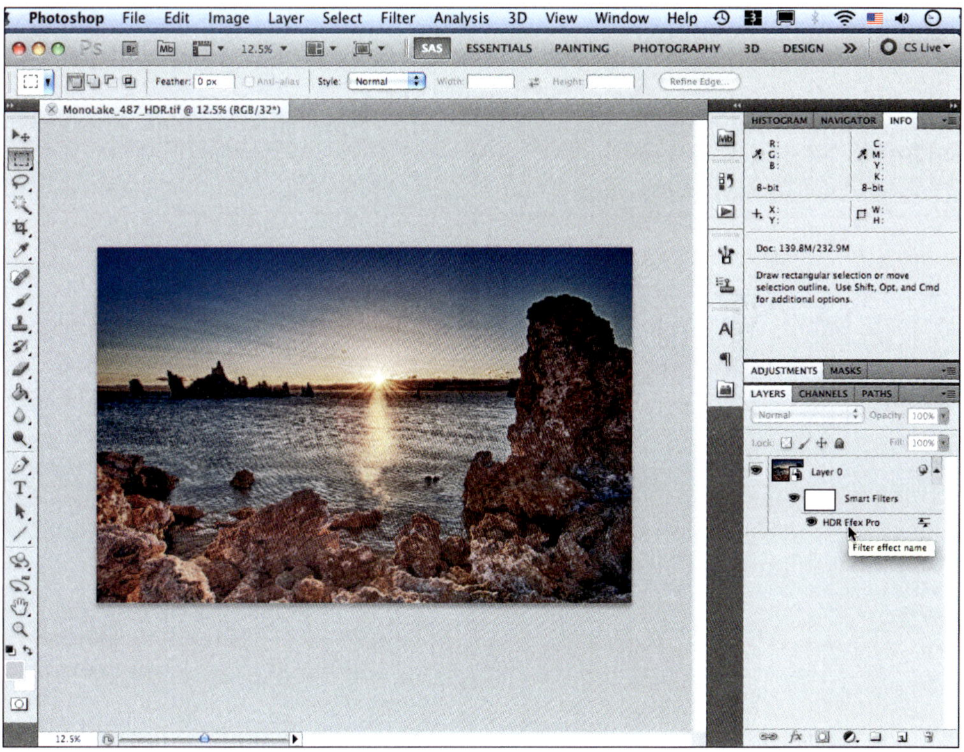

Figure 10.52

Choose File→Save or File→Save As and name the file. There are a number of available file formats in which to save the 32-bit HDR image, as shown in Figure 10.53. Unless you plan on working on the image in another 32-bit HDR program, select the TIFF option and the remaining defaults and click Save.

This opens the TIFF Options dialog box, as shown in Figure 10.54. Use the default settings and click OK. The file is saved as a 32-bit TIFF Smart Object file. Whenever the file is reopened in Photoshop, the interface will look like Figure 10.52. Click HDR Efex Pro in the Layers palette and the image reopens in HDR Efex Pro with all the tone compression, global adjustments, Control Points, and finishing adjustments intact.

At some point you will want to share this HDR image with others. There isn't much you can do with a 32-bit file, so it must be flattened and saved at a lower bit depth.

With the Smart Object HDR image open in Photoshop after saving it, click the Layers menu and scroll to the bottom to select Flatten Image.

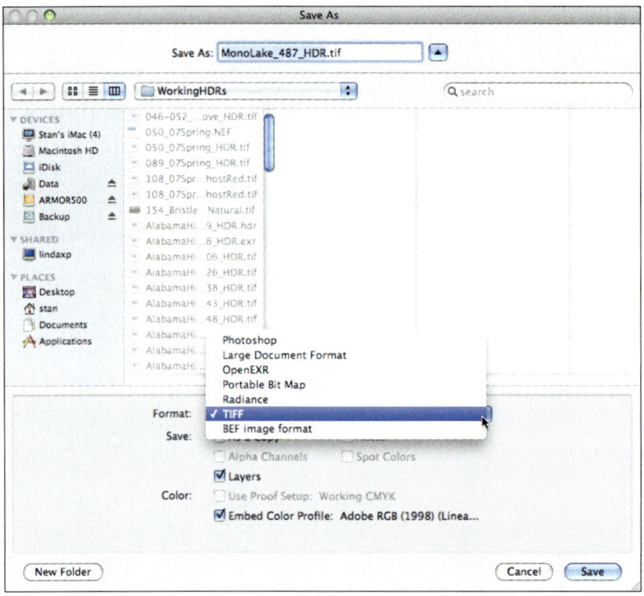

Figure 10.53

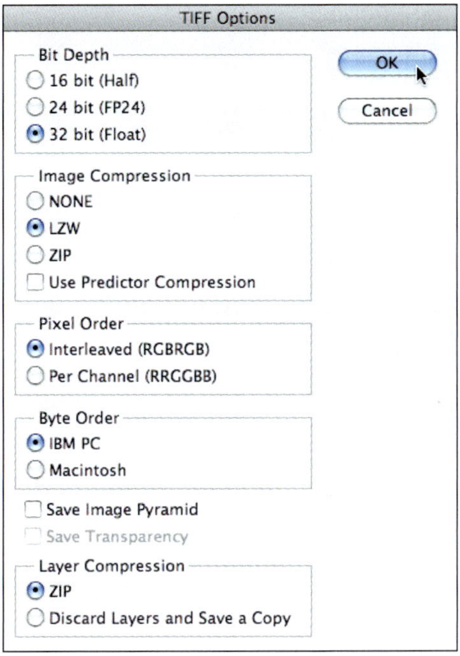

Figure 10.54

Next, in the Image menu, select Mode, and then select 8 Bits/Channel or 16 Bits/Channel. The choice is up to you. This opens the Photoshop HDR Toning dialog box, as shown in Figure 10.55.

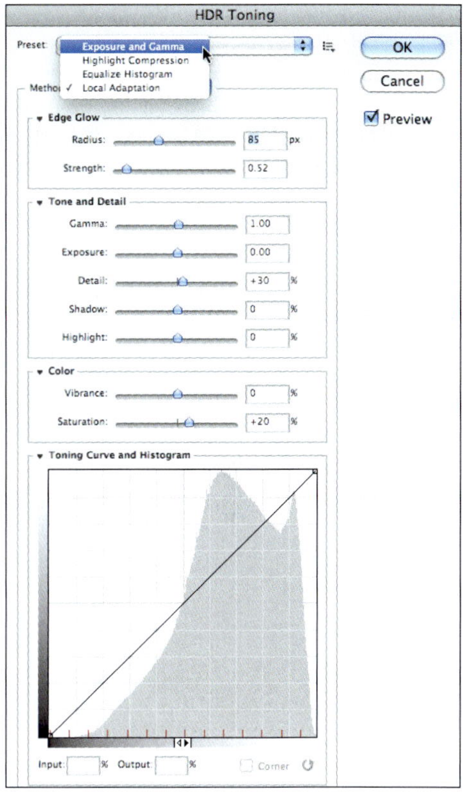

Figure 10.55

In the Method drop-down menu shown in Figure 10.55, choose Exposure and Gamma.

The HDR Toning dialog box changes to the Exposure and Gamma view shown in Figure 10.56. Leave the default settings, click OK, and you are back in Photoshop with an 8- or 16-bit flattened version of your HDR image.

At this point all the Photoshop tools that are not available for a 32-bit image are now available. Save the image with a unique filename in your favorite file format so that you don't overwrite the Smart Object version. Your workflow is complete, and you are ready to share your creation.

Figure 10.56

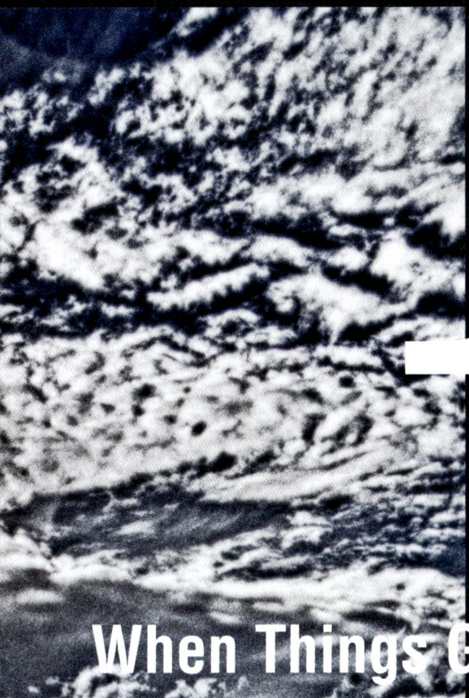

11

When Things Go Wrong

Many HDR images created with HDR Efex Pro contain a wealth of tonal information and image detail that almost demands that the images be viewed as large prints. However, as you examine the final HDR image at 100 percent on your monitor, you may notice that some areas didn't turn out quite as you expected. Something may have gone wrong during the complex HDR processing, or there may be artifacts or defects in the HDR image that you hadn't noticed in the originals.

This chapter offers suggestions for dealing with some common issues that you may not have expected in your HDR image. Problems can be corrected while you're working with the images in HDR Efex Pro, before the images are exported to HDR Efex Pro, or after the final HDR is flattened and saved. And sometimes the image issues simply can't be corrected without additional work in Photoshop.

Dealing with Alignment Issues

For an HDR image to be as sharp as possible, each image in the series must overlay in perfect register with every other image. The first step in guaranteeing this is to use a tripod during image capture. If you shoot with the camera on a tripod, in HDR Efex Pro you can usually leave the Alignment check box deselected and the images align without a problem.

Sometimes it just isn't possible to shoot with a tripod and you capture an image series while handholding the camera. This is when the Alignment check box becomes important.

I was driving across Baja California close to sunset and wishing that the sun would break through a cloud bank so I could shoot an HDR. I had given up hope when the sun broke through right before it was about to disappear below the horizon. I stopped the car, grabbed my camera, and knew I wouldn't have time to set up the tripod. So I shot seven handheld exposures and hoped that the alignment function in HDR Efex Pro would save me.

Opening the image series through Lightroom with the Alignment check box deselected produced the result in Figure 11.1. The alignment is way off and there is even a ghost of the cactus visible.

Because the image series was exported from Lightroom to HDR Efex Pro, the Alignment & Ghost Reduction button was visible in the upper menu bar. After I clicked the button and waited while HDR Efex Pro performed the Alignment and Ghost Reduction, Figure 11.2 was the result.

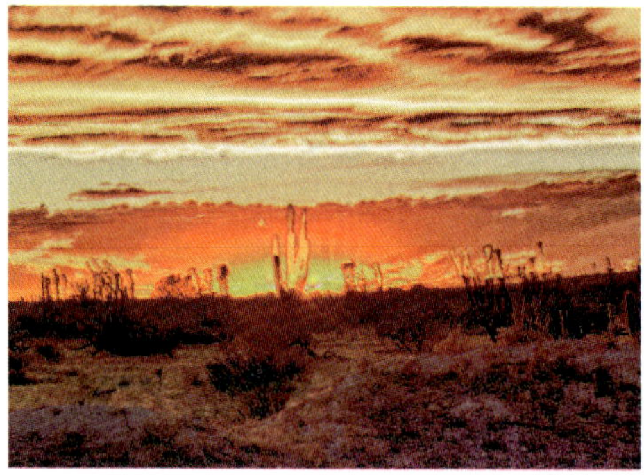

Figure 11.1

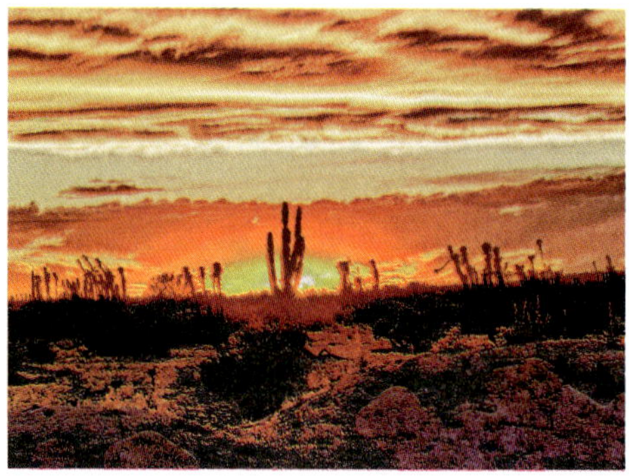

Figure 11.2

Using a tripod doesn't always solve the alignment issue, however. Even with the camera on a tripod, if you move the camera or tripod when you press the release button or if the wind is strong enough, you can still have alignment issues. I discovered this when I shot in a strong wind and exported the image series to HDR Efex Pro through Bridge with the Alignment check box deselected. The result is shown in Figure 11.3.

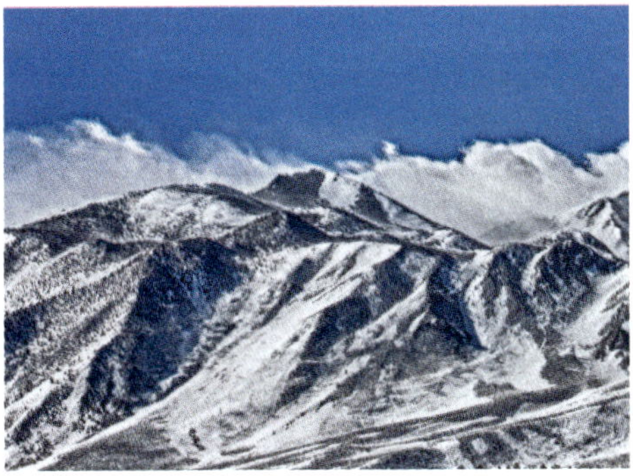

Figure 11.3

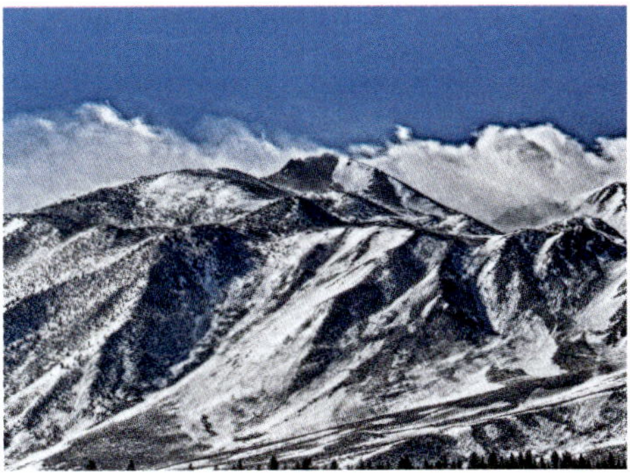

Figure 11.4

There is no way to align the images in HDR Efex Pro if they are exported through Bridge or Photoshop, so I needed to exit HDR Efex Pro and begin the process again with the Alignment check box selected this time. The result is shown in Figure 11.4.

My recommendation is to leave the Alignment check box selected for every export from Bridge or Photoshop to HDR Efex Pro. The extra time spent aligning the images is much less than the time required in starting the process over again if you realize that an alignment correction is needed.

Dealing with Ghosting

If there is any type of movement in the original scene, there is often a ghost of the moving object in the HDR image when you open it in HDR Efex Pro. *Ghosts* are artifacts in the HDR image that generally look like semitransparent images of the object that moved.

see also

Chapter 3 discusses the Ghost Reduction settings in detail.

Figure 11.4 was exported to HDR Efex Pro from Bridge with the Ghost Reduction check box deselected. The strong wind that was shaking my tripod was also rapidly blowing the clouds across the sky, so the image has ghosts of the edges of the clouds in the sky.

The clouds were moving horizontally through the frame, calling for the use of the Global option for Ghost Reduction. I chose the High setting and reprocessed the image with both the Alignment and Ghost Reduction check boxes selected. Figure 11.5 is the result.

Unfortunately, there is no real improvement in the ghosting. Sometimes this happens, and the only recourse is to live with the ghosting or spend additional time in Photoshop to correct it.

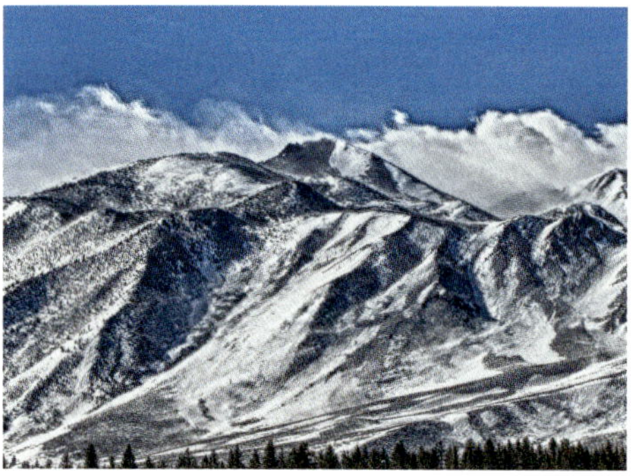

Figure 11.5

With other images, the Ghost Reduction tool works better, but the image may still need some additional work in Photoshop.

The image series for Figure 11.6 has two ghosting problems: the flag blowing in the breeze on the lifeguard tower and the people walking along the shore. Figure 11.6 was created through Bridge with the Alignment check box selected, but the Ghost Reduction check box deselected. Ghosting is clearly visible in the flag and in the people.

Both the movement of the flag and the movement of the people are random in the scene. This calls for the Adaptive Ghost Reduction Method. I tried the Adaptive Method the first time at the Medium setting and there was still ghosting present. Redoing the images with the Adaptive Ghost Reduction Method set to High helps the issues with the people, but not the flag (see Figure 11.7). Additional work is required for both issues.

Not satisfied with this result, I tried again with the Ghost Reduction set to Global at the High setting. The result in Figure 11.8 is perfect for the flag and much improved for the people.

There may even be times when you think it is impossible to create an HDR image because

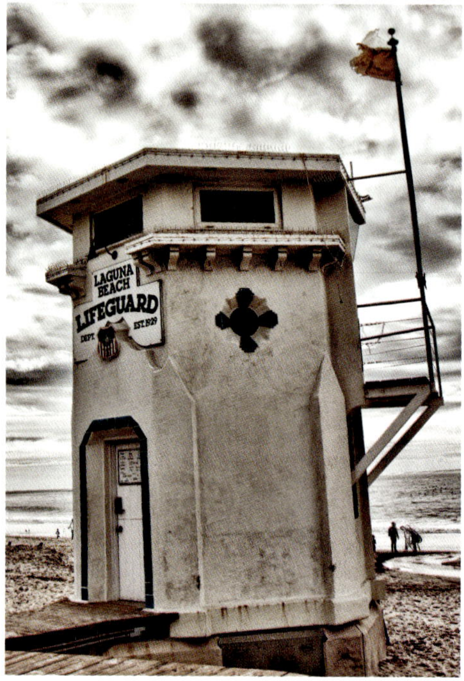

Figure 11.6

there is so much activity in the scene, such as in a busy hotel lobby. I shot a five-exposure bracket just to see if HDR Efex Pro could deal with it. The initial HDR without Ghost Reduction is shown in Figure 11.9.

Reprocessing the image with Global Ghost Reduction set to High produces the nearly perfect result in Figure 11.10. There is some interesting blurring left in the faces of some people, but no ghosting.

A good deal of the success in HDR imaging is the result of trying different options until you find one that works for you and is appropriate to the image. HDR Efex Pro has many options that you can experiment with to find the one that works.

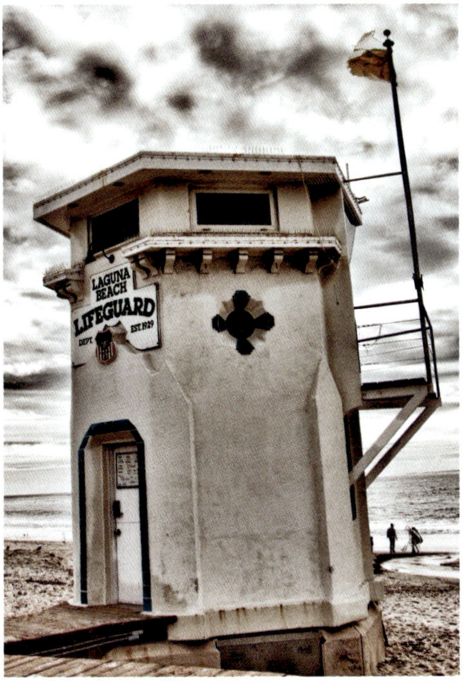

Figure 11.7

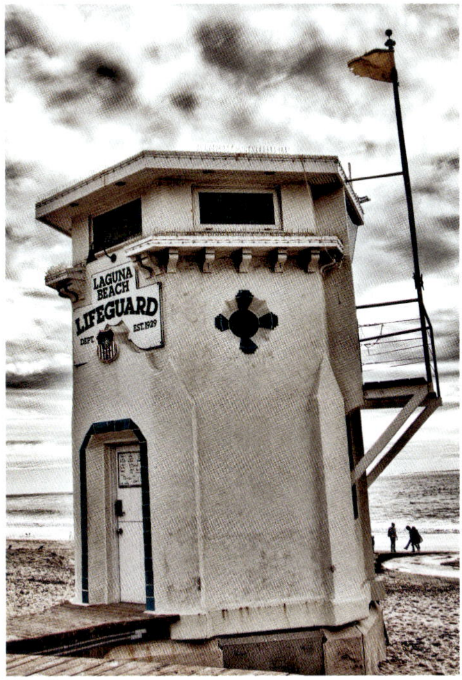

Figure 11.8

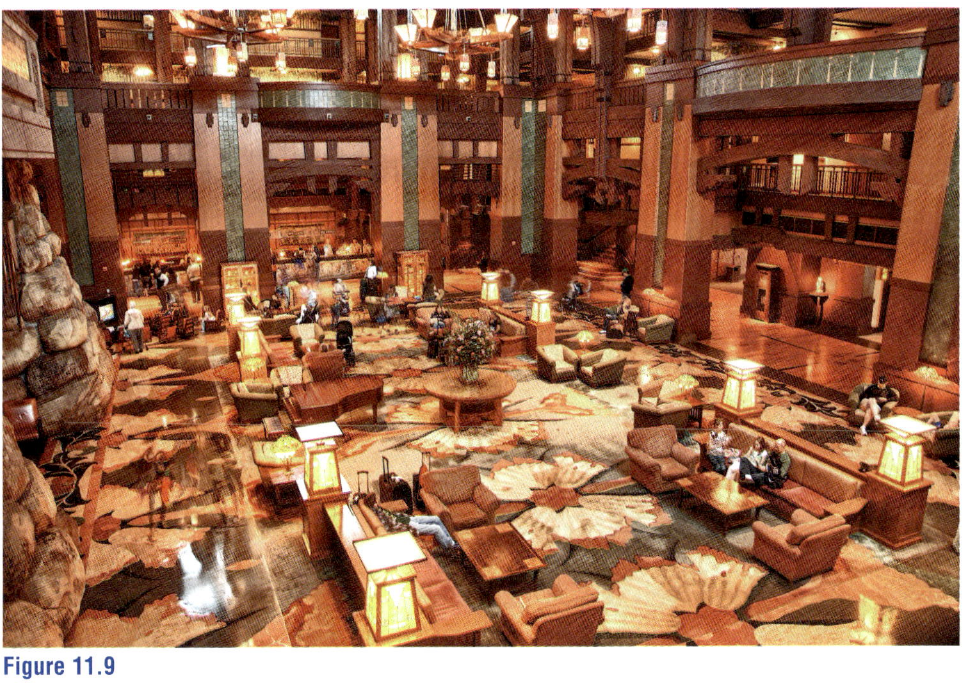
Figure 11.9

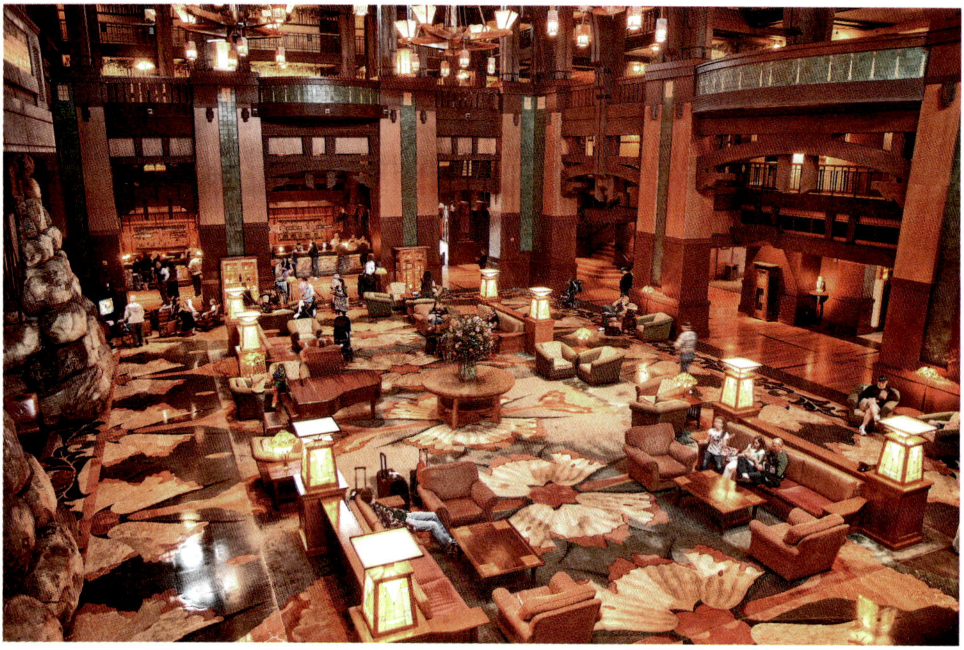

Figure 11.10

Dealing with Noise

When you shoot with most digital cameras at ISO settings higher than 400, noise is often an issue in the shadows. With HDR imaging, noise is even an issue at lower ISO settings with many digital cameras because the HDR process pulls information out of the shadow areas of several exposures and overlays the noise along with the image information.

For some photographers, noise is an issue, particularly when it appears in areas other than the deep shadows. For others, noise isn't a problem at all. If the amount of noise at the ISO you are using to capture an HDR image series with your camera is an issue for you, your workflow should include a noise-reduction step before you merge the images in HDR Efex Pro.

The earlier you perform noise reduction the better. HDR Efex Pro has no provision for removing noise during the HDR processing, and if you wait until the HDR image is final the amount of noise reduction you need to apply will be much higher than if you reduce noise before processing.

The method you use to reduce noise is up to you. When I want to be especially accurate with my noise reduction and brush it into the shadow areas or use Control Points so that I do not sharpen skin areas, I use Nik Software's Dfine 2.0 noise-reduction program.

But most of the time I'm after global noise reduction when creating HDR images, and I use the noise-reduction controls in Lightroom 3. I apply luminance and color noise reduction while viewing one of the RAW files in the image series at 100% in Lightroom. Then I sync the other images in the series to it with the same noise-reduction settings.

Without any noise reduction applied, the noise in an HDR of a concert hall shot at ISO 800 looks like Figure 11.11.

Making a noise reduction adjustment to the images before exporting them for HDR processing in HDR Efex Pro produced the result in Figure 11.12, a definite improvement in noise reduction and with little loss of sharpness.

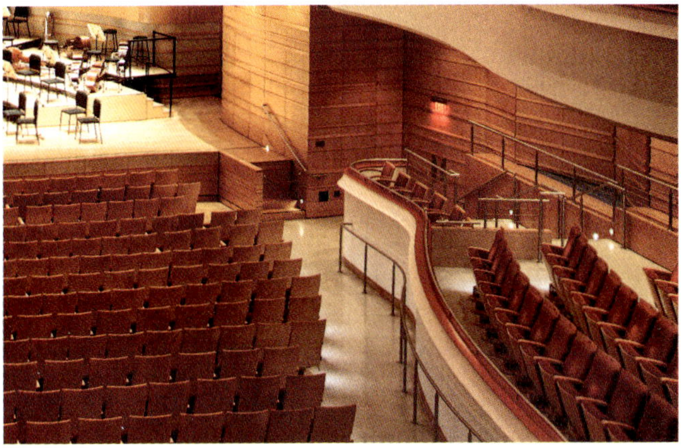

Figure 11.11

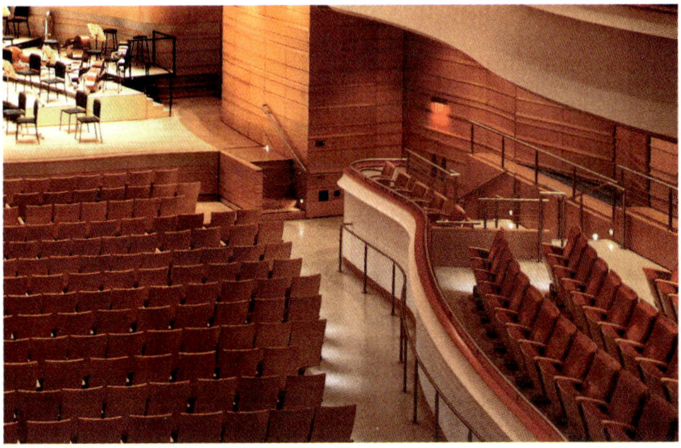

Figure 11.12

Dealing with Color Fringing

As with noise, color fringing, also called chromatic aberration, is a fact of life in digital photography and HDR imaging seems to enhance its presence. Color fringing is the presence of bands of non-image-related color on either side of an object, usually in an area of high contrast in the image. An example is shown in Figure 11.13.

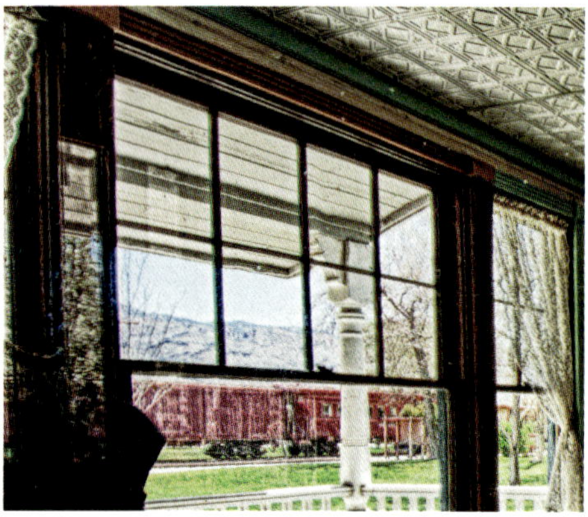

Figure 11.13

There is no general agreement on what causes color fringing or if it can be legitimately called a chromatic aberration, but there is no denying the presence of color aberration in HDR images. It is usually characterized by a cyan, purple, or red fringe that bleeds into the image on either side of a dark object against a lighter background. You can easily miss the color fringing unless you zoom the image to 100% and look around the edges of the HDR image.

Color fringing is most often found around dark tree branches against a light sky, or in the image in Figure 11.13, dark wood against a light exterior. But it can also occur with larger objects

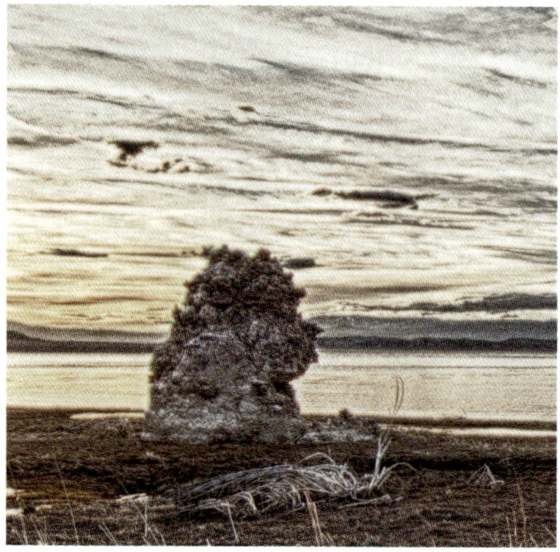

Figure 11.14

close to the image frame, such as the formation in Figure 11.14.

There is no tool in HDR Efex Pro designed to deal with color fringing. You must deal with it outside of the program. As with noise reduction, there are a number of ways to minimize color fringing, and again I prefer to use the tools in Lightroom.

It may be difficult to see color fringing in a single image of the image series when you open it in Lightroom. I usually end up seeing it in the HDR image in HDR Efex Pro, exiting HDR Efex Pro, and then opening one of the image series in Lightroom to correct the issue.

After making the correction to one image and syncing the other images in the series with the same correction, I reopen the image series through Lightroom or Bridge and proceed with the HDR image creation in HDR Efex Pro. With this workflow, the color fringing can be totally eliminated, as in Figure 11.15.

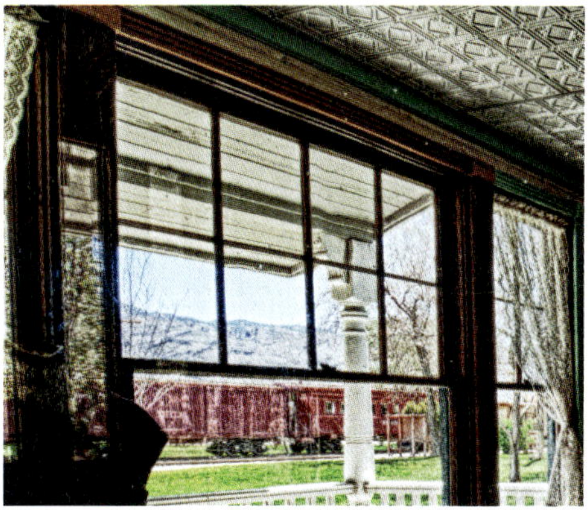

Figure 11.15

Dealing with Digital Artifacts

HDR imaging enhances other digital artifacts besides color fringing. The most common one I have seen is a single or even a series of round dark dots, as shown in Figure 11.16.

I'm guessing that these result from something present on the image sensor, as they generally disappear or move to a different location when I clean the sensor. The spots aren't obviously visible in a single image in the series (as you can see from Figure 11.17), but as the HDR is created they become very obvious.

Figure 11.16 has other problems besides the dark dots, which are also visible in Figure 11.17. The roundish spot is an internal reflection of the lens diaphragm. The origin of the light vertical streak to the left of the diaphragm reflection is a mystery to me. It is barely visible in the original image (Figure 11.17) but obvious in the HDR image (Figure 11.16).

These digital artifacts are present in the original image, whether or not they are obvious, and independent of the HDR process. There is no way to correct them in HDR Efex Pro. But some straightforward cleanup on the final flattened HDR image in Photoshop fixes the problems, as shown in Figure 11.18.

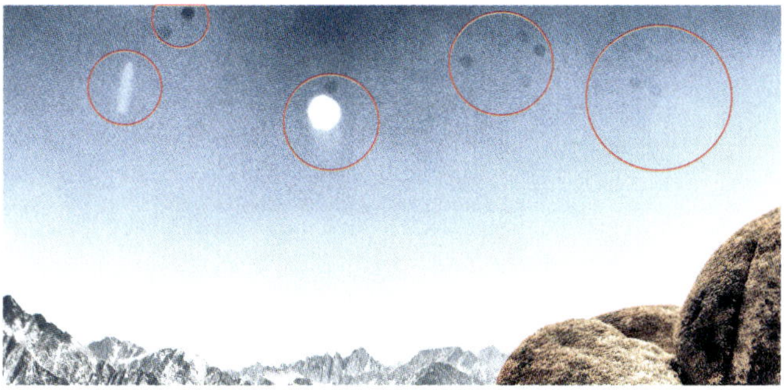

Figure 11.16

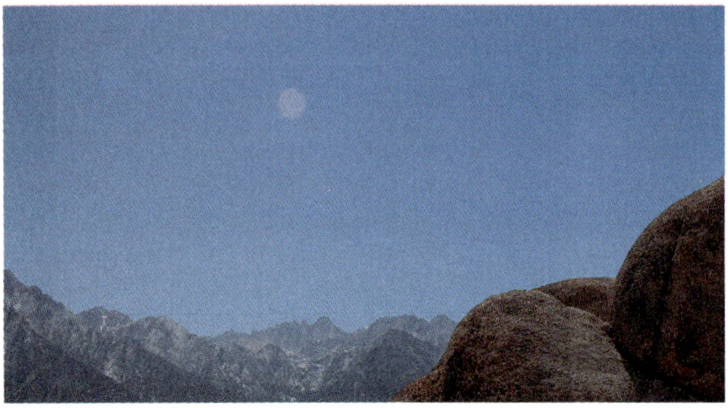

Figure 11.17

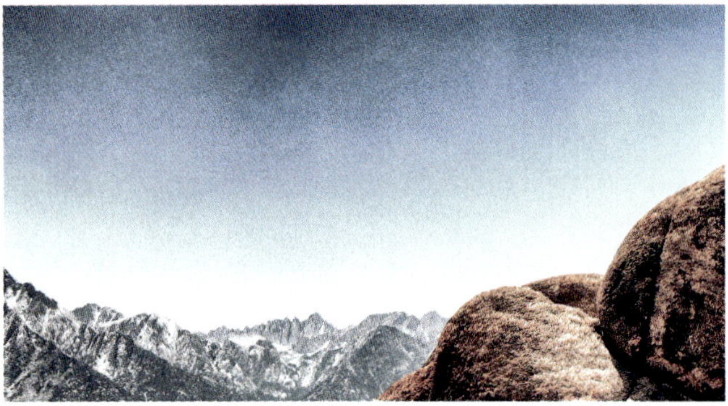

Figure 11.18

Dealing with Halos

Along with alignment and ghosting, another issue that is closely related to the HDR process is the presence of light outlines around dark objects in areas of high contrast. These outlines are called *halos* and can appear as a thin band outlining the objects (see Figure 11.19) or as large wide bands that break up the sky into patches, as shown in Figure 11.20.

The appearance of the halo depends on the HDR Method chosen, the position of the Contrast and Structure sliders, and the amount of tone compression. Adjusting any of these will change the look of the halo, or even eliminate the halo entirely.

Halos, while considered unnatural and therefore undesirable, are not all that uncommon. You can

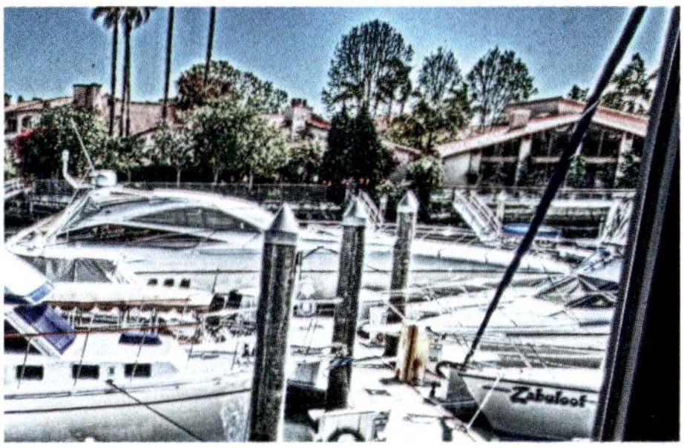

Figure 11.19

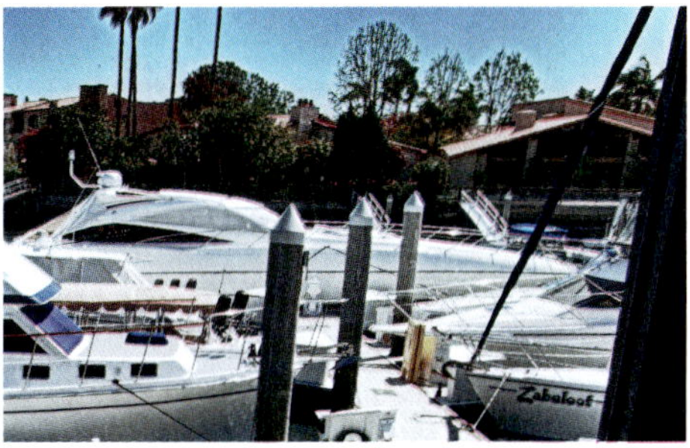

Figure 11.20

create halos in many non-HDR images by cranking up the image contrast. And if you carefully examine many fine-art black-and-white landscape images, you see halos around trees against a dark sky caused by the buildup of bromides in the processing.

The tone-mapping algorithms in HDR processing certainly contribute to haloing. HDR Efex Pro includes a Halo Reduction HDR Method that can be effective with the right combination of its Method Strength slider and the other sliders in the Global Adjustments section. If the halos in the image look wrong to you, try the Halo Reduction Method. As HDR imaging technology progresses, the presence of halos should decrease and new tools should become available to deal with halos when they occur.

Appendix A: Keyboard Shortcuts

Table AA.1

Interface

Tool	*Windows*	*Mac*
Undo	Ctrl+Z	⌘+Z
Redo	Ctrl+Y	⌘+Y
Full screen	F	F
Preview	P	P
Show/Hide palettes	Tab	Tab
Apply filter	Enter	Return
Cancel filter	Esc	Esc
Zoom in	Ctrl+–	⌘+–
Zoom out	Ctrl+=	⌘+=
Increase/decrease slider by one unit	left/right arrows	left/right arrows
Increase/decrease slider by 10 units	Shift+left/right arrows	Shift+left/right arrows
Zoom	spacebar	spacebar

Table AA.2
Control Points

Tool	*Windows*	*Mac*
Add Control Point	Ctrl+Shift+A	⌘+Shift+A
Delete Control Point	Delete	Delete
Duplicate Control Point	Ctrl+D	⌘+D
	Alt+drag	Option+drag
Copy Control Point	Ctrl+C	⌘+C
Paste Control Point	Ctrl+V	⌘+V
Expand/Collapse Control Point	E	E
Select all Control Points	Ctrl+A	⌘+A
Move a selected Control Point	arrows (all)	arrows (all)
Increase/decrease slider by one unit	left/right arrows	left/right arrows
Increase/decrease slider by 10 units	Shift+left/right arrows	Shift+left/right arrows
Select previous/next Control Point when one is selected	up/down arrows	up/down arrows
Group Control Points	Ctrl+G	⌘+G
Ungroup Control Points	Ctrl+Shift+G	⌘+Shift+G

Appendix B: Presets

Table AB.1

HDR Efex Pro Prebuilt Presets

Preset	*HDR Method*	*Preset Category*
Default	Natural	Realistic
Realistic (Subtle)	Natural	Realistic
Realistic (Balanced)	Clean	Realistic
Realistic (Strong)	Sharp	Realistic
Realistic Gradients 1	Gradual Medium	Realistic
Realistic Gradients 2	Gradual Large	Realistic
Fine Structures	Bright Textures	Artistic
Subdued Contrasts	Crisp	Artistic
Structured Skies	Fresco	Artistic
Vibrant Textures	Sharp	Artistic
Vibrant Details & Colors	Bright Textures	Artistic
Monochrome, Contrasty	Textured	Artistic
Monochrome, Soft	Diffused	Artistic
The Old Cottage	Soft	Surreal
Night On Earth	Dark Soft	Surreal
Vintage Colors	Bright Textures	Surreal
Granny's Attic	Natural	Surreal
End of the Road	Soft	Surreal
Bleach Bypass Look	Harsh Details	Surreal
Full Scene Compression	Natural	Landscape
Vibrant Scenery	Sharp	Landscape
Gradual Contrasts 1	Gradual Large	Landscape
Gradual Contrasts 2	Gradual Medium	Landscape
Postcard Paradise	Dark Soft	Landscape
Clean City 1	Clean	Architecture
Clean City 2	Clean	Architecture
Friendly Scenery	Clean	Architecture
Bright Room 1	Bright Soft	Architecture

Preset	HDR Method	Preset Category
Bright Room 2	Soft	Architecture
Strong Counterlight	Subtle	Architecture
Very Low Compression	Natural	Special
Single Exposure 1	Subtle	Special
Single Exposure 2	Sharp	Special

Glossary

Adobe RGB (1998) A common color space in digital imaging. It contains more colors than the sRGB color space, but less than the ProPhoto RGB color space. If possible, digital captures for HDR imaging should be made in the Adobe RGB (1998) color space.

algorithm A set of mathematical instructions used to calculate a final result. HDR Efex Pro uses algorithms to produce and adjust the HDR image.

anchor point A point on the curve of the Curves diagram in HDR Efex Pro where an adjustment is made to the shape of the curve.

aperture The opening through which light travels in a camera lens. The lens aperture is determined by the size of the diaphragm inside the lens. In bracketing for HDR imaging, the aperture remains fixed and the shutter speed varies.

artifact An undesirable alteration of image data caused by some factor in the digital process.

autobracketing The ability of a camera to automatically capture an image sequence with different exposure values.

banding The appearance of bands of tone rather than a smooth tone in areas of an image where the tonal value is changing.

bit A contraction of binary digit. The smallest unit of information used by a computer.

bit depth The number of bits per pixel used to store information in an image. An image with 1 bit per pixel would be black and white with no gray tones. An 8-bit-per-pixel image would be capable of containing 256 colors or gray tones per pixel for each color channel. A 16-bit-per-pixel image could contain 65,536 colors per pixel per channel. A 32-bit-per-pixel HDR image could contain 4,294,967,296 colors per pixel per channel.

bracketing The photographic technique of varying exposure. In HDR imaging, bracketing is accomplished by varying the shutter speed at a fixed aperture in order to create an image series of the same subject with varying exposures.

brightness The intensity of light present in a color. Often used interchangeably with the term luminance, brightness can vary due to viewing conditions while luminance is a measurable fixed quantity.

burning The process of selectively darkening an area of an image.

clipping The loss of image detail in the highlights or shadows. Clipping occurs when the color values of a pixel are higher than the highest value or lower than the lowest value that can be represented in the image. Overly bright values are clipped to output white, and overly dark values are clipped to output black.

color channel One of the red, green or blue components that make up the digital image. The channel is a grayscale representation of either the red, green or blue information in the image.

color noise A type of noise that looks like splotches of color under high magnification. Color noise arises from the flow of electrons in an image sensor that occurs even in the absence of light. See also *noise*.

color space A mathematical representation of a color model mapped onto an absolute color space depicting a range of colors. Common color spaces in HDR imaging include Adobe RGB (1998), ProPhoto RGB, and sRGB.

contrast The difference in brightness between the brightest and darkest areas of the image. Also called global contrast as opposed to microcontrast. HDR Efex Pro provides sliders in the Global Adjustments section and in Control Points to change contrast.

Control Point A feature unique to Nik Software's patented U Point Technology that allows for local control of the image without requiring the user to create masks.

depth of field The distance between the nearest and farthest points in a scene that are rendered in acceptably sharp focus.

dodging The process of selectively lightening an area of an image.

dynamic range The ratio between the maximum and minimum values of a measurement. Human vision can accommodate a dynamic range of about 10,000,000:1 from moonlight to bright sunlight. For daylight scenes, the dynamic range can easily exceed 100,000:1.

EDR image Extended Dynamic Range image. An image created by HDR software from a single image capture. See also *HDR image* and *LDR image.*

EV Exposure Value. An interval on the photographic exposure scale. A step of 1EV corresponds to an interval of 1 f-stop.

EXIF Exchangeable Image File Format. A set of nonimage data written by many cameras that travels with the image. The data consists of camera settings and other information gathered while the image is captured.

ghost In an HDR image a ghost is an artifact in the image that doesn't belong. It is created because an object moved during the exposure sequence.

golden hour The hour around sunrise and around sunset when contrast is low and colors are warm.

halo Bright halos appear in areas of high contrast in HDR images. Halos are caused by the local tone-mapping operator brightening areas around dark objects in order to maintain the local contrast in the image.

HDR image High Dynamic Range image. An image created in the computer with a dynamic range approximating 100,000:1 and capable of capturing the full tonal range of scenes in the real world.

highlight values The lightest tones in an image.

histogram A graphical representation of the tonal range of an image. The horizontal axis represents tonal values from shadow to highlight. The vertical axis shows the amount of information in the image for each tonal value. Histograms with red, green, and blue lines show the distribution of tonal values for each of those colors, usually accompanied by a black line to show the composite of red, green, and blue values.

hue A specific shade of color that can be represented by an RGB value.

image series A set of bracketed exposures used to create an HDR image.

IPTC International Press Telecommunications Council. A standardized set of fields that photographers can fill in about themselves and their image that travels with the image but is not image information.

ISO International Organization for Standardization. ISO sensitivity is a measure of the digital image sensor's sensitivity to light. Low ISO values such as ISO 100 denote lower light sensitivity than higher ISO values such as ISO 1600.

JPEG Joint Photographic Experts Group. A compressed industry-standard digital file format. JPEG captures are not recommended for HDR imaging.

LDR image Low Dynamic Range image. A single image capture. See also *HDR image* and *EDR image*.

luminance noise A type of noise that looks like black dots, something like film grain but more uniform. Luminance noise is caused by random luminance variation between pixels. See also *noise*.

metadata Data about data. In digital imaging metadata is nonimage information added to the digital image by the camera (EXIF data) or the user (IPTC data).

microcontrast The local contrast in an image. Many tools in HDR Efex Pro affect microcontrast, including tone compression, choice of HDR Method, and the Structure sliders.

noise Random variation of brightness or color values in an image. There are two types of noise, luminance noise and color noise. Both types increase as the temperature of the sensor increases, the size of the pixels decrease and the amplification of the signal from each pixel increases; that is, at higher ISO ratings. See also *luminance noise* and *color noise*.

ProPhoto RGB An RGB color space containing nearly as many colors as the human eye can perceive. When exporting an image series for processing in HDR Efex Pro, ProPhoto RGB is the best color space to use.

RAW The catchall term for the proprietary image file formats of many digital cameras. RAW files contain image information taken directly from the image sensor with minimum processing. RAW files are the recommended capture file format for HDR imaging.

RGB Red, Green, Blue. The three color channels of an RGB image.

saturation The amount of gray present in a color. The higher the saturation, the less gray is present. Also called chroma.

shadow values The darkest tones in an image.

shutter speed The effective time that the camera's shutter is open. In bracketing for HDR imaging, the shutter speed is changed while the aperture remains fixed.

sRGB A color space in digital imaging commonly used for JPEG captures. The range of colors available is limited and it should be avoided for HDR imaging. However, it is an appropriate choice when finalizing an HDR image for low-quality color printing or for display on the Internet.

TIFF Tagged Image File Format. A lossless industry-standard digital file format. TIFF files can be used as a capture format for HDR imaging, but RAW files are better.

tone compression The process of reducing the tonal range of an image so that it reproduces or displays on a specific device.

tone mapping The process of converting the tonal range of an image with a high dynamic range to an image of lower dynamic range.

U Point technology Nik Software's patented selection technology that allows the user to create a mask and adjust settings by creating a Control Point in the image.

vignette The loss of clarity or resolution at the edges of an image compared to that in the center.

Index

Continued

Printed in Great Britain
by Amazon

74036936R00228